Agnostic Capability [428] How can multi-purpose service logic be made effectively consumable and composable?

 Agnostic Context [429] How can multi-purpose service logic be positioned as an effective enterprise resource?

 Agnostic Sub-Controller [430] How can agnostic, cross-entity composition logic be separated, reused, and governed independently?

 Asynchronous Queuing [431] How can a service and its consumers accommodate isolated failures and avoid unnecessarily locking resources?

 Atomic Service Transaction [432] How can a transaction with rollback capability be propagated across messaging-based services?

 Brokered Authentication [433] How can a service efficiently verify consumer credentials if the consumer and service do not trust each other or if the consumer requires access to multiple services?

 Canonical Expression [434] How can service contracts be consistently understood and interpreted?

 Canonical Protocol [435] How can services be designed to avoid protcol bridging?

 Canonical Resources [436] How can unnecessary infrastructure resource disparity be avoided?

 Canonical Schema [437] How can services be designed to avoid data model transformation?

Canonical Schema Bus [438]

 Canonical Versioning [439] How can service contracts within the same service inventory be versioned with minimal impact?

 Capability Composition [440] How can a service capability solve a problem that requires logic outside of the service boundary?

 Capability Recomposition [441] How can the same capability be used to help solve multiple problems?

 Compatible Change [442] How can a service contract be modified without impacting consumers?

MW00991128

 ...positions be implemented to minimize loss of autonomy?

 Concurrent Contracts [445] How can a service facilitate multi-consumer coupling requirements and abstraction concerns at the same time?

 Content Negotiation [446] How can a service capability accommodate service consumers with different data format or representation requirements?

 Contract Centralization [447] How can direct consumer-to-implementation coupling be avoided?

 Contract Denormalization [448] How can a service contract facilitate consumer programs with differing data exchange requirements?

 Cross-Domain Utility Layer [449] How can redundant utility logic be avoided across domain service inventories?

 Data Confidentiality [450] How can data within a message be protected so that it is not disclosed to unintended recipients while in transit?

 Data Format Transformation [451] How can services interact with programs that communicate with different data formats?

 Data Model Transformation [452] How can services interoperate when using different data models for the same type of data?

 Data Origin Authentication [453] How can a service verify that a message originates from a known sender and that the message has not been tampered with in transit?

 Decomposed Capability [454] How can a service be designed to minimize the chances of capability logic deconstruction?

 Decoupled Contract [455] How can a service express its capabilities independently of its implementation?

 Direct Authentication [456] How can a service verify the credentials provided by a consumer?

(pattern list continued on inside back cover)

Praise for this Book

"This book illuminates the connection of the two domains—SOA and REST—in a manner that is concrete and practical, providing concise application to everyday architectural challenges. Fantastic!"

—Ryan Frazier, Technology Strategist, Microsoft

"SOA can be done in many different ways, and REST has become the most visible newcomer in the space of potential implementation frameworks. This book illustrates what architects and developers need to know about *RESTful* SOA and most importantly drives home the main point that REST makes as a style for SOA: It is all about designing service ecosystems and providing clients an easy way to use resources in those ecosystems and even connect them across individual services. This book undoubtedly will help SOA to reap the benefits from the main value propositions of Web architecture: decentralization, loose coupling, connectedness, self-describing services, and service interfaces that are independent from service implementations."

—Dr. Erik Wilde, Architect, EMC Corporation

"*SOA with REST* is a tour de force that elegantly applies REST principles to the industry-standard SOA framework described in prior titles in this series. The book provides useful guidance to practitioners while staying true in form and spirit to the REST constraints defined in Roy Fielding's thesis. The chapters on RESTful contract design in and of themselves justify the cost of purchase. This book is a must-read for anyone developing REST services."

—Dave Slotnick, Enterprise Architect, Rackspace Hosting

"An excellent repertoire of service-oriented patterns that will prove handy when solving problems in the real world. The REST perspectives and principles will provide complete coverage of modern-day Web 2.0 style approaches. Highly recommended."

—Sid Sanyal, IT Architect, Zurich Financial Services

"REST is so much more than just another type of interface implementation—*SOA with REST* shows how the ecosystem of service compositions changes as new opportunities arise for service composition architecture designs. A comprehensive guide and a must-read for any serious IT architect considering REST-style services for application architectures."

—Roger Stoffers, Solution Architect, Hewlett Packard

"Service-orientation and REST both are architectural styles that are cornerstones of modern applications and cloud computing. Both aim to deliver scalable, interoperable solutions, but their different roots don't always make them a natural fit. *SOA with REST* explains how the two styles can work together in enterprise environments. It discusses a design process for a services portfolio that meets the goals of SOA and at the same time designs services that comply with the established REST constraints. It also shows pragmatic approaches to meet enterprise-grade requirements with the REST programming style but relaxes constraints where necessary."

—Christoph Schittko, Director of Cloud Strategy, Microsoft

"An inspirational book that provides deep insight into the design and development of next-generation service-oriented systems based on the use of REST. This book clarifies the convergence of SOA and REST with no-nonsense content that addresses common questions and issues head-on. An essential 'instrument of modern service implementation' and a powerful body of knowledge for software designers, architects, and consultants."

—Pethuru Raj, Ph.D., Enterprise Architecture (EA) Consultant, Wipro Consulting Services

"*The Service Technology Series from Thomas Erl* continues its tradition of using simple examples to elucidate complicated concepts. With the latest in the series, *SOA with REST*, the authors have created a resource that discusses REST through the lenses of the common SOA pattern language. *SOA with REST* is a fantastic resource for the enterprise architect and developer alike!"

—Kevin P. Davis, Ph.D., Software Architect

"Unlike many other texts on the subject, *SOA with REST* is a well-rounded, easy-to-read narrative, including real-world case studies that appeal to both developers and analysts. This makes it an indispensable source for any SOA practitioner or any professional who is planning to initiate an SOA project."

—Theodore T. Morrison, Certified SOA Analyst, CSM, Geocent, LLC

"The book is a must-read for any IT architect or software engineer who wants to gain a deep understanding of the principles, patterns, and implementation concepts that pertain to building REST-based applications for service-oriented architectures. It goes well beyond fundamental topics to explore the relationship between REST and various specific SOA principles and patterns."

—*Sanjay Singh, Certified SOA Architect, Development Manager, NorthgateArinso*

"An authoritative, well-written reference for enterprise architects, analysts, developers, and others. This book shows not only the elegance, simplicity, and versatility of REST, it also gives us a clear understanding of how REST synergizes with SOA and service-orientation, how REST can impact SOA design goals, how we can design and develop REST services, and how we can address the unique challenges of integrating REST-fulness into service-orientation. This book is required reading for anyone who desires technical mastery of building service-oriented architectures with REST."

—*Philip Wik, MSS Technology*

"This is a comprehensive and fundamental book to understand how to employ REST in service-oriented architectures. The many examples provided and the patterns described will be an invaluable help to any practitioner interested in service orientation."

—*Gustavo Alonso, Department of Computer Science, ETH Zurich*

"SOA and REST are two very important architectural styles for distributed computing. SOA is successfully adopted by most enterprises, and the REST style is getting more attention from both researcher and industry users. The book *SOA with REST* introduces a new architectural style that is ingeniously combining both SOA and REST styles and clearly reveals how SOA and REST can work together to generate successful enterprise SOA strategies with REST, along with guidance for making architecture design decisions. This book is a bible of best practices for designing and implementing SOA architecture with REST. It is a must-have reference book for both IT practitioners and researchers."

—*Longji Tang, FedEx IT Senior Technical Advisor, Ph.D. in CSSE*

"REST and SOA are two of the most misunderstood terms in the software industry over the past decade. Yet the REST architectural style coupled with modern RESTful framework implementations provides a scalable and reliable approach to SOA. This book covers all you need to know about how to take the principles of REST and apply them in small and large SOA developments. If you are familiar with REST and thinking about SOA, then you need this book. If you have not considered REST in your SOA work, then this book is for you, too. Covering concepts of both REST and SOA, as well as design patterns and when to use them, the book is a wonderful companion and a good tool for architects and engineers."

—Dr. Mark Little, CTO JBoss, Red Hat

"This book is an excellent introduction into how SOA methodology can be used with services implementing a RESTful architectural style. Thomas Erl and his co-authors help SOA architects to better understand the implications of utilizing and the requirements for integrating REST into the service-oriented architecting process."

—Gerald Beuchelt, MITRE

SOA with REST

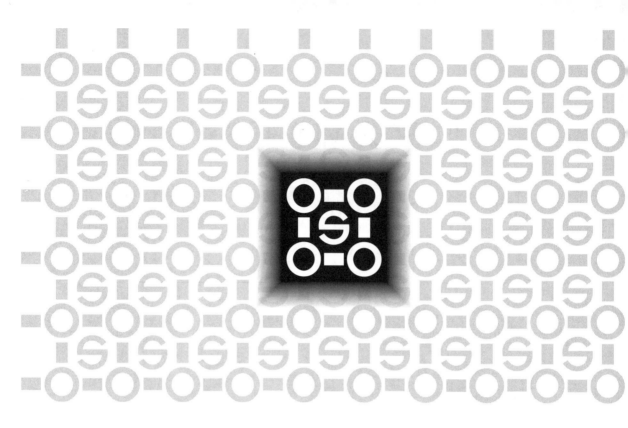

The Prentice Hall Service Technology Series
from Thomas Erl aims to provide the IT industry with
a consistent level of unbiased, practical, and
comprehensive guidance and instruction in the areas
of service technology application and innovation.

Each title in this book series is authored in relation to
other titles so as to establish a library of complementary
knowledge. Although the series covers a broad spectrum
of service technology-related topics, each title is authored
in compliance with common language, vocabulary, and
illustration conventions so as to enable readers to
continually explore cross-topic research and education.

For more information, visit www.servicetechbooks.com.

SOA with REST

Principles, Patterns & Constraints
for Building Enterprise Solutions with REST

Thomas Erl, Benjamin Carlyle, Cesare Pautasso, and Raj Balasubramanian

PRENTICE HALL

PRENTICE HALL

UPPER SADDLE RIVER, NJ • BOSTON • INDIANAPOLIS • SAN FRANCISCO

NEW YORK • TORONTO • MONTREAL • LONDON • MUNICH • PARIS • MADRID

CAPE TOWN • SYDNEY • TOKYO • SINGAPORE • MEXICO CITY

Many of the designations used by manufacturers and sellers to distinguish their products are claimed as trademarks. Where those designations appear in this book, and the publisher was aware of a trademark claim, the designations have been printed with initial capital letters or in all capitals.

The authors and publisher have taken care in the preparation of this book, but make no expressed or implied warranty of any kind and assume no responsibility for errors or omissions. No liability is assumed for incidental or consequential damages in connection with or arising out of the use of the information or programs contained herein.

The publisher offers excellent discounts on this book when ordered in quantity for bulk purchases or special sales, which may include electronic versions and/or custom covers and content particular to your business, training goals, marketing focus, and branding interests. For more information, please contact:

> U.S. Corporate and Government Sales
> (800) 382-3419
> corpsales@pearsontechgroup.com

For sales outside the United States, please contact:

> International Sales
> international@pearsoned.com

Visit us on the Web: informit.com/ph

Library of Congress Cataloging-in-Publication Data

SOA with REST : principles, patterns & constraints for building enterprise solutions with REST / Thomas Erl ... [et al.].

p. cm.

ISBN 978-0-13-701251-0 (hardcover : alk. paper)

1. Service-oriented architecture (Computer science) 2. Representational State Transfer (Software architecture) I. Erl, Thomas.

TK5105.5828.S64 2012

004.6'54--dc23

2011034777

ISBN-13: 978-0-13-701251-0
ISBN-10: 0-13-701251-9

Text printed in the United States on recycled paper.
Second printing: April 2014

Editor-in-Chief
Mark L. Taub

Development Editors
Infinet Creative Group
Jillian Warren

Managing Editor
Kristy Hart

Project Editor
Betsy Harris

Project Coordinator
Pamela Janice Yau

Copy Editor
Infinet Creative Group

Senior Indexer
Cheryl Lenser

Proofreaders
Abigail Gavin
Melissa Mok
Williams Woods
Publishing

Publishing Coordinator
Kim Boedigheimer

Cover Designer
Thomas Erl

Compositor
Bumpy Design

Photos
Thomas Erl

Graphics
Demian Richardson
Kan Kwai Lui

This book is dedicated to Christoph Schittko, whose uninhibited review comments led us to alter the course of this book after the original draft of the manuscript had already been submitted for production. The subsequent changes improved the manuscript dramatically.

—Thomas Erl

To my darling wife Michelle, to my parents Rob and Sue, and to my children Genevieve and Matthew. Thank you for your years of support and encouragement.

—Benjamin Carlyle

To my family and my Esperanza.

—Cesare Pautasso

To my parents for their sacrifice and support.

—Raj Balasubramanian

Contents at a Glance

Foreword xxix

CHAPTER 1: Introduction 1

CHAPTER 2: Case Study Background 13

PART I: FUNDAMENTALS

CHAPTER 3: Introduction to Services 23

CHAPTER 4: SOA Terminology and Concepts 31

CHAPTER 5: REST Constraints and Goals. 51

PART II: RESTFUL SERVICE-ORIENTATION

CHAPTER 6: Service Contracts with REST 67

CHAPTER 7: Service-Orientation with REST 93

PART III: SERVICE-ORIENTED ANALYSIS AND DESIGN WITH REST

CHAPTER 8: Mainstream SOA Methodology and REST 127

CHAPTER 9: Analysis and Service Modeling with REST 139

CHAPTER 10: Service-Oriented Design with REST 173

PART IV: SERVICE COMPOSITION WITH REST

CHAPTER 11: Fundamental Service Composition with REST 231

CHAPTER 12: Advanced Service Composition with REST. 261

CHAPTER 13: Service Composition with REST Case Study 305

PART V: SUPPLEMENTAL

CHAPTER 14: Design Patterns for SOA with REST 327

CHAPTER 15: Service Versioning with REST. 343

CHAPTER 16: Uniform Contract Profiles. 361

PART VI: APPENDICES

APPENDIX A: Case Study Conclusion 383

APPENDIX B: Industry Standards Supporting the Web 387

APPENDIX C: REST Constraints Reference 391

APPENDIX D: Service-Orientation Principles Reference 409

APPENDIX E: SOA Design Patterns Reference 425

APPENDIX F: State Concepts and Types 521

APPENDIX G: The Annotated SOA Manifesto. 533

APPENDIX H: Additional Resources 547

About the Authors 553

About the Pattern Co-Contributors 555

About the Foreword Contributor 557

Index 559

Contents

Foreword by Stefan Tilkov . . . . **xxix**

Acknowledgments . . . . **xxxiii**

CHAPTER 1: **Introduction** 1

    1.1 About this Book 2

        Who this Book is For 2

        What this Book Does Not Cover 3

    1.2 Recommended Reading 3

    1.3 How this Book is Organized 4

        Part I: Fundamentals 4

        Chapter 3: Introduction to Services .4

        Chapter 4: SOA Terminology and Concepts 5

        Chapter 5: REST Constraints and Goals 5

        Part II: RESTful Service-Orientation 5

        Chapter 6: Service Contracts with REST 5

        Chapter 7: Service-Orientation with REST 5

        Part III: Service-Oriented Analysis and Design with REST 5

        Chapter 8: Mainstream SOA Methodology and REST 5

        Chapter 9: Analysis and Service Modeling with REST 5

        Chapter 10: Service-Oriented Design with REST 6

        Part IV: Service Composition with REST 6

        Chapter 11: Fundamental Service Composition with REST 6

        Chapter 12: Advanced Service Composition with REST 6

        Chapter 13: Service Composition with REST Case Study 6

        Part V: Supplemental 6

        Chapter 14: Design Patterns for SOA with REST 6

        Chapter 15: Service Versioning with REST 6

        Chapter 16: Uniform Contract Profiles 7

        Part VI: Appendices 7

        Appendix A: Case Study Conclusion .7

        Appendix B: Industry Standards Supporting the Web 7

        Appendix C: REST Constraints Reference 7

        Appendix D: Service-Orientation Principles Reference 7

Appendix E: SOA Design Patterns Reference 7
Appendix F: State Concepts and Types 7
Appendix G: The Annotated SOA Manifesto 7
Appendix H: Additional Resources 8

1.4 Conventions 8
   Use of the Color Red 8
   Design Constraints, Principles, and Patterns:
   Page References and Capitalization 8
   Design Goals: Capitalization 9
   Symbol Legend 9

1.5 Additional Information 10
   Updates, Errata, and Resources (www.servicetechbooks.com) . . 10
   Master Glossary (www.soaglossary.com) 10
   Service-Orientation (www.serviceorientation.com) 10
   What Is REST? (www.whatisrest.com) 10
   Referenced Specifications (www.servicetechspecs.com) 10
   The Service Technology Magazine (www.servicetechmag.com) . . 10
   SOASchool.com® SOA Certified Professional (SOACP) 11
   CloudSchool.com™ Cloud Certified (CCP) Professional 11
   Notification Service 11

CHAPTER 2: Case Study Background **13**

2.1 How Case Studies Are Used 14

2.2 Case Study Background #1: Midwest University
Association (MUA) 14
   History 14
   IT Environment 14
   Business Goals and Obstacles 16
      1. Build Reusable Business Services 18
      2. Consolidate Systems and Information 18
      3. Improve Channel Experience 18
      4. Build Services Infrastructure 18

2.3 Case Study Background #2: KioskEtc Co. 18
   History 19
   IT Environment 19
   Business Goals and Obstacles 19

PART I: FUNDAMENTALS

CHAPTER 3: Introduction to Services **23**

    3.1 Service Terminology 24

        Service 24

        Service Contract. 24

        Service Capability 26

        Service Consumer 26

        Service Agent. 27

        Service Composition 27

    3.2 Service Terminology Context 29

        Services and REST 29

        Services and SOA 29

        REST Services and SOA 29

CHAPTER 4: SOA Terminology and Concepts **31**

    4.1 Basic Terminology and Concepts 32

        Service-Oriented Computing. 33

        Service-Orientation 34

        Service-Oriented Architecture (SOA). 37

        SOA Manifesto 38

        Services 39

        Cloud Computing. 40

        IT Resources 41

        Service Models. 41

           Agnostic Logic and Non-Agnostic Logic *42*

        Service Inventory 42

        Service Portfolio 43

        Service Candidate 44

        Service Contract. 44

        Service-Related Granularity. 45

        Service Profiles. 46

        SOA Design Patterns 46

    4.2 Further Reading 49

    4.3 Case Study Example. 50

CHAPTER 5: REST Constraints and Goals 51

    5.1 REST Constraints 52

        Client-Server 53

        Stateless 54

        Cache 55

        Interface/Uniform Contract 55

        Layered System 56

        Code-On-Demand 57

    5.2 Goals of the REST Architectural Style 58

        Performance 58

        Scalability 59

        Simplicity 60

        Modifiability 61

        Visibility 61

        Portability 62

        Reliability 62

    Case Study Example 63

PART II: RESTFUL SERVICE-ORIENTATION

CHAPTER 6: Service Contracts with REST 67

    6.1 Uniform Contract Elements 68

        Resource Identifier Syntax (and Resources) 69

           URIs (and URLs and URNs) *69*

           Resource Identifiers and REST Services *71*

        Methods 71

        Media Types 73

    6.2 REST Service Capabilities and REST Service Contracts . . 75

    6.3 REST Service Contracts vs. Non-REST Service Contracts 77

        Non-REST Service with Custom Service Contract 77

        REST Service with Uniform Contract 79

        HTTP Messaging vs. SOAP Messaging 81

        REST Service Contracts with WSDL? 82

6.4 The Role of Hypermedia 83

   URI Templates and Resource Queries 86

6.5 REST Service Contracts and Late Binding 87

Case Study Example 90

CHAPTER 7: Service-Orientation with REST **93**

7.1 "SOA vs. REST" or "SOA + REST"? 95

7.2 Design Goals 97

   Increased Intrinsic Interoperability 97

   Increased Federation 98

   Increased Vendor Diversity Options 99

   Increased Business and Technology Alignment 100

   Increased ROI 100

   Increased Organizational Agility 102

   Reduced IT Burden 102

   Common Goals 103

7.3 Design Principles and Constraints 104

   Standardized Service Contract 104

   Service Loose Coupling 105

   Service Abstraction 107

   Service Reusability 109

   Service Autonomy 110

   Service Statelessness 111

   Service Discoverability 113

   Service Composability 114

   Common Conflicts 114

      Stateful Interactions 115

      Service-Specific Contract Details 115

Case Study Example 116

PART III: SERVICE-ORIENTED ANALYSIS AND DESIGN WITH REST

CHAPTER 8: Mainstream SOA Methodology and REST. . . . 127

8.1 Service Inventory Analysis. 131

8.2 Service-Oriented Analysis (Service Modeling) 133

8.3 Service-Oriented Design (Service Contract). 135

8.4 Service Logic Design 137

8.5 Service Discovery. 137

8.6 Service Versioning and Retirement 138

CHAPTER 9: Analysis and Service Modeling with REST . . 139

9.1 Uniform Contract Modeling and REST Service Inventory
Modeling 141
    REST Constraints and Uniform Contract Modeling 144
    REST Service Centralization and Normalization 146

9.2 REST Service Modeling 147
    REST Service Capability Granularity 148
    Resources vs. Entities 149
    REST Service Modeling Process 150
    Case Study Example 152
    Step 1: Decompose Business Process (into Granular Actions). . 152
    Case Study Example 152
    Step 2: Filter Out Unsuitable Actions 154
    Case Study Example 154
    Step 3: Identify Agnostic Service Candidates 155
    Case Study Example 157
        Event Service Candidate (Entity). 157
        Award Service Candidate (Entity) 158
        Student Service Candidate (Entity). 158
        Notification Service Candidate (Utility) 159
        Document Service Candidate (Utility). 159
    Step 4: Identify Process-Specific Logic. 160

Case Study Example 160
Confer Student Award Service Candidate (Task) 161
Step 5: Identify Resources 161
Case Study Example 162
Step 6: Associate Service Capabilities with Resources
and Methods 163
Case Study Example 164
Confer Student Award Service Candidate (Task) 164
Event Service Candidate (Entity) 164
Award Service Candidate (Entity) 165
Student Service Candidate (Entity) 165
Notification Service Candidate (Utility) 166
Document Service Candidate (Utility) 166
Step 7: Apply Service-Orientation 167
Case Study Example 167
Step 8: Identify Candidate Service Compositions 167
Case Study Example 168
Step 9: Analyze Processing Requirements 169
Step 10: Define Utility Service Candidates 170
Step 11: Associate Utility-Centric Service Capabilities
with Resources and Methods 171
Step 12: Apply Service-Orientation 171
Step 13: Revise Candidate Service Compositions 171
Step 14: Revise Resource Definitions 171
Step 15: Revise Capability Candidate Grouping 172
Additional Considerations 172

CHAPTER 10: Service-Oriented Design with REST 173

10.1 Uniform Contract Design Considerations 175
Designing and Standardizing Methods 175
Designing and Standardizing HTTP Headers 177
Designing and Standardizing HTTP Response Codes 179
Customizing Response Codes 184
Designing Media Types 186
Designing Schemas for Media Types 188
Service-Specific XML Schemas 189

10.2 REST Service Contract Design 191

   Designing Services Based on Service Models 191

      Task Services 191

      Entity Services 192

      Utility Services. 193

   Designing and Standardizing Resource Identifiers 194

      Service Names in Resource Identifiers. 195

      Other URI Components. 196

      Resource Identifier Overlap 197

      Resource Identifier Design Guidelines 199

   Designing with and Standardizing REST Constraints 201

      Stateless 201

      Cache 202

      Uniform Contract. 203

      Layered System. 204

   Case Study Example 205

      Confer Student Award Service Contract (Task). 205

      Event Service Contract (Entity) 207

      Award Service Contract (Entity). 207

      Student Transcript Service Contract (Entity) 208

   Notification and Document Service Contracts (Utility). 209

10.3 Complex Method Design 211

   Stateless Complex Methods. 214

      Fetch Method 214

      Store Method. 215

      Delta Method. 217

      Async Method 219

   Stateful Complex Methods. 221

      Trans Method 221

      PubSub Method 222

Case Study Example 224

   OptLock Complex Method. 224

   PesLock Complex Method. 226

PART IV: SERVICE COMPOSITION WITH REST

CHAPTER 11: Fundamental Service Composition with REST 231

11.1 Service Composition Terminology 233
   Compositions and Composition Instances 233
   Composition Members and Controllers 234
      Service Compositions Are Actually Service Capability
      Compositions 235
      Designated Controllers 236
      Collective Composability. 236
   Service Activities 238
   Composition Initiators. 239
   Point-to-Point Data Exchanges and Compositions 240

11.2 Service Composition Design Influences 241
   Service-Orientation Principles and Composition Design. 241
      Standardized Service Contract and the Uniform Contract 242
      Service Loose Coupling and the Uniform Contract. 243
      Service Abstraction and Composition Information Hiding 244
      Service Reusability for Repeatable Composition 245
      Service Autonomy and Composition Autonomy Loss. 245
      Service Statelessness and Stateless 246
      Service Composability and Service-Orientation 246
   REST Constraints and Composition Design. 247
      Stateless and Stateful Compositions. 247
      Cache and Layered System 248
      Code-on-Demand and Composition Logic Deferral. 248
      Uniform Contract and Composition Coupling 248

11.3 Composition Hierarchies and Layers. 249
   Task Services Composing Entity Services. 250
   Entity Services Composing Entity Services 251

11.4 REST Service Composition Design Considerations. 253
   Synchronous and Asynchronous Service Compositions 253
   Idempotent Service Activities. 254
   Lingering Composition State 255
   Binding Between Composition Participants. 255

11.5 A Step-by-Step Service Activity. .258

    1. Request to Purchase a Ticket. 258

    2. Verify the Requested Flight Details 258

    3. Confirm a Seat on the Flight. 259

    4. Generate an Invoice 259

    5. Create the Ticket 260

    Summary 260

**CHAPTER 12: Advanced Service Composition
with REST. 261**

12.1 Service Compositions and Stateless 263

    Composition Design with Service Statelessness 264

    Composition Design with Stateless 265

12.2 Cross-Service Transactions with REST 266

    REST-Friendly Atomic Service Transactions 267

        Phase 1: Initialize. *267*

        Phase 2: Reserve *268*

        Phase 3A: Confirm *269*

        Phase 3B: Cancel *269*

        Phase 3C: Timeout *270*

        Compliance with Stateless *271*

        Additional Considerations. *272*

    REST-Friendly Compensating Service Transactions 272

        Phase 1: Begin *273*

        Phase 2: Do *273*

        Phase 3A: Complete. *274*

        Phase 3B: Undo *274*

        Phase 3C: Timeout *275*

    Compliance with Stateless. 276

        Additional Considerations. *276*

    Non-REST-Friendly Atomic Service Transactions 276

        Phase 1: Initialize *277*

        Phase 2: Do. *277*

        Phase 3: Prepare. *278*

        Phase 4A: Commit *279*

        Phase 4B: Rollback. *279*

        Phase 4C: Timeout *280*

Compliance with Stateless *280*
Additional Considerations *281*

12.3 Event-Driven Interactions with REST 282
Event-Driven Messaging 282
Compliance with Stateless *283*
Message Polling 285
Compliance with Stateless *287*

12.4 Service Composition with Dynamic Binding and
Logic Deferral 288
Denormalized Capabilities Across Normalized Services 289
Composition Deepening 292
Dynamically Binding with Common Properties 294
Runtime Logic Deferral 297

12.5 Service Composition Across Service Inventories 299
Inventory Endpoint with REST 299
Dynamic Binding Between Service Inventories with Baseline
Standardization 302

**CHAPTER 13: Service Composition with REST
Case Study 305**

13.1 Revisiting the Confer Student Award Process 306

13.2 Application Submission and Task Service Invocation . . .310

13.3 Confer Student Award Service Composition Instance
(Pre-Review Service Activity View) 312
Step 1: Composition Initiator to Confer Student Award
Task Service (A) 312
Step 2: Confer Student Award Task Service to Event
Entity Service (B) 312
Step 3: Event Entity Service to Confer Student Award
Task Service (B) 313
Step 4: Confer Student Award Task Service to Award
Entity Service (E) 314
Step 5: Award Entity Service to Confer Student Award
Task Service (E) 314
Step 6: Confer Student Award Task Service to Award
Entity Service (E) 314

Step 7: Award Entity Service to Confer Student Award
Task Service (E) 315

Step 8: Confer Student Award Task Service to Student
Entity Service (F) 315

Step 9: Student Entity Service to Confer Student Award
Task Service (F) 315

Step 10: Confer Student Award Task Service to Student
Transcript Entity Service (F) 316

Step 11: Student Transcript Entity Service to Confer Student
Award Task Service (F) 316

Step 12: Confer Student Award Task Service to Composition
Initiator 316

13.4 Review of Pending Applications and Task Service
Invocation 317

Confer Student Award Service Composition Instance
(Post-Review Service Activity View) 318

Step 1: Composition Initiator to Confer Student Award
Task Service (L) 320

Step 2: Confer Student Award Task Service to Notification
Utility Service (N) 320

Step 3: Notification Utility Service to Student Entity
Service (N) 320

Step 4: Student Entity Service to Notification Utility
Service (N) 320

Step 5: Notification Utility Service to Confer Student Award
Task Service (N) 321

Intermediate Step: Confer Student Award Task Service to
Transaction Coordinator (P, Q) 321

Intermediate Step: Transaction Coordinator to Confer
Student Award Task Service (P, Q) 321

Step 6: Confer Student Award Task Service to Conferral
Entity Service (P) 322

Intermediate Step: Conferral Entity Service to Transaction
Coordinator (P) 322

Intermediate Step: Transaction Coordinator to Conferral
Entity Service 322

Step 7: Conferral Entity Service to Confer Student Award
Task Service (Q) 322

Step 8: Confer Student Award Task Service to Student
Manuscript Entity Service (Q) 323

Intermediate Step: Student Transcript Entity Service to
Transaction Controller (Q) 323

Intermediate Step: Transaction Controller to Student
Transcript Entity Service (Q) 323

Step 9: Student Transcript Entity Service to Confer Student
Award Service (Q) 324

Intermediate Step: Confer Student Award Task Service to
Transaction Coordinator (P, Q)..........................324

Intermediate Step: Transaction Coordinator to Confer
Student Award Task Service (P, Q) 324

Step 10: Confer Student Award Task Service to Composition
Initiator 324

PART V: SUPPLEMENTAL

CHAPTER 14: Design Patterns for SOA with REST 327

14.1 REST-Inspired SOA Design Patterns 329

Content Negotiation 331

Related Patterns *332*

Related Service-Oriented Computing Goals *332*

Endpoint Redirection 332

Related Patterns *333*

Related Service-Oriented Computing Goals *333*

Entity Linking 333

Related Patterns *335*

Related Service-Oriented Computing Goals *335*

Idempotent Capability 335

Related Patterns *335*

Related Service-Oriented Computing Goals *335*

Lightweight Endpoint 336

Related Patterns *337*

Related Service-Oriented Computing Goals *337*

Reusable Contract 338

Related Patterns *338*

Related Service-Oriented Computing Goals *339*

Uniform Contract 339

14.2 Other Relevant SOA Design Patterns 340

    Contract Centralization. 340

    Contract Denormalization. 340

    Domain Inventory 340

    Schema Centralization 341

    State Messaging. 341

    Validation Abstraction. 342

CHAPTER 15: Service Versioning with REST **343**

15.1 Versioning Basics 346

    REST Service Contract Compatibility 346

        Compatible and Incompatible Changes. *348*

    Uniform Contract Method Compatibility 349

    Uniform Contract Media Type Compatibility 350

        Media Types and Forwards-compatibility. *354*

15.2 Version Identifiers 355

    Using Version Identifiers. 356

    Version Identifiers and the Uniform Contract 358

CHAPTER 16: Uniform Contract Profiles **361**

16.1 Uniform Contract Profile Template 362

    Uniform-Level Structure 363

    Method Profile Structure. 364

    Media Type Profile Structure 365

16.2 REST Service Profile Considerations 367

16.3 Case Study Example. 369

    Uniform-Level Structure: MUAUC 370

    Method Profile Structure: Fetch 371

    Response Code Handling for GET Methods in Fetch Method. . .373

    Method Profile Structure: Store 374

    Response Code Handling for PUT and DELETE Methods
    in Store Method 376

    Method Profile Structure: GET 377

    Method Profile Structure: PUT 378

    Media Type Profile Structure:
    Invoice (`application/vnd.edu.mua.invoice+xml`). 379

PART VI: APPENDICES

APPENDIX A: Case Study Conclusion 383

APPENDIX B: Industry Standards Supporting the Web 387

The Internet Engineering Taskforce (IETF). 388

The World Wide Web Consortium 389

Other Web Standards 390

APPENDIX C: REST Constraints Reference 391

APPENDIX D: Service-Orientation Principles Reference . .409

APPENDIX E: SOA Design Patterns Reference 425

APPENDIX F: State Concepts and Types 521

State Management Explained 522

State Management in Abstract. 522

Origins of State Management. 523

Deferral vs. Delegation. 527

Types of State 527

Active and Passive. 527

Stateless and Stateful. 528

Session and Context Data 528

Measuring Service Statelessness 530

APPENDIX G: The Annotated SOA Manifesto 533

APPENDIX H: Additional Resources. 547

    www.whatisrest.com 548

    Bibliography and References. 548

    Resources 551

        www.servicetechbooks.com 551

        www.soaschool.com, www.cloudschool.com 551

        www.servicetechmag.com. 552

        www.soaglossary.com. 552

        www.servicetechspecs.com 552

        www.soapatterns.org, www.cloudpatterns.org 552

        www.serviceorientation.com, www.soaprinciples.com,

        www.whatissoa.com. 552

        www.servicetechsymposium.com 552

About the Authors 553

    Thomas Erl. 553

    Benjamin Carlyle 553

    Cesare Pautasso 554

    Raj Balasubramanian. 554

About the Pattern Co-Contributors 555

    David Booth, Ph.D.. 555

    Herbjörn Wilhelmsen 555

About the Foreword Contributor .557

    Stefan Tilkov. 557

Index. 559

Foreword
by Stefan Tilkov

When I first heard about REST in early 2002, I was a strong believer in the value of the emerging Web services specifications and standards. I was initially intrigued by the approach, particularly the "uniform interface" idea, but quickly concluded that while REST might be interesting, it was most certainly not applicable in enterprise use cases.

A year or two later, I had started to appreciate the elegance and simplicity of the REST style, and became convinced that in some cases, it was a better choice, while more advanced use cases still required SOAP and WSDL and WS-*. Another year later, I found myself recommending RESTful HTTP over SOAP-style Web services in most situations, and decided that I could call myself a "RESTafarian" by conviction. I had become convinced—and still am—that adhering to the constraints of the REST architectural style not only leads to better systems on the public Web, but also within all kinds of enterprise-internal scenarios.

Today, REST has become mainstream—with all the positive and negative effects this has for any technology. It is now relatively easy to introduce a RESTful approach, even in large enterprises, without raising too many eyebrows. I am still surprised how often it is even viewed as the obvious default choice.

So maybe the REST community should be happy and satisfied, and look forward to all the excellent system development and integration work we will do, both on the public Web and within companies. But there are two problems with this: Not everything that claims to be RESTful actually is so, and often SOA is perceived as the architecture of WS-* style Web services and therefore seen as incompatible with REST.

The Misuse of the "REST" Moniker

Following REST principles when applying Web technologies, such as HTTP and URIs, and using hypermedia formats, such as HTML, leads to systems that are evolvable, dynamic yet stable, and can be connected in new and unforeseen ways. Building or integrating systems in a way that actually deserves being called "RESTful" requires a different kind of design than what most developers have been used to in the past. Choosing REST instead of a Distributed Objects, RPC, or WS-* approach requires expressing an interface's domain using resources, media types, hypermedia, and the uniform interface. The better your understanding of these concepts, the easier you will find it to adhere to the implied constraints, and the more you will be able to exploit REST's benefits.

Due to the fundamental design decision of "transport independence" in the WDSL/ SOAP/WS-* architecture, systems built using it can never be RESTful, and very few people would disagree. But it is just as easy to violate the Web's underlying ideas without ever coming near XML or SOAP, and the Internet is filled with examples of this: Tunneling method calls through HTTP GET or POST, ignoring caching and hypermedia, or treating the characters that make up a URI as a development API. Using JSON, HTTP, and "pretty" URIs does not mean a system is RESTful. Don't assume everything called a "REST API" can serve as a role model.

On the Merits of SOA

The label "SOA" has been thoroughly burned, and in my view, this is mostly due to the fact that many made, and continue to make, a strong association between the abstract, high-level concept of SOA and the Web services technology that initially became a popular way to support it. The many discussions you can find on the Web that talk about "REST vs. SOA" enforce this with their apples to oranges comparison. So let us take a step back and look at the original motivation for SOA.

In practically any company, many individual systems make up the complete IT landscape. They run on different technologies, and they have been built using different tools. Some come from commercial vendors, some may have been built in-house. After a short while, you will want to connect them because there very obviously is value in doing so. You can do this in a point-to-point way, exporting some data here, periodically importing it over there, via files, shared databases, or individual integration solutions. This will lead to a brittle, unmanageable landscape.

Because it is so hard to integrate systems, you (and your vendor) will opt for making them fatter and fatter, unless you have to invest an absurd amount of effort to change them. Introducing a centralized integration middleware bottleneck in the middle is not a good solution, although it might seem tempting at first: You become dependent on the single vendor, who will get bought by somebody else, go out of business, or become legacy after you merge with your competitor who has bought another product of this type more recently.

So what do you do instead? You treat the problem in a reasonable way—by reducing the amount of effort for integrating individual systems by limiting the amount of different technologies used at the interface layer, by picking a good interface abstraction, and by modularizing the big applications into smaller chunks. You take care not to depend on a particular vendor, be it a middleware or an applications vendor; you want to make it easy to (re)use stuff. Few will disagree that this is a reasonable approach.

That is, to me, the essence of SOA: A software architecture that is not applied to an individual system, but to a set of systems within a company; focusing on network/wire interfaces, not implementation; standardizing whatever is necessary to ensure smooth communication and serendipitous re-use, but nothing more. When we authored the SOA Manifesto several years ago, it was the emphasis we placed on achieving intrinsic interoperability that embodied, for me, what SOA and service-orientation were truly about, and it was also what aligned it with REST principles.

In my view service-orientation is very much worth pursuing, and RESTful HTTP is the best way we currently have available to do so. No other architecture is as widely supported, enables reuse with similar ease, and has the same kind of support for continued evolution. Yet the use of REST in SOA scenarios is still in its infancy, and best practices and patterns have, so far, been hard to find.

The Contribution of this Book

The authors have a clear and thorough understanding of what REST is and isn't, and this book will provide you with the knowledge needed to distinguish something that actually is RESTful from something that just claims to be. You will learn about SOA and REST fundamentals, and get to know some of the design patterns that combine service-orientation and REST. You will find out how to design and build both services and service consumers.

There is a strong need for guidance in building RESTful systems and integration scenarios—and it is critical that your guide is not satisfied with the low-hanging fruit, but aims for the long-term benefits. I am convinced the authors are among the best guides that you can find, and I am confident you will become convinced that REST and SOA are not only not in conflict, but a perfect match.

—*Stefan Tilkov, innoQ*

Acknowledgments

- Gustavo Alonso, Department of Computer Science, ETH Zurich

- Gerald Beuchelt, MITRE

- Kevin Davis

- Jean-Paul De Baets, Belgian Government

- Roy Fielding

- Ryan Frazier, Microsoft

- Michael Grube, Nordstrom

- Dolly Kandpal, Qamlo Information Services

- Jana Koehler

- Ivana Lee, Arcitura Education

- Mark Little, Red Hat

- Damian Maschek, Deutsche Bahn Systel

- Theodore Morrison, Geocent

- Pethuru Raj, Ph.D., Wipro Consulting Services

- Ian Robinson

- Sid Sanyal, Zurich Financial Services

- Al Scherer, Follett Higher Education Group

- Christoph Schittko, Microsoft

- Sanjay Singh, NorthgateArinso

- Dave Slotnick, Rackspace

- Roger Stoffers, HP

- Longji Tang, Ph.D., FedEx

- Clemens Utschig-Utschig, Boehringer Ingelheim Pharma

- Philip Wik, MSS

- Erik Wilde, EMC

Chapter 1

Introduction

1.1 About this Book

1.2 Recommended Reading

1.3 How this Book is Organized

1.4 Conventions

1.5 Additional Information

The World Wide Web is based on the most successful technology architecture in the history of IT. It has changed how we view, access, and exchange information and, with the formalization of REST constraints, it has also provided us with compelling new ways to build and improve automation solutions.

How you wield the power that comes with the inherent flexibility and simplicity of REST is up to you. REST provides a great deal of guidance for making an architecture and its automation logic technically sound, but it does not provide guidance to ensure that what you build actually provides on-going value in support of the distinct requirements and goals of your business.

Service-orientation has established a proven method for realizing a specific target state. This target state provides proven strategic business value to many organizations. Achieving this target state requires that we apply service-orientation to a suitable distributed computing medium. This book not only demonstrates that REST is a suitable medium for building service-oriented solutions, but also that the service-oriented architectural model is a suitable (and often necessary) foundation for REST-style technology architectures to realize their full business potential.

1.1 About this Book

The purpose of this book is to document how REST relates to and can be used in conjunction with service-oriented architecture, service-orientation design principles, and associated design patterns.

Who this Book is For

- Architects that design services and distributed solution architectures.

- Developers interested in working with REST technologies to build service-oriented solutions.

- Enterprise architects who need to understand the benefits and impacts of REST as a service implementation medium for SOA.

- Analysts who may need to model services specifically for eventual implementation as REST services.

- REST specialists who want to understand how REST can be used in support of SOA and service-orientation.

- SOA specialists who want to understand the pros and cons of merging REST architecture with service-oriented architecture.

What this Book Does Not Cover

This is neither a REST tutorial, nor a comprehensive guide to learning SOA or service-orientation. Although introductory chapters cover some fundamentals, the bulk of this book is dedicated to exploring how service-orientation can be applied to REST service design and how REST architecture influences service-oriented solution design and the complexion of service-oriented technology architectures.

This book maintains a focus on modeling, design, and architecture in relation to principles, patterns, and constraints. It does not explore the hands-on implementation of REST-based service architectures in any great detail, nor does it cover middleware and intermediary components, such as proxies and gateways.

If you are new to REST and/or SOA, it is recommended you explore the resources listed in the upcoming *Recommended Reading* section prior to reading this book.

1.2 Recommended Reading

To further ensure that you have a clear understanding of the key terms used and referenced in the upcoming chapters, you can also visit the online master glossary for this book series at www.soaglossary.com.

Books from this series that elaborate on key topics covered by this title include:

- *SOA Principles of Service Design* – A comprehensive documentation of the service-orientation design paradigm with full descriptions of all of the principles referenced in this book. These principles are also explained at www.soaprinciples.com and in Appendix D.

- *SOA Design Patterns* – This is the official SOA design patterns catalog containing descriptions and examples for most of the patterns referenced in this book. You can also look up concise descriptions for these patterns at www.soapatterns.org and in Appendix E.

Further examples of REST service technologies and designs developed in support of service-orientation are provided in the *SOA with .NET & Windows Azure, SOA with Java,* and *Service-Oriented Infrastructure: On Premise and in the Cloud* books.

For those of you interested in comparing REST service design to Web service design, the series title *Web Service Contract Design & Versioning for SOA* provides a large amount of corresponding coverage, as it pertains to WSDL, SOAP, XML Schema, WS-Policy, and WS-Addressing.

For those of you new to REST, the following titles are recommended:

- *Building Hypermedia APIs with HTML5 and Node* (by Mike Amundsen, O'Reilly Media, 2011)

- *RESTful Web Services: Web Services for the Real World* (by Leonard Richardson and Sam Ruby, O'Reilly Media, 2007)

- *HTTP: The Definitive Guide* (by David Gourley, O'Reilly Media, 2002)

- *REST in Practice: Hypermedia and Systems Architecture* (by Savas Parastatidis, Ian Robinson, Jim Webber, O'Reilly Media, 2010)

- *Restlet in Action: Developing RESTful Web APIs in Java* (by Jerome Louvel, Thierry Templier, and Thierry Boileau, O'Reilly Media, 2009)

- *RESTful .NET* (by Jon Flanders, O'Reilly Media, 2008)

A number of recommended reading resources for REST are provided in Appendix H, including books, papers, and articles from the authors of this book.

1.3 How this Book is Organized

This book begins with Chapters 1 and 2, which supply introductory content and case study background information respectively. Provided here is a brief overview of subsequent chapters.

Part I: Fundamentals

Chapter 3: Introduction to Services

Service-related terminology and concepts can differ in relation to REST and SOA. This chapter provides a gentle introduction to services and includes clarifications necessary to avoid confusion in subsequent chapters.

Chapter 4: SOA Terminology and Concepts

This chapter contains an overview of key terms and concepts associated with SOA, service-orientation, and related topic areas, such as service composition.

Chapter 5: REST Constraints and Goals

This chapter provides a brief overview of REST constraints and architectural design goals. For those of you already familiar with REST, be sure to at least read through the Interface constraint description to understand how this book uses the term "Uniform Contract" for this constraint instead.

Part II: RESTful Service-Orientation

Chapter 6: Service Contracts with REST

Building upon Chapters 3, 4, and 5, this chapter explores the fundamentals of REST service contracts and compares their characteristics and usage to non-REST variations. Also introduced is a distinct diagram symbol notation used to represent REST service contracts and service capabilities.

Chapter 7: Service-Orientation with REST

This chapter includes sections that map service-orientation design principles to REST constraints and architectural properties, and then further explores how REST can impact the goals of service-oriented computing.

Part III: Service-Oriented Analysis and Design with REST

Chapter 8: Mainstream SOA Methodology and REST

A brief introduction to the SOA project delivery phases is provided, along with content relating key stages to REST.

Chapter 9: Analysis and Service Modeling with REST

The complete service-oriented analysis process is explored, with case study examples and augmented for the modeling of REST-based service candidates, service capability candidates, and service composition candidates.

Chapter 10: Service-Oriented Design with REST

A varied collection of design-related topics is provided in this chapter to provide guidance for the creation of custom REST-based service contracts.

Part IV: Service Composition with REST

Chapter 11: Fundamental Service Composition with REST

The unique design considerations that come with building service compositions comprised of REST services are addressed by a set of topics that tackle areas such as service models, service layers, and idempotency. The chapter concludes with a step-by-step sample scenario.

Chapter 12: Advanced Service Composition with REST

Some of the more challenging areas of REST-based service composition are covered in this dense chapter, including cross-service transactions, event-driven messaging, dynamic binding, and cross-service inventory interactions. A recurring theme throughout this chapter is compliance issues with the Stateless {395} constraint.

Chapter 13: Service Composition with REST Case Study

The services modeled and designed in the case study examples from Chapters 9 and 10 are now aggregated into a REST-based service composition architecture. This in-depth case study steps through two runtime scenarios and maps automated actions to original business process steps.

Part V: Supplemental

Chapter 14: Design Patterns for SOA with REST

This important chapter provides plain English descriptions of the seven new REST-inspired SOA design patterns that have been added to the SOA design patterns catalog. Each of the explained patterns is officially represented via a profile in Appendix E.

Chapter 15: Service Versioning with REST

This chapter uses some basic versioning content from the series title *Web Service Contract Design & Versioning for SOA* and supplements it with REST service versioning topics and examples.

Chapter 16: Uniform Contract Profiles

The uniform contract profile template is introduced, along with content describing a variation of the established service profile augmented to document REST service characteristics. The chapter concludes with a case study example in which a sample uniform contract profile is documented.

Part VI: Appendices

Appendix A: Case Study Conclusion

This appendix provides a conclusion of the case study storyline.

Appendix B: Industry Standards Supporting the Web

An overview of industry standards organizations and published specifications relevant to REST are provided in this appendix.

Appendix C: REST Constraints Reference

This appendix provides the profile tables for the REST design constraints referenced in this book.

Appendix D: Service-Orientation Principles Reference

This appendix provides the profile tables (originally from *SOA Principles of Service Design*) for the service-orientation design principles referenced in this book.

Appendix E: SOA Design Patterns Reference

This appendix provides the profile tables for the SOA design patterns referenced in this book, including 14 new REST-inspired design patterns.

Appendix F: State Concepts and Types

Fundamental terms and concepts originally introduced in Chapter 11 of *SOA Principles of Service Design* are provided primarily in support of content in Part IV of this book.

Appendix G: The Annotated SOA Manifesto

This appendix provides the annotated version of the SOA Manifesto declaration, which is also published at www.soa-manifesto.com.

Appendix H: Additional Resources

A list of relevant Web sites and supplementary resources is provided in this final appendix, including a bibliography of additional publications.

1.4 Conventions

Use of the Color Red

Text and code fragments are colored red sporadically throughout this book. Red text is used sparingly within general chapter content to help highlight key statements. Within code samples, fragments are generally colored red when they relate to the preceding description text for the given *Example* section.

Design Constraints, Principles, and Patterns:
Page References and Capitalization

Each design constraint, principle, and pattern discussed in this book has a corresponding profile. A profile is a concise definition that summarizes key design aspects and considerations. A primary and on-going topic area of this book is the exploration of how constraints, principles, and patterns relate to and affect each other. You are therefore encouraged to repeatedly refer to the profiles whenever encountering a constraint, principle, or pattern in a context that is unclear to you.

In order to facilitate the quick reference of profiles, a special convention is used. Each principle, pattern, and constraint name is always capitalized and followed by a page number that points to the corresponding profile page. This is a convention that was established by the design patterns community and is further being extended to design principles and design constraints in this book.

All page references point to profile tables located in appendices. The profile tables for constraints are provided in Appendix C, and those for principles and patterns are located in Appendices D and E, respectively.

To maintain an immediately recognizable distinction between constraints, principles, and patterns throughout this book, each uses a different delimiter for page numbers. The page number for each constraint is displayed in curly braces, for each principle it is placed in rounded parentheses, and for patterns, square brackets are used, as follows:

- Constraint Name {page number}
- Principle Name (page number)
- Pattern Name [page number]

For example, the following statement first references a service-orientation design principle, then an SOA design pattern, and finally a REST constraint:

"… the Service Loose Coupling (413) principle is supported via the application of the Decoupled Contract [455] pattern and the Stateless {395} constraint …"

In this statement, each reference is explicitly qualified as a principle, pattern, or constraint. Most of the references in this book (especially in later chapters) omit this qualifier in order to allow for more concise content.

For example, the preceding statement will more commonly be worded as follows:

"… Service Loose Coupling (413) is supported via the application of Decoupled Contract [455] and Stateless {395} …"

This wording convention also has origins within the design patterns community. As previously stated, if you run into a reference without an explicit qualifier, use the page number delimiter (parentheses, square brackets, or curly braces) to identify its type (principle, pattern, or constraint).

Design Goals: Capitalization

Both the REST architectural design goals and the strategic goals of service-oriented computing are capitalized throughout this book. This convention is introduced to help distinguish references to design goals, primarily for comparison purposes.

Unlike design constraints, principles, and patterns, design goals do not have profiles. The REST architectural design goals are explained in Chapter 5 and the service-oriented computing design goals are covered in Chapter 4.

Symbol Legend

This book contains a series of diagrams that are referred to as *figures*. The primary symbols used throughout all figures are individually described in the symbol legend located on the inside of the book cover.

1.5 Additional Information

The following sections provide supplementary information and resources for the *Prentice Hall Service Technology Series from Thomas Erl*.

Updates, Errata, and Resources (www.servicetechbooks.com)

Information about other series titles and various supporting resources can be found at www.servicetechbooks.com. You are encouraged to visit this site regularly to check for content changes and corrections.

Master Glossary (www.soaglossary.com)

To avoid content overlap and to ensure constant content currency, the books in this series do not contain glossaries. Instead, a dedicated Web site at www.soaglossary.com provides a master glossary for all series titles. This site continues to grow and expand with new glossary definitions as new series titles are developed and released.

Service-Orientation (www.serviceorientation.com)

This site provide papers, book excerpts, and various content dedicated to describing and defining the service-orientation paradigm, associated principles, and the service-oriented technology architectural model.

What Is REST? (www.whatisrest.com)

This Web site contains excerpts from this book and related content to provide a concise overview of REST architecture and constraints.

Referenced Specifications (www.servicetechspecs.com)

The chapters throughout this book reference various industry specifications and standards. The www.servicetechspecs.com Web site provides a central portal to the original specification documents created and maintained by the primary standards organizations.

The Service Technology Magazine (www.servicetechmag.com)

The Service Technology Magazine (formerly the *SOA Magazine*) is a regular publication provided by Arcitura Education Inc. and Prentice Hall and is officially associated with the *Prentice Hall Service Technology Series from Thomas Erl. The Service Technology Magazine* is dedicated to publishing specialized articles, case studies, and papers by industry experts and professionals.

SOASchool.com® SOA Certified Professional (SOACP)

The SOA Certified Professional curriculum is dedicated to specialized areas of service-oriented architecture and service-orientation, including analysis, architecture, governance, security, .NET development, Java development, and quality assurance.

For more information, visit www.soaschool.com.

CloudSchool.com™ Cloud Certified (CCP) Professional

The Cloud Certified Professional curriculum is dedicated to specialized areas of cloud computing, including technology, architecture, governance, security, and storage.

For more information, visit www.cloudschool.com.

Notification Service

If you'd like to be automatically notified of new book releases in this series, new supplementary content for this title, or key changes to the previously listed Web sites, use the notification form at www.servicetechbooks.com.

Chapter 2

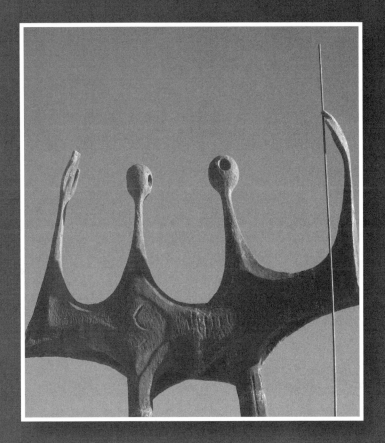

Case Study Background

2.1 How Case Studies Are Used

2.2 Case Study Background #1: Midwest University Association (MUA)

2.3 Case Study Background #2: KioskEtc Co.

2.1 How Case Studies Are Used

Case study examples are an effective means of exploring abstract topics within real world scenarios. The background information provided in this brief chapter establishes the basis for an on-going storyline. Some of the upcoming chapters conclude with *Case Study Example* sections that relate to the scenarios described in this chapter. In order to more easily identify these sections, a light gray background is used.

The case studies examine the IT and business environments of two organizations: Midwest University Association (MUA), a large academic institution, and KioskEtc Co., a medium-sized corporation.

2.2 Case Study Background #1: Midwest University Association (MUA)

Midwest University Association is one of the oldest educational institutions west of the Mississippi in the continental US. It's rated among the top 10 leading universities in the engineering and research fields and has six remote locations along with the main campus (Figure 2.1) that employ over 6,000 faculty and staff.

History

MUA was founded in the mid-1800s as the continental US was expanding. The initial establishment was created to educate next generation scholars in arts and sciences. Over the past century, it evolved into a premier engineering and research institution, while still preserving its existing academic programs. In the last decade it forged relationships with other schools in Europe and Asia. These partnerships have enabled MUA to offer its degree programs in foreign countries, in addition to launching online curricula and extended certification programs.

IT Environment

Over the last three decades, the technical infrastructure of the university has grown exponentially to accommodate the emergence of remote campuses, online learning, and the custom B2B systems that came from forming partnerships with foreign institutions. All campuses have both wired and wireless connectivity to the university network.

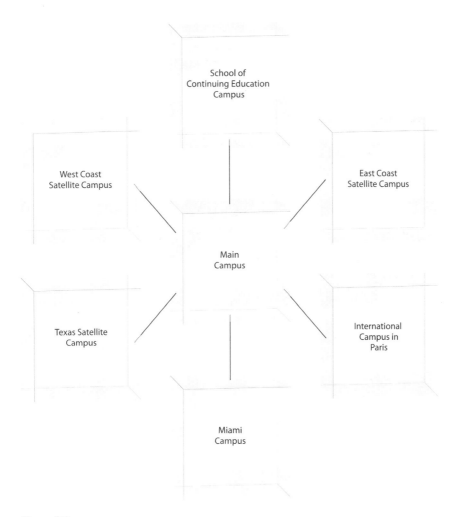

Figure 2.1
MUA's main campus and satellite locations are geographically dispersed.

Various types of supporting servers and network devices span a diverse set of operating systems.

Each program within the university has an independent IT staff and budget to support systems management. The remote campuses also have their own IT department. The collaboration with foreign institutions is governed by an independent, central enterprise architecture group.

There are various automated solutions for common processes, such as student enrollment, course cataloging, accounting, financials, as well as grading and reporting. The primary system for record keeping is an IBM Mainframe which is reconciled every night with a batch feed from the individual remote locations. The different schools themselves employ a variety of technologies and platforms, but several have common traits, as follows:

- Many of the course catalogs and transactional systems are available online, with databases running on IBM DB2 and Oracle. Some newer instances of the course catalogs have migrated to MySQL and Microsoft SQL Server.

- The most prevalent technology for hosting Web applications is PHP and J2EE with some applications based on .NET technologies.

- Most of the staff handling student information (enrollment, grades, financial aid, etc.) use 3270 emulation to access mainframes.

- Students access the course catalogs, enroll in classes, and check exam statuses using a Web-based application built with PHP. Some of these functions require each student to be on campus for security purposes. To pay tuition (if not handled via student aid or loans), students are required to physically visit the accounting office on the main campus.

- There are some kiosks on campus that let students swipe an ID card to instantly get information about courses.

A high-level view of the MUA IT enterprise is shown in Figure 2.2.

Business Goals and Obstacles

Due to increasing enrollment, MUA has seen a need to move all transactional systems online so students can access it remotely via the Web. The university has further noticed an increase in the number of part-time students and commuters who do not live on campus. Many of these students are employed and need timely access to university information from wherever they may be. This has caused changes in the revenue collected from tuition and there is now a call for a strategy that "can do more with less."

In addition, recent economic factors have forced the university to reduce IT staff and to consider the consolidation of systems for centralized management. To this end, the following goals have been defined:

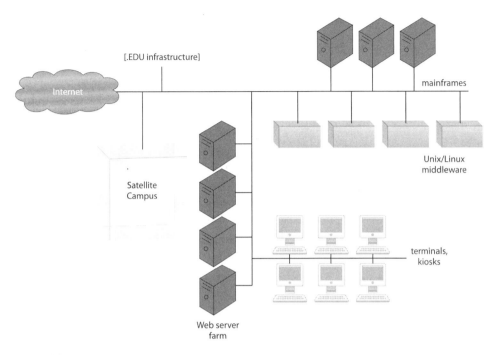

Figure 2.2
An overview of the various IT resources that comprise the MUA IT ecosystem.

- Create a single IT department to manage systems and IT support for all MUA campuses and partnered schools. Although the systems management and development of core services will be centralized, the individual schools need to have their own application development staff to handle school-specific requirements.

- Move toward "information-on-demand," where a student can access pertinent information and conduct transactions in real-time, from anywhere.

- Provide a personalized educational experience for students to help improve the successful usage of new online systems with minimal impact on support staff.

After a careful assessment of the existing infrastructure it has further been decided to re-engineer the IT systems to a service-oriented architecture that will preserve legacy assets, simplify integration between various internal and external systems, and improve channel experience for both the students and staff. The enterprise architecture group at MUA has proposed a phased adoption based on the following steps:

1. Build Reusable Business Services

Reduce the tight coupling between the channel applications and the backend systems, as well as the systems within a given school, by building a layer of reusable services that can be consumed by various platforms. These services will need to be leveraged across schools and from remote locations and must further be defined in such a way that their implementation is technology independent.

2. Consolidate Systems and Information

Provide a consolidated view of student, course, and staff information. This will be done by either consolidating back-end applications or by federating the data in the back-end, as applicable. A common view of each student will allow the faculty to make appropriate recommendations, immaterial of which school the student is affiliated with. Likewise, students can view the course and faculty information from across campuses to opt in or out of classes, or to work with faculty in schools outside of their own.

3. Improve Channel Experience

Leverage common reusable services to provide a personalized experience for the student and staff by building a highly responsive Web-based portal. These services will also be consumed by clients on mobile devices and will leverage external services where appropriate to deliver functionality based on the context.

4. Build Services Infrastructure

Enhance the current Web-based and middleware infrastructure to allow for the hosting of services, while still maintaining all the "qualities of service" mandated by university policies. In addition, the infrastructure must address message broadcasting in the case of an emergency or a significant event.

2.3 Case Study Background #2: KioskEtc Co.

KioskEtc Co. is a medium-sized coffee franchise that was started in the Midwest US with shops in and around university campuses. KioskEtc sells a range of specialty coffees and teas in addition to various baked goods.

History

KioskEtc was established in the early 1990s on the MUA main campus by a student association. It was eventually bought out by a private company and has since expanded across other campuses in the Midwest. It now has over 200 locations, with more than 60% of its revenue coming from on-campus establishments. The initial store expansions were carried out by the original KioskEtc management team who employed a strategy of using low-rent campus buildings to set-up many of the first-series coffee shops. However, for the past two years, the strategy of expansion has shifted to acquiring local coffee shops and using a franchise model.

IT Environment

KioskEtc has a very small IT staff compared to MUA. IT personnel are still centralized and operate out of the head office located a few miles from the MUA main campus. Each of the stores has its own system to handle on-going transactions. The systems are periodically synced with the main systems at the head office. All of the common functions, such as business reporting, financials, Web hosting, supply chain management, and human resources are performed out of this central IT department. Most of the custom solutions were built using open source software and have evolved over time, with some vendor-specific products, to run key back-office applications.

KioskEtc also built a Store Management Portfolio (SMP) that consists of several systems, ranging from inventory management to order processing to timesheet management. For scalability reasons, the SMP Web front-end has recently been migrated to a JEE platform on an open source Servlet container. The native client is a Windows desktop with embedded systems. Most of the functions in the SMP use asynchronous messaging to communicate between stores and the head office. There is limited functionality that relies on real-time synchronous communication via the Web interface. The asynchronous messaging is implemented using a variety of message queuing protocols, with the primary ones being Microsoft MS MQ and IBM WebSphere MQ. Newer variations use JMS to abstract underlying vendor-specific message queuing products. The simplified view of the current environment is provided in Figure 2.3.

Business Goals and Obstacles

KioskEtc has been growing rapidly in the past few years. In most instances local shops have been transformed to adopt the KioskEtc franchise model, which carries over the requirement to adopt KioskEtc automation systems.

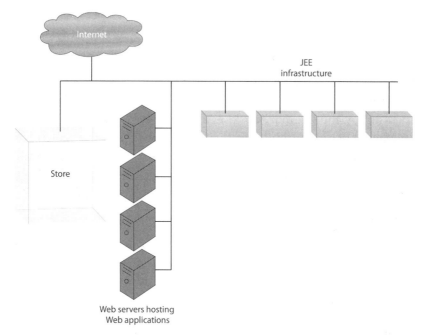

Figure 2.3
KioskEtc's SMP environment.

The KioskEtc management team would like to establish an enhanced franchising model where new stores will be managed and owned by independent business owners. KioskEtc will lend its name, business model, and products, while the franchisee will maintain full ownership of the store. This has been projected as the fastest way to reach the next plateau of 100 new stores. Franchisees can choose to run any system in their stores, as long as it supports (or can integrate with) the SMP.

Coinciding with this new franchising model, KioskEtc has expanded its menu to include hot breakfast items. This is seen as having the potential to significantly increase revenue, but the necessary changes will add complexity to existing information systems, including the SMP. There will also be new suppliers and vendors that KioskEtc will need to interface with due to the additional procurement needed to support the new items on the hot breakfast menu.

The head of KioskEtc IT has been asked to propose a phased approach to accommodate the franchising model as well as to support the expanded menu options. To this effect, the lead architect at KioskEtc has been working on a service inventory blueprint to establish a series of services that will build upon the already SOA-compliant SMP system.

Part I

Fundamentals

Chapter 3: Introduction to Services

Chapter 4: SOA Terminology and Concepts

Chapter 5: REST Constraints and Goals

Chapter 3

Introduction to Services

3.1 Service Terminology

3.2 Service Terminology Context

The term "service" can assume different meanings and implications depending on the context in which it is used. This brief chapter acts as a prelude to upcoming chapters to establish some basic distinctions pertaining to service terminology.

We begin by introducing the following terms:

- Service
- Service Contract
- Service Capability
- Service Consumer
- Service Agent
- Service Composition

The chapter concludes with the *Service Terminology Context* section that explains how the context of these terms can differ in relation to REST and SOA.

3.1 Service Terminology

Service

From a general perspective, a *service* is a software program that makes its functionality available via a published technical interface, called a *service contract*. The symbol used to depict a service (without providing any detail regarding its service contract) is shown in Figure 3.1.

Figure 3.1
The symbol used to represent an abstract service.

Service Contract

The symbol used to represent a service contract is displayed in Figure 3.2. Note how REST service contracts have a distinct notation (as explained in Chapter 6).

The view provided in Figure 3.2 is required when modeling services and designing service contracts. When an architectural view of a service is needed, the contract is shown as one artifact wedged among others within the service's implementation, as demonstrated in Figure 3.3.

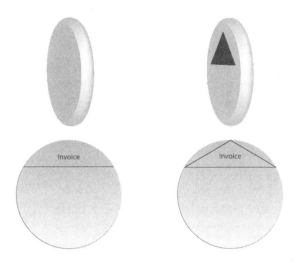

Figure 3.2

The chorded circle symbol used to display an Invoice service
contract (left) and a variation of this symbol used specifically for
REST service contracts (right).

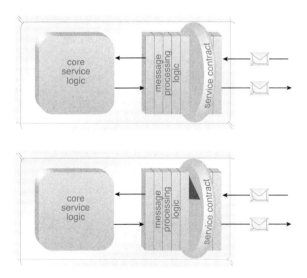

Figure 3.3

The service contract as part of a service architecture (top) and a
variation of the architecture that incorporates a REST service contract
(bottom).

Service Capability

A service contract can be broken down into a set of *service capabilities*, each of which expresses a function offered by the service to other software programs. Figure 3.4 illustrates the service contract symbol together with a set of service capabilities.

Service Consumer

A *service consumer* is the runtime role assumed by a software program when it accesses and invokes a service—or, more specifically, when it sends a message to a service capability expressed in the service contract. Upon receiving the

Figure 3.4
A Purchase Order service contract with four service capabilities.

request, the service begins processing and it may or may not return a corresponding response message to the service consumer. Figure 3.5 shows how any number of programs can act as a service consumer, including other services.

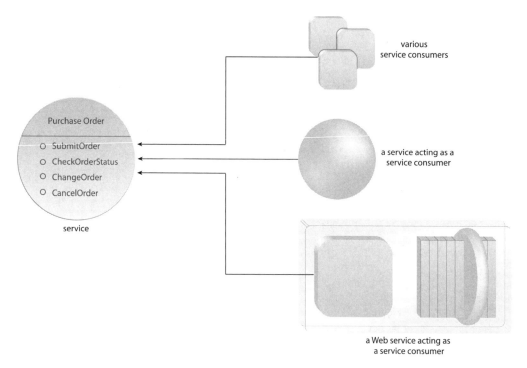

Figure 3.5
The Purchase Order service can be accessed by a range of service consumers.

Service Agent

A *service agent* is an event-driven program (often referred to as a interceptor, listener, or filter) that does not provide a published technical interface. Instead, it is designed to act as an intermediary capable of intercepting messages at runtime. When a message is intercepted, the service agent can perform *active* or *passive* processing upon the message. Agent processing logic is generally considered active when it ends up altering the message content, whereas passive processing logic does not. An example of passive processing logic is updating a separate log file used to trace messages.

Service agents play a significant role in both REST and Web service architectures. This type of software program is formally documented by the Service Agent [495] design pattern. See also the symbol legend on the inside book cover for the distinct symbol used to represent service agents in diagrams.

Service Composition

Different services are often required to work together to complete a task. A *service composition* is an aggregate of services collectively composed to automate a common task. Figure 3.6 shows the symbol used to represent an abstract service composition and Figure 3.7 illustrates a service composition from a service contract perspective that highlights which service capabilities are being invoked in a particular sequence.

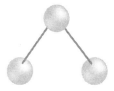

Figure 3.6

A generic symbol used to represent a service composition.

NOTE
There are several additional terms and topic areas associated with the field of service composition. These are introduced in the *Service Composition Terminology* section in Chapter 11.

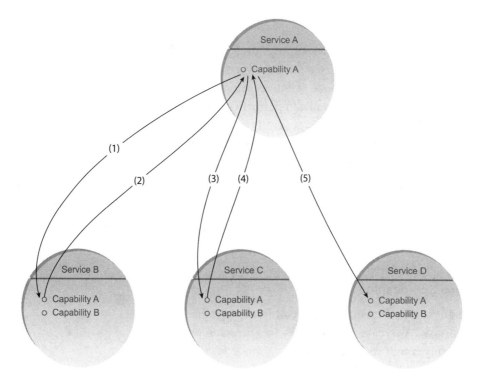

Figure 3.7

A service composition comprised of four services. Service A is acting as the service consumer of Services B, C, and D. The arrows indicate a sequence of modeled message exchanges. Note arrow #5 representing a one-way, asynchronous data delivery from Service A to Service D.

SUMMARY OF KEY POINTS

- From a general perspective, a service can be considered a software program that makes its functionality available via a published technical interface, called a service contract.

- A service contract can be broken down into a set of service capabilities, each of which expresses a function offered by the service to other software programs.

- A service consumer is the runtime role assumed by a software program when it invokes and interacts with a service.

- A service composition is an aggregate of services collectively composed to automate a common task.

3.2 Service Terminology Context

Services and REST

REST is one of several implementation mediums that can be used to create services. Another common implementation medium is Web services, a technology platform based on the use of industry standards, such as WSDL and SOAP. This book is dedicated specifically to exploring REST service design, but does make occasional reference to non-REST service mediums (such as Web services) for comparison purposes. (More information about Web services can be found in the series title *Web Service Contract Design & Versioning for SOA.*)

REST services have distinct characteristics that are introduced in Chapter 5 and further explored in subsequent chapters. REST enforces a number of design and architectural constraints upon the service contract and logic, but it does not restrict how and for what purpose services can be designed and used individually and in relation to each other. Therefore, you have a great deal of freedom as to how you can carry out a process for modeling and designing REST services intended to automate business logic.

Services and SOA

Chapter 4 introduces a series of terms specific to SOA and its associated design paradigm, service-orientation. Within the context of SOA and service-orientation the term "service" takes on a special meaning, beyond what we defined at the beginning of this chapter. A service still represents a software program with a published service contract, but both the program logic and the contract are subjected to design practices that further establish characteristics that restrict how and for what purpose individual services can be designed and used individually and in relation to each other.

REST Services and SOA

Whereas REST can be viewed as providing a service technology medium with architectural and technology-specific design requirements, service-orientation (and SOA) can be viewed as providing a technology-neutral approach to service design that can be applied to a number of service technology mediums, including Web services and REST.

Each service technology medium (or service implementation medium) has its own unique collection of technologies, design requirements, and technology architecture artifacts and properties, some of which support different service-orientation principles to lesser or greater extents.

This book is dedicated to exploring specifically how service-orientation can be applied to REST services (Figure 3.8). The upcoming chapters will highlight areas of convergence as well as gaps that will allow you to make educated decisions about how and when REST services should and should not be leveraged in support of SOA.

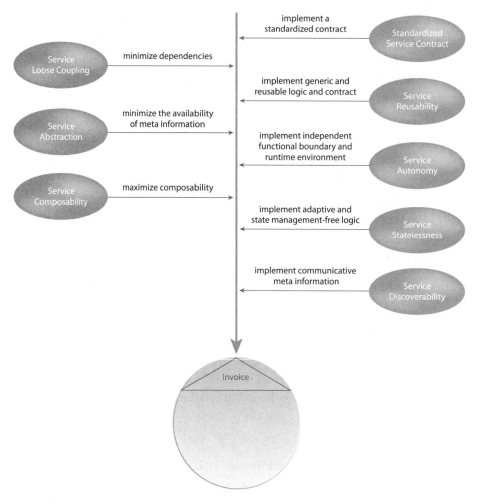

Figure 3.8
Service-orientation is comprised of a set of design principles that are collectively applied to shape software programs into service-oriented units of logic. Chapters 4 and 7 and Appendix D provide more information about these principles.

Chapter 4

SOA Terminology and Concepts

4.1 Basic Terminology and Concepts

4.2 Further Reading

4.3 Case Study Example

This chapter describes fundamental terms and concepts associated with service-oriented computing.

4.1 Basic Terminology and Concepts

Definitions for the following items are provided in this section:

- Service-Oriented Computing
- Service-Orientation
- Service-Oriented Architecture (SOA)
- SOA Manifesto
- Services
- Cloud Computing
- IT Resources
- Service Models
- Service Inventory
- Service Portfolio
- Service Candidate
- Service Contract
- Service-Related Granularity
- Service Profiles
- SOA Design Patterns

These terms are used throughout this book.

Service-Oriented Computing

Service-oriented computing is an umbrella term that represents a distinct distributed computing platform. As such, it encompasses many things, including its own design paradigm and design principles, design pattern catalogs, pattern languages, and a distinct architectural model, along with related concepts, technologies, and frameworks.

Service-orientation emerged as a formal method in support of achieving the following goals and benefits (Figure 4.1) associated with service-oriented computing:

- *Increased Intrinsic Interoperability* – Services within a given boundary are designed to be naturally compatible so they can be effectively assembled and reconfigured in response to changing business requirements.

- *Increased Federation* – Services establish a standardized contract layer that is federated, enabling it to hide underlying disparity that allows services to be individually governed and evolved.

- *Increased Vendor Diversification Options* – A service-oriented environment is based on a vendor-neutral architectural model, allowing the organization to evolve the architecture in tandem with the business without being limited to proprietary vendor platform characteristics.

- *Increased Business and Technology Alignment* – Some services are designed with a business-centric functional context, allowing them to mirror and evolve with the business of the organization.

- *Increased ROI* – Most services are delivered and viewed as IT assets that are expected to provide repeated value that surpasses the cost of delivery and ownership.

- *Increased Organizational Agility* – New and changing business requirements can be fulfilled more rapidly by establishing an environment in which solutions can be assembled or augmented with reduced effort by leveraging the reusability and native interoperability of existing services.

- *Reduced IT Burden* – The enterprise as a whole is streamlined as a result of the previously described goals and benefits, allowing IT itself to better support the organization by providing more value with less cost and less overall burden.

These goals collectively represent the target state we look to achieve when we consistently apply service-orientation to the design of software programs. Various chapters in this book identify how REST relates to the attainment of these goals.

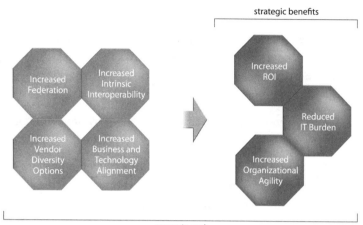

Figure 4.1

The latter three goals listed in the previous list represent target strategic benefits that are achieved when attaining the preceding four goals.

NOTE
The strategic goals of service-oriented computing are also commonly associated with SOA, as explained in the *SOA Manifesto* section.

Service-Orientation

Service-orientation is a design paradigm intended for the creation of solution logic units that are individually shaped so they can be collectively and repeatedly utilized in support of the realization of the specific strategic goals and benefits associated with service-oriented computing.

Solution logic designed in accordance with service-orientation can be qualified with "service-oriented," and units of service-oriented solution logic are referred to as "services." As a design paradigm for distributed computing, service-orientation can be compared to object-orientation (or object-oriented design). Service-orientation, in fact, has many roots in object-orientation and has also been influenced by other industry developments (Figure 4.2).

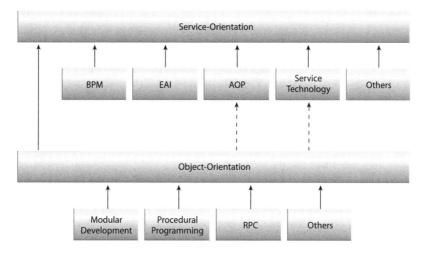

Figure 4.2

Service-orientation is an evolutionary design paradigm that owes much of its existence to established design practices and technology platforms.

The service-orientation design paradigm is primarily comprised of eight specific design principles (Figure 4.3):

- *Standardized Service Contract (411)* – "Services within the same service inventory are in compliance with the same contract design standards."

- *Service Loose Coupling (413)* – "Service contracts impose low consumer coupling requirements and are themselves decoupled from their surrounding environment."

- *Service Abstraction (414)* – "Service contracts only contain essential information and information about services is limited to what is published in service contracts."

- *Service Reusability (415)* – "Services contain and express agnostic logic and can be positioned as reusable enterprise resources."

- *Service Autonomy (417)* – "Services exercise a high level of control over their under-lying runtime execution environment."

- *Service Statelessness (418)* – "Services minimize resource consumption by deferring the management of state information when necessary."

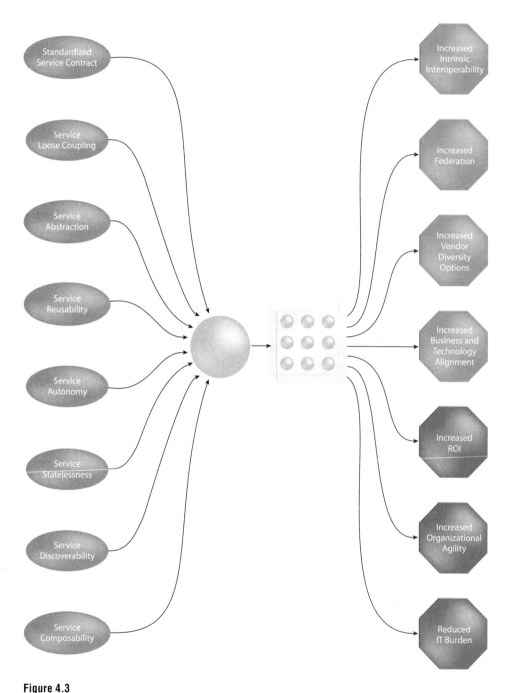

Figure 4.3

The repeated application of service-orientation principles, to services that are delivered as part of a collection, leads to a target state based on the manifestation of the strategic goals associated with service-oriented computing. (Note the container symbol represents a "service inventory," a term that is described later in this chapter.)

- *Service Discoverability (420)* – "Services are supplemented with communicative meta data by which they can be effectively discovered and interpreted."

- *Service Composability (422)* – "Services are effective composition participants, regardless of the size and complexity of the composition."

Much of this book is dedicated to the application of these principles to REST services. Various aspects of this are covered, including positive and negative impacts, relationships with REST constraints, and guidance for REST service design and development with service-orientation.

Service-Oriented Architecture (SOA)

Service-oriented architecture is a technology architectural model for service-oriented solutions with distinct characteristics in support of realizing service-orientation and the strategic goals associated with service-oriented computing. Different types of service-oriented architecture can exist, depending on the scope of its application (Figure 4.4).

Figure 4.4

The layered SOA model establishes the four common SOA types: service architecture, service composition architecture, service inventory architecture, and service-oriented enterprise architecture. (These different architectural types are explained in detail in the book *SOA Design Patterns*.)

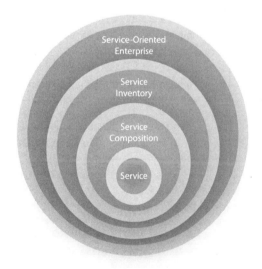

As a form of technology architecture, an SOA implementation can consist of a combination of technologies, products, APIs, supporting infrastructure extensions, and various other parts. The actual complexion of a deployed service-oriented architecture is unique within each enterprise; however, it is typified by the introduction of new technologies and platforms that specifically support the creation, execution, and evolution of service-oriented solutions. As a result, building a technology architecture with the SOA model establishes an environment suitable for solution logic that has been designed in compliance with service-orientation design principles.

SOA is defined in terms of characteristics that must exist to support the application of service-orientation principles, rather than formal constraints like those of REST-style architecture. These differences are expanded upon in subsequent chapters.

NOTE

Let's briefly recap the previous three terms to clearly establish how they relate to each other and specifically how they lead to a definition of SOA:

- There is a set of strategic goals associated with service-oriented computing.

- These goals represent a specific target state.

- Service-orientation is the paradigm that provides a proven method for achieving this target state.

- When we apply service-orientation to the design of software, we build units of logic called "services."

- Service-oriented solutions are comprised of one or more services.

- To build successful service-oriented solutions, we need a distributed technology architecture with specific characteristics.

- These characteristics distinguish the technology architecture as being service-oriented. This is SOA.

SOA Manifesto

Historically, the term "service-oriented architecture" (or "SOA") has been used so broadly by the media and within vendor marketing literature that it almost became synonymous with service-oriented computing itself. The SOA Manifesto (published at www.soa-manifesto.org) is a formal declaration authored by a diverse working group comprised of industry thought leaders during the 2nd International SOA Symposium in Rotterdam in 2009. This document establishes, at a high level, a clear separation of service-oriented architecture and service-orientation in order to address the ambiguity that had been causing confusion in relation to the meaning of the term "SOA."

The Annotated SOA Manifesto is published at www.soa-manifesto.com and in Appendix G of this book. This version of the SOA Manifesto is recommended reading as it elaborates on statements made in the original SOA Manifesto.

Services

Chapter 3 introduced the term "service" from a general perspective. From a service-orientation perspective, a *service* is a unit of logic to which service-orientation has been applied to a meaningful extent. It is the application of service-orientation design principles that distinguishes a unit of logic as a service compared to units of logic that may exist solely as objects, components, Web services, REST services, or cloud-based services.

Subsequent to conceptual service modeling, service-oriented design and development stages implement a service as a physically independent software program with specific design characteristics that support the attainment of the strategic goals associated with service-oriented computing. Each service is assigned its own distinct functional context and is comprised of a set of capabilities related to this context. Therefore, a service can be considered a container of capabilities associated with a common purpose (or functional context).

It is important to view and position SOA and service-orientation as being neutral to any one technology platform. By doing so, you have the freedom to continually pursue the strategic goals associated with service-oriented computing by leveraging on-going service technology advancements.

Any implementation technology that can be used to create a distributed system may be suitable for the application of service-orientation. In addition to Web services and REST services, distributed components can also be used to create legitimate service-oriented solutions (Figure 4.5).

Figure 4.5

These are the symbols used to represent a component. The symbol on the left is a generic component that may or may not have been designed as a service, whereas the symbol on the right highlights the embedded service contract, and is therefore labeled to indicate that it has been designed as a service.

core
service
logic

service contract

NOTE
Building service-oriented components is one of the topics covered in the books *SOA with .NET & Windows Azure* and *SOA with Java*, both titles in the *Prentice Hall Service Technology Series from Thomas Erl*.

Cloud Computing

Cloud computing is a specialized form of distributed computing that introduces utilization models for remotely provisioning scalable and measured IT resources. The primary benefits associated with cloud computing are:

- *Reduced Investment and Proportional Costs* – Cloud consumers that use cloud-based IT resources can generally lease them with a pay-for-use model, which allows them to pay a usage fee for only the amount of the IT resource actually used, resulting in directly proportional costs. This gives an organization access to IT resources without having to purchase its own, resulting in reduced investment requirements. By lowering required investments and incurring costs that are proportional to their needs, cloud consumers can scale their IT enterprise effectively and pro-actively.

- *Increased Scalability* – IT resources can be flexibly acquired from a cloud provider, almost instantaneously and at a wide variety of usage levels. By scaling with cloud-based IT resources, cloud consumers can leverage this flexibility to increase their responsiveness to foreseen and unforeseen changes.

- *Increased Availability and Reliability* – Cloud providers generally offer resilient IT resources for which they are able to guarantee high levels of availability. Cloud environments can be based on a modular architecture that provides extensive failover support to further increase reliability. Cloud consumers that lease access to cloud-based IT resources can therefore benefit from increased availability and reliability.

When appropriate, these benefits can help realize the strategic goals of service-oriented computing by extending and enhancing service-oriented architectures and increasing the potential of realizing certain service-orientation principles.

IT Resources

An IT resource is a broad term to refer to any physical or virtual IT-related artifact (software or hardware). For example, a physical server, a virtual server, a database, and a service implementation are all forms of IT resources.

Even though a service is considered an IT resource, it is important to acknowledge that a service architecture will commonly encapsulate and connect to other IT resources. This distinction is especially important in cloud-based environments, where a cloud service is classified as a remotely accessible IT resource, which may encompass and depend on various additional cloud-based IT resources that are only accessible from within the cloud.

Service Models

A *service model* is a classification used to indicate that a service belongs to one of several predefined types based on the nature of the logic it encapsulates, the reuse potential of this logic, and how the service may relate to domains within its enterprise.

The following three service models are common to most enterprise environments and therefore common to most SOA projects:

- *Task Service* – A service with a non-agnostic functional context that generally corresponds to single-purpose, parent business process logic. A task service will usually encapsulate the composition logic required to compose several other services in order to complete its task.

- *Entity Service* – A reusable service with an agnostic functional context associated with one or more related business entities (such as invoice, customer, claim, etc.). For example, a Purchase Order service has a functional context associated with the processing of purchase order-related data and logic.

- *Utility Service* – Also a reusable service with an agnostic functional context, but this type of service is intentionally not derived from business analysis specifications and models. It encapsulates low-level technology-centric functions, such as notification, logging, and security processing.

Service models play an important role during service-oriented analysis and service-oriented design phases. Although the aforementioned set of service models is well established, it is not uncommon for an organization to create its own service models (which are often derived from established ones).

Agnostic Logic and Non-Agnostic Logic

The term "agnostic" originated from Greek and means "without knowledge." Therefore, logic that is sufficiently generic so that it is not specific to (has no knowledge of) a particular parent task is classified as *agnostic* logic. Because knowledge specific to single purpose tasks is intentionally omitted, agnostic logic is considered multi-purpose. On the flipside, logic that is specific to (contains knowledge of) a single-purpose task is labeled as *non-agnostic* logic.

Another way of thinking about agnostic and non-agnostic logic is to focus on the extent to which the logic can be repurposed. Because agnostic logic is expected to be multi-purpose, it is subject to the Service Reusability (415) principle with the intention of turning it into highly reusable logic. Once reusable, this logic is truly multi-purpose in that it, as a single software program (or service), can be used to help automate multiple business processes.

Non-agnostic logic does not have these types of expectations. It is deliberately designed as a single-purpose software program (or service) and therefore has different characteristics and requirements.

Service Inventory

A *service inventory* is an independently standardized and governed collection of complementary services within a boundary that represents an enterprise or a meaningful segment of an enterprise. When an organization has multiple service inventories, this term is further qualified as *domain service inventory*.

Service inventories are typically created through top-down delivery processes that result in the definition of *service inventory blueprints*. The subsequent application of service-orientation design principles and custom design standards throughout a service inventory is of paramount importance so as to establish a high degree of native inter-service interoperability. This supports the repeated creation of effective service compositions in response to new and changing business requirements (Figure 4.6).

NOTE
Service composition-related terminology is covered in the *Service Composition Terminology* section in Chapter 11.

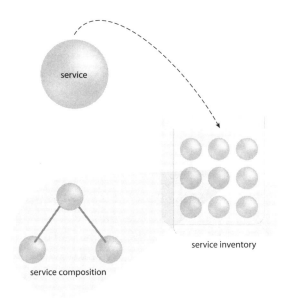

Figure 4.6
Services (top) are delivered into a service inventory (right) from
which service compositions (bottom) are drawn.

Service Portfolio

Service portfolio (also commonly referred to as a "service catalog") is a separate term
used to represent a set of the services within a given IT enterprise. The distinction
between service inventory and service portfolio is important as these and related terms
are used within different contexts, as follows:

- A service inventory represents a collection of implemented services that are independently owned and governed.

- The service inventory analysis is a modeling process by which service candidates
  are defined for a new or existing service inventory.

- A service inventory blueprint is a technical specification that represents the result
  of having performed a service inventory analysis. Subsequent iterations of the
  service inventory analysis process can expand or further refine a service inventory
  blueprint.

- The term "service portfolio" has a less specific definition than service inventory in
  that it can represent all or a subset of the services within an IT enterprise.

- A service portfolio often exists as a high-level documentation of services used for planning purposes.

- A service portfolio most commonly encompasses one or multiple service inventories.

Service portfolio management is the practice of planning the definition, delivery, and evolution of collections of services.

Service Candidate

When conceptualizing services during the service-oriented analysis and service modeling processes, services are defined on a preliminary basis and are still subject to a great deal of change and refinement before they are handed over to the service-oriented design project stage responsible for producing physical service contracts. The term "service candidate" is used to help distinguish a conceptualized service from a service that has actually been implemented.

Service Contract

As first explained in Chapter 3, a *service contract* expresses the technical interface of a service. It can be comprised of one or more published documents that express meta information about a service, which essentially establish an API into the functionality offered by the service via its capabilities.

When services are implemented as Web services, the most common service description documents are the WSDL definition, XML Schema definition, and WS-Policy definition. A Web service generally has one WSDL definition, which can link to multiple XML Schema and WS-Policy definitions. When services are implemented as components, the technical service contract is comprised of a technology-specific API.

Services implemented as REST services are accessed via a uniform contract, such as the one provided by HTTP and Web media types. Service contracts are depicted differently depending on whether a uniform contract is involved (as explained in Chapters 3 and 6).

A service contract can be further comprised of human-readable documents, such as a Service Level Agreement (SLA) that describes additional quality-of-service guarantees, behaviors, and limitations. Several SLA-related requirements can also be expressed in machine-readable format as policies.

Within service-orientation, the design of the service contract is of paramount importance—so much so, that the Standardized Service Contract (411) design principle and the aforementioned service-oriented design process are dedicated solely to the standardized creation of service contracts.

Service-Related Granularity

When designing services, there are different granularity levels that need to be taken into consideration, as follows:

- *Service Granularity* – This represents the functional scope of a service. For example, fine-grained service granularity indicates that there is a small quantity of logic associated with the service's overall functional context.

- *Capability Granularity* – The functional scope of individual service capabilities is represented by this granularity level. For example, a GetDetail capability will tend to have a finer measure of granularity than a GetDocument capability.

- *Constraint Granularity* – The level of validation logic detail is measured by constraint granularity. For example, the more coarse the constraint granularity is, the less constraints (or smaller the amount of data validation logic) a given capability will have.

- *Data Granularity* – This granularity level represents the quantity of data processed. For example, a fine level of data granularity is equivalent to a small amount of data.

Because the level of service granularity determines the functional scope of a service, it is usually determined during analysis and modeling stages that precede service contract design. Once a service's functional scope has been established, the other granularity types come into play and affect both the modeling and physical design of a service contract (Figure 4.7).

Granularity is generally measured in terms of fine and coarse levels. It is worth acknowledging that the use of the terms "fine-grained" and "coarse-grained" is highly subjective. What may be fine-grained in one case may not be in another. The point is to understand how these terms can be applied when comparing parts of a service or when comparing services with each other.

NOTE

As already established, the term "constraint granularity" is not associated with the term "constraint" as it pertains to REST. To avoid any confusion, the term *validation constraint granularity* is used instead in this book.

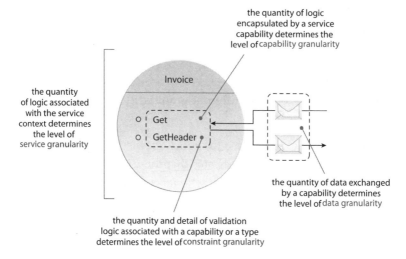

Figure 4.7

The four granularity levels that represent various characteristics of a service and its contract.
Note that these granularity types are, for the most part, independent of each other.

Service Profiles

The document used to record details about a service throughout its lifecycle is the *service profile* (Figure 4.8). A service profile is typically maintained by the owner or custodian of a service and is based on a template that is standardized throughout a service inventory. Chapter 16 covers the service profile documents in relation to REST, and further introduces a new template for a uniform contract profile.

SOA Design Patterns

A design pattern is a proven solution to a common design problem. The SOA design patterns catalog provides a collection of design patterns (Figure 4.9) that provide practices and techniques for solving common problems in support of service-orientation. This book further expands this catalog by introducing eight new REST-inspired SOA design patterns in Appendix E.

NOTE

Profiles of SOA design patterns are provided in Appendix E of this book and are also published online at www.soapatterns.org.

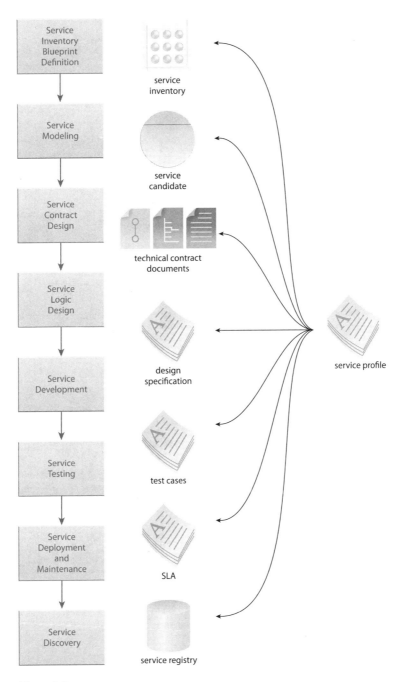

Figure 4.8

A service profile is generally created when a service is first conceptualized, and is then updated and maintained throughout subsequent lifecycle phases.

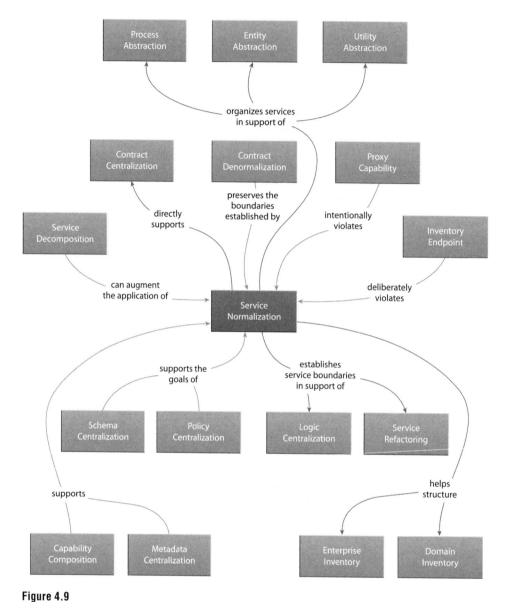

Figure 4.9

SOA design patterns form a design pattern language that allows patterns to be applied in different combinations and in different sequences in order to solve various complex design problems.

4.2 Further Reading

- Explanations of the service-oriented computing goals and benefits are available at www.serviceorientation.com and in Chapter 3 of *SOA Principles of Service Design*.

- For information about SOA types and the distinct characteristics of the service-oriented technology architecture, see Chapter 4 of *SOA Design Patterns*.

- Design principles are referenced throughout this book but represent a separate subject matter that is covered in *SOA Principles of Service Design*. Introductory coverage of service-orientation as a whole is also available at www.serviceorientation.com and all eight principle profile tables are provided in Appendix D of this book.

- For a comparison of service-orientation and object-orientation concepts and principles, see Chapter 14 in *SOA Principles of Service Design*.

- Numerous design patterns are discussed in the upcoming chapters. These patterns are part of a greater SOA design patterns catalog that was published in the book *SOA Design Patterns*. Pattern profiles are available online at the www.soapatterns.org community site, and pattern profile tables for design patterns referenced in this book are further provided in Appendix E.

- For an explanation of how SOA design patterns relate to service-orientation design principles, see Chapter 5 in the *SOA Design Patterns* book.

- For general coverage of SOA project stages and associated organization roles and governance controls, see *SOA Governance: Governing Shared Services On-Premise and in the Cloud*.

- For detailed coverage of service-oriented analysis and service-oriented design process steps, see *Service-Oriented Architecture: Concepts, Technology, and Design*.

- Definitions for the terms introduced in this chapter can also be found at www.soaglossary.com.

- Read the Annotated SOA Manifesto in Appendix G (also published at www.soa-manifesto.com) for a high level description of SOA and service-orientation (without references to specific principles or patterns).

See www.servicetechbooks.com for additional reading resources.

4.3 CASE STUDY EXAMPLE

MUA architects are dedicated to adopting SOA and applying service-orientation as part of a key strategy to consolidate systems and data. They decide to focus on entity services that track the information assets of the various campuses. This initial set of services is to be deployed on the main campus first, so that IT staff can monitor maintenance requirements. Individual campuses are then to build solutions based on the same centralized service inventory. Solutions that introduce new task services will be allocated to virtual machines in the main campus to allow them to be moved to independent hardware and onto dedicated server farms, should the need arise in the future.

Back-end mainframe systems will be wrapped up by a utility services layer in order to effectively access the information and logic they hold. New Web-based interfaces will replace the terminal-based access to these systems, except for direct administration purposes. The Web server layer will primarily interact with task and entity services in order to access information and perform business processes. New proposed linkages between mainframe systems will go through an assessment process to determine whether the mainframes should instead interact with each other through services.

It is determined that a cohesive security model will also be needed to ensure that requests from untrusted sources, such as the Internet, are adequately authenticated and these interfaces secured. All users will be assigned unique federated identities which will be used by services at all levels to determine whether requests should be authorized to proceed. Some of this security processing will also be centralized within dedicated utility services.

Chapter 5

REST Constraints and Goals

5.1 REST Constraints

5.2 Goals of the REST Architectural Style

This chapter introduces fundamental concepts relevant to REST service design and architecture. The objectives of REST are primarily technical in nature and must be achieved by making clear design decisions to produce a technology architecture that closely resembles the Web. These design decisions are defined through *constraints* that are associated with *architectural properties* that represent *design goals*.

5.1 REST Constraints

REST constraints are design rules that are applied to establish the distinct characteristics of the REST architectural style.

The formal REST constraints are:

- Client-Server {393}

- Stateless {395}

- Cache {398}

- Interface/Uniform Contract {400}

- Layered System {404}

- Code-On-Demand {407}

Each constraint is a pre-determined design decision that can have both positive and negative impacts. The intent is for the positives of each constraint to balance out the negatives to produce an overall architecture that resembles the best features of the Web.

An architecture that weakens or eliminates a given REST constraint is generally considered to no longer conform to REST. Deviating from REST constraints can result in various combinations of additional positive and negative consequences. This requires that educated decisions be made to understand the potential trade-offs when deliberately deviating from the application of REST constraints.

Client-Server {393}

Perhaps the most foundational constraint, Client-Server {393} enforces the separation of concerns in the form of a client-server architecture. This helps establish a fundamental distributed architecture, thereby supporting the independent evolution of the client-side logic and server-side logic.

The Client-Server {393} constraint requires that a service offer one or more capabilities and listen for requests on these capabilities. A consumer invokes a capability by sending the corresponding request message, and the service either rejects the request or performs the requested task before sending a response message back to the consumer (Figure 5.1). Exceptions that prevent the task from proceeding are raised back to the consumer, and the consumer is responsible for taking corrective action.

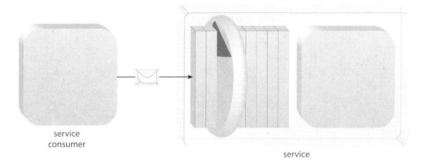

service
consumer

service

Figure 5.1

Client-Server {393} introduces a clear separation between a service and its consumers.

NOTE
When discussing REST, it is common to use the terms "client" and "server" to refer to the initiator and recipient of a request message, respectively. In this book, REST is explored specifically within the context of services. As established in Chapters 3 and 4, a software program issuing a request to a service assumes the role of service consumer. Therefore, from here on, the term "client" is generally replaced with "service consumer" and for the term "server" the term "service" is used instead.

Stateless {395}

The communication between service consumer (client) and service (server) must be stateless between requests. This means that each request from a service consumer should contain all the necessary information for the service to understand the meaning of the request, and all session state data should then be returned to the service consumer at the end of each request.

Statelessness is one of the primary influences over service contract design in REST-style architecture. It imposes significant restrictions on the kinds of communication allowed between services and their consumers in order to achieve its design goals (Figure 5.2). The application of the Cache {398} and Layered System {404} constraints helps to compensate for limitations resulting from Stateless {395}.

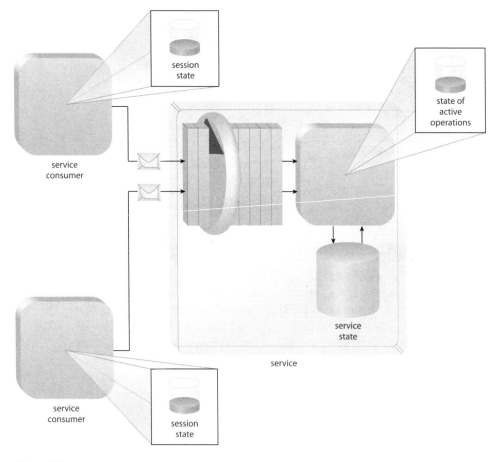

Figure 5.2
Statelessness {395} ensures that each service consumer request can be treated independently by the service.

Cache {398}

Response messages from the service to its consumers are explicitly labeled as cacheable or non-cacheable. This way, the service, the consumer, or one of the intermediary middleware components can cache the response for reuse in later requests.

The Cache {398} constraint builds upon Client-Server {393} and Stateless {395} with a requirement that responses are implicitly or explicitly labeled as cacheable or non-cacheable. Requests are passed through a cache component, which may reuse previous responses to partially or completely eliminate some interactions over the network (Figure 5.3). This form of elimination can improve efficiency and scalability, and can further improve user-perceived performance by reducing the average latency during a series of interactions. However, a common reason for incorporating caching as a native part of a REST architecture is as a counterbalance to some of the negative impacts of applying the Stateless {395} constraint.

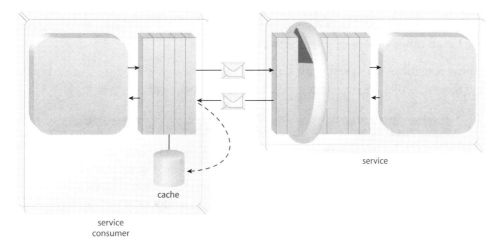

service

cache

service
consumer

Figure 5.3
Responses may be cached by the consumer to avoid resubmitting the same requests to the service.

Interface/Uniform Contract {400}

The Interface {400} constraint (also known as "Uniform Interface") states that all services and service consumers within a REST-compliant architecture must share a single, overarching technical interface. As the primary constraint that distinguishes REST from other architecture types, Interface {400} is generally applied using the methods and media types provided by HTTP and other Internet standards (Figure 5.4).

Figure 5.4

The triangle symbol is used to represent the elements of a uniform contract: methods, media types, and resource identifier syntax (as further explained at the beginning of Chapter 6).

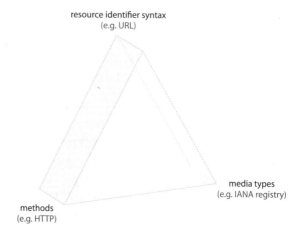

The technical contract established by Interface {400} is typically free of business context because, in order to be reusable by a wide range of services and service consumers, it needs to provide generic, high-level capabilities that are abstract enough to accommodate a broad range of service interaction requirements.

Business-specific or service-specific data and meaning are isolated to specific portions of the messages that are exchanged via the uniform technical contract.

> **NOTE**
>
> In this book, the Interface {400} constraint is deliberately referred to as the Uniform Contract {400} constraint to avoid confusion or watering down of the generic term "interface," and to further provide a clear contrast with the general concept of service contracts (as further explained in Chapter 6).

Layered System {404}

A REST-based solution can be comprised of multiple architectural layers, and no one layer can "see past" the next. Layers can be added, removed, modified, or reordered in response to how the solution needs to evolve.

The Layered System {404} constraint builds on Client-Server {393} to add middleware components (which can exist as services or service agents) to an architecture. Specifically, Layered System {404} requires that this middleware be inserted transparently so that interaction between a given service and consumer is consistent, regardless of whether the consumer is communicating with a service residing in a middleware layer or a service that represents the ultimate receiver of a message. Similarly, a service does not need to be aware of whether its consumer sent its request message directly, or whether the message passed through one or more service agents along its delivery path.

This form of information hiding simplifies distributed architecture and allows individual architectural layers to be deployed and evolved independently of specific services and consumers.

Code-On-Demand {407}

This optional constraint is primarily intended to allow logic within clients (such as Web browsers) to be updated independently from server-side logic. Code-On-Demand {407} typically relies on the use of Web-based technologies, such as Web browser plug-ins, applets, or client-side scripting languages (i.e. JavaScript).

Code-On-Demand {407} can further be applied to services and service consumers. For example, a service can be designed to dynamically defer portions of logic to service consumer programs. For example, this type of functionality can be used in support of Stateless {395}, which dictates when session state should be deferred back to the service consumer. Code-On-Demand {407} can also build upon this by further deferring the processing effort. This approach may be justifiable when service logic can be executed by the consumer more efficiently or effectively.

NOTE

Because Code-On-Demand {407} is classified as optional, architectures that do not use this feature can still be considered RESTful.

SUMMARY OF KEY POINTS

- REST provides a set of design constraints that, when collectively applied, result in a RESTful technology architecture.

- All REST constraints are required, with the exception of Code-On-Demand {407}.

5.2 Goals of the REST Architectural Style

REST provides the following set of "Architectural Properties of Key Interest" that help establish the design goals that lie behind the application of REST constraints:

- Performance

- Scalability

- Simplicity

- Modifiability

- Visibility

- Portability

- Reliability

These properties represent a target state of a technology architecture that resembles the World Wide Web. Although many of the design decisions carried out during the application of REST constraints assist in achieving these goals, several of these properties can be further realized or improved by making additional design decisions that are not necessarily formal parts of REST.

Performance

Two fundamental characteristics that distinguish distributed architectures from ones designed to operate on a single machine are the performance and reliability of communication. With performance we need to contend with issues such as network latency and limited network bandwidth. Unreliable networks can also affect performance by losing, reordering, or delaying packets or messages, and requiring that they be retried or resent.

We often think of network performance as absolute, but it is driven by a number of factors, some of which are impacted by architectural decisions. First and foremost is the issue of what data actually needs to be transferred over the network. Data has to move if it is needed for processing at a different location from where it is stored. Therefore, architectures that keep data close to where it is processed naturally perform better than those that have to move it before it can be processed.

Once it is clear that all data flows are essential, the next question is how those flows occur and what type of overhead is involved. The fewer messages and round trips over the network taken to transfer the data and the less overhead that is included in those messages, the more efficient the transfer will be (Figure 5.5). Protocol overhead can be incurred as an interaction is started or a connection is established, and as each message or packet is sent as part of the interaction. Overhead can also be introduced by transferring irrelevant data that will not be used by its recipient.

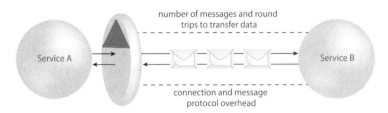

Figure 5.5
Explicit design decisions can improve or negatively impact overall performance.

User perception is also often a performance concern. For example, a large database query that takes 30 seconds to complete but returns the first page of results in 5 seconds is perceived to perform better than a similar query that returns all results simultaneously after 30 seconds.

REST can negatively impact performance through its Uniform Contract {400} constraint. For example, forcing services and consumers to always share a common technical contract can:

- prevent data exchange optimizations

- result in increased messages or round trips for a given activity to complete

- add redundant overhead to message content

REST can support the performance goal by using caches to keep available data close to where it is being processed. It can further help by minimizing overhead associated with setting up complex interactions by keeping each interaction simple and self-contained (as a request-response pair).

Scalability

Scalability addresses an architecture's need to support a large number of instances or concurrent interactions. Four basic approaches for dealing with scalability demands are identified and can be combined in various ways:

- *scaling up* – increasing the capacity of services, consumers, and network devices

- *scaling out* – distributing load across services and programs

- *smoothing out* – evening out the number of interactions over peak and non-peak periods to optimize the infrastructure (thereby reducing the impact of the peaks to avoid the infrastructure sitting idle at other times)

- *decoupling the consumption of finite resources* – such as memory from concurrent consumers

Most REST constraints do little to support scaling up or smoothing out the number of interactions, but the focus is on supporting the scaling out of service instances and on aligning finite resource consumption to the number of active requests (rather than the number of concurrent consumers).

REST-style architectures support load balancing across service instances via the Layered System {404} and Uniform Contract {400} constraints. These constraints allow services to use off-the-shelf load balancing solutions as the first tier in handling requests on behalf of a service without changing its technical service contract. This can be further simplified through the Stateless {395} constraint, which structures interactions as request-response pairs that can each be handled by services independently of other requests. There is no need to keep directing the same service consumer to the same service instance or to synchronize session state explicitly between service instances; the session data is contained in each request.

Simplicity

A solution's distributed architecture is ideally designed to reduce complexity by separating functionality in such a manner that each unit of functionality is distinct and easily understood. The simplicity design goal is based on the proper application of the separation of concerns.

Simplicity is a focus for REST because it impacts how services are defined, discovered, and eventually used (or reused) and further determines how easily services can be evolved independently.

The application of Uniform Contract {400} results in an architecture whereby every interaction between services, consumers, and middleware uses the same message types. The application of Stateless {395} enables every request to be understood in its own right without needing to refer to earlier messages that were sent as part of the same session. The Client-Server {393} and Layered System {404} constraints result in service logic, consumer logic, and middleware logic that only need to be understood via defined technical contracts.

Modifiability

The requirements for a technology architecture are bound to change over time. Modifiability represents the ease at which changes can be made to an architecture.

Modifiability in a REST-style architecture is further broken down into the following areas:

- *evolvability* – the ability to refactor and redeploy a service, consumer, or middleware component without impacting other parts of the architecture (even when the upgrade occurs while applications are running)

- *extensibility* – the ability to add functionality to the architecture (even while solutions are running)

- *customizability* – the ability to temporarily modify parts of a solution to perform special types of tasks

- *configurability* – the ability to permanently modify parts of an architecture

- *reusability* – the ability to add new solutions to an architecture that reuse existing services, middleware, methods, and media types, without modification

Modifiability is particularly important for larger distributed architectures where it is not possible to redeploy the entire environment every time an architectural improvement is made.

Visibility

Involvement in and understanding of the communication between services and their consumers allows middleware to monitor and mediate that communication.

Within the context of REST, visibility refers to the ability of parts of an architecture to monitor and regulate the interaction between other parts of the same architecture. Most commonly, this translates into establishing middleware-based service agents that keep track of messages passed between services and consumers.

The focus of these service agents is usually on improving administrative control over the architecture and optimizing its performance. Typical features provided by utility-centric service agents include:

- shared caching of responses

- improving scalability through layers that aggregate requests and reduce the direct impact on services

- improving reliability by ensuring requests always reach a service replica that is currently available

- supported enforcement of security policies by inspecting and filtering interactions at network firewalls

The design goal of visibility relates to how much generic information a service agent can extract from a message without knowing any service-specific contract details. REST primarily supports visibility through the Uniform Contract {400} constraint.

Portability

The ease at which services and solutions can be moved from one platform to another is represented by the goal of portability. Considerations that should be taken into account include the level of compatible standardization across environments, the ability to keep both data and logic grouped, and how portable a given software program can be. For example, third-party public cloud environments can impose proprietary architectural characteristics that can inhibit the portability of Web-based solutions. In contrast, a fragment of JavaScript transferred from a Web server to a Web browser is highly portable due to the level of platform standardization. An explicit means by which Code-on-Demand {407} supports this goal is to help standardize execution environments.

Reliability

Reliability of a distributed architecture is the degree to which its solutions and services (and underlying infrastructure) are susceptible to failure. The reliability of an architecture can be improved by avoiding single points of failure, using failover mechanisms, and relying on monitoring features that can dynamically anticipate and respond to failure conditions.

SUMMARY OF KEY POINTS

- REST highlights a set of architectural properties that represent key design goals of applying REST constraints.

- The design goals (architectural properties) are Performance, Scalability, Simplicity, Modifiability, Visibility, Portability, and Reliability.

CASE STUDY EXAMPLE

To carry out the service delivery plans listed in the *Case Study Example* section from Chapter 4, MUA architects have chosen REST as the primary service implementation medium. They recognize that most REST constraints will help establish a viable foundation for realizing their architectural goals in support of their SOA initiative. They plan to develop a series of REST services through a new technology rollout in order to contain complexity and to support the required system scale and performance as inexpensively as possible.

The plan will be carried out as follows:

• A caching infrastructure is deployed throughout the various campus sites to ensure efficient use of network bandwidth as well as to improve performance for users. These caches are centrally monitored by IT staff on the main campus to guarantee their ongoing efficiency and to raise awareness of any problems with inefficient cache directives back to IT staff at individual campuses.

• With the range of technologies available for supporting large Web server deployments, HTTP is chosen as the uniform contract for providing methods and URIs for resource identification. Entity and task services will return a range of centrally-governed media types to their consumers, including HTML for direct consumption by Web browsers.

• The focus of governance is on centralized IT infrastructure. A uniform contract specification is developed that refers to the existing HTTP and URI specifications for the definition of methods and resource identifiers. A small registry of extension methods for HTTP is established to accommodate special communication patterns that are not used on the Web.

• A new registry of media types will be created to ensure this set is normalized, that each media type has an evolution path defined, and that each is uniquely identified. Because of the HTTP foundations, Internet media types will be used with a `vnd` prefix. For example, machine-readable course descriptions are recorded as having an `application/vnd.edu.mua.courses+xml` media type. An equivalent URI-based identifier is also used in some circumstances. In this case, it is `http://mua.edu/media-types/courses`.

A search will be performed before registering new media types to determine whether a better, more widely-standardized form for the data can be found before inventing a new one in-house. Each new type will also be scrutinized to consider whether the data really needs to be machine-readable, or whether it could simply be encoded as HTML, ATOM, or a more generic type for lists and other human-facing data.

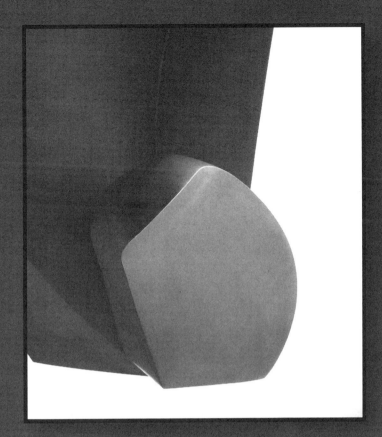

Part II

RESTful Service-Orientation

Chapter 6: Service Contracts with REST

Chapter 7: Service-Orientation with REST

Chapter 6

Service Contracts with REST

6.1 Uniform Contract Elements

6.2 REST Service Capabilities and REST Service Contracts

6.3 REST Service Contracts vs. Non-REST Service Contracts

6.4 The Role of Hypermedia

6.5 REST Service Contracts and Late Binding

D ue to its fundamental reliance on the Uniform Contract {400} constraint, REST-style architecture introduces distinct service contract characteristics that further carry over into a distinct service contract diagram notation. This chapter explains how REST service contracts are comprised and expressed, and further provides a comparison with non-REST service contracts.

6.1 Uniform Contract Elements

The REST uniform contract is based on three fundamental elements:

1. *resource identifier syntax* – How can we express where the data is being transferred to or from?

2. *methods* – What are the protocol mechanisms used to transfer the data?

3. *media types* – What type of data is being transferred?

These elements are commonly represented using a triangle symbol, as shown in Figure 6.1.

As explained later in this chapter, individual REST services use these elements in different combinations to expose their service capabilities. However, it is important to understand that what makes this type of service contract "uniform" is the fact that a master

Figure 6.1
The REST triangle.

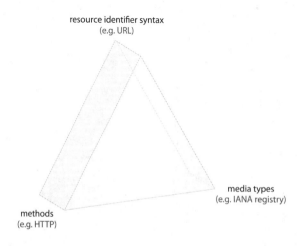

resource identifier syntax
(e.g. URL)

media types
(e.g. IANA registry)

methods
(e.g. HTTP)

set of these elements is defined for use by a collection (or inventory) of services. This essentially allows us to standardize the baseline elements of the service contract.

The three elements of the REST triangle are deliberately orthogonal in order to limit the impact of changes to any one element. For example, the resources for a given service inventory are defined separately from the set of methods used for that same inventory, and separately again from the set of supported media types.

Let's take a closer look at each of the uniform contract elements.

Resource Identifier Syntax (and Resources)

Resource identifiers represent the actual resources that a service exposes. A resource can be data, processing logic, files, or anything else that a service may have access to. A resource identifier is like a unique ID assigned to one or more service resources.

It's important to understand that a uniform contract does not standardize resource identifiers. It standardizes the *syntax* used to express them. The most common syntax used to express resource identifiers is the Web's Uniform Resource Identifier (URI) syntax.

Before we continue exploring resource identifiers, let's briefly cover some of the URI basics. (If you are already familiar with URI syntax, then skip ahead to the *Resource Identifiers and REST Services* section.)

URIs (and URLs and URNs)

The Uniform Resource Identifier (URI) standard is defined by the IETF, and provides a syntax that includes a list of allowed and prohibited characters, a generic structure for identifiers, and further defines the concepts of Uniform Resource Locators (URLs) and Uniform Resource Names (URNs). The relationship between URIs, URLs, and URNs is highlighted in Figure 6.2.

- URIs are simply sequences of characters that conform to the standardized syntax.

- URLs are URIs that can be used in requests. Referring to concepts in a way that can be used directly as a resource to send messages to its underlying service is so useful that most URIs used in REST service architectures are also URLs. This makes the terms somewhat equivalent, which is the reason they are often used interchangeably.

- URNs are URIs that can be used as unique identifiers for resources, such as business entities. Many identifiers in REST are URIs, URLs, and URNs at the same time.

Figure 6.2

How URIs, URLs, and URNs relate
to each other.

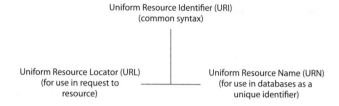

For example `http://invoices.example.com/invoice/INV042` is a URI because it conforms to the generic syntax. It is also a URL because we can use it as a resource identifier and invoke methods upon it. Finally, it is a URN because we will always refer to the invoice using this identifier outside of the Invoice service itself. This combination of URI, URL, and URN work together to ensure that the discovery of resources, and the ability to access the data they refer to, usually occur at the same time.

The generic syntax for URIs is as follows:

`{scheme}://{authority}{path}?{query}`

This syntax can be extended to form a URI reference by adding a fragment component:

`{scheme}://{authority}{path}?{query}#{fragment}`

The different elements of the syntax denote the beginning or end of each component, and whether the component is present or not:

- the colon ":" after scheme indicates the presence of the scheme

- the double-slash "//" before authority indicates an authority is present

- path is always present, and generally begins with a slash "/"

- query is denoted by a leading question mark "?"

- fragment is denoted by a leading hash symbol "#"

An example URI reference that uses all of these components is:

`http://invoices.example.com/invoices?total-less-than=100USD#page2`

- `http` is the scheme, denoting the use of the Hypertext Transfer Protocol for URLs

- `invoices.example.com` is the authority

- `/invoices` is the path

- `total-less-than=100USD` is the query

- `page2` is the fragment component

The preceding examples are continued and expanded upon in the *Designing and Standardizing Resource Identifiers* section in Chapter 10.

Resource Identifiers and REST Services

Each resource identifier can be service-specific, and one REST service can provide many resource identifiers for use by its service consumers.

Because REST services can have a functional context and scope, the same way other kinds of services can, a given REST service can be based on a service model (explained in Chapter 3). This means a REST service can be agnostic or non-agnostic—and—business-centric or utility-centric. The REST service's functional context carries over into the types of resources it encapsulates, which in turn determines the types of resource identifiers we define for a REST service.

For example, we could have an entity REST service called Customer. This service would be responsible for encapsulating agnostic, customer-related resources. A resource identifier we could create to provide the ability for the Customer service to retrieve data about a specific customer record might look something like this:

`http://customer.example.com/customer/C081`

In this example, the `C081` part of the URL represents the customer record ID provided by the service consumer requesting specific customer data (indicated by the `/customer` path), while the `http://customer.example.com/` part of the URL represents the Customer service itself.

Methods

A method is a type of function provided by a uniform contract to process resource identifiers and data. While resource identifiers are generally specific to a REST service, methods are usually not. The uniform contract establishes a set of methods that are expected to be reused by services within a given collection or inventory. Therefore, together with standardizing the resource identifier syntax, the uniform contract standardizes the methods used to process resource identifiers.

Because of the need for methods to be reusable across services, they tend to be highly generic (or uniform). A typical uniform contract will provide a modest set of high-level methods capable of performing basic processing functions. Anything more specific that a service consumer requires of a REST service is expressed in the resource identifier that is processed by the method.

You may have noticed that earlier we referred to methods as the "protocol mechanisms" used to transfer data. This means that when we discuss methods as an element of a uniform contract, we further define (and standardize) the actual protocol technology used to express and transport the generic functions. The most common type of protocol technology used in REST architecture is HTTP.

HTTP provides us with a set of generic methods, such as GET, PUT, POST, DELETE, HEAD and OPTIONS, that are pre-defined in the HTTP specification. The complete protocol interactions in this specification further include a set of response codes, plus syntax for expressing various parameters that can be encoded in HTTP messages.

Let's expand on our previous example by showing how the generated HTTP message expresses the GET statement in the message header, as follows:

```
GET /customer/C081 HTTP/1.1
```

In this statement we indicate that by using the GET method, the content associated with a specific customer record (as determined by using the C081 identifier) is requested by the service consumer. (Also indicated by this header statement is the version of HTTP being used.)

Earlier we stated that the uniform contract standardizes the methods that services (within an inventory) use to transfer data. It's important to point out that the uniform contract establishes the available methods services can use. When we design an individual REST service, we can choose which of the available parent uniform contract methods we want our service to support and expose. How this relates to the definition of REST service contracts is discussed shortly in this chapter.

> **NOTE**
>
> The use of resource identifiers and methods in REST mirrors the basic mechanics of the World Wide Web. For example, cooking Web sites may provide the ability to search, update and/or view recipes. Instead of exposing these features via a custom API, they offer them as resources that share a common contract (HTTP). A generic service consumer (the Web browser) can access these resources by providing specific resource identifiers (URLs) that are processed by generic methods (supplied by HTTP), as illustrated in Figure 6.3.

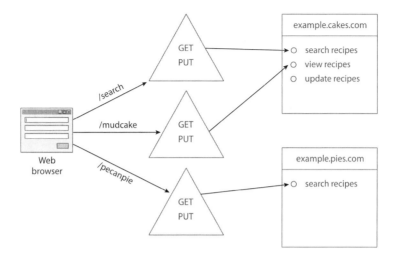

Figure 6.3
The Web browser accesses Web resources by providing URLs processed by HTTP methods.

Media Types

When defining methods for REST services, we can further specify the types of data a given method can process. For example, a GET method may be able to transfer plain text, XML, and JPG images. Each is represented by its own media type.

We can also make a media type more specific in terms of indicating the type of payload content a method is able to transfer. For example, in addition to stating that we want the GET method to transfer XML data, we can also limit it to transferring XML data associated with a business context, such as customer.

A media type can therefore be generic and based on a pre-defined industry media type (such as XML and JPG) or it can be further customized to represent unique types of content, such as those based on organization-specific business documents and records.

The most common forms of industry media types used with HTTP are those registered with IANA, which follow a standardized syntax that is also applied to custom media types.

For example, the following statement expresses a media type that supports XML-based customer content:

```
application/vnd.com.example.customer+xml
```

As with a GET statement, the media type statement is located in the HTTP message header. The request message issued by the service consumer can provide one or more of the media types it is able to support by using the Accept header, as shown here:

```
Accept: application/vnd.com.example.customer+xml
```

Upon returning the requested content, the response HTTP message provides a Content-Type header that confirms the media type of the content being returned to the service consumer:

```
Content-Type: application/vnd.com.example.customer+xml
```

Allowable media types are determined when designing a uniform contract, making the media type the third element to be naturally standardized for the collection of services using the uniform contract. You may recall that the uniform contract establishes a set of parent methods from which we can choose to have a service support a subset. Similarly, the uniform contract establishes a set of parent media types for these methods. When designing a service, we can choose which of the available media types we want the service to use for a method.

NOTE

HTTP, URI, and Internet media types are the most common technologies and industry standards used to implement methods, resource identifiers, and media type elements of a REST uniform contract. The remainder of this book therefore focuses almost exclusively on their usage. Because the focus of this book is on how REST relates to SOA and service-orientation, there are no tutorials provided for these or other REST-related industry standards. See Appendix B for online resources covering industry standards referenced in this book.

It is also worth noting that alternative technologies and industry standards may also be used within a REST architecture, as long as their usage does not require the violation of REST constraints.

SUMMARY OF KEY POINTS

- A uniform contract is comprised of three elements: resource identifier syntax, methods, and media types.

- Resource identifier syntax is used to express identifiers that point to resources provided by REST services.

- Methods are used to process resource identifiers and data.

- Media types are used to indicate the types of data that can be processed by methods.

6.2 REST Service Capabilities and REST Service Contracts

Uniform contract methods are extremely generic and multi-purpose. Therefore, they have little meaning beyond basic, high-level functions (such as Get Something or Update Something). For this reason, a uniform contract alone does not constitute a REST service contract.

The high-level method of the uniform contract invoked by the service consumer determines the parent context of the service consumer request (such as Get Something) and the provided resource identifier determines the specific function requested by the service consumer (such as "Customer Record Data for ID C081"). Together, these two parts of the service consumer request message give the REST service what it needs to carry out a specific function (such as Get Customer Record).

This means that:

- a REST service capability can be considered a combination of a uniform contract method and resource identifier

- a REST service contract establishes a functional context that encapsulates one or more REST service capabilities associated with the functional context

In Chapter 3 we introduced the symbol used to distinguish a REST service contract from a non-REST service contract. Throughout this book, the notation established by this symbol is used to express REST service capabilities as combinations of HTTP methods and resource identifiers.

As further reiterated in Figure 6.4, each service capability is expressed on one or more grouped lines where the single uniform method precedes the resource identifier, expressed as a URL (or a URI template).

Figure 6.4

A non-REST service contract (left) alongside a REST service contract (right). Note how REST-compliant service contracts are denoted with a triangle annotation to indicate their dependency on the uniform contract.

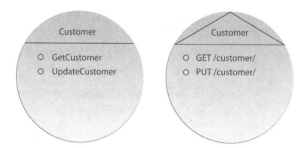

The service contracts displayed in Figure 6.4 provide minimal information about the service capabilities. This concise form of notation is typically used as a starting point during service modeling processes as part of early analysis project stages. To indicate the input data required by a service capability, a more detailed variation of the notation can be used, as shown in Figure 6.5.

Figure 6.5

Both REST and non-REST service capabilities can be further detailed with input data information. In these examples, the id value represents the input expected by each service capability.

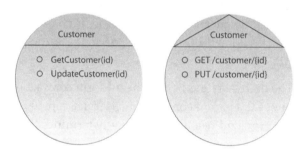

When depicting REST service contracts in runtime scenarios, the input data placeholder can be replaced with the actual expected input data value (the full resource identification), as illustrated in the next section, in Figures 6.6 and 6.7.

NOTE

Media type support also represents a characteristic of a service capability that can optionally be expressed in the service contract notation. For example, media types may be included by appending one or more allowable media types to the service capability statement, as follows:

```
GET /customer/customer/{id}/address: application/
vcard+xml
```

As an alternative, it may be preferable to use a system of standardized, condensed codes to represent the list of supported media types.

SUMMARY OF KEY POINTS

- A REST service capability can be considered a combination of a uniform contract method and resource identifier, plus supported media types.

- A REST service contract represents a set of related service capabilities.

- The REST service contract has a distinct symbol notation that incorporates a triangle symbol.

6.3 REST Service Contracts vs. Non-REST Service Contracts

For those of you interested in better understanding how the interaction between a service consumer and a REST service differs from that of a non-REST service, this section provides a step-by-step comparison.

A common form of a non-REST service contract is a Web service based on the use of WSDL and SOAP. In this case, the service contract is comprised of a custom definition containing a set of embedded, custom service capabilities. A Web service contract is usually specific to one Web service.

In both of the upcoming examples, the logic is based on the following steps for printing the mailing label of a customer invoice:

1. An invoice is requested and retrieved from the Invoice service.

2. The associated customer record is requested and retrieved from the Customer service.

3. The address of the customer is sent to a print queue in order to produce a mailing label.

Non-REST Service with Custom Service Contract

Let's start by studying the interaction between a service consumer and a service that provides a custom service contract:

1. Issue a SOAP message to request invoice data by invoking the getInvoice service capability, as pre-defined in the WSDL definition of the Invoice service contract.

2. Receive the requested invoice data in a SOAP response message issued by the getInvoice service capability of the Invoice service.

3. Issue a SOAP message to request customer data by invoking the GetCustomer service capability, as pre-defined in the WSDL definition of the Customer service contract.

4. Receive the requested customer data in a SOAP response message issued by the GetCustomer service capability of the Customer service.

5. Issue a SOAP message requesting to have the customer address added to the print queue by invoking the print service capability of the Printer service, as pre-defined in the WSDL definition of the Printer service contract.

6. Receive a SOAP response message indicating that the action was successful (or not).

Figure 6.6 and the following example help demonstrate this interaction scenario.

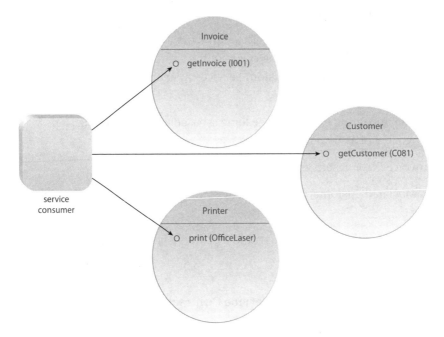

Figure 6.6
The steps required for a service consumer to interact with three services, each with a custom service contract.

Provided here is a sample code fragment that shows how this interaction would need to be programmed within the service consumer.

```
Invoice invoice =
  InvoiceService(http://invoice.example.com/).getInvoice(I001)
Customer customer =
  CustomerService(http://customer.example.com/).getCustomer(
    invoice.getCustomerId() // customer id is C081
    )
PrinterService(http://printer.example.com/).print(
  OfficeLaser, customer.getAddress()
  )
```

At the network level, the messages exchanged are service-specific. Without further annotation, any middleware that may be involved in the exchanges will be unable to determine whether these are read or write functions, or make any optimizations or perform any checks based on this information.

REST Service with Uniform Contract

When using a REST service, a resource is requested by the service consumer. This request occurs via a uniform contract that will be standardized throughout an IT enterprise, or at least throughout a meaningful domain of the IT enterprise. This level of standardization reduces the coupling requirements between the service consumer and services.

Let's take a look at the processing steps required by a REST service to carry out the same task:

1. Issue a request for invoice data by accessing the Invoice service using a resource identifier processed via the HTTP GET method.

2. Receive the requested invoice data in an HTTP response message issued by the Invoice service.

3. Issue a request for customer data by accessing the Customer service using a resource identifier processed via the HTTP GET method.

4. Receive the requested customer data in an HTTP response message issued by the Customer service.

5. Issue a request to have the customer address added to the print queue by accessing the Printer service using a resource identifier processed via the HTTP POST method.

6. Receive an HTTP response indicating that the action was successful (or not).

By using a uniform contract, REST services generally require the same number of steps to be performed. Figure 6.7 and the following example further explain the interaction between the service consumer and the three REST services.

```
Invoice invoice =
  Resource(http://invoice.example.com/invoice/I001).GET
    (Invoice.type);

Customer customer =
  // customer id is http://customer.example.com/customer/C081
  Resource(invoice.getCustomerId()).GET(Customer.type);

Resource(http://printer.example.com/printer/OfficeLaser).POST
  (customer.getAddress())
```

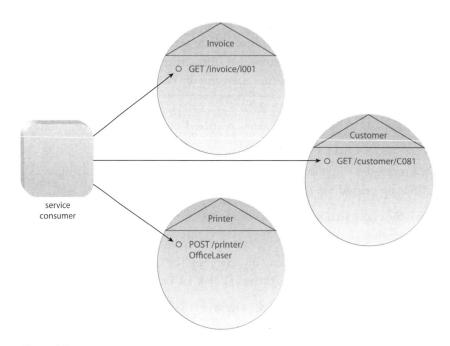

Figure 6.7
The steps required for a service consumer to interact with three REST services, each using the same uniform contract.

HTTP Messaging vs. SOAP Messaging

Using WSDL and SOAP-based Web service messaging as a point of comparison, let's get a deeper insight into what distinguishes REST services messaging from HTTP.

In the following example, a simple SOAP message is sent to a WSDL-based service contract to request an invoice based on its ID:

```
<soap:Envelope>
  <soap:Header>
    <wsa:To>http://invoice/</wsa:To>
  </soap:Header>
  <soap:Body>
    <getInvoice>
      <invoice-id>I123</invoice-id>
    </getInvoice>
  </soap:Body>
</soap:Envelope>
```

Next we have the response message returned by the Web service, providing a SOAP message containing the invoice content:

```
<soap:Envelope>
  <soap:Body>
    <getInvoiceResponse>
      <Invoice> ...invoice content... </Invoice>
    </getInvoiceResponse>
  </soap:Body>
</soap:Envelope>
```

The equivalent exchange with a REST service relying on the use of HTTP methods would be as follows:

```
GET http://invoice/invoice/I123 HTTP/1.1
Accept: application/vnd.com.example.invoice+xml
```

The response HTTP message that is returned to the service consumer contains a success code, the media type header statement, and the same XML fragment as the response message from the Web service, as highlighted here:

```
200 OK
Content-Type: application/vnd.com.example.invoice+xml
<Invoice> ...invoice content... </Invoice>
```

The SOAP messages exchanged with the WSDL-based Web service require the service consumer to know:

- the service name: `http://invoice/`

- the service-specific operation (service capability): `getInvoice`

- the service-specific invoice document identifier: `I123`

- how to invoke the service capability

- how to interpret service-specific response messages

- how to interpret service-specific exceptions

The messages exchanged via HTTP require the service consumer to know:

- the generic method for retrieving the invoice document: `GET`

- the resource identifier for the invoice document: `http://invoice/invoice/I123`

- how to invoke the service capability (method + resource identifier)

- how to interpret the received invoice content (for example, using the `application/vnd.com.example.invoice+xml` media type)

- how to interpret generic HTTP response codes (such as `200 OK`)

- how to interpret generic HTTP exceptions

Throughout a service inventory with REST services, this particular invoice will not be referred to as `I123`, but instead as `http://invoice.example.com/invoice/I123`. Whenever a service consumer is required to retrieve the identified invoice, it needs to be prepared to invoke the HTTP GET method. In doing this (on what it knows is an invoice resource) the service consumer is already expected to be able to process invoice data in the corresponding response.

It is further expected that throughout the service inventory, all services and service consumers that interact with invoice resources understand the uniform contract media type for invoice data: `application/vnd.com.example.invoice+xml`

REST Service Contracts with WSDL?

It is worth repeating that HTTP is not the only implementation technology available for building service-oriented architectures based on REST. For example, a uniform contract approach could be taken in conjunction with WSDL by defining a set of generic, uniform operations for a service inventory in a centralized WSDL definition. The resulting architecture would be at odds with some of the features in the WS-* specifications, but can still result in a legitimate REST architecture, as long as service capabilities are not defined solely in the WSDL definition. In other words, individual service contracts would not be able to rely on WSDL, but instead would refer to the centralized WSDL.

SUMMARY OF KEY POINTS

- REST service contracts do not introduce new methods or media types. Instead, they introduce service capabilities that reuse the uniform contract's methods and media types, and rely on a common resource identifier syntax.

- Service consumers interacting with non-REST service contracts (such as those based on the use of WSDL and SOAP) are required to directly invoke service capabilities specific to each service.

- Service consumers interacting with REST service contracts are required to invoke service capabilities by providing service-specific resource identifiers that are processed by (non-service-specific) methods.

6.4 The Role of Hypermedia

Hypermedia is a broad term used to represent environments and resources related through the use of hyperlinks. The World Wide Web is a classic example of hypermedia. Given that the primary goal of REST architecture is to mirror the architecture of the Web, hypermedia results as a natural characteristic that can be leveraged to create relationships between resources.

These intrinsic relationships can help loosen the coupling between service consumers and REST services by enabling REST services to provide resources with hyperlinks to other resources (provided by the same or other REST services). The service consumer can receive these hyperlinks at runtime and act upon them. Although the service consumer would need to have been designed to look for and process a hyperlinked resource identifier, it would not have needed prior knowledge of the nature of the resource identifier, nor the location of the resource.

To demonstrate, let's revisit the interaction scenario we explored in the previous section. In this variation of the scenario, our service consumer has the following information prior to beginning its interaction with the REST services:

- the resource identifier for the invoice: `http://invoice.example.com/invoice/I001`

- knowledge that the invoice will include a hyperlink to a customer record

- the resource identifier of the print queue to use for the label: `http://printer.example.com/printer/OfficeLaser`

As illustrated in Figure 6.8, the service consumer begins by invoking the Invoice service using the invoice resource identifier, which points to a resource provided by the Invoice service. In order to retrieve data from this resource, the service consumer uses the GET method.

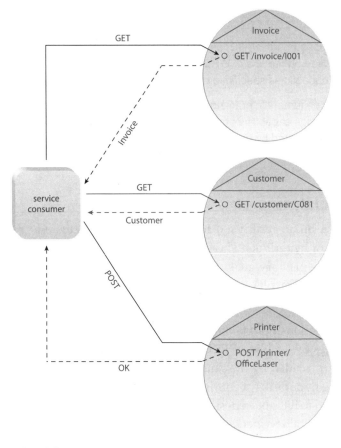

Figure 6.8

The service consumer interacts with the Invoice, Customer, and Printer services at runtime. However, at design-time, the service consumer is only aware of the Invoice and Printer services. The interaction with the Customer service (highlighted in red) occurs as a result of a hyperlink provided by the Invoice service.

Upon receiving the requested invoice, the service consumer "discovers" an embedded hyperlink pointing to a required customer resource. The service consumer logic is designed such that it is able to follow the hyperlink to the invoice's customer record in order to extract the customer mailing address. Finally, the service consumer invokes the Printer service to add a document containing the customer address to the print queue.

The more loosely coupled the relationship between the service consumer and the Customer service is, the more flexible the overall service composition architecture will be because it is less likely that the service consumer will be impacted by change.

Here are some examples of changes or factors from which the service consumer can be protected:

- the Invoice and Customer services could be the same service initially and different services at a later point

- the Customer service could be further split up and refactored

- there may be one Customer service, or there may be many (for example, each individual customer might maintain their own Customer service to ensure contact information is completely up to date)

- the requested Customer resource identifier could change

Figure 6.9 further highlights where direct coupling does and does not exist among the resources involved in this interaction.

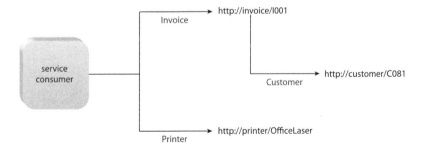

Figure 6.9

The service consumer follows a hypermedia link to access a resource provided by the Customer service. The hypermedia link is provided to the service consumer by the Invoice service at runtime.

It is worth noting that aside from resources dynamically providing hyperlinks via HTTP messages, there are other means by which linked resource identifiers can be provided to service consumers in a loosely coupled manner.

For example:

- hyperlinks stored within configuration files that are loaded by the service consumer logic at startup

- resource identifiers input by human users via forms or command-line statements

Each of these is an example of hypermedia, or simply "linking."

URI Templates and Resource Queries

Resources that capture the result of specific queries can pose a problem for conventional hypermedia. Service consumers that receive a hyperlinked resource identifier at runtime for which they want to perform an ad-hoc query will often need a way to supply the necessary query parameters.

For example, a service consumer may receive the resource identifier `http://invoice/reports/` for a resource that provides invoice reporting functionality. All the service consumer has at hand is the base URL, plus knowledge of what it wants to query. It does not have knowledge of the syntax required to append the query parameters to the `http://invoice/reports/` resource in a manner that will be understood by the service.

A URI template establishes the structure of a URI by indicating what additional values can be added (and what these values represent). A sample URI template for the aforementioned resource could be:

```
http://invoice/reports/{year}/{month}
```

So, what the service consumer needs is this template in order to assemble the resource identifier according to the resource's pre-defined requirements. The template could be hard-coded into the service consumer logic, but this would undermine the loose coupling benefit of hypermedia we discussed earlier.

To address this particular situation, there are two common techniques:

1. Have a service designated to provide URI templates at runtime. This way, upon receiving the base URI, the service consumer can further request and retrieve its corresponding template at runtime.

2. Standardize query-related parts of URIs across all REST services within a given service inventory. This way, the service consumer can contain hard-coded logic enabling it to assemble the query statement on its own. The service consumer will then end up being coupled to a standardized resource identifier structure, as opposed to a structure specific to the Invoice service.

These techniques can also be applied for other forms of parameter-driven resource interaction.

SUMMARY OF KEY POINTS

- By using hypermedia features, REST services can provide and work with hyperlinked resources at runtime.
- The use of hyperlinked resource identifiers can reduce consumer-to-service coupling requirements.
- Special techniques are required to query hyperlinked resources in order to avoid negative forms of coupling.

6.5 REST Service Contracts and Late Binding

Within the context of REST service contracts, late binding occurs when a service consumer discovers a resource identifier that it uses at runtime rather than having been designed to use the resource identifier at design time. By taking advantage of opportunities to apply late binding, we can loosen the coupling between services while simplifying and increasing the flexibility of service contracts. REST service contracts can often be designed to minimize published information (and support late binding) by removing select resource identifier details.

Consider the following service capability used to retrieve a manifest for a shipment:

```
GET /shipping/manifest/{id}
```

This statement implies that the core service logic might invoke something along the lines of a getManifest(id) function within the core service logic API, which would require the consumer logic to be designed to specifically provide this ID value with each invocation.

As an alternative, we design a looser coupled relationship between the service and its consumers by allowing the manifest ID to be "discovered" with its complete resource identifier at runtime.

So, upon receiving a resource identifier statement like this:

```
http://shipping/manifest/34
```

...the service consumer could extract the ID value "34" by parsing it out of the resource identifier, but the consumer would be simpler and more loosely coupled if it just forwards the resource identifier "as is" to the REST service.

With this type of flexibility, the REST service capability content in the service contract can be reduced to:

```
GET {+manifest}
```

...where the plus ("+") symbol is used to indicate that the service capability accepts a range of resource identifiers of "type" manifest. The exact syntax of these resource identifiers may be defined internally by the Shipping service.

NOTE

The use of the plus ("+") symbol for this purpose originates from the RFC6570 URI Template industry standard, where {+some-identifier} is considered a parameter that makes up part of the structure of the URL. Braces without the plus notation indicate a simple identifier that doesn't include any special delimiters such as slash ("/"). The plus symbol indicates a more complex identifier that can include major sections of the resource identifier or that can act as the placeholder for a whole resource identifier.

There are other types of resources that can be considered more as properties of a parent entity rather than entities in their own right. These can pose a challenge when attempting to streamline the level of resource identifier abstraction, because we need to start trading off between the amount of knowledge that consumers have about the service contract and the number of officially registered relationship types that exist as part of the uniform contract.

For example:

```
GET /customer/customer/{id}/address
```

...could be optimized in the published service contract either as:

```
GET {+customer}/address
```

...or as:

```
GET {+address}
```

...where the `address` URL can be found by querying a known customer resource.

The first of these alternatives requires less complex composition logic and fewer messages than the second. Despite this, the second option may be more desirable. The reasons for this are multi-layered and do not necessarily start with a normalized service inventory in mind:

- The consumer may need to interact with a different service that has a slightly different resource identifier structure; for example, a future version of the service or a Customer service from another service inventory that shares a common contract with this Customer service.

- The service may actually wish to delegate this service capability to a dedicated Address service (either now or in the future), rather than handle address-related requests itself.

One other possibility to increase the level of abstraction of a service contract is to rely on the uniform contract to define parts of the contract. For example, if a customer resource contains an "address" hyperlink to the address resource, then sufficient information may be present in the customer media type to understand how to access the related address resource. In theory we could remove the address resource from the published service contract because any consumer would need to access the customer resource and could determine that the related address resource exists without the need for an explicit service contract entry.

SUMMARY OF KEY POINTS

- REST service contracts can be designed to enable the late binding of resource identifiers.

- Late binding of resource identifiers requires a service consumer to contain logic capable of receiving and processing a range of resource identifiers at runtime.

- REST service contracts support late binding by reducing resource identifier-specific content via the use of coarse-grained parameters (that can be expressed using a plus symbol notation).

CASE STUDY EXAMPLE

Due to a recent increase in smart phone users, there have been several requests made at KioskEtc stores to have a convenient way to find store locations via mobile devices. In addition, the student union of MUA wants a portal for its members to find campus buildings in a given radius that meet certain criteria. The union also requests that KioskEtc provide—via a service—the location, hours of operation, and menu of each on-campus store.

These new business demands motivate KioskEtc to create a service based on their current Store Finder application that is available via their public Web site. This application provides the location (address, city and zip code) of stores, along with phone and hours of operation. They would need to enhance the application logic to include store-specific menus, as well as the latitude and longitude of each store location.

The KioskEtc Store Operations team has tasked its IT department to design and deploy a Web-based service to deliver this functionality. An SOA project team is assigned to deliver this service. Their first order of business is to review the requirements outlined by their business client (the Store Operations team), and document them as follows:

- any consumer should be able to provide a zip code and get a list of stores within a 10 mile radius, as well as basic contact information about the store

- any consumer should be able to ask for a specific store number and obtain the store details, including the name and contact information of the store manager

An internal service data model is developed, as shown in Figure 6.10.

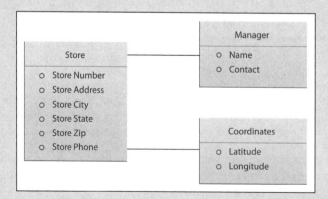

Figure 6.10
The data model to be used by the planned Store service.

The first decision the team makes is to use a REST service to expose the Store Finder functionality. Using the data model, the team identifies the following resources:

- Store: /store/{storenumber}

- Manager for a Store: /store/{storenumber}/manager

- Search Stores in a Zip Code: /stores?zip={zip}

- Search Stores near a Zip Code: /stores?zip={zip}&rad={radius (miles)}

Store URIs are opaque to service consumers and each of these URIs is used consistently as the identifier of a store throughout the service inventory. The latter two Stores/Zip Code URIs need to be constructed by service consumers, which is why the variable portion has been explicitly split out into the query part of the URI. The zip and rad parameters are registered within the service inventory as part of the relevant uniform contract to ensure that other services accepting similar data as URI parameters use the same parameter names.

The only method this service exposes is GET, as per the Stores service contract displayed in Figure 6.11.

Figure 6.11

The Stores service contract, limited to a series of GET-based service capabilities.

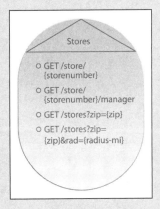

Next, response codes and exceptions are defined for the Stores service.

The success response code is set at:

- 200 OK when the resource is accessed with GET or HEAD methods together with valid credentials. 200 OK will also be returned in cases where searches return no results in the form of an empty results list.

The exception codes are set at:

- `401 Unauthorized` when the consumer does not provide valid credentials.

- `404 Not Found` when an invalid resource (for example, an incorrect store number) is requested.

- `405 Method Not Allowed` when PUT, POST or DELETE is invoked (because this is a read-only service).

Different media types are considered for the various URI templates. Store lists are consumed both directly by humans with Web browsers as well as automated service consumer programs.

HTML is chosen for interfaces requiring human interaction because of its support for the encoding of the hyperlinks from the list of stores to the individual store resources. Since the result set is simply a list of store URIs, support is added for the standard `text/uri-list` media type from the IANA media type registry.

This format defines a text file with one URI per line, as follows:

```
http://stores.example.com/store/00123MUAMainCampus
http://stores.example.com/store/00332MUAWestCoastCampus
```

Store data is also returned in a human-readable and machine-readable form. For machine-readable data based on the supplied schema the standard `text/directory;profile=vCard` media type is chosen (a media type commonly used with email clients to exchange contact information). However, this is a fairly complex text-only format. As such, architects decide to provide alternatives, including:

- `application/xhtml+xml` with `hCard` markup (as per microformats.org)

- `application/vnd.com.kiosketc+rdf+xml` (a vendor-specific media type identifier that extends the corresponding W3C encoding of vCard objects into RDF, as per www.w3.org/TR/vcard-rdf)

Manager resources contain a schema similar to the one used for store data. Therefore, the same media types are used. When accessed by authorized service consumers, Manager resources can further provide a special hyperlink to a given manager's Employee ID, which can be used as a query parameter for a separate Staff service.

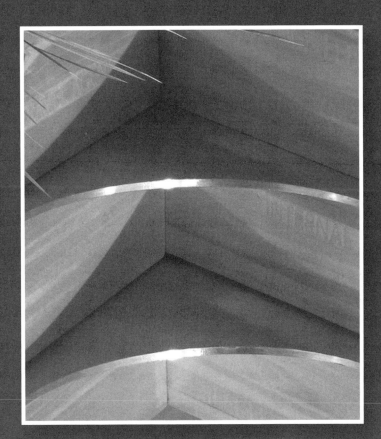

Chapter 7

Service-Orientation with REST

7.1 "SOA vs. REST" or "SOA + REST"?

7.2 Design Goals

7.3 Design Principles and Constraints

PRINCIPLES, PATTERNS, AND CONSTRAINTS REFERENCED IN THIS CHAPTER:

- Cache {398}

- Client-Server {393}

- Code-On-Demand {407}

- Content Negotiation [446]

- Contract Centralization [447]

- Endpoint Redirection [460]

- Event-Driven Messaging [465]

- Layered System {404}

- Lightweight Endpoint [474]

- Logic Centralization [475]

- Reusable Contract [492]

- Schema Centralization [494]

- Service Abstraction (414)

- Service Autonomy (417)

- Service Composability (422)

- Service Discoverability (420)

- Service Loose Coupling (413)

- Service Reusability (415)

- Service Statelessness (418)

- Standardized Service Contract (411)

- State Messaging [509]

- Stateless {395}

- Uniform Contract {400}

To better pinpoint the areas of convergence between SOA and REST, we need to take a closer look at the different parts that comprise the service-orientation paradigm and how those parts relate to the design goals and constraints of REST.

7.1 "SOA vs. REST" or "SOA + REST"?

Both SOA and REST are commonly described as distinct architectural styles, each with its own design approach that is carried out to attain specific design goals. On the surface, it may appear as though we need to choose one architectural style over the other, depending on our individual preferences and goals. However, that is not the case.

When looking back at the design goals of service-oriented computing introduced in Chapter 4 and the design goals of REST covered in Chapter 5, it is evident that these respective sets of goals are not direct alternatives. One is a medium by which the other can be implemented.

To further illustrate this, let's look at the following points of comparison:

- Service-oriented computing goals are strategic and business-centric.

- REST goals are technology-centric and can help achieve strategic or tactical business goals.

- While not all REST design goals are relevant to each service-oriented computing goal, most REST design goals are directly supportive of service-oriented computing goals.

- There are no conflicts between REST and service-oriented computing goals.

REST aims to establish application architecture that emulates the World Wide Web. This represents the target state we look to achieve when applying REST constraints. The strategic goals of service-oriented computing seek to produce a target state that realizes specific business benefits. This represents the target state we plan to attain when applying service-orientation principles.

For a technology architecture to be considered service-oriented, it must have the following characteristics that enable applications to support the goals of service-oriented computing:

- Business-Driven

- Vendor-Neutral

- Composition-Centric

- Enterprise-Centric

These characteristics are commonly realized naturally when applying service-orientation principles throughout the scope of a technology architecture. They are the primary means by which SOA is distinguished as a formal type of technology architecture.

As we stated earlier, REST is also classified as a distinct type of technology architecture because it too is defined by the realization of specific properties that are supported by the application of design constraints:

- Performance

- Scalability

- Simplicity

- Modifiability

- Visibility

- Portability

- Reliability

The preceding two lists represent sets of distinguishing characteristics that apply at different levels of technology architecture. SOA characteristics are defined at a higher level, without reference as to how they can or should be implemented. What's important, from an SOA perspective, is that the technology architecture supports these qualities collectively and consistently. REST characteristics are defined at an implementation level. They represent Web application architecture ideals that are specific to the moving parts that implement the technology architecture.

Therefore, REST architecture provides a medium by which service-oriented architecture can be implemented. The choice is not between SOA and REST, but rather:

- whether REST is the correct implementation medium for a service-oriented technology architecture, or…

- whether service-oriented architecture is the correct architectural model by which a REST architecture should be formalized.

The answer to either question depends on the business requirements that need to be fulfilled.

The upcoming sections dive a bit deeper in the relationships between goals, principles, and constraints. Their purpose is to provide an overview of where the synergies and gaps between SOA and REST lie.

> **NOTE**
>
> You may have noticed that with this chapter we begin listing referenced design principles, patterns, and constraints. While service-orientation principles and REST constraints are primary topic areas explored in this book, SOA design patterns are mostly referenced for informational purposes.
>
> As explained in Chapter 1, each principle, pattern, and constraint is followed by a page number that points to an official profile provided in an appendix. When you encounter a reference to a principle, pattern, or constraint that is unfamiliar, you are encouraged to look up the corresponding profile page prior to continuing.

7.2 Design Goals

The seven strategic goals of service-oriented computing introduced in Chapter 4 collectively represent the target state we aim to achieve as a result of adopting SOA and applying service-orientation principles. The following sections point out some of the ways in which service-oriented computing goals relate to REST design goals, and further how their attainment can be influenced by REST constraints.

Performance	x
Scalability	x
Simplicity	
Modifiability	x
Visibility	
Portability	
Reliability	x

Increased Intrinsic Interoperability

Services within a given boundary are designed to be naturally compatible so that they can be effectively assembled and reconfigured in response to changing business requirements.

All of the REST design goals directly or indirectly support and enhance the interoperability potential of services within a service inventory. Those goals checked off in the reference table are directly relevant to this service-oriented computing goal because they affect the service architecture design, its runtime behavior, and its maintainability.

The service inventory-wide usage of a common, overarching technical contract establishes a baseline level of intrinsic interoperability among all services, which makes the Uniform Contract {400} constraint a direct contributor to this goal. This REST constraint builds on the premise of established SOA patterns, such as Contract Centralization [447] and Schema Centralization [494], to centralize the definition of common methods and associated communication patterns required to move data freely between services and their consumers, both individually and as part of service compositions.

Client-Server	
Stateless	
Cache	
Uniform Contract	x
Layered System	
Code-On-Demand	

Other constraints, such as Stateless {395} and Cache {398}, can indirectly support this goal by improving the runtime performance of services (especially shared services).

Increased Federation

Services establish a uniform contract layer that hides underlying disparity, allowing them to be individually governed and evolved.

A service-oriented architecture is required to establish a layer of federated service endpoints that provide a common front that is exposed to service consumers, while allowing each underlying service implementation to exist and evolve independently. This relates to the Simplicity goal, which supports the proper application of the separation of concerns whereby each service endpoint is clearly distinct from the other in terms of functional context and scope.

Performance	
Scalability	
Simplicity	x
Modifiability	
Visibility	
Portability	
Reliability	

Federation is a prominent part of REST architecture due to the Uniform Contract {400} and Client-Server {393} constraints. Uniform Contract {400} provides a standardized layer that can be used to access information and functionality regardless of its business context. Client-Server {393} introduces the information hiding requirement that protects service consumers from forming unhealthy dependencies on underlying service implementation details by limiting them to positive forms of coupling (in other words, limiting them to coupling with the federated service endpoint layer only).

Client-Server	x
Stateless	
Cache	
Uniform Contract	x
Layered System	
Code-On-Demand	

Both REST and service-orientation have similar effects on federation. While the application of REST constraints can lead to consistency across service contracts with freedom from business context, service-orientation can add architectural layers that can drive an organization to achieve federation over a broader scope, within the enterprise and in alignment with required business contexts.

Increased Vendor Diversity Options

A service-oriented environment is based on a vendor-neutral architectural model, allowing the organization to evolve the architecture in tandem with the business without being limited to proprietary vendor platform characteristics.

Performance	
Scalability	
Simplicity	
Modifiability	
Visibility	
Portability	x
Reliability	

The importance for a technology architecture to not be locked into a given vendor product platform enables it to leverage best-of-breed products from different vendors, when justified to maximize business requirement fulfillment. This important goal is directly related to the REST design goal of Portability, which aims to allow REST-based services and solutions to remain mobile across different environments.

Service-orientation principles and REST constraints both have similar objectives for establishing an environment that can support the on-going option of diversifying vendor technologies. The basic Client-Server {393} constraint separates consumers from services and Layered System {404} further introduces potential architecture layers comprised of middleware. The distributed nature of REST allows different parts of a solution or even of an entire service inventory to be based on different vendor technologies, as required. This flexibility is intentional in that it enables each part to evolve independently; a consideration especially relevant to shared services.

Client-Server	x
Stateless	
Cache	
Uniform Contract	x
Layered System	x
Code-On-Demand	

Both service-oriented architecture and REST-style architecture advocate abstracting away service implementation details from service consumers to avoid negative forms of coupling that can inhibit this type of product vendor independence. With REST, the Uniform Contract {400} constraint is a direct contributor to this form of abstraction.

Increased Business and Technology Alignment

Some services are designed with business-centric functional contexts, allowing them to mirror and evolve with the business of the organization.

Establishing and maintaining alignment between IT automation systems and the ever-changing business requirements is foundational to service-orientation, and further corresponds to the Business-Driven characteristic of service-oriented architecture.

Increasing alignment between business and technology is neither a focus of REST, nor does it work against this outcome. The primary means by which REST can support this goal is in its emphasis on building flexibility into technology architecture. Specifically, the Modifiability goal is dedicated to facilitating low-impact changes to operational solutions.

The layers of abstraction and separation resulting from the Layered System {404} constraint help a technology architecture evolve in response to change. Each architectural layer can be independently evolved as long as there are no immediate impacts upon dependent software programs. The Code-On-Demand {407} constraint provides further flexibility by allowing updates to clients and consumers to be made dynamically.

Performance	
Scalability	
Simplicity	
Modifiability	x
Visibility	
Portability	
Reliability	

Client-Server	
Stateless	
Cache	
Uniform Contract	
Layered System	x
Code-On-Demand	x

Increased ROI

Most services are delivered and viewed as IT assets that are expected to provide repeated value that surpasses the cost of delivery and ownership.

With SOA, shared services are positioned as IT assets with expectations that repeated usage will lead to returns significantly higher than the investment required to build and maintain them. Service-orientation has a primary focus on achieving increased ROI through reusability, normalized service inventories, and mechanisms that enable the effective composition and re-composition of services. When combined with REST, these objectives are amplified with the ability for services and service consumers to be delivered with an inherent level of intrinsic interoperability.

Reusability is one of the aspects of the Modifiability design goal in that REST advocates leveraging reuse as a means of modifying, evolving, and adding solution logic. Increased ROI is further supported by the Simplicity design goal because of its relationship to realizing reusable services. Simplicity requires that we apply the separation of concerns in a manner that results in distinct functional contexts. The more distinct the functional boundaries of services, the less redundancy across services, and the more reuse (and ROI) potential we end up with.

Performance	
Scalability	
Simplicity	x
Modifiability	x
Visibility	
Portability	
Reliability	

As stated in Chapter 5, one of the objectives of Modifiability is to enable "the ability to add new solutions to an architecture that reuse existing services, middleware, methods, and media types, without modification." These objectives correspond directly with those of the Service Reusability (415) principle and various design patterns that support reuse and ROI via normalized service inventories, and mechanisms that enable the effective composition and re-composition of services.

When combined with REST constraints, these objectives are amplified with the ability for services and service consumers to be delivered with an inherent level of intrinsic interoperability. The application of the Uniform Contract {400} constraint provides a foundational means of building reusability into the service inventory architecture by establishing a set of common and generic data exchange methods.

Client-Server	x
Stateless	
Cache	
Uniform Contract	x
Layered System	x
Code-On-Demand	

The separation of logic resulting from the Client-Server {393} and Layered System {404} constraints further supports this goal by increasing the potential of repeated ROI by enabling the isolation of reusable logic into independent services.

REST further supports reusability with its support for hypermedia (explained in Chapter 6).

Increased Organizational Agility

New and changing business requirements can be fulfilled more rapidly by establishing an environment in which solutions can be assembled or augmented with reduced effort by leveraging the reusability and native interoperability of existing services.

Organizational agility is a business-centric goal not directly addressed by REST. However, when using REST as a means of implementing SOA, each REST design goal can directly contribute to improving an organization's responsiveness

Not all REST design goals necessarily apply at the same time or to the same set of circumstances that demand an agile response. It is up to those applying service-orientation to determine how to best leverage REST architecture in support of creating an inventory with services that are naturally interoperable and composable, and can therefore be recomposed, augmented, and refactored in support of business-driven change.

The REST constraints that directly contribute to agility on an organizational level are those that support abstraction, evolvability, and unforeseen change. The separation resulting from Client-Server {393} and Layered System {404} establishes a foundation that allows a service inventory architecture to be comprised of distributed parts that can be individually modified, extended, or otherwise repurposed. The reduced coupling requirements of the Uniform Contract {400} further increase responsiveness as changes to service interaction and data flow will more likely be implemented on the message level. Finally, the optional Code-On-Demand {407} constraint can facilitate forms of changes that result in the need for dynamic client-side (or consumer-side) updates.

Performance	x
Scalability	x
Simplicity	x
Modifiability	x
Visibility	x
Portability	x
Reliability	x

Client-Server	x
Stateless	
Cache	
Uniform Contract	x
Layered System	x
Code-On-Demand	x

Reduced IT Burden

The enterprise as a whole is streamlined as a result of the previously described goals and benefits, allowing IT itself to better support the organization by providing more value with less cost and less overall burden.

The IT burden of an organization can be increased each time a new software program is added to its ecosystem, and especially each time two or more disparate software programs need to be integrated in order to force data exchange. SOA subdues this by breaking down departmental silos, reusing and recomposing services, and decoupling services from their consumers so that they can be upgraded independently.

Performance	x
Scalability	x
Simplicity	x
Modifiability	x
Visibility	x
Portability	x
Reliability	x

All REST goals and most REST constraints can contribute to the Reduced IT Burden goal, as per the positive convergence of goals and constraints documented so far in this section. REST constraints make scaling services more efficient, individual services more reliable, and service upgrades more practical. These, together with other positive impacts of adopting REST, help realize this ultimate goal.

As will be discussed in the upcoming section, a common point of conflict between SOA and REST originates with the Stateless {395} constraint and its requirement to limit state deferral to the message layer. Stateless {395} is therefore not checked off as a constraint that supports the goal of Reduced IT Burden, because this goal is specific to the successful application and adoption of SOA.

Client-Server	x
Stateless	
Cache	x
Uniform Contract	x
Layered System	x
Code-On-Demand	x

Common Goals

As per the preceding comparisons, the following design goals are considered common to REST architecture and service-oriented architecture:

- Increased Standardization

- Increased Scalability

- Increased Reusability

- Increased Interoperability

- Increased Vendor Neutrality

- Increased Responsiveness to Change

Combining REST technology and practices, together with the service-orientation paradigm and the service-oriented architectural model, improves the benefit potential of achieving these goals. This is positive as long as the potential for fulfilling business requirements is correspondingly improved.

SUMMARY OF KEY POINTS

- REST constraints generally have a positive or neutral impact on the strategic design goals of service-orientation.

- REST and service-orientation share a set of common goals. When studying these common goals, we can identify the primary benefits of using REST and service-orientation together.

7.3 Design Principles and Constraints

This section highlights the effects of applying service-orientation principles to REST services by explaining how REST constraints do and do not comply with individual service-orientation principles.

Standardized Service Contract (411)

"Services within the same service inventory are in compliance with the same contract design standards."

The use of the Uniform Contract {400} constraint naturally applies a measure of the Standardized Service Contract (411) principle by:

- establishing generic, reusable, and standardized methods and media types that are shared by REST services throughout the service inventory

- standardizing the syntax used to express resource identifiers

When applying Standardized Service Contract (411) to REST, service contract content (as well as the technologies used to express and process service contracts) is typically further standardized.

Let's explore a few possibilities:

- The application of Standardized Service Contract (411) can extend to the standardization of the resource identifier syntax used to express and access resources. For example, recall the issues raised in the *URI Templates and Resource Queries* section from Chapter 6. One of the proposed techniques for overcoming the problem that service consumers face when encountering hyperlinked resource identifiers that need to be used for queries is to standardize the query-related URI syntax. This is something that would be addressed directly by Standardized Service Contract (411).

- The usage of HTTP methods can be standardized for the service inventory. For example, there may be a standard that requires that POST always be used instead of PUT. Or, there may be a standard that limits the use of the OPTIONS method.

- Standardized Service Contract (411) will especially be important for standardizing custom media types used to identify and represent common business documents exchanged by REST services. Both the media type identifier syntax and perhaps even the versioning syntax for canonical business documents can be standardized.

- The use of a common notation for expressing service contracts and service capabilities (such as the notation introduced in Chapter 6) can be considered a design-time convention very much related to Standardized Service Contract (411).

Both REST and SOA place a great deal of emphasis on contracts. The fact that Uniform Contract {400} and Standardized Service Contract (411) are compatible and the fact that their combined application is mutually beneficial to their respective design goals establishes a solid foundation for realizing SOA with REST.

Service Loose Coupling (413)

"Service contracts impose low consumer coupling requirements and are themselves decoupled from their surrounding environment."

Coupling refers to a connection or relationship between two things. A measure of coupling is comparable to a level of dependency. This principle advocates the creation of a specific type of relationship within and outside of service boundaries, with a constant emphasis on reducing ("loosening") dependencies between service contracts, service implementations, and service consumers.

The service contract within a REST service architecture is physically decoupled from other aspects of the service's underlying implementation environment. The names of REST services generally appear in resource identifiers rather than the names of specific hosts or other implementation details. Likewise, technology dependencies are not exposed through centralized methods or media types, and also not through resource identifiers.

Applying REST to services can significantly help in achieving loose coupling by making all aspects of a service contract conform to a uniform contract that is shared between all services. Service consumers are directly coupled to the uniform contract, but not necessarily to any individual service. The uniform contract is governed to avoid service-specific detail from ever becoming incorporated within it. REST services that form dependencies on uniform contract methods can be considered loosely coupled in that the contract (or parts of the contract) is implemented by a range of services across the service inventory.

The principle of Service Loose Coupling (413) promotes the independent design and evolution of a REST service's logic and implementation while still guaranteeing baseline interoperability with service consumers that have come to rely on the service's capabilities. Coupling is loosened both in terms of uniform contract methods and media types, as well as via discovered resource identifiers provided by the service.

The built-in evolutionary mechanisms of a typical REST service architecture include Endpoint Redirection [460], Lightweight Endpoint [474], Content Negotiation [446], and media type versioning. As demonstrated on the Web, a REST-style approach can achieve longevity for services and consumers alike.

Applying the Service Loose Coupling (413) principle to REST services can require:

- ensuring that service contracts are not unnecessarily subjected to change when underlying logic changes (for example, when generating contract data from implementation details to ensure that such details are stable and support a "contract first" methodology)

- disallowing technology details to find their way into uniform contract facets or into service contracts

- not allowing other implementation details, such as internal APIs or data structures of particular services, to excessively impact their service contracts or the uniform contract

- applying the Reusable Contract [492] pattern by defining service contracts that are sufficiently agnostic to their business context to allow them to be reused in multiple applications

- optimizing service contracts to minimize published resource identifier syntax detail in support of late binding (as described in Chapter 6)

- keeping uniform contracts free of service-specific details

- not allowing the structure of the resource identifier set exposed by a service to be built into service consumer implementations (such as hard-coding URI templates in consumer logic; where consumers need to start with a definite business context, provide resource identifiers as configuration data input; defer service consumers discovering information about any service resources or the structure of a service's resource identifiers until they are able to do so at runtime through hypermedia)

- applying Endpoint Redirection [460] and Content Negotiation [446] patterns in support of centralized methods and as part of standard service consumer implementations

- including document extension points in centralized media types

- being conservative in what a service sends and liberal in interpreting what is received (especially when validating input against what may turn out to be outdated validation logic)

There are, of course, features of REST that also naturally support the application of Service Loose Coupling (413). The use of hypermedia, for example, can dramatically decrease the level of consumer-to-service coupling requirements by instead promoting service consumer logic capable of processing various hyperlinked resource identifiers at runtime.

Service Abstraction (414)

"Service contracts only contain essential information and information about services is limited to what is published in service contracts."

Abstraction ties into many aspects of service-orientation. On a fundamental level, this information hiding principle emphasizes the need to remove access to as much of the underlying details of a service architecture as possible, especially from developers of service consumer logic. Doing so directly enables and preserves the goals of the Service

Loose Coupling (413) principle. Service Abstraction (414) also plays a significant role in the design of service compositions.

Various forms of metadata come into the picture when assessing appropriate abstraction levels, and the extent of abstraction applied can affect service resource granularity and can further influence the ultimate cost and effort of governing services.

As originally documented in the book *SOA Principles of Service Design*, Service Abstraction (414) covers four main abstraction types:

1. *Functional* – the level of abstraction of capabilities in a service contract

2. *Technology Information* – the level of exposed information relating to the implementation technology of the service

3. *Programmatic Logic* – the level of exposed information relating to the logic that implements the service contract

4. *Quality of Service* – the level of information relating to responsiveness, capacity, reliability, and other non-functional properties of the service

A service architecture based on REST frames the question of abstraction around how much information is present within the uniform contract, how much information is present in the service contract, and who has access to service contracts.

The application of Uniform Contract {400} automatically hides a great deal of information by stripping the service contract of detail. However, even a REST service contract cannot be completely hidden. Portions of the contract must be available to those responsible for configuring the service consumer logic. As a result, some elements of the contract may flow into the service logic through the semantics of the configuration data. Developers of service consumers that need to link to resources within a service contract must have knowledge of the contract and it's through that knowledge that the service consumers also end up coupled to the contract.

Applying the Service Abstraction (414) principle to REST services means:

- preventing service-specific contract detail, or other details, from leaking into uniform contract elements (uniform contract details are abstracted from service functions, underlying technology, and implementation details and are applicable to a wide variety of services)

- separating service consumer logic from configuration data, and abstracting as much service contract detail away as possible when feeding a resource identifier to service logic through configuration data

- restricting the access of service consumer developers to service contract information, while still leaving sufficient information available for developers to configure the logic, and discover capabilities for reuse purposes (it can be a difficult balancing act to avoid excessive service contract detail leaking into the logic)

- ensuring capabilities expressed through resource identifiers are functionally abstract and can support a degree of change over time, without modifying the set of resources or their methods

- being able to avoid revealing technology details through service contracts (particularly in relation to URL extensions, such as .php or .aspx)

- being able to avoid exposing internal state or interim logic steps through resource identifiers, except where this information constitutes opaque deferred session state

- publishing service level agreement information for consumption by humans, and maintaining minimum standards for all invocations of a given method

The use of hypermedia is worth mentioning again here. By limiting the amount of hard-coded references to resource identifiers within service consumer logic, we not only gain the advantages of decreased coupling, but we also end up hiding more information about resources that a service consumer may need to access and process. This level of abstraction is what enables hyperlinked resource identifiers to change with less impact to service consumers.

Service Reusability (415)

"Services contain and express agnostic logic and can be positioned as reusable enterprise resources."

The reduced coupling and increased abstraction introduced naturally by Uniform Contract {400} can foster reuse by making generic functionality more easily accessible. However, the Service Reusability (415) principle is really about separating agnostic (multi-purpose) logic from non-agnostic (single-purpose) logic, and encapsulating the agnostic functions and data in designated services. The processes and decisions that lead to the definition of reusable service logic are not greatly impacted by using REST as a service implementation medium.

When applying this principle, REST services follow established analysis and modeling approaches for identifying and grouping reusable logic as part of the service inventory blueprint definition process. This is positive because it continues to allow SOA analysts to model candidate services without being concerned with how they will ultimately be implemented.

After agnostic REST services enter subsequent delivery lifecycle stages, commercial design and testing techniques are typically applied to ensure that each service is functionally coherent, correctly abstracts agnostic logic, and is ready for concurrent production usage.

Applying the Service Reusability (415) principle to REST services means:

- producing a normalized service inventory, where each service has well-defined functional boundaries

- applying Logic Centralization [475] to ensure that any given piece of logic that is expressed in a single REST service can be accessed through that service's resources

- considering the level of abstraction each service is operating at (task, entity, utility, etc.) and avoiding the overlap of these different levels of abstraction in a single service (in order to avoid hindering its reusability by trying to do too much in one place)

- producing and centralizing interpretable information about a service so that it is discoverable at design-time, effectively allowing potential service consumer builders to reuse existing services instead of creating new variations of existing service logic

- planning for and leveraging runtime discoverability so that it becomes a reliable and feasible part of the service inventory architecture, to whatever extent appropriate

It is worth noting that the extent to which Service Reusability (415) can be realized is often dependent on the extent to which the Service Composability (422) principle can be successfully applied. Therefore, the challenges highlighted in the upcoming *Service Composability* (422) section, as well as in Chapter 11, are directly relevant to Service Reusability (415).

Service Autonomy (417)

"Services exercise a high level of control over their underlying runtime execution environment."

As with Service Reusability (415), the Service Autonomy (417) principle applies to REST services as it would to other service implementation mediums. REST does not specifically address how coupled the implementation of one service should be from another. Service-orientation is clearer in this regard, stating that the implementation of services should neither be bound up in back-door interfaces with other co-located services, nor, ideally, should it share databases or other resources that can compromise the service's behavioral predictability because it will be difficult to tease these apart should demands on the service grow.

Applying the Service Autonomy (417) principle to REST services means:

- ensuring that services only rely on each other in arrangements that allow each to continue meeting its own service level agreement commitments (as they change)

- ensuring that services are deployed on independent hardware (virtual or otherwise) in a way that supports rapid capacity increases and reasonably straightforward migration (when required)

Note that Layered System {404} can hide the autonomy of underlying services in such a way that Service Autonomy (417) within dependent service consumers can unknowingly be negatively impacted. For example, more and more layers can be inserted into a service architecture over time. Other services can form dependencies on this service architecture by composing its service capabilities (in which case those services are acting as service consumers, as explained in Chapter 4). In this case, their collective autonomy can be decreased by the introduction of the additional architectural layers.

Service Statelessness (418)

"Services minimize resource consumption by deferring the management of state information when necessary."

The management of state information can compromise the availability of a service and undermine its scalability potential. Services should only remain stateful (retaining consumer-specific session state) when required. The Service Statelessness (418) principle positions state deferral as an effective way of improving scalability and availability.

REST and service-orientation are bound to different interpretations of statelessness. Services in a REST architecture are stateless *between* requests. Any session state that must be retained (between requests) is passed back to the service consumer and then returned to the service as part of each subsequent request. This definition of statelessness operates at a communication protocol level to restrict the kinds of interaction a service consumer can engage in with a given service.

The REST Stateless {395} constraint rules out a number of useful communication patterns based on an argument that they cannot scale to the size of the Web. For example, publish-subscribe communication (as per the Event-Driven Messaging [465] pattern) based on push-notification is effectively outlawed in REST. Syndication is a common alternative, where information is published as resources that are not specific to any service consumer, and are accessed through polling by consumers.

However, from the sole perspective of this principle, there is no direct conflict between the Service Statelessness (418) principle and the Stateless {395} constraint, even when applying the constraint to its full potential. Conversely, as discussed in upcoming chapters, it is possible to consider weakening the Statelessness {395} constraint for architectures that don't need to operate at the same scale as the Web.

Applying the Service Statelessness (418) principle to REST services means:

- incorporating appropriate state deferral mechanisms within interactions between the uniform contract (and REST service contracts in general) that require a service to retain state data for extended periods

- allowing session state to flow "tidally" back and forth between services and their consumers

- deferring any additional session state back to the consumer at the end of each request, generally in the form of one or more resource identifiers and surrounding context

When intending to apply Service Statelessness (418) together with Stateless {395}, the use of the State Messaging [509] pattern will likely be repeatedly required. This pattern embodies a typical messaging mechanism in compliance with the Stateless {395} constraint.

STATE CONCEPTS AND TYPES

Appendix F provides an overview of state-related terminology and concepts, as well as descriptions of the following types of state conditions and data:

- active and passive states

- stateful and stateless conditions

- context, session, and business state data

- context data and context rules

Be sure to read through this introductory content as several of the described terms are referenced in subsequent chapters, especially those in Part IV pertaining to service composition topics.

Service Discoverability (420)

"Services are supplemented with communicative metadata by which they can be effectively discovered and interpreted."

Service-orientation provides a basis for building solutions on top of a set of reusable services and service compositions. In order for services to be effectively reused, they must be discoverable. Services must be identified and described in a centralized registry that provides service consumers the information they need to exploit reuse opportunities.

When applying the Service Discoverability (420) principle to REST services, the focus at design-time for service logic is *not* on discovering services, but on discovering specifications for elements of the uniform contract (such as methods and media types). This contract definition should be easily accessible to developers that need to design service consumers based on the uniform contract. However, as we move to a normalized service inventory, the discoverability of service contracts comes into play. These contract definitions should provide enough information for consumer programs to interact with services at runtime by following links from an initial set of configured URLs.

Combining the two styles leads to a positive outcome: a highly-discoverable uniform contract incorporated into service consumers at design-time, a registry of available services, along with a published subset of resource identifiers available for human consumption. These parts unite to exploit reuse opportunities and to provide adequate configuration data and runtime hyperlinks.

What makes the runtime aspect of Service Discoverability (420) with REST services distinct is the expectation that REST services (through the use of hypermedia) can be designed to receive resource identifiers (at runtime) that lead them to services not part of the fixed service composition architecture.

Applying the Service Discoverability (420) principle to REST services means:

- ensuring that all facets of the uniform contract are readily available to service consumers at design-time

- ensuring that service contract descriptions are easy for humans to access and understand in order to configure service consumers accordingly

- ensuring that, where appropriate, REST services contain logic capable of working with hypermedia

Service Composability (422)

"Services are effective composition participants, regardless of the size and complexity of the composition."

Services are expected to be reused not just individually, but *repeatedly*, in multiple service compositions. This principle supports and rounds out many of the preceding principles with the overarching objective that services are reliable, predictable, and perform well when composed concurrently and repeatedly.

REST provides features, such as hypermedia, that support this principle and further provides constraint-related rules that can limit its application. For example, the runtime discoverability of REST services opens up new forms of service composition. Complex service compositions may require features hindered by Stateless {395}, such as cross-service transactions.

Common Conflicts

There are times when REST constraints should not be applied, whether it is to overcome some of the previously explained restrictions that REST can impose on a service-oriented architecture, or whether it is warranted simply in support of specific business requirements and preferences. It is further important for SOA governance specialists to consider whether REST constraints should be weakened or ignored in order to enable or support specific interactions within the service-oriented architecture.

The following sections focus on the Stateless {395} and Uniform Contract {400} constraints to discuss how and when their application may need to be weakened in support of service-orientation.

NOTE

Any deviation from a REST constraint means that a service inventory architecture is no longer considered REST-compliant. When stepping away from REST constraints, it can be helpful to remove the "REST" label from the underlying architecture for clarity and to better enable planning for the potential impacts of relaxing REST criteria.

Stateful Interactions

The Stateless {395} constraint of REST is based on Internet-scale considerations that may be irrelevant to the requirements of a given solution. Existing services may already demonstrate that stateful designs prohibited by REST are, in fact, more appropriate for the scale of an IT enterprise (or a service inventory architecture). Additionally, restricting service interactions to those that fit Stateless {395} can eliminate vital features important to current and future service composition architectures.

Service-oriented architectures that weaken Stateless {395} can still enjoy many of the features afforded by the use of a uniform contract. For example, a stateful publish-subscribe mechanism using uniform contract methods can be applied to any resource without needing special-purpose consumer or middleware logic.

On the other hand, weakening statelessness can increase the costs for service scaling and for guaranteeing high levels of reliability to larger numbers of service consumers. As already explained in the preceding coverage of the Service Composability (422) principle, by weakening this constraint we can essentially restrain the performance potential of service composition architectures, while increasing the freedom with which service compositions can be designed.

Service-Specific Contract Details

The application of Uniform Contract {400} is of most benefit in support of:

- generic service consumer functions, such as caching, logging, debugging and browsing
- de-normalized services, such as when interacting with services that perform similar functions across different business contexts

An isolated and highly-normalized service inventory that has little need for generic features can accommodate deviations from the uniform contract in ways that de-normalized services cannot. In this respect, it can be easier to build special service contract features or service-specific media types in support of business contexts that are distinct to the service, rather than to come up with an appropriate uniform contract alternative.

Architects who breach Uniform Contract {400} should do so with great care to avoid locking the service inventory architecture out of useful features that may be supported by generic middleware or service consumer programs. The Uniform Contract {400} constraint is key to most of the positive impacts of REST, and should therefore be broken only with a clear understanding of future implications and impacts.

SUMMARY OF KEY POINTS

- REST constraints mostly have a positive or neutral impact on the application of service-orientation design principles.

- Many REST constraints and features can introduce new options and opportunities for applying service-orientation principles, while some can limit the application of select principles.

- In comparing the focus of REST constraints to service-orientation principles it is evident that while some overlap exists, they are mostly focused on addressing different problem areas. The strategic business problems addressed by service-orientation are largely orthogonal to the technical problems addressed by REST.

- REST is designed for the massive scale and diversity of the World Wide Web, and some weakening of REST constraints can be justified for service inventory architectures that do not require Internet-scale performance.

- The Stateless {395} constraint can improve the performance and reliability of a service composition, but can also restrict the composability of services by eliminating some forms of transaction and event notification.

- Uniform contract elements that are only used within one service contract are no more reusable than a service-specific contract. A REST service capability that cannot be expressed in terms of existing generic uniform contract methods should simply be identified as being service-specific.

CASE STUDY EXAMPLE

Throughout the first several months of MUA's SOA initiative, a series of REST services were deployed and placed into production use. During the weeks following these service implementations, a number of problems arose, followed by complaints and demands for improvements. MUA stakeholders decided to temporarily suspend further service delivery, subject to a review of the project goals and status.

Three weeks later, hired consultants produced a report highlighting that the existing REST services were:

- out of alignment with the overarching goals of the SOA project

- unable to fulfill the strategic business requirements that were to be addressed by the SOA project

- performing below expectations, even in response to immediate automation requirements

The report's executive summary concluded that these issues were the result of poor analysis and design approaches employed during the initial service delivery project stages.

The report went on to detail some of the specific areas of concern:

- Caching semantics have been inappropriately defined for some services, meaning that much of the caching infrastructure installed in individual campuses is sitting idle.

- Some HTTP methods were used incorrectly, and new media types have been invented without going through the correct uniform contract change management process. In some cases this led to tunneling of other messages through the HTTP methods and to a lack of visibility by caching and security infrastructure.

- .php, .jsp, .aspx and other extensions have crept into resource identifiers, and these have led to ugly workarounds when some of the early technology foundations were replaced with the new standard platform for services.

- Some session states that were deferred back to service consumers were found during the audit to contain transaction identifiers that could cause the Enrollments entity service data to become out of sync with course catalog information if it were lost or corrupted.

- Some developers unnecessarily hard-coded resource identifiers into service consumer logic instead of following the provided hyperlinks. These service consumers required extra (and avoidable) development effort when changes were made to the resource identifiers.

- In order to avoid coupling, some service developers refused to release their service contracts to downstream developers. This meant that those developers were unable to effectively seed their services with the starting URLs they needed and, in some cases, they were unable to discover the service at all (leading to the need to create redundant services).

After many discussions, all campus IT groups agreed that the SOA project had not been managed properly. The critical missing piece to how SOA adoption was being approached was the absence of standard service-oriented analysis and design processes in which service-orientation principles are consistently applied. While these principles alone will not address all of the outstanding problems, their application has become a priority.

MUA stakeholders agree to fund the development of a new project plan based on formal processes defined in the Mainstream SOA Methodology (MSOAM). It is acknowledged that the existing REST services will need to be redeveloped in the near future to bring the service-oriented technology architecture to a state comparable to initial expectations. In the meantime, however, the SOA project team is asked to proceed with the new SOA methodology by delivering a new service as part of an initiative to create a community-centric offering for MUA students.

Specifically, they are planning to extend the core student profile to include social contacts (friends) of students within MUA campuses. This will allow students to find and locate friends on campus for study and extra-curricular events. The resulting project focuses on the delivery of an application on the MUA student portal to manage lists of friends and their public connections.

As the application enters the planning stage, architects are presented with two requests:

- one from a remote campus to expose the application functionality as a service (as there were some custom kiosks that did not have regular Web browsers)

- the other from the Dean's Office to provide course selection functionality based on choices a student's friend might have made in past semesters or were planning on enrolling in upcoming semesters

This leads to the decision to create a service to deliver the student profile and, for each student profile record, an associated friends network.

The intent for this service is to have the ability to create, view, and update student profile descriptions along with the ability to instantiate one or more friends networks categorized by communities of interest. It also needs to allow for students to add and remove friends, as required. The service will need to be sensitive to the student's privacy guidelines and make only the information available which the student has approved as shareable.

The initiative is rebranded as the Student Friends Network (SFN) project, and moves on to the service-oriented analysis stage during which current student profile data is reviewed. The team discovers that this existing student profile data is kept in three separate locations:

- a contact database housed by the Admissions department

- a student profile database with some basic curriculum information with the Dean's Office

- department-specific student data (for example, concerning specific projects carried out) stored in a range of repositories

The current MUA portal presents, by default, the student profile from the Admissions department's database, but also merges this data with query results from the Dean's Office's database. There are no clear URIs for accessing the student profile uniformly across the MUA service inventory.

The IT team proposes centralizing the student profiles into a common repository with the key data they need to display in the portal application. They identify that in addition to the elimination of duplicates and missing data from the three sources, they also need to access a course registration system that contains student enrollment data. In this process, they find that the Academic Office has already embarked on such an integration project which will provide a centralized store of student profile information that will serve as the Student Master repository for ongoing projects. Further, architects determine that the Academic Office will provide their own Student Master service with a WSDL definition (Figure 7.1) offering basic query features for student profile data.

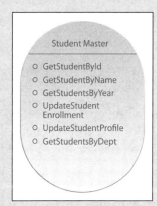

Figure 7.1
The Student Master service contract.

The project team proposes that a REST-based SFN service be introduced to also expose data access functions for the Student Master repository.

They point out the following reasons for doing so:

- to bring interface standards into line with other universities, so that generic service consumers can browse their way between student friend networks across campuses and organizations

- to support reuse caching and security enforcement infrastructure built into the existing MUA Web presence

- to make data access for the Student Master repository more broadly available via the World Wide Web

Upon receiving approval to proceed, architects begin by identifying resources based on the data model shown in Figure 7.2.

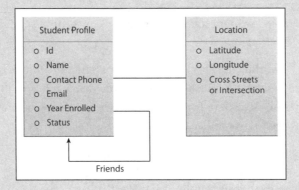

Figure 7.2
The data model to be used for the new SFN REST service.

Further analysis and design effort results in the definition of the following list of functional requirements for the SFN service:

- expose student profile data

- provide access to the friends network of each student

- provide the ability to update student profile attributes as well as the current location of a student

- provide the ability to add and remove a friend to/from the friends network of a student

Before the project team proceeds to the service-oriented design stage during which they will be tasked with designing the SFN service contract and its service capabilities, they review the new considerations they need to take into account, as a result of applying service-orientation design principles.

Specifically, there are four principles that directly affect the design of service contracts:

- Standardized Service Contract (411)

- Service Loose Coupling (413)

- Service Abstraction (414)

- Service Discoverability (420)

They focus first on applying Standardized Service Contract (411). They learn that, in support of this principle, the enterprise architect group has already put together a series of service contract design standards that will need to be applied to all services within the new MUA service inventory. The SFN service is the first to be subjected to these standards.

The standards immediately relevant are:

- The `application/vnd.edu.mua.foaf+rdf+xml` media type (based on the REF FOAF vocabulary) is to be used when it is required to accommodate links to records by resource identifier and the associations with those records needed for DELETE actions.

- Each REST service must, at minimum, be able to return standard HTTP codes `200`, `401`, and `404`.

- Business-related terms in resource identifier statements must comply to a pre-defined vocabulary.

- When multiple terms are required for a single segment in a resource identifier, those terms must be separated by a hyphen symbol.

In compliance with these design standards, the following service capabilities are defined:

- `GET /student/{id}`

- `GET /students?name={name}`

- `GET /students?year={year}`

- `GET /students?department={department}`

- `POST /student/{id}/enrollments`

- `POST /student/{id}/profile`

- `DELETE /friend-association/{student};{student}`

- `PUT /friend-association/{student};{student}`

- `PUT /student/{id}/location`

- `DELETE /student/{id}/location`

- `GET /student/{id}/location`

The application of Service Abstraction (414) further results in an optimized set of resource identifiers for use in the published service contracts, as follows:

- Student: `{+student}`

- Base URL for search queries: `/students`

- Student Enrollments: `{+student enrollments}`

- Student Profile: `{+student profile}`

- Student Location: `{+student location}`

- Student Friends List (included in Student resource, if authorized)

- Friend Association: `{+friend association}`

Before proceeding, architects reconsider one aspect of their service contract design. It is proposed that the PUT method be used instead of the POST method for updating the friends network with new friends, for the following reasons:

- The core functionality provided is that of appending a friend to an existing network. Therefore, the friend becomes a subordinate to the main URI when the method is invoked on the friends network resource (`/student/{id}/friends`), and since the consumer already knows the ID for adding friend records, using PUT makes sense.

- The PUT method is idempotent and the students can safely retry adding a friend to their network and it will always be treated as if it was the first request. This brings an additional advantage, since there could be students making updates from mobile devices.

- Choosing the POST method is not necessary, as the consumer is always creating a new contact in their network with a known friend ID. They are not updating the entire friends network—just attaching existing nodes. (If they had to use POST to support existing Web browsers, then the service capability would look like: `POST /student/{id}/friends`.)

Subsequent to some discussion, the team decides to proceed with the PUT method. They further inform the enterprise architecture group of this change, in case there is the potential for this to become the basis of another service contract design standard.

The revised SFN service capabilities expose GET, PUT and DELETE methods, as shown in Figure 7.3.

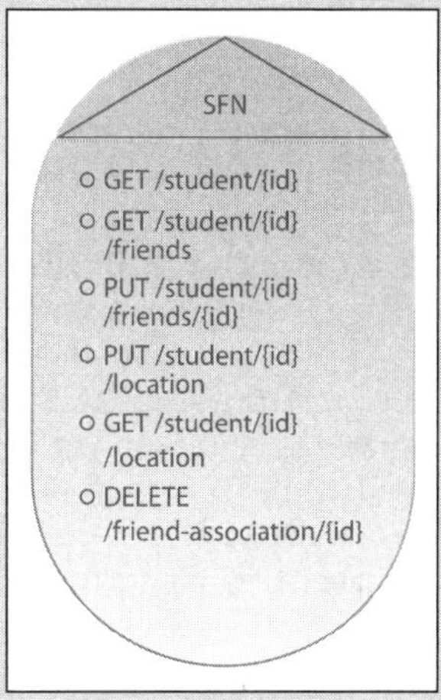

The next step in the design process is to establish response codes and exceptions in compliance with design standards.

The following codes are identified:

SFN

- ○ GET /student/{id}
- ○ GET /student/{id} /friends
- ○ PUT /student/{id} /friends/{id}
- ○ PUT /student/{id} /location
- ○ GET /student/{id} /location
- ○ DELETE /friend-association/{id}

- `200 OK` when the resource is available and accessed with a GET or HEAD method and with valid credentials

Figure 7.3
A partially revised (unpublished) SFN service contract.

- `401 Unauthorized` when the consumer doesn't provide valid credentials

- `404 Not Found` when an invalid resource is requested

- `405 Method Not Allowed` when POST is invoked

Following the similar approach, the design team starts looking at requirements for media types. Since there are two key resources (student and student's friends), the team intends to define two resource representations using a common base, preferably an industry standard.

The student information again correlates closely with vCard; however, it extends the concept with the year the student enrolled. The architects determine that "year enrolled" is a valid extension of vCard, and use the three media types already identified for vCard use with the additional year enrolled data encoded into a `X-YEAR-ENROLLED` extension element.

As per the service contract design standards, the list of friends for the student is encoded into the `application/vnd.edu.mua.foaf+rdf+xml` media type because support is required for links to both the friends of a student by student resource identifier and the associations with those friends needed for DELETE actions:

```
<rdf:RDF>
  <foaf:Person rdf:about=
    "http://sfn.mua.edu/student/335810">
    <foaf:knows rdf:ID="association1 ">
      <foaf:Person rdf:about=
        "http://sfn.mua.edu/student/335815"/>
      </foaf:knows>
    <rdf:Description rdf:about="#association1 ">
      <owl:sameAs rdf:resource=
        "http://sfn.mua.edu/friend-association/123"/>
    </rdf:Description>
  </foaf:Person>
</rdf:RDF>
```

Example 7.1

Other relation types are also defined to allow hyperlinks from the student to be related to enrollment, profile, location, and friends list resources, as required. As much as possible, these relationship types are defined in a way that is applicable to other entity types, and to student entities at institutions elsewhere.

Part III

Service-Oriented Analysis and Design with REST

Chapter 8: Mainstream SOA Methodology and REST

Chapter 9: Analysis and Service Modeling with REST

Chapter 10: Service-Oriented Design with REST

Chapter 8

Mainstream SOA Methodology and REST

8.1 Service Inventory Analysis

8.2 Service-Oriented Analysis (Service Modeling)

8.3 Service-Oriented Design (Service Contract)

8.4 Service Logic Design

8.5 Service Discovery

8.6 Service Versioning and Retirement

SOA projects are comprised of a common set of stages that transition the delivery of services from conceptualization to implementation to evolution through a pre-defined lifecycle. Formal, SOA-specific processes have been established for several of these stages.

Although Figure 8.1 displays these stages sequentially, how and when each stage and process is carried out depends on the delivery strategy being used. Different approaches can be considered, depending on the nature and scope of the overall SOA project, the size and extent of standardization of the service inventory for which services are being delivered, and the manner in which tactical (short-term) requirements are being prioritized in relation to strategic (long-term) requirements.

The generic processes and delivery strategies that have been established are part of a mainstream SOA methodology (MSOAM) that has been documented across several titles (in this series and in other books) over the past decade.

REST introduces specific considerations and requirements that we need to take into account when delivering REST services for service-oriented solutions.

In particular, we need to raise some key questions:

- *How can a uniform contract be modeled in alignment with a service inventory blueprint—and—prior to the design of dependent service contracts?*

- *How can REST services be modeled in advance of their physical design— and—in alignment with uniform contract characteristics?*

- *How can a uniform contract be designed with features and boundaries that support the distinct requirements of a service inventory?*

- *How can REST service contracts be designed in accordance with service contract-related service-orientation principles and relevant patterns— and—the distinct features and limitations of the over-arching uniform contract?*

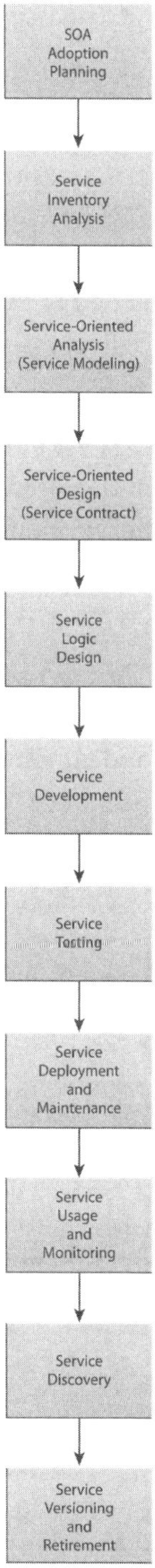

Figure 8.1

Common mainstream SOA project stages.

- *How can uniform contracts and REST service contracts be effectively versioned?*

- *How can REST service compositions be designed in accordance with service-orientation principles and relevant patterns?*

To answer the preceding list of questions, we need to determine how and where unique REST service delivery considerations can be incorporated into the SOA project delivery lifecycle. The outcome of merging REST analysis and design requirements with established SOA methodology is a set of formal processes expanded and optimized for the delivery of REST services and service-oriented solutions.

This chapter provides an overview of relevant SOA project stages and associated MSOAM processes in preparation for upcoming chapters that document new processes and cover various additional topics specific to merging SOA with REST for real-world applications. The end-result is a significant extension to the mainstream SOA methodology that takes into account the distinct characteristics and design goals sought when creating Web-centric architecture.

The SOA project stages are repeated in Table 8.1. Those grayed out are not of direct relevance due to this book's specific focus on the application of design principles, patterns, and constraints. However, it is important to acknowledge that all project stages are of relevance to the overall delivery of REST services for SOA projects.

SOA Adoption Planning	–
Service Inventory Analysis	Chapter 9
Service-Oriented Analysis (Service Modeling)	Chapter 9
Service-Oriented Design (Service Contract)	Chapter 10
Service Logic Design *(as it pertains to service composition only)*	Chapters 11, 12
Service Development	–
Service Testing	–
Service Deployment and Maintenance	–
Service Usage and Monitoring	–

Service Discovery (as it pertains to service composition only)	Chapters 6, 12
Service Versioning and Retirement	Chapter 15

Table 8.1
SOA project stages and relevant chapters.

The upcoming sections briefly describe the relevant project stages.

8.1 Service Inventory Analysis

As explained in Chapter 4, a service inventory represents a collection of independently standardized, owned, and governed services. The scope of a service inventory is expected to be meaningfully "cross-silo," which generally implies that it encompasses multiple business processes or operational areas within an organization.

This service inventory analysis stage is dedicated to conceptually defining an inventory of services. It is comprised of a cycle (Figure 8.2) during which the service-oriented analysis stage (explained shortly) is carried out once during each iteration. Each completion of a service-oriented analysis results in the definition of new service candidates or the refinement of existing ones. The cycle is repeated until all business processes that fall within the domain of the service inventory are analyzed and decomposed into individual actions suitable for service encapsulation.

Figure 8.2
The service inventory analysis cycle. The highlighted step refers to the service inventory blueprint that represents the primary deliverable of this stage.

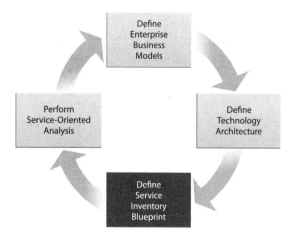

As individual service candidates are identified they are assigned appropriate functional contexts in relation to each other. This ensures that services (within the service inventory boundary) are normalized so that they don't functionally overlap. As a result, service reuse is maximized and the separation of concerns is cleanly carried out. A primary deliverable produced during this stage is the *service inventory blueprint*.

The scope of the initiative and the size of the target service inventory tend to determine the amount of up-front effort required to create a complete service inventory blueprint. More up-front analysis results in a better defined conceptual blueprint, which is intended to lead to the creation of a better quality inventory of services. Less up-front analysis leads to partial or less well-defined service inventory blueprints.

Here are brief descriptions of the primary cycle steps:

- *Define Enterprise Business Models* – Business models and specifications (such as business process definitions, business entity models, logical data models, etc.) are identified, defined, and, if necessary, brought up-to-date and further refined. These models are used as the primary business analysis input.

- *Define Technology Architecture* – Based on what we learn of business automation and service encapsulation requirements, we are able to define preliminary technology architecture characteristics and constraints. This provides a preview of the service inventory environment that can raise practical considerations that may impact how we define service candidates. As explained in Chapter 9, this step represents the point during this cycle at which a REST-based service inventory's uniform contract can be modeled.

- *Define Service Inventory Blueprint* – After an initial definition that establishes the scope and structure of the planned service inventory, this blueprint acts as the master specification wherein modeled service candidates are documented.

- *Perform Service-Oriented Analysis* – Each iteration of the service inventory lifecycle executes a service-oriented analysis process. (The service-oriented analysis stage is explained in the next section, as well as in Chapter 9.)

The service inventory blueprint is incrementally defined as a result of repeated iterations of steps that include the service-oriented analysis.

8.2 Service-Oriented Analysis (Service Modeling)

Service-oriented analysis represents one of the early stages in an SOA initiative and the first phase in the service delivery cycle. It is a process that begins with preparatory information gathering steps that are completed in support of a service modeling sub-process that results in the creation of conceptual service candidates, service capability candidates, and service composition candidates (Figures 8.3 and 8.4).

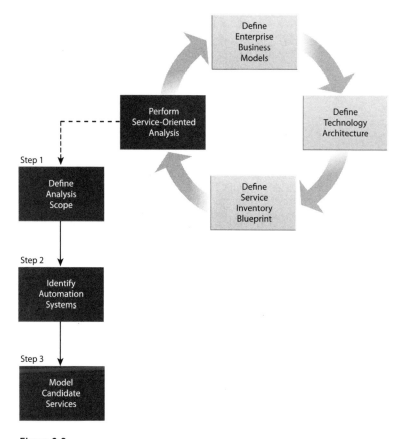

Figure 8.3

A generic service-oriented analysis process in which the first two steps collect information in preparation for a detailed service modeling sub-process represented by the Model Candidate Services step.

The service-oriented analysis process is commonly carried out iteratively, once for each business process. Typically, the delivery of a service inventory determines a scope that represents a meaningful domain of the enterprise, or the enterprise as a whole. All iterations of a service-oriented analysis then pertain to that scope, with each iteration contributing to the service inventory blueprint.

Figure 8.4 displays the service modeling process, a sub-process of service-oriented analysis. In Chapter 9 we discuss how this process can be further augmented in support of REST service modeling.

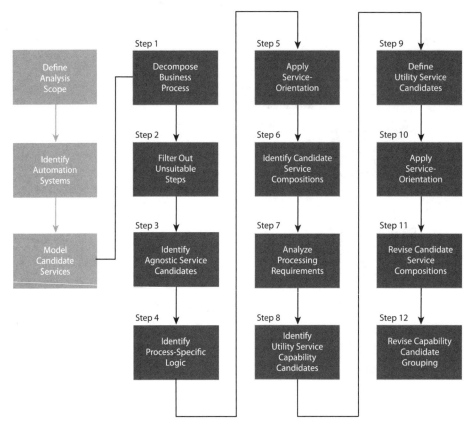

Figure 8.4

A generic service modeling process comprised of steps that raise key service definition considerations.

8.3 Service-Oriented Design (Service Contract)

The service-oriented design phase represents a service delivery lifecycle stage dedicated to producing service contracts in support of the well-established "contract-first" approach to software development.

The typical starting point for the service-oriented design process is a service candidate that was produced as a result of completing all required iterations of the service-oriented analysis process (Figure 8.5). Service-oriented design subjects this service candidate to additional considerations that shape it into a technical service contract in alignment with other service contracts being produced for the same service inventory.

As a precursor to the service logic design stage, service-oriented design is comprised of a process that steps service architects through a series of considerations to ensure that the service contract being produced fulfills business requirements while representing a normalized functional context that further adheres to service-orientation principles. Part of this process further includes the authoring of the SLA, which may be especially of significance for cloud-based services being offered to a broader consumer base.

Chapter 10 is dedicated to exploring considerations and practices specific to REST service contract design and uniform contract design.

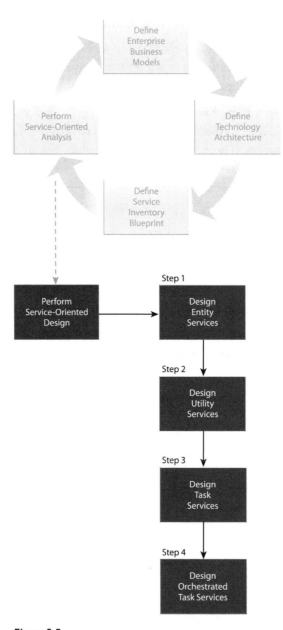

Figure 8.5

When a given service is deemed to have received sufficient analysis
effort, it is subjected to a service-oriented design process specific
to its service model. Each such process produces a physical service
contract.

8.4 Service Logic Design

By preceding the design of service logic with the service-oriented design process, the service contract is established and finalized prior to the underlying service architecture and the logic that will be responsible for carrying out the functionality expressed in the service contract. This deliberate sequence of project stages is in support of the Standardized Service Contract (411) principle, which states that service contracts should be standardized in relation to each other within a given service inventory boundary.

How service logic is designed is dictated by the business automation requirements that need to be fulfilled by the service. With service-oriented solutions, a given service may be able to address business requirements individually or (more commonly) as part of a service composition.

Chapter 11 delves into the various design considerations of service compositions, as they pertain to services that participate in composition, as well as the composition architecture as a whole.

8.5 Service Discovery

In order to ensure the consistent reuse of agnostic services and service capabilities, project teams carry out a separate and explicitly defined service discovery process. The primary goal of this process is to identify one or more existing agnostic services (such as utility or entity services) within a given service inventory that can fulfill generic requirements for whatever business process the project team is tasked with automating.

The communications quality of the metadata and service contract documents play a significant role in how successfully this process can be carried out. This is why one of the eight service-orientation principles—Service Discoverability (420)—is dedicated solely to ensuring that information published about services is highly interpretable and discoverable.

Chapter 12 makes reference to the discoverability of services in relation to service composition design.

8.6 Service Versioning and Retirement

After a service has been implemented and used in production environments, the need may arise to make changes to the existing service logic or to increase the functional scope of the service. In cases like this, a new version of the service logic and/or the service contract will likely need to be introduced. To ensure that the versioning of a service can be carried out with minimal impact and disruption to service consumers that have already formed dependencies on the service, a formal service versioning process needs to be in place. There are different versioning strategies, each of which introduces its own set of rules and priorities when it comes to managing the backwards and forwards compatibilities of services.

Chapter 15 provides a series of best practices for versioning REST services.

Chapter 9

Analysis and Service Modeling with REST

9.1 Uniform Contract Modeling and REST Service Inventory Modeling

9.2 REST Service Modeling

PRINCIPLES, PATTERNS, AND CONSTRAINTS REFERENCED IN THIS CHAPTER:

- Cache {398}

- Domain Inventory [458]

- Enterprise Inventory [461]

- Entity Abstraction [463]

- Layered System {404}

- Logic Centralization [475]

- Process Abstraction [486]

- Service Autonomy (417)

- Service Normalization [506]

- Stateless {395}

- Three-Layer Inventory [513]

- Uniform Contract {400}

- Utility Abstraction [517]

A fundamental characteristic of SOA projects is that they emphasize the need for working toward a strategic target state that the delivery of each service is intended to support. In order to realize this, some level of increased up-front analysis effort is generally necessary. Therefore, a primary way in which SOA project delivery methodologies differ is in how they position and prioritize analysis-related phases. This consideration is equally relevant to any service implementation medium. In fact, the actual medium and associated technology that will be used to physically design and develop services may not actually be known during initial analysis stages. It may be better to determine whether REST or another medium is the most suitable choice after having had the opportunity to model a number of planned service candidates and study their anticipated composition and interaction requirements.

There are two primary analysis phases in a typical SOA project:

- the analysis of individual services in relation to business process automation

- the collective analysis of a service inventory

The service-oriented analysis phase is dedicated to producing conceptual service definitions (service candidates) as part of the functional decomposition of business process logic. The service inventory analysis establishes a cycle whereby the service-oriented analysis process is carried out iteratively to whatever extent the project methodology will allow.

9.1 Uniform Contract Modeling and REST Service Inventory Modeling

As explained in Chapter 4, a service inventory is a collection of services that are independently owned, governed, and standardized. When we apply the Uniform Contract {400} constraint during an SOA project, we typically do so for a specific service inventory. This is because a uniform contract will end up standardizing a number of aspects pertaining to service capability representation, data representation, message exchange, and message processing. *The definition of a uniform contract is ideally performed in advance of individual REST service contract design because each REST service contract will be required to form dependencies on and operate within the scope of the features offered by its associated uniform contract.*

Organizations that apply Enterprise Inventory [461] to build a single inventory of REST services will typically rely on a single over-arching uniform contract to establish baseline communication standards. Those that proceed with the Domain Inventory [458] approach instead will most likely need to define a separate uniform contract for each domain service inventory. Because domain service inventories tend to vary in terms of standardization and governance, separate uniform contracts can be created to accommodate these individual requirements. This is why uniform contract modeling can be part of the service inventory analysis project stage.

In the *Service Inventory Analysis* section from Chapter 8, we explained that the purpose of this stage is to enable a project team to first define the scope of a service inventory via the authoring of a service inventory blueprint. This specification is populated by the repeated execution of the service inventory analysis cycle. Once all (or as many iterations as are allowed) are completed, we have a set of service candidates that have been (hopefully) well-defined, individually and in relation to each other. The next step after that is to proceed with the design of the respective service contracts.

When we know in advance that we will be delivering these services using REST, it is beneficial to incorporate the modeling of the inventory's uniform contract during the modeling of the service inventory itself. This is because as we perform each service-oriented analysis process and as we model and refine each service candidate and each service capability candidate, we gather more and more intelligence about the business automation requirements that are distinct to that service inventory. Some of this information will be relevant to how we define the methods and media types of the uniform contract.

For example:

- understanding the types of information and documents that will need to be exchanged and processed can help define necessary media types

- understanding the service models (entity, utility, task, etc.) in use by service candidates can help determine which available methods should be supported

- understanding policies and rules that are required to regulate certain types of interaction can help determine when certain methods should not be used, or help define special features that may be required by some methods

- understanding how service capability candidates may need to be composed can help determine suitable methods

- understanding certain quality-of-service requirements (especially in relation to reliability, security, transactions, etc.) can help determine the need to support special features of methods, and may further help identify the need to issue a set of pre-defined messages that can be standardized as complex methods (as explained in Chapter 10)

A practical means of incorporating the task of uniform contract modeling as part of the service inventory analysis is to group it with the *Define Technology Architecture* step (Figure 9.1). It is during this step that general service inventory architecture characteristics and requirements are identified from the same types of intelligence we collect for the definition of uniform contract features. In this context, the uniform contract is essentially being defined as an extension to the standardized technology architecture for the service inventory.

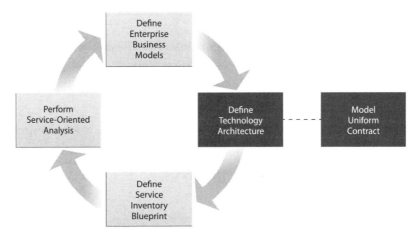

Figure 9.1

The service inventory analysis cycle diagram from Chapter 8 augmented to include uniform contract modeling as an iterative task.

If combining the *Model Uniform Contract* task with the *Define Technology Architecture* step turns out to be an unsuitable grouping, then the *Model Uniform Contract* task can be positioned as its own step within the cycle.

When we begin working on the uniform contract definition, one of the key decisions will be to determine the sources to be used to populate its methods and media types. As a general starting point, we can look to the HTTP specification for an initial set of methods, and the IANA Media Type Registry for the initial media types. Further media types and possibly further methods may come from a variety of internal and external sources.

> **NOTE**
>
> It is also worth noting that methods and media types can be standardized independently of a service inventory. For example, HTTP methods are defined by the IETF. A service inventory that uses these methods will include a reference to the IETF specification as part of the service inventory uniform contract definition. Media types may be specified on an ongoing basis by external bodies, such as the W3C, the IETF, and industry bodies across various supply chains, or even within an IT enterprise.

Before continuing, have a quick look at Figure 9.4 in the upcoming *REST Service Modeling Process* section. Note how the symbols for Steps 6 and 11 contain an asterisk in the top right corner. As explained in this section, this indicates that during this step we are modeling REST service candidates that either:

- incorporate methods and/or media types already modeled for the uniform contract, or...

- introduce the need to add or augment methods and/or media types for the uniform contract.

This type of two-way relationship between the *Perform Service-Oriented Analysis* step (which encompasses the REST service modeling process) and the *Model Uniform Contract* task is a natural dynamic of the service inventory analysis cycle.

> **NOTE**
>
> It is usually during the *Model Uniform Contract* task that a uniform contract profile is first populated with preliminary characteristics and properties. This profile document is then further refined as the uniform contract is physically designed and maintained over time. See Chapter 16 for an exploration of the template that these types of profiles can be based on.

REST Constraints and Uniform Contract Modeling

Although REST constraints are primarily applied during the physical design of service architectures, it can be helpful to take them into consideration as the uniform contract takes shape during the service-oriented analysis stage.

For example:

- *Stateless {395}* – From the data exchange requirements we are able to model between service candidates, can we determine whether services will be able to remain stateless between requests?

- *Cache {398}* – Are we able to identify any request messages with responses that can be cached and returned for subsequent requests instead of needing to be processed redundantly?

- *Uniform Contract {400}* – Can all methods and media types we are associating with the uniform contract during this stage be genuinely reused by service candidates?

- *Layered System {404}* – Do we know enough about the underlying technology architecture to determine whether services and their consumers can tell the difference between communicating directly or communicating via intermediary middleware?

The extent to which concrete aspects of REST constraint application can be factored into how we model the uniform contract will depend directly on:

- the extent to which the service inventory technology architecture is defined during iterations of the service inventory analysis cycle, and…

- the extent to which we learn about a given business process's underlying automation requirements during Step 2 of the service-oriented analysis process (as explained in Chapter 8).

Much of this will be dependent on the amount of information we have and are able to gather about the underlying infrastructure and overall ecosystem in which the inventory of services will reside. For example, if we know in advance that we are delivering a set of services within an environment riddled with existing legacy systems and middleware, we will be able to gain access to many information sources that will help determine boundaries, limitations, and options when it comes to service and uniform contract definition. On the other hand, if we are planning to build a brand new environment for our service inventory, there will usually be many more options for creating and tuning the technology architecture in support of how the services (and the uniform contract) can best fulfill business automation requirements.

REST Service Centralization and Normalization

Logic Centralization [475] attempts to avoid many of the pitfalls associated with redundant logic implemented across services by centralizing the logic in the form of a single normalized service. Redundant logic can lead to increased maintenance overhead both on an on-going basis and when business requirements change. It can further lead to governance and configuration management issues, especially in cases where the redundant logic is owned by different groups within an organization.

Because, within REST service implementations, the service contract is not "packaged" with the service architecture and logic, it is relatively easy for others in an IT department to add new REST services to a service inventory, particularly in the absence of a contract-first design approach. This tends to result in service capabilities that perform functions redundant with those provided by existing REST services. For example, a new REST service may inadvertently add an entity-centric service capability that belongs to the functional context of an existing REST entity service.

This issue can be addressed by applying Service Normalization [506], a pattern related to Logic Centralization [475], but one that views the design of services from a service inventory perspective. A normalized service inventory is designed with a clear blueprint and careful attention to service boundaries. These boundaries are defined on a functional basis. New logic that needs to be incorporated into a service inventory is first analyzed for its coherency in relation to the functional boundaries of existing services (Figure 9.2).

Normalizing a REST-centric service inventory requires up-front analysis, established governance practices, and a "whole-of-inventory" perspective to be applied. Normalization makes it easier for service consumers to find and correctly use the functionality they need in a consistent, logically partitioned space of REST service capabilities grouped into distinct functional contexts.

Figure 9.2

A service inventory comprised of REST services, each with a distinct functional boundary. When no one boundary overlaps the other, Service Normalization [506] has been applied to its full extent.

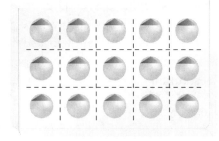

normalized
service inventory
with REST services

SUMMARY OF KEY POINTS

- The modeling of the uniform contract is closely associated with the service inventory analysis project stage.

- The initial definition of the uniform contract should be carried out prior to REST service contract design because individual REST service contracts will be dependent on the uniform contract features and limitations.

- A straight-forward means of incorporating the task of modeling the uniform contract with the service inventory analysis lifecycle is to combine it with the existing *Define Technology Architecture* step or to establish it as an independent step.

9.2 REST Service Modeling

The need to build a particular service can originate from various sources and under different circumstances.

For example:

- A service might be identified as being necessary based on a service inventory blueprint that maps out required functions and allocates them to functional contexts that form the basis of existing and future services.

- A service might be identified through change requests when it is determined that new functionality is needed and that this new functionality does not belong in any existing functional service contexts.

- A service might be identified through the analysis of legacy systems not yet encapsulated within the scope of a service inventory.

In any case, the service candidate is typically defined with whatever service capability candidates result from the service-oriented analysis process, during which we carry out a service modeling process that decomposes business process logic into granular actions that form the basis of service capability candidates.

The incorporation of resources and uniform contract features add new dimensions to service modeling. When we are aware that a given service candidate is being modeled specifically for a REST implementation, we can take these considerations into account by extending the service modeling process to include steps to better shape the service candidate as a basis for a REST service contract.

The upcoming *REST Service Modeling Process* section documents a generic service modeling process optimized for REST services. In preparation for the step-by-step coverage of this process, the next two sections highlight some key characteristics of REST service candidate definition.

REST Service Capability Granularity

When actions are defined at this stage, they are considered fine-grained in that each action is clearly distinguished with a specific purpose. However, within the scope of that purpose they can often still be somewhat vague and can easily encompass a range of possible variations.

Defining conceptual service candidates using this level of action granularity is common with mainstream service modeling approaches. It has proven sufficient for SOAP-based Web services because service capabilities that need to support variations of functionality can still be effectively mapped to WSDL-based operations capable of handling a range of input and output parameters.

With REST service contracts, service capabilities are required to incorporate methods (and media types) defined by an overarching uniform contract. As already discussed in the preceding section, the uniform contract for a given service inventory can be modeled alongside and in collaboration with the modeling of service candidates, as long as we know in advance that REST will act as the primary service implementation medium.

Whereas a WSDL-based service contract can incorporate custom parameter lists and other service-specific features, REST puts an upper bound on the granularity of message exchanges at the level of the most complex or most general purpose method and media type. This may, in some cases, lead to the need to define finer-grained service capabilities.

Figure 9.3 highlights the difference between a service candidate modeled in an implementation-neutral manner, versus one modeled specifically for the REST service implementation medium.

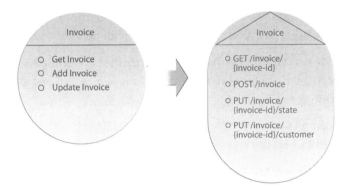

Figure 9.3

A REST service candidate can be modeled specifically to incorporate uniform contract characteristics. The Update Invoice service capability candidate is split into two variations—one that updates the invoice state value and another that updates the invoice customer value.

Resources vs. Entities

Part of the upcoming REST service modeling process explores the identification of resource candidates. It is through the definition of these resource candidates that we begin to introduce a Web-centric view of a service inventory. As discussed previously in Chapter 6, resources represent the "things" that need to be accessed and processed by service consumers.

What we are also interested in establishing during the service-oriented analysis stage is the encapsulation of entity logic, as explained in the coverage of the entity service model provided in Chapter 4. As with resources, entities also often represent "things" that need to be accessed and processed by service consumers.

What then is the difference between a resource and an entity? To understand REST service modeling, we need to clearly understand this distinction:

- Entities are business-centric and are derived from enterprise business models, such as entity relationship diagrams, logical data models, and ontologies.

- Resources can be business-centric or non-business-centric. A resource is any given "thing" associated with the business automation logic enabled by the service inventory.

- Entities are commonly limited to business artifacts and documents, such as invoices, claims, customers, etc.

- Some entities are more coarse-grained than others. Some entities can encapsulate others. For example, an invoice entity may encapsulate an invoice detail entity.

- Resources can also vary in granularity, but are often fine-grained. It is less common to have formally defined coarse-grained resources that encapsulate fine-grained resources.

- All entities can relate to or be based on resources. Not all resources can be associated with entities because some resources are non-business-centric.

The extent to which we need to formalize the mapping between business-centric resources and entities is up to us. In the upcoming REST service modeling process there are steps that encourage us to define and standardize resources as part of the service inventory blueprint so that we gain a better understanding of how and where resources need to be consumed.

From a pure modeling perspective we are further encouraged to relate business-centric resources to business entities so that we maintain a constant alignment with how business-centric artifacts and documents exist within our business. This perspective is especially valuable as the business and its automation requirements continue to evolve over time.

REST Service Modeling Process

We now introduce a formal process for modeling REST services. This section is divided into a series of parts that describe each process step. About half of the step descriptions are further supplemented with a string of case study examples that demonstrate how a set of service candidates are defined and refined to form a simple service composition candidate.

Figure 9.4 summarizes the process by providing a variation of the original mainstream service modeling process (first introduced in Chapter 8) containing modifications and additional steps incorporated in support of REST service modeling.

NOTE

As with any MSOAM process or model, the REST service modeling process should be considered a generic approach that can be further customized to incorporate preferences and requirements specific to the organization and its IT enterprise. The purpose of this process is to provide a starting point that highlights key considerations and steps commonly required to effectively model service candidates in support of REST implementation.

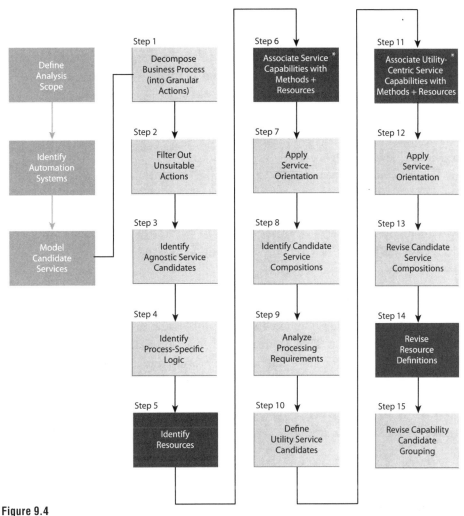

Figure 9.4

A RESTful version of the MSOAM service modeling process extended to include new steps (highlighted with dark grey) in support of modeling services specifically for REST implementation. The asterisk on the top-right of Steps 6 and 11 indicates a connection with the Model Uniform Contract task from the service inventory analysis cycle (as previously explained in the *Uniform Contract Modeling and REST Service Inventory Modeling* section).

Let's take a closer look at the individual steps of the REST service modeling process. We'll begin with a case study example that establishes the business process logic that will act as our primary input into the process steps.

CASE STUDY EXAMPLE

Existing MUA charter agreements with partner schools explicitly refer to the need to acknowledge individual academic achievements. This makes the correct conferral of awards important to the reputation of MUA and its elite students.

MUA assembles a service modeling team comprised of SOA architects, SOA analysts, and business analysts. The team begins with a REST service modeling process for the Student Achievement Award Conferral business process. As detailed in Figure 9.5, this business process logic represents the procedures followed for the assessment, conference, and rejection of individual achievement award applications submitted by students. An application that is approved results in the conferral of the achievement award and a notification of the conferral to the student. An application that is rejected results in a notification of the rejection to the student.

Step 1: Decompose Business Process (into Granular Actions)

We begin by taking the documented business process and breaking it down into a series of granular process steps. This requires further analysis of the process logic, during which we attempt to decompose the business process into a set of individual granular actions.

CASE STUDY EXAMPLE

The original Student Award Conferral business process is broken down into the following granular actions:

- Initiate Conferral Application

- Get Event Details

- Verify Event Details

- If Event is Invalid or Ineligible for Award, Cancel Process

- Get Award Details

- Get Student Transcript

- Verify Student Transcript Qualifies for Award Based on Award Conferral Rules

- If Student Transcript does not Qualify, Initiate Rejection

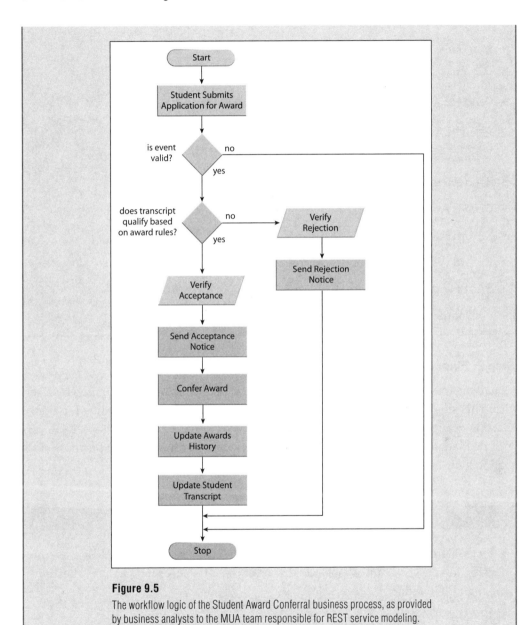

Figure 9.5

The workflow logic of the Student Award Conferral business process, as provided by business analysts to the MUA team responsible for REST service modeling.

- Manually Verify Rejection

- Print Rejection Notice

- Send Rejection Notice

- Manually Verify Acceptance

- Print Acceptance Notice

- Send Acceptance Notice

- Confer Award

- Record Award Conferral in Student Transcript

- Record Award Conferral in Awards Database

- Print Hard Copy of Award Conferral Record

- File Hard Copy of Award Conferral Record

Step 2: Filter Out Unsuitable Actions

Not all business process logic is suitable for automation and/or encapsulation by a service. This step requires us to single out any of the granular actions identified in Step 1 that do not appear to be suitable for subsequent REST service modeling steps. Examples include manual process steps that need to be performed by humans and business automation logic being carried out by legacy systems that cannot be wrapped by a service.

CASE STUDY EXAMPLE

After assessing each of the decomposed actions, a subset is identified as being unsuitable for automation or unsuitable for service encapsulation, as indicated by the items highlighted in red:

- Initiate Conferral Application

- Get Event Details

- Verify Event Details

- If Event is Invalid or Ineligible for Award, Cancel Process

- Get Award Details

- Get Student Transcript

- Verify Student Transcript Qualifies for Award Based on Award Conferral Rules

- If Student Transcript does not Qualify, Initiate Rejection

- Manually Verify Rejection

- Print Rejection Notice

- Send Rejection Notice

- Manually Verify Acceptance

- Print Acceptance Notice

- Send Acceptance Notice

- Confer Award

- Record Award Conferral in Student Transcript

- Record Award Conferral in Awards Database

- Print Hard Copy of Award Conferral Record

- File Hard Copy of Award Conferral Record

Step 3: Identify Agnostic Service Candidates

By filtering out unsuitable actions during Step 2, we are left with only those actions relevant to our REST service modeling effort.

A primary objective of service-orientation is to carry out a separation of concerns whereby agnostic logic is cleanly partitioned from non-agnostic logic. By reviewing the actions that have been identified so far, we can begin to further separate those that have an evident level of reuse potential. This essentially provides us with a preliminary set of agnostic service capability candidates.

We then determine how these service capability candidates should be grouped to form the basis of functional service boundaries.

Common factors we can take into account include:

1. Which service capability candidates defined so far are closely related to each other?

2. Are identified service capability candidates business-centric or utility-centric?

3. What types of functional service contexts are suitable, given the overarching business context of the service inventory?

Item #2 on the list of factors pertains to the organization of service candidates within logical service layers based on service models (see Chapter 4). The Entity Abstraction [463] and Utility Abstraction [517] patterns are applied in particular as these provide the necessary criteria used to distinguish:

- business-centric agnostic logic suitable for entity services

- non-business-centric agnostic logic suitable for utility services

Due to the business-centric level of documentation that typically goes into the authoring of business process models and specifications and associated workflows, the emphasis during this step will naturally be more on the definition of entity service candidates. The upcoming *Identify Utility Service Capability Candidates* and *Define Utility Service Candidates* steps are dedicated to developing the utility service layer.

Finally, Item #3 on the preceding list of factors relates to how we may choose to establish functional service boundaries not only in relation to the current business process we are decomposing, but also in relation to the overall nature of the service inventory. This broader consideration helps us determine whether there are generic functional contexts that we can define that will be useful for the automation of multiple business processes.

> **NOTE**
>
> Both the previously referenced Logic Centralization [475] and Service Normalization [506] patterns play a key role during this step to ensure we keep agnostic service candidates aligned to each other, without allowing functional overlap.

CASE STUDY EXAMPLE

By analyzing the remaining actions from Step 2, the MUA service modeling team identifies and categorizes those considered agnostic. Actions that are non-agnostic are highlighted:

- Initiate Conferral Application

- Get Event Details

- Verify Event Details

- If Event is Invalid or Ineligible for Award ,Cancel Process

- Get Award Details

- Get Student Transcript

- Verify Student Transcript Qualifies for Award Based on Award Conferral Rules

- If Student Transcript does not Qualify ,Initiate Rejection

- Print Rejection Notice

- Send Rejection Notice

- Print Acceptance Notice

- Record Award Conferral in Student Transcript

- Record Award Conferral in Awards Database

- Print Hard Copy of Award Conferral Record

Agnostic actions are classified as preliminary service capability candidates and are grouped accordingly into service candidates, as follows:

Event Service Candidate (Entity)

The original Get Event Details action is positioned as a Get Details service capability candidate as part of an entity service candidate named Event (Figure 9.6).

Note that it was determined that the Verify Event Details action was not agnostic because it carried out logic specific to the Student Award Conferral process.

Figure 9.6

The Event service candidate with one service capability candidate.

Award Service Candidate (Entity)

As a central part of this business process, the Award business entity becomes the basis of an Award entity service candidate (Figure 9.7).

Figure 9.7

The Award service candidate with three service capability candidates, including two that are based on the same action.

The Get Award Details action establishes a Get Details service capability candidate. The Record Award Conferral in Awards Database action is split into two service capability candidates:

• Confer

• Update History

The Confer capability is required to officially issue an award for an event, which requires updates in the internal MUA Awards database, as well as an update to an external National Academic Recognition System shared by schools throughout the US. Furthermore, based on the award conferral policies, this service capability is required to issue a conferral notification and forward the award conferral record information to be printed in hard copy format. Therefore, it is expected that the Confer service capability will invoke corresponding utility services to perform these functions automatically, upon each conferral.

The Update History capability will issue a further update of student and event details within a separate part of the internal Awards database. It is deemed necessary to keep the capabilities separate as the Update History capability can be used independently and for different purposes than the Confer capability.

Student Service Candidate (Entity)

The need for a Student entity service within a school is self-evident. This service will eventually provide a wide range of student-related functions. In support of the

Student Award Conferral business process specifically, the Get Student Transcript and Record Award Conferral in Student Transcript actions are positioned as individual service capability candidates named Get Transcript and Update Transcript (Figure 9.8).

Figure 9.8

The Student service candidate with two service capability candidates.

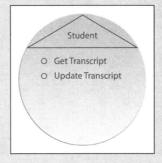

Notification Service Candidate (Utility)

The Print Rejection Notice and Print Acceptance Notice actions are combined into one generic Send service capability candidate as part of a utility service called Notification (Figure 9.9). The Send capability will accept a range of input values, enabling it to issue approval and rejection notifications, among others.

Figure 9.9

The Notification service candidate with a sole service capability candidate that processes two of the actions identified for the parent business process.

Document Service Candidate (Utility)

The MUA service modeling team originally created a Document Printing utility service, but then realized its functional scope was too limiting. Instead, it broadened its scope to encompass generic document processing functions. For the time being, this service candidate will only include a Print service capability candidate to accommodate the Print Hard Copy of Award Conferral Record action (Figure 9.10). In the future, this utility service will include other service capabilities that perform generic document processing tasks, such as faxing, routing, and parsing.

Figure 9.10
The Document service candidate with a generic Print service capability candidate.

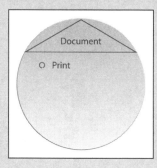

Step 4: Identify Process-Specific Logic

Any parts of the business process logic remaining after we complete Step 3 will likely need to be classified as non-agnostic or specific to the business process. Common types of actions that fall into this category include business rules, conditional logic, exception logic, and the sequence logic used to execute the individual business process actions.

Process-specific logic is separated into its own logical service layer, as per the Process Abstraction [486] pattern. For a given business process, this type of logic is commonly grouped into a single task service or a service consumer acting as the composition controller.

CASE STUDY EXAMPLE

The following actions are considered non-agnostic because they are specific to the Student Award Conferral process:

- If Student Transcript does not Qualify, Initiate Rejection

- Verify Student Transcript Qualifies for Award Based on Award Conferral Rules

- If Event is Invalid or Ineligible for Award, Cancel Process

- Verify Event Details

- Initiate Conferral Application

The first action on this list forms the basis of a service capability candidate, as explained shortly in the Confer Student Award task service candidate description. The remaining actions (highlighted in red) do not correspond to service capability candidates. Instead, they are identified as logic that occurs internally within the Confer Student Award task service.

Confer Student Award Service Candidate (Task)

The Initiate Conferral Application action is translated into a simple Start service capability candidate as part of a Confer Student Award task service candidate (Figure 9.11). It is expected that the Start capability will be invoked by a separate software program. (Such a program would be acting as a composition initiator, as explained in Chapter 11.)

Figure 9.11

The Confer Student Award task service candidate with a single service capability that launches the automation of the Student Award Conferral business process.

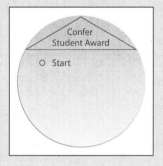

Step 5: Identify Resources

By examining the functional contexts associated with individual actions we can begin to make a list of how these contexts relate to or form the basis of resources. It can be helpful to further qualify identified resources as agnostic (multi-purpose) or non-agnostic (single-purpose), depending on how specific we determine their usage and existence are to the parent business process.

Step 3 explained how labeling a service candidate or a service capability candidate as "agnostic" has significant implications as to how we approach the modeling of that service. This is not the case with resources. From a modeling perspective, agnostic resources can be incorporated into agnostic service and capability candidates without limitation. The benefit to identifying agnostic resources is to earmark them as parts of the enterprise that are likely to be shared and reused more frequently than non-agnostic resources. This can help us prepare necessary infrastructure or perhaps even limit their access in how we model (and subsequently design) the service capabilities that encompass them.

Note that resources identified at this stage can be expressed using the forward slash as a delimiter. This is not intended to result in URL-compliant statements; rather, it is a means by which to recognize the parts of service capability candidates that pertain to resources. Similarly, modeled resources are intentionally represented in a simplified form. Later, in the service-oriented design stage, the syntactically correct resource identifier statements are used to represent resources, including any necessary partitioning into multi-part URL statements (as per resource identifier syntax standards being used).

CASE STUDY EXAMPLE

Subsequent to a review of the processing requirements of the service capability candidates defined so far, the following potential resources are identified:

- /Process/
- /Application/
- /Event/
- /Award/
- /Student Transcript/
- /Notice Sender/
- /Printer/

Before proceeding, the MUA service modeling team decides to further qualify the /Process/ and /Application/ resource candidates to better associate them with the nature of the overarching business processing logic, as follows:

- /Student Award Conferral Process/
- /Conferral Application/

These qualifiers help distinguish similar resources that may exist as other forms of applications or rules.

Because the service modeling process has, so far, already produced a set of entity services, each of which represents a business entity, it is further decided to establish some preliminary mapping between identified resources and entities, as follows:

Entity	Resource
Event	/Event/
Award	/Award/
Student	/Student Transcript/

Table 9.1
Mapping business entities to resources.

Additional resources are not mapped because they do not currently relate to known business entities. They may end up being mapped during future iterations of the service modeling process.

Step 6: Associate Service Capabilities with Resources and Methods

We now associate the service capability candidates defined in Steps 3 and 4 with the resources defined in Step 5, as well as with available uniform contract methods that may have been established. If we discover that a given service capability candidate requires a method that does not yet exist in the uniform contract definition, the method can be proposed as input for the next iteration of the *Model Uniform Contract* task that is part of the service inventory analysis cycle.

We continue to use the same service candidate and service capability candidate notation, but we append service capability candidates with their associated method + resource combinations. This allows for a descriptive and flexible expression of a preliminary service contract that can be further changed and refined during subsequent iterations of the service-oriented analysis process.

NOTE

At this stage, it is common to associate actions with regular HTTP methods, as defined via uniform contract modeling efforts. In Chapter 12 we introduce the notion of complex methods that can be comprised of pre-defined sets and/or sequences of regular method invocations. If complex methods are defined at the service modeling stage, then they can also be associated, as appropriate.

CASE STUDY EXAMPLE

The MUA service modeling team continues to expand upon their original service candidate definitions by adding the appropriate uniform contract methods and resources, as follows:

Confer Student Award Service Candidate (Task)

The business document required as the primary input to kick-off the Student Award Conferral business process is the application submitted by the student. It was initially assumed that a /Conferral Application/ resource would be required to represent this document. However, upon further analysis, it turns out that all the Start service capability candidate needs is a POST method to forward the application document to a resource named after the business process itself (Figure 9.12).

Figure 9.12
The Confer Student Award service candidate with method and resource association.

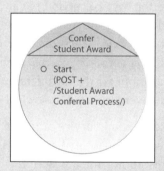

Event Service Candidate (Entity)

The sole Get Details service capability candidate is appended with the GET method and the /Event/ resource (Figure 9.13).

Figure 9.13

The Event service candidate with method and resource association.

Award Service Candidate (Entity)

The Get Details service capability is correspondingly associated with a GET method plus /Award/ resource combination. The Confer and Update History service capability candidates each require input data that will update resource data, and therefore are expanded with a preliminary POST method and the /Awards/ resource (Figure 9.14). This method may later be refined during the service-oriented design phase.

Figure 9.14

The Award service candidate with method and resource associations.

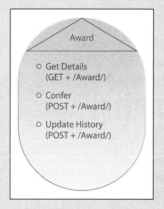

Student Service Candidate (Entity)

The Get Transcript service capability candidate is associated with the GET method and the /Student Transcript/ resource. The Update Transcript is appended with the POST method together again with the /Student Transcript/ resource (Figure 9.15).

Figure 9.15

The Student service candidate with method and resource associations.

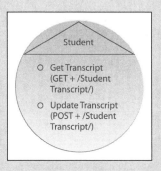

Notification Service Candidate (Utility)

The Send service capability candidate is expanded with the POST method and the /Notice Sender/ resource (Figure 9.16).

Figure 9.16

The Notification service candidate with method and resource association.

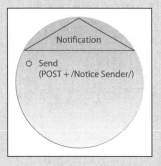

Document Service Candidate (Utility)

The highly generic Print service capability candidate is expanded with a POST method and the /Printer/ resource (Figure 9.17). Any document sent to the Print capability will be posted to the /Printer/ resource and, resultantly, printed.

Figure 9.17

The Document service candidate with method and resource association.

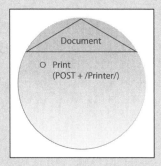

Step 7: Apply Service-Orientation

The business process documentation we used as input for the service modeling process may provide us with a level of knowledge as to the underlying processing required by each of the identified REST service capability candidates. Based on this knowledge, we may be able to further shape the definition and scope of service capabilities, as well as their parent service candidates, by taking a relevant subset of the service-orientation principles into consideration.

CASE STUDY EXAMPLE

When applying this step, the MUA service modeling team is faced with various practical concerns, based on what participating SOA architects can provide in terms of knowledge of the implementation environment that the services will be deployed in.

For example, they identify that a given set of resources is related to data provided by a large legacy system. This impacts functional service boundaries by the extent to which the Service Autonomy (417) principle can be applied.

Step 8: Identify Candidate Service Compositions

Here we document the most common service capability interactions that can take place during the execution of the business process logic. Different interactions are mapped out based on the success and failure scenarios that can occur during the possible action sequences within the business process workflow.

Mapping these interaction scenarios to the required service capability candidates enables us to model candidate service compositions. If we have applied the Process Abstraction [486], Entity Abstraction [463], and Utility Abstraction [517] patterns previously, we can establish a composition hierarchy that is likely to fall under the Three-Layer Inventory [513] compound pattern.

It is through this type of view that we can get a preview of the size and complexity of potential service compositions that result from how we defined the scope and granularity of agnostic and non-agnostic service candidates (and capability candidates) so far. For example, if we determine that the service composition will need to involve too many service capability invocations, we still have an opportunity to revisit our service candidates.

It is also at this stage that we begin to take a closer look at data exchange requirements (because in order for services to compose each other, they must exchange data). This may provide us with enough information to begin identifying required media types based on what has already been defined for the uniform contract. Alternatively, we may determine the need for new media types that have not yet been modeled. In the latter case, we may be gathering information that will act as input for the *Model Uniform Contract* task that is part of the service inventory analysis cycle (as explained earlier, in the *Uniform Contract Modeling and REST Service Inventory Modeling* section).

NOTE

The depth of service compositions can particularly impact method definition. It is important to pose questions about the possible failure scenarios that can occur during service composition execution.

CASE STUDY EXAMPLE

The MUA service modeling team explores a set of service composition scenarios that correspond to success and failure conditions that may arise when the Student Award Conferral process is executed.

Figure 9.18 illustrates the composition hierarchy of service candidates that is relatively consistent across these scenarios. In each case, the Confer Student Award task service invokes the Event, Award, and Student entity services. The Award entity service further composes the Notification utility service to issue acceptance or rejection notifications and, if the award is conferred, the Document utility service to print the award record.

NOTE

This next series of steps is optional and more suited for complex business processes and larger service inventory architectures. It requires that we more closely study the underlying processing requirements of all service capability candidates in order to abstract further utility-centric service candidates.

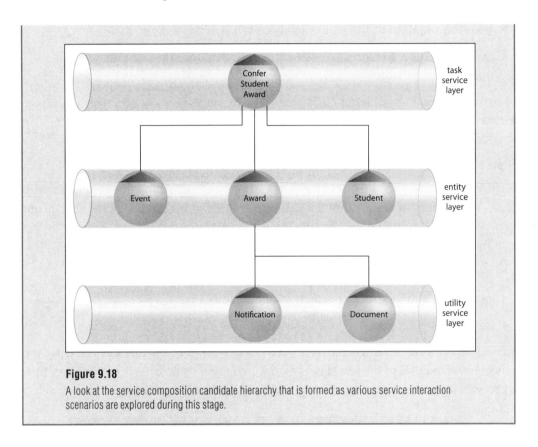

Figure 9.18
A look at the service composition candidate hierarchy that is formed as various service interaction scenarios are explored during this stage.

Step 9: Analyze Processing Requirements

As mentioned in the description for Step 3, the emphasis so far in this service modeling process will likely have been on business-centric processing logic. This is to be expected when working with business process definitions that are primarily based on a business view of automation. However, it is prudent to look under the hood of the business logic defined so far in order to identify the need for any further utility logic.

To accomplish this, we need to consider the following:

- Which of the resources identified so far can be considered utility-centric?

- Can actions performed on business-centric resources be considered utility-centric (such as reporting actions)?

- What underlying utility logic needs to be executed in order to process the actions and/or resources encompassed by a service capability candidate?

- Does any required utility logic already exist?

- Does any required utility logic span application boundaries? (In other words, is more than one system required to complete the action?)

Note that information gathered during the Identify Automation Systems step of the parent service-oriented analysis process will be referenced at this point.

Step 10: Define Utility Service Candidates

In this step, we group utility-centric processing steps according to predefined contexts. With utility service candidates, the primary context is a logical relationship between capability candidates. This relationship can be based on any number of factors, including:

- association with a specific legacy system

- association with one or more solution components

- logical grouping according to type of function

Various other issues are considered once service candidates are subjected to the service-oriented design process. For now, this grouping establishes a preliminary utility service layer.

> **NOTE**
>
> It is important to acknowledge that Steps 9 and 10 are not responsible for defining all utility service candidates. We will have likely already defined some preliminary utility service candidates during Step 3. The optional steps in this modeling process (Steps 9 through 15) encourage us to drill-down into the detailed processing requirements of the service-enabled automation logic we defined and organized so far. They therefore help us establish additional utility processing requirements that can impact our service inventory blueprint via the:
>
> - identification of new utility service candidates and capability candidates
>
> - augmentation, refinement, or consolidation of previously defined utility service candidates and capability candidates

Modeling utility service candidates is notoriously more difficult than entity service candidates. Unlike entity services where we base functional contexts and boundaries upon already documented enterprise business models and specifications (such as taxonomies, ontologies, entity relationships, etc.), there are usually no such models for utility logic. Therefore, it is common for the functional scope and context of utility service candidates to be continually revised during iterations of the service inventory analysis cycle.

Step 11: Associate Utility-Centric Service Capabilities with Resources and Methods

Here we break down each utility logic processing requirement we identified in Step 9 into a series of granular actions. As with Step 6, we associate resources and methods with actions to establish a set of REST-friendly service capability candidates.

Step 12: Apply Service-Orientation

This step is a repeat of Step 7 provided here specifically for any new utility service candidates that may have emerged from the completion of Steps 9 and 10.

Step 13: Revise Candidate Service Compositions

Now we revisit the original service composition candidate scenarios we identified in Step 8 to incorporate new or revised utility service candidates. The result is typically an expansion of the service composition scope where more utility service capabilities find themselves participating in the business process automation.

Step 14: Revise Resource Definitions

Both business-centric and utility-centric resources can be accessed or processed by utility services. Therefore, any new utility-related processing logic identified in the preceding steps can result in opportunities to further add to and/or revise the set of resources modeled so far.

Step 15: Revise Capability Candidate Grouping

This final step in the REST service modeling process asks us to check the grouping of all modeled service capability candidates.

Reasons why we may need to make further adjustments to these groupings include:

- Utility service capability candidates defined in Steps 9 and 10 may remove some of the required actions that comprised entity service capability candidates defined earlier, in Step 3.

- The introduction of new utility service candidates may affect (or assimilate) the functional scopes of already defined utility service candidates.

- The modeling of larger and potentially more complex service composition candidates in Step 13 may lead to the need to reduce or increase the granularity of some service capability candidates.

Additional Considerations

The preceding service modeling process was presented with the assumption that it is being carried out during the first iteration of the service inventory analysis cycle. Subsequent iterations will have already produced entity service candidates, utility service candidates, resources, and various input for uniform contract methods and media types. As a result, subsequent execution of Steps 3, 5, 8, 9, 10, and 14 will require an extra discovery task during which we determine what relevant service candidates, resources, and uniform contract properties exist, prior to defining or proposing new ones.

SUMMARY OF KEY POINTS

- When carrying out the service modeling process it may not yet be known what service implementation medium will be used in subsequent project stages. If we know in advance that services we are modeling are going to be implemented using REST, we can carry out a service modeling process augmented specifically for REST services.

- The base service modeling process can be augmented and extended in a number of areas to accommodate distinct REST service modeling requirements, such as the incorporation of resources and uniform contract features.

Chapter 10

Service-Oriented Design with REST

10.1 Uniform Contract Design Considerations

10.2 REST Service Contract Design

10.3 Complex Method Design

PRINCIPLES, PATTERNS, AND CONSTRAINTS REFERENCED IN THIS CHAPTER:

- Atomic Transaction [432]

- Cache {398}

- Canonical Expression [434]

- Canonical Schema [437]

- Entity Abstraction [463]

- Event-Driven Messaging [465]

- Idempotent Capability [470]

- Layered System {404}

- Legacy Wrapper [473]

- Logic Centralization [475]

- Process Abstraction [486]

- Service Abstraction (414)

- Service Discoverability (420)

- Service Loose Coupling (413)

- Stateless {395}

- Uniform Contract {400}

- Utility Abstraction [517]

- Validation Abstraction [518]

Using the conceptual service candidates modeled during the preceding service-oriented analysis process as a starting point, service-oriented design is dedicated to the physical design of service contracts. When it comes to contract design with REST, we need to be concerned with two particular areas:

1. The design of a uniform contract for a service inventory.

2. The design of individual service contracts within the service inventory and in compliance with the uniform contract.

The uniform contract needs to be firmly established before we begin creating service contracts that will be required to form dependencies on uniform contract features. As a service inventory grows and evolves, new services can still influence the design of a uniform contract, but uniform contract features are generally changed and added at a very deliberate pace.

Following the preceding sequence, this chapter begins with coverage of uniform contract design topics and then moves on to topics that pertain to the design of REST service contracts. The chapter concludes with a section on complex methods, an optional field of REST contract design and one suitable mainly for use within controlled environments, such as internal service inventories.

10.1 Uniform Contract Design Considerations

When creating a uniform contract for a service inventory, we have a responsibility to equip and limit its features so that it is streamlined to effectively accommodate requirements and restrictions unique to the service inventory. The default characteristics of Web-centric technology architecture can provide an effective basis for a service inventory's uniform contract, although additional forms of standardization and customization are likely to be required for non-trivial service inventory architectures.

The following sections explore how common elements of a uniform contract (methods, media types, and exceptions in particular) can be customized to meet the needs of individual service inventories.

Designing and Standardizing Methods

When we discuss methods in relation to the uniform contract, it is considered shorthand for a request-response communications mechanism that also includes methods, headers, response codes, and exceptions. Methods are centralized as part of the uniform contract in order to ensure that there are always a small number of ways of moving information around within a particular service inventory, and that existing service consumers will work correctly with new or modified services as they are added to the inventory. Whereas it is important to minimize the number of methods in the uniform contract, methods can and should be added when service inventory interaction requirements demand it. This is a natural part of evolving a service inventory in response to business change.

HTTP provides a solid foundation by supplying the basic set of methods (such as GET, PUT, DELETE, POST) proven by use on the Web and widely supported by off-the-shelf software components and hardware devices. But the need may arise to express other types of interactions for a service inventory. For example, you may decide to add a special method that can be used to reliably trigger a resource to execute a task at most once, rather than using the less reliable HTTP POST method.

HTTP is designed to be extended in these ways. The HTTP specification explicitly supports the notion of extension methods, customized headers, and extensibility in other areas. Leveraging this feature of HTTP can be effective, as long as new extensions are added carefully and at a rate appropriate for the number of services that implement HTTP within an inventory. This way, the total number of options for moving data around (that services and consumers are required to understand) remains manageable.

> Less well-known HTTP methods have come and gone in the past. For example, at various times the HTTP specification has included a PATCH method consistent with a partial update or partial store communications mechanism. PATCH is currently specified separately from HTTP methods in the IETF's RFC 5789 document. Other IETF specifications, such as WebDAV's RFC 4918 and the Session Initiation Protocol's RFC 3261, introduced new methods as well as new headers and response codes (or special interpretations thereof).

NOTE

Later in this chapter we explore a set of sample, extended methods (referred to as *complex methods*), each of which utilizes multiple basic HTTP methods or utilizes a single basic HTTP method multiple times, to perform pre-defined, standardized interactions.

Common circumstances that can warrant the creation of new methods include:

- Hyperlinks may be used to facilitate a sequence of request-response pairs. When they start to read like verbs instead of nouns and tend to suggest that only a single method will be valid on the target of a hyperlink, we can consider introducing a new method instead. For example the "customer" hyperlink for an invoice resource suggests that GET and PUT requests might be equally valid for the customer resource. But a "begin transaction" hyperlink or a "subscribe" hyperlink suggest only POST is valid and may indicate the need for a new method instead.

- Data with must-understand semantics may be needed within message headers. In this case, a service that ignores this metadata can cause incorrect runtime behavior. HTTP does not include a facility for identifying individual headers or information within headers as "must-understand." A new method can be used to enforce this requirement because the custom method will be automatically rejected by a service that doesn't understand the request (whereas falling back on a default HTTP method will allow the service to ignore the new header information).

It is important to acknowledge that introducing custom methods can have negative impacts when exploring vendor diversity within an implementation environment. It may prevent off-the-shelf components (such as caches, load balancers, firewalls, and various HTTP-based software frameworks) from being fully functional within the service inventory. Stepping away from HTTP and its default methods should only be attempted in mature service inventories when the effects on the underlying technology architecture and infrastructure are fully understood.

Some alternatives to creating new methods can also be explored. For example, service interactions that require a number of steps can use hyperlinks to guide consumers through the requests they need to make. The HTTP Link header (RFC 5988) can be considered to keep these hyperlinks separate from the actual document content.

Designing and Standardizing HTTP Headers

Exchanging messages with metadata is common in service-oriented solution design. Because of the emphasis of composing a set of services together to collectively automate a given task at runtime, there is often a need for a message to provide a range of header information that pertains to how the message should be processed by intermediary service agents and services along its message path.

Built-in HTTP headers can be used in a number of ways:

• They can be used to add parameters related to a request method as an alternative to using query strings to represent the parameters within the URL. For example, the `Accept` header can supplement the GET method by providing content negotiation data.

• They can be used to add parameters related to a response code. For example the `Location` header can be used with the `201 Created` response code to indicate the identifier of a newly created resource.

• They can be used to communicate general information about the service or consumer. For example the `Upgrade` header can indicate that a service consumer supports and prefers a different protocol, while the `Referrer` header can indicate which resource the consumer came from while following a series of hyperlinks.

This type of general metadata may be used in conjunction with any HTTP method.

HTTP headers can also be utilized to add rich metadata. For this purpose custom headers are generally required, which re-introduces the need to determine whether or not the message content must be understood by recipients or whether it can optionally be ignored. This association of must-understand semantics with new methods and must-ignore semantics with new message headers is not an inherent feature of REST, but it is a feature of HTTP.

When introducing custom HTTP headers that can be ignored by services, regular HTTP methods can safely be used. This also makes the use of custom headers backwards-compatible when creating new versions of existing message types.

As previously stated in the *Designing and Standardizing Methods* section, new HTTP methods can be introduced to enforce must-understand content by requiring services to either be designed to support the custom method or to reject the method invocation attempt altogether. In support of this behavior, a new `Must-Understand` header can be created in the same format as the existing `Connection` header, which would list all of the headers that need to be understood by message recipients.

If this type of modification is made to HTTP, it would be the responsibility of the SOA Governance Program Office responsible for the service inventory to ensure that these semantics are implemented consistently as part of inventory-wide design standards. If custom, must-understand HTTP headers are successfully established within a service inventory, we can explore a range of applications of messaging metadata. For example, we can determine whether it is possible or feasible to emulate messaging metadata such as what is commonly used in SOAP messaging frameworks based on WS-* standards.

While custom headers that enforce reliability or routing content (as per the WS-ReliableMessaging and WS-Addressing standards) can be added to recreate acknowledgement and intelligent load balancing interactions, other forms of WS-* functions are subject to built-in limitations of the HTTP protocol. The most prominent example is the use of WS-Security to enable message-level security features, such as encryption and digital signatures. Message-level security protects messages by actually transforming the content so that intermediaries along a message path are unable to read or alter message content. Only those message recipients with prior authorization are able to access the content.

This type of message transformation is not supported in HTTP/1.1. HTTP does have some basic features for transforming the body of the message alone through its `Content-Encoding` header, but this is generally limited to compression of the message body and does not include the transformation of headers. If this feature was used for encryption purposes the meaning of the message could still be modified or inspected in transit, even though the body part of the message could be protected. Message signatures are also not possible in HTTP/1.1 as there is no canonical form for an HTTP message to sign, and no industry standard that determines what modifications intermediaries would be allowed to make to such a message.

Designing and Standardizing HTTP Response Codes

HTTP was originally designed as a synchronous, client-server protocol for the exchange of HTML pages over the World Wide Web. These characteristics are compatible with REST constraints and make it also suitable as a protocol used to invoke REST service capabilities.

Developing a service using HTTP is very similar to publishing dynamic content on a Web server. Each HTTP request invokes a REST service capability and that invocation concludes with the sending of a response message back to the service consumer.

A given response message can contain any one of a wide variety of HTTP codes, each of which has a designated number. Certain ranges of code numbers are associated with particular types of conditions, as follows:

- `100-199` are informational codes used as low level signaling mechanisms, such as a confirmation of a request to change protocols.

- 200-299 are general success codes used to describe various kinds of success conditions.

- 300-399 are redirection codes used to request that the consumer retry a request to a different resource identifier, or via a different intermediary.

- 400-499 represent consumer-side error codes that indicate that the consumer has produced a request that is invalid for some reason.

- 500-599 represent service-side error codes that indicate that the consumer's request may have been valid but that the service has been unable to process it for internal reasons.

The consumer-side and service-side exception categories are helpful for "assigning blame," but do little to actually enable service consumers to recover from failure. This is because, while the codes and reasons provided by HTTP are standardized, how service consumers are required to behave upon receiving response codes is not. When standardizing service design for a service inventory, it is necessary to establish a set of conventions that assign response codes concrete meaning and treatment.

Table 10.1 provides common descriptions of how service consumers can be designed to respond to common response codes.

Response Code	Reason Phrase	Treatment
100	Continue	Indeterminate
101	Switching Protocols	Indeterminate
1xx	Any other 1xx code	Failure
200	OK	Success
201	Created	Success
202	Accepted	Success
203	Non-Authoritative Information	Success
204	No Content	Success

Response Code	Reason Phrase	Treatment
205	Reset Content	Success
206	Partial Content	Success
2xx	Any other 2xx code	Success
300	Multiple Choices	Failure
301	Moved Permanently	Indeterminate (Common Behavior: Modify resource identifier and retry.)
302	Found	Indeterminate
303	See Other	(Common Behavior: Change request to a GET and retry using nominated resource identifier.)
304	Not Modified	Success (Common Behavior: Use cached response.)
305	Use Proxy	Indeterminate (Common Behavior: Connect to identified proxy and resend original message.)
307	Temporary Redirect	Indeterminate (Common Behavior: Retry once to nominated resource identifier.)
3xx	Any other 3xx code	Failure
400	Bad Request	Failure

continues

Response Code	Reason Phrase	Treatment
401	Unauthorized	Indeterminate (Common Behavior: Retry with correct credentials.)
402	Payment Required	Failure
403	Forbidden	Failure
404	Not Found	Success if request was DELETE, else Failure
405	Method Not Allowed	Failure
406	Not Acceptable	Failure
407	Proxy Authentication Required	Indeterminate (Common Behavior: Retry with correct credentials.)
408	Request Timeout	Failure
409	Conflict	Failure
410	Gone	Success if request was DELETE, else Failure
411	Length Required	Failure
412	Precondition Failed	Failure
413	Request Entity Too Large	Failure
414	Request-URI Too Long	Failure
415	Unsupported Media Type	Failure
416	Requested Range Not Satisfiable	Failure
417	Expectation Failed	Failure

Response Code	Reason Phrase	Treatment
4xx	Any other 4xx code	Failure
500	Internal Server Error	Failure
501	Not Implemented	Failure
502	Bad Gateway	Failure
503	Service Unavailable	Repeat if Retry-After header is specified. Otherwise, Failure.
504	Gateway Timeout	Repeat if request is idempotent. Otherwise, Failure.
505	HTTP Version Not Supported	Failure
5xx	Any other 5xx code	Failure

Table 10.1
HTTP response codes, and typical corresponding consumer behavior.

As is evident when reviewing Table 10.1, HTTP response codes go well beyond the simple distinction between success and failure. They provide an indication of how consumers can respond to and recover from exceptions.

Let's take a closer look at some of the values from the Treatment column in Table 10.1:

- *Repeat* means that the consumer is encouraged to repeat the request, taking into account any delay specified in responses such as `503 Service Unavailable`. This may mean sleeping before trying again. If the consumer chooses not to repeat the request, it must treat the method as failed.

- *Success* means the consumer should treat the message transmission as a successful action and must therefore not repeat it. (Note that specific success codes may require more subtle interpretation.)

- *Failed* means that the consumer must not repeat the request unchanged, although it may issue a new request that takes the response into account. The consumer should treat this as a failed method if a new request cannot be generated. (Note that specific failure codes may require more subtle interpretation.)

- *Indeterminate* means that the consumer needs to modify its request in the manner indicated. The request must not be repeated unchanged and a new request that takes the response into account should be generated. The final outcome of the interaction will depend on the new request. If the consumer is unable to generate a new request, then this code must be treated as failed.

Because HTTP is a protocol, not a set of message processing logic, it is up to the service to decide what status code (success, failure, or otherwise) to return. As previously mentioned, because consumer behavior is not always sufficiently standardized by HTTP for machine-to-machine interactions, it needs to be explicitly and meaningfully standardized as part of an SOA project.

For example, indeterminate codes tend to indicate that service consumers must handle a situation using their own custom logic. We can standardize these types of codes in two ways:

- Design standards can determine which indeterminate codes can and cannot be issued by service logic.

- Design standards can determine how service consumer logic must interpret those indeterminate codes that are allowed.

Customizing Response Codes

The HTTP specification allows for extensions to response codes. This extension feature is primarily there to allow future versions of HTTP to introduce new codes. It is also used by some other specifications (such as WebDAV) to define custom codes. This is typically done with numbers that are not likely to collide with new HTTP codes, which can be achieved by putting them near the end of the particular range (for example, 299 is unlikely to ever be used by the main HTTP standard).

Specific service inventories can follow this approach by introducing custom response codes as part of the service inventory design standards. In support of the Uniform Contract {400} constraint, custom response codes should only be defined at the uniform contract level, not at the REST service contract level.

When creating custom response codes, it is important that they be numbered based on the range they fall in. For example, 2xx codes should be communicating success, while 4xx codes should only represent failure conditions.

Additionally, it is good practice to standardize the insertion of human-readable content into the HTTP response message via the Reason Phrase. For example, the code 400 has a default reason phrase of "Bad Request." This is enough for a service consumer to handle the response as a general failure, but it doesn't tell a human anything useful about the actual problem. Setting the reason phrase to "The service consumer request is missing the Customer address field." or perhaps even "Request body failed validation against schema http://example.com/customer" is more helpful, especially when reviewing logs of exception conditions that may not have the full document attached.

Consumers can associate generic logic to handle response codes in each of these ranges, but may also need to associate specific logic to specific codes. Some codes can be limited so that they are only generated if the consumer requests a special feature of HTTP, which means that some codes can be left unimplemented by consumers that do not request these features.

Uniform contract exceptions are generally standardized within the context of a particular new type of interaction that is required between services and consumers. They will typically be introduced along with one or more new methods and/or headers. This context will guide the kind of exceptions that are created. For example, it may be necessary to introduce a new response code to indicate that a request cannot be fulfilled due to a lock on a resource. (WebDAV provides the `423 Locked` code for this purpose.)

When introducing and standardizing custom response codes for a service inventory uniform contract we need to ensure that:

- each custom code is appropriate and absolutely necessary

- the custom code is generic and highly reusable by services

- the extent to which service consumer behavior is regulated is not too restrictive so that the code can apply to a large range of potential situations

- code values are set to avoid potential collision with response codes from relevant external protocol specifications

- code values are set to avoid collision with custom codes from other service inventories (in support of potential cross-service inventory message exchanges that may be required)

Response code numeric ranges can be considered a form of exception inheritance. Any code within a particular range is expected to be handled by a default set of logic, just as if the range were the parent type for each exception within that range.

In this section, we have briefly explored response codes within the context of HTTP. However, it is worth noting that REST can be applied with other protocols (and other exception models). It is ultimately the base protocol of a service inventory architecture that will determine how normal and exceptional conditions are reported.

For example, you could consider having a REST-based service inventory standardized on the use of SOAP messages that result in SOAP-based exceptions instead of HTTP exception codes. This allows the response code ranges to be substituted for inheritance of exceptions.

Designing Media Types

During the lifetime of a service inventory architecture we can expect more changes will be required to the set of a uniform contract's media types than to its methods. For example, a new media type will be required whenever a service or consumer needs to communicate machine-readable information that does not match the format or schema requirements of any existing media type.

Some common media types from the Web to consider for service inventories and service contracts include:

- `text/plain; charset=utf-8` for simple representations, such as integer and string data. Primitive data can be encoded as strings, as per built-in XML Schema data types.

- `application/xhtml+xml` for more complex lists, tables, human-readable text, hypermedia links with explicit relationship types, and additional data based on microformats.org and other specifications.

- `text/uri-list` for plain lists of URIs.

- `application/atom+xml` for feeds of human-readable event information or other data collections that are time-related (or time ordered).

More standard media types can be found in the IANA media type registry, as explained in Appendix B. Before inventing new media types for use within a service inventory, it is advisable to first carry out a search of established industry media types that may be suitable.

Whether choosing existing media types or creating custom ones, it is helpful to consider the following best practices:

- Each specific media type should ideally be specific to a schema. For example, `application/xml` or `application/json` are not schema-specific, while `application/atom+xml` used as a syndication format is specific enough to be useful for content negotiation and to identify how to process documents.

- Media types should be abstract in that they specify only as much information as their recipients need to extract via their schemas. Keeping media types abstract allows them to be reused within more service contracts.

- New media types should reuse mature vocabularies and concepts from industry specifications whenever appropriate. This reduces the risk that key concepts have been missed or poorly constructed, and further improves compatibility with other applications of the same vocabularies.

- A media type should include a hyperlink whenever it needs to refer to a related resource whose representation is located outside the immediate document. Link relation types may be defined by the media type's schema or, in some cases, separately, as part of a link relation profile.

- Custom media types should be defined with must-ignore semantics or other extension points that allow new data to be added to future versions of the media type without old services and consumers rejecting the new version.

- Media types should be defined with standard processing instructions that describe how a new processor should handle old documents that may be missing some information. Usually these processing instructions ensure that earlier versions of a document have compatible semantics. This way, new services and consumers do not have to reject the old versions.

All media types that are either invented for a particular service inventory or reused from another source should be documented in the uniform contract profile, alongside the definition of uniform methods.

HTTP uses Internet media type identifiers that conform to a specific syntax. Custom media types are usually identified with the notation:

`application/vnd.organization.type+supertype`

...where `application` is a common prefix that indicates that the type is used for machine consumption and standards. The `organization` field identifies the vendor namespace, which can optionally be registered with IANA.

The `type` part is a unique name for the media type within the organization, while the `supertype` indicates that this type is a refinement of another media type. For example, `application/vnd.com.examplebooks.purchase-order+xml` may indicate that:

- the type is meant for machine consumption

- the type is vendor-specific, and the organization that has defined the type is "examplebooks.com"

- the type is for purchase orders (and may be associated with a canonical Purchase Order XML schema)

- the type is derived from XML, meaning that recipients can unambiguously handle the content with XML parsers

Types meant for more general inter-organizational use can be defined with the media type namespace of the organization ultimately responsible for defining the type. Alternatively, they can be defined without the vendor identification information in place by registering each type directly, following the process defined in the RFC 4288 specification.

Designing Schemas for Media Types

Within a service inventory, most custom media types created to represent business data and documents will be defined together with XML schemas. This essentially applies the Canonical Schema [437] pattern in that it establishes a set of standardized data models that are reused by REST services within the inventory to whatever extent feasible.

For this to be successful, especially with larger collections of services, schemas need to be designed to be flexible. This means that it is generally preferable for schemas to enforce a coarse level of validation constraint granularity that allows each schema to be applicable for use with a broader range of data interaction requirements.

REST requires media types and their schemas to be defined only at the uniform contract level. If a service capability requires a unique data structure for a response message, it must still use one of the canonical media types provided by the uniform contract. Designing schemas to be flexible and weakly typed can accommodate a variety of service-specific message exchange requirements.

> **NOTE**
>
> To explore techniques for weakly typing XML Schema definitions, see
> Chapters 6, 12, and 13 in the book *Web Service Contract Design & Ver-
> sioning for SOA*, as well as the description for the Validation Abstraction
> [518] pattern.

```xsd
<xsd:schema xmlns:xsd="http://www.w3.org/2001/XMLSchema"
  targetNamespace="http://example.com/schema/po"
  xmlns="http://example.com/schema/po">
  <xsd:element name="LineItemList" type="LineItemListType"/>
  <xsd:complexType name="LineItemListType">
    <xsd:element name="LineItem" type="LineItemType"
      minOccurs="0"/>
  </xsd:complexType>
  <xsd:complexType name="LineItemType">
    <xsd:sequence>
      <xsd:element name="productID" type="xsd:anyURI"/>
      <xsd:element name="productName" type="xsd:string"/>
      <xsd:element name="available" type="xsd:boolean"
        minOccurs="0"/>
    </xsd:sequence>
  </xsd:complexType>
</xsd:schema>
```

Example 10.1

One of the most straightforward ways of making a media type more reusable is to
design the schema to support a list of zero or more items. This enables the media type
to permit one instance of the underlying type, but also allows queries that return zero
or more instances. Making individual elements within the document optional can also
increase reuse potential.

Service-Specific XML Schemas

It is technically possible for individual REST service contracts to introduce contract-
specific XML schemas, but in doing so we need to accept that the Uniform Contract
{400} constraint will be violated.

This may be warranted when a service capability needs to generate a response message containing unique data (or a unique combination of data) for which:

- no suitable canonical schemas exist

- no new canonical schema should be created due to the fact that it would not be reusable by other services.

A consequence of non-compliance to Uniform Contract {400} is potentially increased levels of negative coupling between service consumers and the service offering service capabilities based on service-specific media types. Service-specific media types should be clearly identified and effort should be made to minimize the quantity of logic that is directly exposed to and made dependent upon these types.

SUMMARY OF KEY POINTS

- We can design and standardize custom HTTP methods and response codes. We can also standardize how built-in HTTP methods and response codes are used (or whether they are used).

- There are numerous existing media types we can choose to use (and reuse) within a service inventory, many of which are registered with the IANA (and other industry bodies). We can also design and standardize custom media types to represent common types of data and documents that are exchanged within the service inventory.

- Schemas encompassed by media types are naturally standardized when made part of a uniform contract. For schemas to be reusable, they generally need to be designed with flexibility in mind, ensuring reduced levels of validation constraint granularity.

10.2 REST Service Contract Design

This next section explores design techniques and considerations specific to individual REST service contracts and how they relate to their overarching uniform contract.

Designing Services Based on Service Models

In Chapters 4 and 9 we described the three common service models used to establish base functional contexts that categorize and group services within a service inventory into three common logical layers. The choice of service model for a given REST service can affect our approach to service contract design. The following sections briefly raise some key considerations and provide one sample REST service contract design for each service model.

Task Services

Task services will typically have few service capabilities, sometimes limited to only a single one (Figure 10.1). This is due to the fact that a task service contract's primary use is for the execution of automated business process (or task) logic. The service capability can be based on a simple verb, such as Start or Process. That verb, together with the name of the task service (that will indicate the nature of the task) is often all that is required for synchronous tasks.

Figure 10.1

A sample task service, recognizable by the verb in its name. The contract only provides a single service capability that will be used by the composition initiator to trigger the execution of the Validate Timesheet business process that the task service logic encapsulates. In this case, the service capability receives a timesheet resource identifier that will be used as the basis of the validation logic, plus a unique consumer-generated request identifier that supports reliable triggering of the process. (Note that the composition initiator is explained in Chapter 11.)

Additional service capabilities can be added to support asynchronous interactions as shown in Figure 10.2. For example, tasks that involve human interaction or batch processing will retain the state of the on-going business process between requests and will typically allow access to this state by exposing service capabilities for this purpose.

Figure 10.2

Two additional service capabilities are added to allow consumers to asynchronously check on the progress of the timesheet validation task, and to cancel the task while it is in progress.

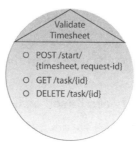

Validate Timesheet

○ POST /start/
  {timesheet, request-id}
○ GET /task/{id}
○ DELETE /task/{id}

REST-based task services will often have service capabilities triggered by a POST request. However, this method is not inherently reliable. A number of techniques exist to achieve a reliable POST, including the inclusion of additional headers and handling of response messages, or the inclusion of a unique consumer-generated request identifier in the resource identifier.

To provide input to a parameterized task service it will make sense for the task service contract to include various identifiers into the capability's resource identifier template (that might have been parameters in a SOAP message). This frees up the service to expose additional resources rather than defining a custom media type as input to its processing.

If the task service automates a long-running business process it will return an interim response to its consumer while further processing steps may still need to take place. If the task service includes additional capabilities to check on or interact with the state of the business process (or composition instance), it will typically include a hyperlink to one or more resources related to this state in the initial response message.

Entity Services

Each entity service establishes a functional boundary associated with one or more related business entities (such as invoice, claim, customer, etc.). Entity services are the prime means by which Logic Centralization [475] is applied to business logic within a service inventory. The types of service capabilities exposed by a typical entity service are focused on functions that process the underlying data associated with the entity (or entities). Figure 10.3 provides some examples.

Entity service contracts are typically dominated by service capabilities that include inherently idempotent and reliable GET, PUT, or DELETE methods. However, more complex methods may be needed. Many entity services will need to support updating

Figure 10.3

An entity service based on the invoice business entity that defines a functional scope that limits the service capabilities to performing invoice-related processing only. This agnostic Invoice service will be reused and composed by any automated business process that needs to work with or process invoice records. For example, the Invoice service may be invoked by the Validate Timesheet task service to retrieve invoice data linked to client information collected from a timesheet record. The Validate Timesheet service may then use this data to verify that what the client was billed matches what the employee logged in the timesheet.

their state consistently with changes to other entity services. Entity services will also often include query capabilities for finding entities or parts of entities that match certain criteria, and therefore return hyperlinks to related and relevant entities.

Utility Services

Utility services are, like entity services, expected to be agnostic and reusable. However, unlike entity services, they do not usually have pre-defined functional scopes. While individual utility services group related service capabilities, the services' functional boundaries can vary dramatically. The example illustrated in Figure 10.4 is a utility service acting as a wrapper for a legacy system (as per the Legacy Wrapper [473] pattern).

NOTE

To learn more about service models and service layers, see the Process Abstraction [486], Entity Abstraction [463], and Utility Abstraction [517] patterns.

Figure 10.4

This utility service is based on the application of the Legacy Wrapper [473] pattern in that it provides a service contract that encapsulates a legacy HR system (and is accordingly named the HR System service). The service capabilities it exposes provide generic, read-only data access functions against the data stored in the underlying legacy repository. For example, the Employee entity service (composed by the Verify Timesheet task service) may invoke an employee data-related service capability to retrieve data. This type of utility service may provide access to one of several available sources of employee and HR-related data.

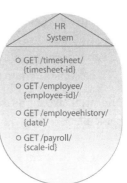

Designing and Standardizing Resource Identifiers

The fundamental requirement of an effective REST service contract design is its ability to express the identity of resources that consumers can interact with as part of their service capability invocations.

At a technical level the structure of a resource identifier is often irrelevant to a service consumer. Any service consumer that follows a simple hyperlink only cares that the destination of the hyperlink is the correct resource. It doesn't try to interpret the meaning of the resource identifier itself, past the information required to actually make the connection to the responsible service.

With that said there are a number of reasons we proceed past the point of standardizing the syntax of resource identifiers to the point of standardizing structure and vocabulary within resource identifiers:

1. The more descriptive and consistent the structure of resource identifiers is for similar service capabilities, the easier it is for humans to interpret and understand services and their capabilities. This directly supports the application of Service Discoverability (420).

2. Some resource identifier structures lend themselves better to the future needs of their service contract than others. They do so by providing obvious places where additional resources and related capabilities can be inserted in the resource identifier namespace.

3. Designing flexible resource identifiers can reduce negative coupling, while increasing backwards compatibility and, potentially, forwards compatibility (as explained in Chapter 15).

4. In some cases, service consumers need to insert information into resource identifiers, either by adding data values into the query component of a URL using a standard syntax, or by following a URL template to insert data throughout the URL. If the vocabulary is not reusable between multiple services then these variable portions of URLs become a back door for negative forms of coupling between the consumers to the service contract.

The latter two items directly support the application of the Service Loose Coupling (413) principle.

Service Names in Resource Identifiers

The first area of standardization we'll explore is the use of service names within resource identifier statements. This brings us back to the study of URI syntax, which we began in the *URIs (and URLs and URNs)* section in Chapter 6. Briefly revisit this section to re-familiarize yourself with the examples.

In the last example provided in this section:

```
invoices.example.com
```

… identifies the service within the URL:

```
http://invoices.example.com/
```

Another service:

```
customers.example.com
```

… may initially share the same IP address as:

```
invoices.example.com
```

… as a result of being deployed in a shared hosting environment.

When `customers.example.com` is moved to its own separate physical hardware, the IP addresses can be easily updated via the Domain Name System (DNS) without modifying the logical name of the service. Consumers that refer to `customers.example.com` will automatically begin communicating with the new IP address, and therefore will place no further burden on the old hosting environment.

If, instead, the service names were part of the *path* of the URL, the authority would have to refer to the hosting environment itself.

A URL for the Invoice service that starts with:

```
http://services.example.com/invoice
```

… would always resolve to the IP address of:

```
services.example.com
```

… rather than a specific IP address for the service.

If the Customer service were then moved to a new hosting environment, all of the hyperlinks held by service consumers would have to change or the requests sent to the service would still have to continue passing through the `services.example.com` host.

When combining REST with service-orientation, the authority needs to be synonymous with the service name in order to maximize the application potential of the Service Autonomy (SDP) principle. The authority is always what is looked up by the service consumer so that it can make the necessary TCP/IP connections. It is also used to identify proxies between the service and its consumers. Sometimes, multiple services will be hosted within the same virtual server or cluster, and these service names will resolve to the same IP address. But, by ensuring that each service has a unique authority, the service can be easily shifted to other IP addresses as service deployment arrangements change.

Other URI Components

The path and query components of the URI provide context for service capabilities within a given service. This context is combined with the service identifier in the authority and with the method of each request to determine which service capability a given consumer seeks to invoke.

The `{fragment}` component of the URI reference is never sent to the service, and is only used as a placeholder to store instructions for the service consumer to know how to process the response when it arrives. If a service consumer needs to use the aforementioned URI reference to invoke a GET request, it would send the part of the URI reference up to and including the query. The `{fragment}` component would be intentionally omitted. For example, a `page2` fragment may indicate to the service consumer that it should start processing at page 2 in the returned document. Where exactly to find such a point in the document depends on the media type of the document.

If some of the components of a URI are missing, the URI reference may become a relative URI. In that case, the context of the URI is used to determine what exactly it is pointing to.

For example, a relative URI of:

```
/invoices/INV042
```

... would be expanded as:

```
http://invoice.example.com/invoices/INV042
```

Relative URIs are often a useful way to refer to related resources without referring to additional context, such as the name of the service. The base URI to resolve a relative URI against can come from XML directives, HTTP headers, the location that a document was retrieved from, or from a range of other sources, depending on the conventions associated with the media type in use.

Resource Identifier Overlap

Resources can be any specific utility, entity, task, queue, report, statistic, or in fact anything related to the service that can be referred to in a context. The identifier for a resource can contain as much or as little context as is needed to specify the concept the resource embodies. A resource could be "today's weather in Vancouver, Canada." A separate resource could capture "yesterday's weather in Vancouver, Canada" while yet another family of resources could capture the weather in Vancouver for specific historical dates. The concepts that resources embody will sometimes overlap, so that some or all of the same data is retrieved via different resource identifiers. Other resources will encapsulate concepts that are distinct in their own right and do not overlap.

We can imagine that a URI such as:

```
http://weather/canada/vancouver/date/today
```

… will return the same value when retrieved as the URI:

```
http://weather/canada/vancouver/date/{date}
```

… with a date set to today's date. However, these are different resources and perhaps even different service capabilities. When the date switches over to the next day, the `today` resource will point to the new day's weather. The resource based on the old `{date}` will still refer to the historical weather at that particular date.

Similarly, an invoice might appear as its own URI but may also have its data summarized as part of an invoice list or report resource. The invoice URI may further have subordinate resources, such as a special resource indicating its paid status. In all of these cases, the URIs are different, but the data and the service logic that implement requests to each one overlap.

The context of the resource as identified in its URI may be dynamic or session-specific. For example, the following URI:

```
http://mybank/accounts/myaccount?after=XACT102
```

... may refer to the transactions in a bank account that occurred after transaction number 102. This may have been returned from the service to a particular consumer as a placeholder between transactions the consumer has reconciled and those that have not yet been reconciled. This kind of resource captures session information and acts as a container for session state, allowing the service to avoid having to retain these details.

Queries can also be encapsulated in resource identifiers. Query terms, such as a required temperature range or the maximum temperature value past a particular date, can be included in a resource identifier. When the first request is sent to this identifier the resource automatically springs into existence, performs its processing, and returns a result. The consumer and any middleware are not aware of whether a resource is static or dynamic. The interface to the resource does not change, and features such as caching, work just as well with static and dynamic resources. The implementation of each resource is hidden from consumers.

In Chapter 6 we covered the use of forms and resource identifier templates to allow service consumers to input parameters into resource identifiers without introducing service-specific coupling. If URIs are being constructed by human users, forms can be provided for them to fill out as part of producing the URI. This does not introduce tight coupling between the service and service consumer, as the consumer does not need to understand the data that passes through it. Only the human user needs to determine what data to place in which form fields. However, a service consumer that is not being driven by a human user will need to know which specific variables to insert into a given resource identifier. If automated service consumers are supplying parameters directly as part of URIs, it is advisable to clearly differentiate between elements of the URI that consumers are considered likely to have, in order to populate themselves and to identify these fields in a way that is documented in the uniform contract profile for the service inventory.

For example, the aforementioned bank account URI:

```
http://mybank/accounts/myaccount?after=XACT102
```

... suggests to readers of the service contract that it is likely to be the service consumer that fills out the `after` field within the URI. In order for an automated service consumer to avoid tight coupling with the service contract, the `after` field should become part of the uniform contract. When `after` is used, it should have the same meaning, regardless of which service the consumer is talking to.

NOTE
Resource identifiers contain data for their corresponding services to inter- pret. In order to invoke the correct service capability, the business context of a request must be specified by the consumer and understood by the service. As explained in previous chapters, resource identifiers can be discovered by a service consumer through hyperlinking, or by direct entry of resource identifiers into configuration data. In these cases the resource identifier can usually be treated as opaque by the service consumer. The consumer does not attempt to parse information out of the identifier, nor does it need to insert additional information. Resource identifier templates allow consumers to insert data into resource identifiers in predefined ways, while treating the overall structure of the resource identifiers as being opaque.
Resource identifiers that are handled in this manner by the service con- sumer act as a message from the service that is held onto by the con- sumer and passed back to the service with subsequent requests. These messages can contain identifiers for entities, session state data, or any other data the service will need the next time a request comes in for pro- cessing. Treating resource identifiers as opaque within service consumers means that we can reduce (or loosen) the coupling between a service and its consumers. The service can change the content or structure of its resource identifiers without needing corresponding changes to service consumer logic.

Resource Identifier Design Guidelines

Here are a few tips for optimizing resource identifiers in support of SOA. Each of these can form the basis of a design standard in support of the Canonical Expression [434] pattern:

- Try to avoid including a variable part of the URL as the first path segment, or any- where not preceded by a static path segment describing the context. For example, avoid `http://invoice.example.com/{invoice}`. Although we may use this type of notation for simplicity's sake early in the service capability modeling lifecycle, once we enter the service-oriented design stage it can make it difficult to extend the namespace. This is because any new path could be interpreted as including an invoice identifier. Consider introducing a prefix to qualify the variable part, for example using `http://invoice.example.com/invoice/{invoice}`, instead.

- Trailing slashes usually indicate a collection of resources. One common convention is that a GET request to a URL with a trailing slash will retrieve a list of these resources, while a POST to the URL will create a new resource. For example, `http://invoice.example.com/unpaid/` may support a GET request to obtain all unpaid invoices, while a POST to `http://invoice.example.com/invoice/` may create an invoice with a resource identifier of `http://invoice.example.com/invoice/INV042`. This again is a departure from the notation used during the service-oriented analysis project stage, where we use the trailing slash, together with the initial slash, as delimiters to represent a resource.

- Single out those resource identifiers that are canonical names (URNs), and make these URLs as simple as possible. Avoid including a query component in the resource identifier and avoid special characters such as ';', '=', and '&'. For example, `http://invoice.example.com/?invoice=INV042` is not a good identifier for invoice number 42, while `http://invoice.example.com/invoice/INV042` is a better choice. Simpler identifiers are easier to embed into other resource identifiers, and easier for a human to read and understand; a prime requirement of the Service Discoverability (420) principle.

- Always refer to canonical names (URNs) by their full resource identifier. For example, the `http://invoice.example.com/query{?customer}` URL should be expanded to `http://invoice.example.com/query?customer=http://customer.example.com/customer/C1234`. This allows the Invoice service to directly interact with the customer resource for additional information (if required), without needing to construct its own resource identifier for the customer.

- Explicitly separate query parameters expected to be inserted by human users or service consumers into resource identifiers in the query component of the URL. For example, `http://invoice.example.com/search{?paid,due-date, min-amount,max-amount,customer}` can be interpreted as indicating that `paid`, `due-date`, `min-amount`, `max-amount`, and `customer` are all likely to be inserted into the resource identifier via human input or by a service consumer. The vocabulary used in the query component of the resource identifier is likely to come under increased governance scrutiny compared to other components of the resource.

- Variables that a service consumer needs to insert into URL templates can produce undesirable forms of coupling to be introduced between the consumer and the service contract. This is in direct opposition to the design goals of the Service Loose Coupling (413) principle. Each variable to be inserted needs to have an agreed upon meaning among a service and its consumers. The simplest way to tackle this is to standardize the names, syntax, data types, and meaning of variables across multiple services as part of the uniform contract definition. It is straightforward to consider standardizing variable names such as `dtstart` and `dtend` to identify the start and end dates and times of a given query. For example, this type of vocabulary can be reused to query an invoice service as `http://invoice.example.com/query?dtstart=2015-03-06T10:00:00&dtend=2015-04-06T10:00:00`, a calendar of events, or a correspondence log for particular time periods.

> **NOTE**
>
> Business entities are prime targets for inclusion in a controlled resource identifier vocabulary. We have already seen examples in this chapter where a consumer queries the Invoice entity service for a list of invoices related to a particular customer. In this case, the expansion of this parameter would be the full resource identifier for that entity. As new service capabilities are defined, new vocabulary will be discovered. It will be important to keep the vocabulary up-to-date and to be able to identify which elements of the vocabulary are genuinely reused in practice across different service contracts, versus those that are service-specific.

Designing with and Standardizing REST Constraints

Although the set of REST constraints are, individually, separate and distinct design rules with corresponding design goals, there is room for interpretation concerning whether each constraint should be strictly applied. Due to the importance of standardizing how services are built as part of a service inventory, it is recommended that how REST constraints themselves are applied also be clearly standardized.

Stateless {395}

The two basic interpretations of rules established by the Stateless {395} constraint are:

- The looser interpretation is that session state is any data that a request message might refer to that does not have an explicit resource identifier. Under this definition, session state can be given a resource identifier within the service to transform it into service state. It can then be deferred by the service into a database or other dedicated repository. Further requests (by the same consumer or by other consumers) refer to the state by its resource identifier and so they can be understood independently of previous requests.

- A stricter interpretation is that session state is any data bound to a specific service consumer that would normally need to be destroyed when that consumer exits an on-going service activity, or when that consumer stops interacting with the service. Under this interpretation, associating a resource identifier with the data does not transform it into service state and it must still not be retained by the service between requests.

The usage of the Stateless {395} constraint requires a clear design standard, both in regards to the interpretation of the constraint as well as the extent to which it is applied to the service inventory.

Additionally, if any exceptions to or violations of Stateless {395} are allowed, these need to be well-defined so that there is an opportunity to adjust the service inventory's underlying infrastructure accordingly.

Cache {398}

As explained in Chapter 5, this constraint requires that any request whose response could potentially be reused for subsequent requests needs to incorporate the facility to include cache control metadata. This constraint mostly applies to data retrieval methods, such as GET and HEAD. However, it can also apply to some uses of POST and other forms of requests that can be classified as primarily retrieving data from a service.

Two basic forms of caching exist:

- A response message is considered reusable for a particular period of time. For example, a message containing report data can state that its content will remain valid for 24 hours. This allows the caching infrastructure to continue returning the same response without having to re-invoke the service for the duration of that period. The HTTP header used for this kind of caching is `Cache-Control` with a `maxage` field.

- A response message is considered reusable only if its validity is checked each time it is used. For example, a log of recent transactions may be reused until a new transaction is added. In this case, each time a cache handles a request it explicitly checks with the service to ensure that no further transactions have occurred before returning the cached response. The HTTP headers used for this kind of caching are `ETag` in responses and `If-None-Match` in requests.

In order to decide whether to even attempt to reuse a cached response the cache needs a mechanism for determining whether two requests are equivalent for caching purposes. Requests are often equivalent if their method and resource identifier are the same;

however, request headers can play a role in whether requests are equivalent or not. In support of this, it can be helpful to introduce a design standard regarding the usage of the HTTP `Vary` header that can be applied to identify which request headers were used as part of generating a response and, by a process of elimination, which headers were ignored. This feature allows requests that are slightly different to still reuse the same cached response.

In addition to a response being able to identify which request headers were used in generating the response, it is helpful to have a further design standard that establishes a canonical form for request messages so that they can be compared for equivalence. HTTP has a basic canonicalization mechanism that can be used to remove redundant whitespace and to merge duplicate headers.

Uniform Contract {400}

HTTP requires that methods and media types be "standard." In the context of REST this does not simply mean standardization, but instead refers to "reuse in practice" by multiple services. Methods, media types, headers, exception types, resource identifier syntax, and any other element of messages (other than the specific resource identifiers chosen as part of service contracts to expose service capabilities) are all required to be reused by multiple services in order to comply with Uniform Contract {400}. In some cases (as described earlier), even parts of the resource identifiers may be standardized as well.

Although the mere usage of a uniform contract introduces a natural level of service inventory standardization, there are aspects that need further attention and custom standardization.

Design standards need to be in place to address the following:

- New methods and media types added to the uniform contract need to be clearly identified and closely monitored as they progress toward a mature state. If actual reuse by multiple service contracts does not happen, it may be necessary to start treating these new extensions as being service-specific.

- Any methods or media types that are intended to be service-specific need to be governed as such to ensure that the quantity of logic that is directly exposed to these extensions is minimized in favor of coupling logic to more reusable methods and media types.

- Some service contracts may also not lend themselves to compliance with the inventory's overarching uniform contract. It can therefore be useful to have a design standard that determines under what circumstances exceptions may be permitted.

With regards to the last item on the preceding list, there should be strong governance in place to ensure that before allowing service-specific methods and media types, uniform methods and media types are always carefully and thoroughly considered first.

Layered System {404}

Layered System {404} requires that consumers and services not be able to tell whether they are communicating with each other directly, or via a series of intermediaries that understand the uniform contract. To comply with this constraint, new methods need to be analyzed to ensure intermediaries are able to pass requests and responses on towards their intended recipients, and to adequately hide the existence of intermediaries when they are present.

One key requirement of Layered System {404} is that enough information be present in each message for it to reach its intended recipient. This means we cannot, upon making a connection to the service, strip out the data that allowed that connection. For example, it is not valid to remove the service name embedded within a resource identifier after making a connection to the service. If the connection turned out to really only be to an intermediary then the intermediary would not be able to determine which service should receive the message. Instead, all requests should include their full resource identifier.

Another requirement is that consumers should not need to speak a different protocol, use different methods, or use different headers to communicate with an intermediary as compared to communicating with an actual service. If removing the intermediary stops the communication from working, the architecture is in breach of Layered System {404}.

SUMMARY OF KEY POINTS

- Defining the reuse of uniform contract methods and media types is a service inventory responsibility, as is enforcing the compliance of these uniform contract elements to REST constraints as part of design standards.

- Services based on different service models will tend to introduce different service contract design considerations and characteristics.

- The use of resource identifiers can be standardized for a given service inventory at both the syntax and vocabulary levels.

CASE STUDY EXAMPLE

By following proven REST service contract design techniques, together with custom design standards established specifically for the MUA enterprise, MUA architects use the service candidates modeled in Chapter 9 as input for a service-oriented design process.

The results of this effort are documented in the following sections.

Confer Student Award Service Contract (Task)

A student who submits an award conferral application will do so through a Web browser. A separate user interface is therefore designed to allow users to enter the application details. It is the submission of this browser-based form that initiates the task service.

Upon receiving the submission, a server-side script organizes the form data into an XML document based on the following media type:

```
application/vnd.edu.mua.student-award-conferral-application+xhtml+xml
```

Example 10.2 provides a submitted application form completed with sample data collected from the human user. This represents the data set that kick-starts and drives the execution of an entire instance of the Confer Student Award business process.

```
<?xml version="1.0" encoding="UTF-8"?>
<!DOCTYPE html PUBLIC "-//W3C//DTD XHTML 1.1//EN"
  "http://www.w3.org/TR/xhtml11/DTD/xhtml11.dtd">
<html xmlns="http://www.w3.org/1999/xhtml" xml:lang="en" >
  <head>
    <title>Student Award Conferral Application</title>
  </head>
  <body>
    <p>Student:
      <a rel="student"
        href="http://student.mua.edu/student/555333">
        John Smith (Student Number 555333)
      </a>
    </p>
    <p>Award:
      <a rel="award"
        href="http://award.mua.edu/award/BS/CompSci">
        Bachelor of Science with Computer Science Major
```

```
    </a>
  </p>
  <p>Event:
    <a rel="event"
      href="http://event.mua.edu/fall-graduation">
      fall graduation event
    </a>
  </p>
  </body>
</html>
```

Example 10.2
Sample application data, as submitted to the Web server. This document structure contains both human-readable and machine-processable information.

Figure 10.5 displays the Confer Student Award service contract. The preceding media type is deliberately designed to include human-readable and machine-readable data in a form suitable for long-term archival. The document is submitted to a service capability corresponding directly to the Start capability defined in the Confer Student Award service candidate (Figure 9.13).

As also shown in Figure 10.5, during the design process for this service contract it was decided to add new service capabilities to provide the following functions:

Figure 10.5
The Confer Student Award service contract.

- `DELETE /task/{id}` – This capability was added to allow an executing instance of the Confer Student Award business process to be terminated.

- `GET /task/{id}` – This capability allows the state of an executing instance of the Confer Student Award business process to be queried.

Note that the sensitive nature of this kind of application means that the `GET /task/{id}` capability can be accessed only by authorized staff and by the student. The `DELETE /task/{id}` capability is only accessible by the student to cancel the application process.

Event Service Contract (Entity)

The Event entity service is equipped with a `GET /event/{id}` service capability used to query event information and which corresponds to the Get Details capability candidate from the Event service candidate (Figure 9.14).

During the service-oriented design process, architects decided to add further `GET /event/{id}/calendar` and `GET /event/{id}/description` capabilities (Figure 10.6) that allow for the retrieval of more specific event information. These capabilities were not added specifically in support of the Confer Student Award business process, but more so to provide a broader range of anticipated reusable functionality.

Figure 10.6
The Event service contract.

Award Service Contract (Entity)

In addition to implementing the three service capabilities from the original Award service candidate (Figure 9.15), SOA architects within MUA decide to make some further changes.

Back in Step 4 of the REST service modeling process (Chapter 9) MUA analysts determined that the following action was to be encompassed by the Confer Student Award task service logic:

• Verify Student Transcript Qualifies for Award Based on Award Conferral Rules

However, with the rules being specific to each award type they determine that it should be the Award entity service that applies the bulk of these rules. Nevertheless, some generic checks do need to be applied so the logic is divided between the Confer Student Award task service and the Award entity service.

To avoid the task service from needing to pass full transcript details into the Award entity service for verification, it is decided to use a code-on-demand approach. The Award entity service provides the logic, but the logic is executed by the task service. The decision to define the logic centrally within the Award entity service is justified based on the need to produce human-readable output (for students), alongside machine-readable output (for the Confer Student Award service). As a result, the entity service provides a new GET /award/{id}/ conferral-rules service capability (Figure 10.7) that supports the output of two formats for the rules logic: the first in human-readable form and the second in a form that can be readily embedded into the task service's logic.

MUA architects choose JavaScript for this purpose because they find that JavaScript runtimes are readily available for many of the technology platforms that have been used to develop services within the inventory. Choosing JavaScript over other technologies also accounts for it being the language of choice for the user-interface tier of the service inventory.

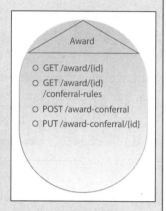

Figure 10.7
The Award service contract.

The same service capability is able to return the conferral rules in JavaScript or as human-readable HTML. The decision as to which transformation to carry out depends on which Accept header was provided by the service consumer. For example, the Confer Student Award task service requests the application/javascript media type, while service consumers requiring human-readable output will request the text/html media type.

Student Transcript Service Contract (Entity)

The Student service was originally intended as a centralized entity service that would encompass all student-related functionality and data access. However, iterations of the REST service modeling process that occurred subsequent to the examples covered in Chapter 9 resulted in a service inventory blueprint that revealed the Student service candidate as being far more coarse grained than any other. This was primarily due to the complexity of the Student entity and its relationships to other related entities.

Upon review of the Student service candidate it was determined to create a set of student-related entity services. One of these more specialized variations became the Student Transcript service candidate (Figure 10.8).

Because the Confer Student Award business process only requires access to student transcript information, it only needs to compose the Student Transcript service, not the actual Student service. As shown in Figure 10.9, the Student Transcript service contains service capabilities that correspond to the service capability candidates provided by the Student Transcript service candidate.

Figure 10.8

The Student Transcript service candidate that was defined subsequent to the Student service candidate from Chapter 9. This service effectively replaces the Student service in the Confer Student Award service composition.

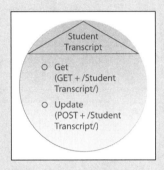

Figure 10.9

The Student Transcript service contract.

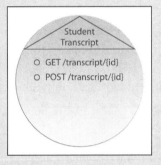

Notification and Document Service Contracts (Utility)

The Notification service and Document service process similar human-readable data. Notifications sent via e-mail or hard copy can both be encoded as a human-readable document format, such as HTML or PDF.

The Notification service is retained for e-mail notifications while the Document service has been evolved into a printer-centric and postal-delivery-centric utility service. The Confer Student Award task service can send a document to the student in the preferred format by looking up the preferred delivery method in the original application form.

As shown in Figure 10.10, the Notification and Document services can each be invoked with the POST method.

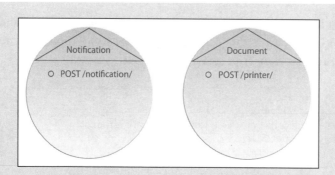

Figure 10.10
The Notification and Document service contracts.

The sample student (John Smith) from the application form used as input for the Confer Student Award task service has nominated his contact preference with a hyperlink to `mailto:s555333@student.mua.edu`. The service inventory standard for handling such an address is to transform the URL into `http://notification.mua.edu/sender?to=s555333@student.mua.edu` and use a POST method for its delivery. John Smith's notification will be delivered via e-mail to this address.

10.3 Complex Method Design

The uniform contract establishes a set of base methods used to perform basic data communication functions. As we've explained, this high-level of functional abstraction is what makes the uniform contract reusable to the extent that we can position it as the sole, over-arching data exchange mechanism for an entire inventory of services. Besides its inherent simplicity, this part of a service inventory architecture automatically results in the baseline standardization of service contract elements and message exchange.

The standardization of HTTP on the World Wide Web results in a protocol specification that describes the things that services and consumers "may," "should," or "must" do to be compliant with the protocol. The resulting level of standardization is intentionally only as high as it needs to be to ensure the basic functioning of the Web. It leaves a number of decisions as to how to respond to different conditions up to the logic within individual services and consumers. This "primitive" level of standardization is important to the Web where we can have numerous foreign service consumers interacting with third-party services at any given time.

A service inventory, however, often represents an environment that is private and controlled within an IT enterprise. This gives us the opportunity to customize this standardization beyond the use of common and primitive methods. This form of customization can be justified when we have requirements for increasing the levels of predictability and quality-of-service beyond what the World Wide Web can provide.

For example, let's say that we would like to introduce a design standard whereby all accounting-related documents (invoices, purchase orders, credit notes, etc.) must be retrieved with logic that, upon encountering a retrieval failure, automatically retries the retrieval a number of times. The logic would further require that subsequent retrieval attempts do not alter the state of the resource representing the business documents (regardless of whether a given attempt is successful).

With this type of design standard, we are essentially introducing a set of rules and requirements as to how the retrieval of a specific type of document needs to be carried out. These are rules and requirements that cannot be expressed or enforced via the base, primitive methods provided by HTTP. Instead, we can apply them in addition to the level of standardization enforced by HTTP by assembling them (together with other possible types of runtime functions) into aggregate interactions. This is the basis of the *complex method*.

A complex method encapsulates a pre-defined set of interactions between a service and a service consumer. These interactions can include the invocation of standard HTTP methods. To better distinguish these base methods from the complex methods that encapsulate them, we'll refer to base HTTP methods as *primitive methods* (a term only used when discussing complex method design.)

Complex methods are qualified as "complex" because they:

- can involve the composition of multiple primitive methods

- can involve the composition of a primitive method multiple times

- can introduce additional functionality beyond method invocation

- can require optional headers or properties to be supported by or included in messages

As previously stated, complex methods are generally customized for and standardized within a given service inventory. For a complex method to be standardized, it needs to be documented as part of the service inventory architecture specification. We can define a number of common complex methods as part of a uniform contract that then become available for implementation by all services within the service inventory.

Complex methods have distinct names. The complex method examples that we cover shortly are called:

- Fetch – A series of GET requests that can recover from various exceptions.

- Store – A series of PUT or DELETE requests that can recover from various exceptions.

- Delta – A series of GET requests that keep a consumer in sync with changing resource state.

- Async – An initial modified request and subsequent interactions that support asynchronous request message processing.

Services that support a complex method communicate this by showing the method name as part of a separate service capability (Figure 10.11), alongside the primitive methods that the complex method is built upon. When project teams create consumer programs for certain services, they can determine the required consumer-side logic for a complex method by identifying what complex methods the service supports, as indicated by its published service contract.

Figure 10.11

An Invoice service contract displaying two service capabilities based on primitive methods and two service capabilities based on complex methods. We can assume that the two complex methods incorporate the use of the two primitive methods, but we can confirm this by studying the design specification that documents the complex methods.

Invoice

o GET /invoice/
  {invoice-id}

o PUT /invoice/
  {invoice-id}/customer

o Fetch /invoice/
  {invoice-id}

o Store /invoice/
  {invoice-id}/customer

NOTE

When applying the Service Abstraction (414) principle to REST service composition design, we may exclude entirely describing some of the primitive methods from the service contract. This can be the result of design standards that only allow the use of a complex method in certain situations. Going back to the previous example about the use of a complex method for retrieving accounting-related documents, we may have a design standard that prohibits these documents from being retrieved via the regular GET method (because the GET method does not enforce the additional reliability requirements).

It is important to note that the use of complex methods is by no means required. Outside of controlled environments in which complex methods can be safely defined, standardized, and applied in support of the Increased Intrinsic Interoperability goal, their use is uncommon and generally not recommended. When building a service inventory architecture we can opt to standardize on certain interactions through the use of complex methods or we can choose to limit REST service interaction to the use of primitive methods only. This decision will be based heavily on the distinct nature of the business requirements addressed and automated by the services in the service inventory.

Despite their name, complex methods are intended to add simplicity to service inventory architecture. For example, let's imagine we choose not to use pre-defined complex methods and then realize that there are common rules or policies that should have been applied to numerous services and their consumers. In this case, we will have built multiple services and consumers that behave unpredictably. When a service returns a redirection code, we can't be sure that all consumers will act upon it, and a temporary communication failure can have unexpected ramifications. Lack of policy can also result in unnecessarily redundant message processing logic. The fact that the implementations will continue to remain out of synch make this a convoluted architecture that is unnecessarily complex. This is exactly the problem that the use of complex methods is intended to avoid.

The upcoming sections introduce a set of sample complex methods organized into two sections:

- Stateless Complex Methods
- Stateful Complex Methods

Note that these methods are by no means industry standard. Their names and the type of message interactions and primitive method invocations they encompass have been customized to address common types of functionality.

> **NOTE**
>
> The *Case Study Example* section at the end of this chapter further explores this subject matter. In this example, in response to specific business requirements, two new complex methods (one stateless, the other stateful) are defined.

Stateless Complex Methods

This first collection of complex methods encapsulate message interactions that are compliant with the Stateless {395} constraint.

Fetch Method

Instead of relying only on a single invocation of the HTTP GET method (and its associated headers and behavior) to retrieve content, we can build a more sophisticated data retrieval method with features such as:

- automatic retry on timeout or connection failure
- required support for runtime content negotiation to ensure the service consumer receives data in a form it understands

- required redirection support to ensure that changes to the service contract can be gracefully accommodated by service consumers

- required cache control directive support by services to ensure minimum latency, minimum bandwidth usage, and minimum processing for redundant requests

We'll refer to this type of enhanced read-only complex method as a Fetch. Figure 10.12 shows an example of a pre-defined message interaction of a Fetch method designed to perform content negotiation and automatic retries.

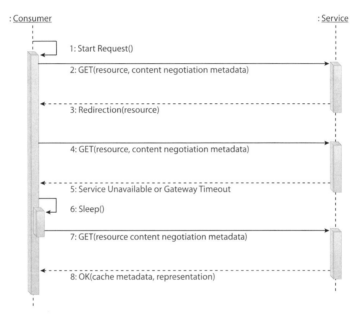

Figure 10.12
An example of a Fetch complex method comprised of consecutive GET method calls.

Store Method

When using the standard PUT or DELETE methods to add new resources, set the state of existing resources, or remove old resources, service consumers can suffer request timeouts or exception responses. Although the HTTP specification explains what each exception means, it does not impose restrictions as to how they should be handled. For this purpose, we can create a custom Store method to standardize necessary behavior.

The Store method can have a number of the same features as a Fetch, such as requiring automatic retry of requests, content negotiation support, and support for redirection exceptions. Using PUT and DELETE, it can also defeat low bandwidth connections by always sending the most recent state requested by the consumer, rather than needing to complete earlier requests first.

The same way that individual primitive HTTP methods can be idempotent, the Store method can be designed to behave idempotently. By building upon primitive idempotent methods, any repeated, successful request messages will have no further effect after the first request message is successfully executed.

For example, when setting an invoice state from "Unpaid" to "Paid":

- a "toggle" request would not be idempotent because repeating the request toggles the state back to "Unpaid."

- the "PUT" request is idempotent when setting the invoice to "Paid" because it has the same effect, no matter how many times the request is repeated

It is important to understand that the Store and its underlying PUT and DELETE requests are requests *to* service logic, not an action carried out on the service's underlying database. As shown in Figure 10.13, these types of requests are stated in an idempotent

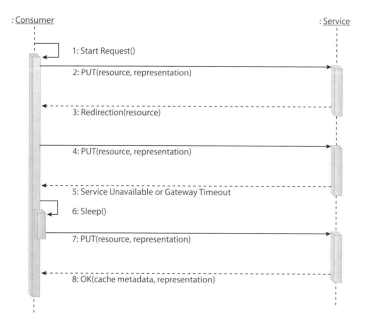

Figure 10.13
An example of the interaction carried out by a Store complex method.

manner in order to efficiently allow for the retrying of requests without the need for sequence numbers to add reliable messaging support.

> **NOTE**
>
> Service capabilities that incorporate this type of method are an example of the application of the Idempotent Capability [470] pattern.

Delta Method

It is often necessary for a service consumer to remain synchronized with the state of a changing resource. The Delta method is a synchronization mechanism that facilitates stateless synchronization of the state of a changing resource between the service that owns this state and consumers that need to stay in alignment with the state.

The Delta method follows processing logic based on the following three basic functions:

1. The service keeps a history of changes to a resource.

2. The consumer gets a URL referring to the location in the history that represents the last time the consumer queried the state of the resource.

3. The next time the consumer queries the resource state, the service (using the URL provided by the consumer) returns a list of changes that have occurred since the last time the consumer queried the resource state.

Figure 10.14 illustrates this using a series of GET invocations.

The service provides a "main" resource that responds to GET requests by returning the current state of the resource. Next to the main resource it provides a collection of "delta" resources that each return the list of changes from a nominated point in the history buffer.

The consumer of the Delta method activates periodically or when requested by the core consumer logic. If it has a delta resource identifier it sends its request to that location. If it does not have a delta resource identifier, it retrieves the main resource to become synchronized. In the corresponding response the consumer receives a link to the delta for the current point in the history buffer. This link will be found in the `Link` header (RFC 5988) with relation type `Delta`.

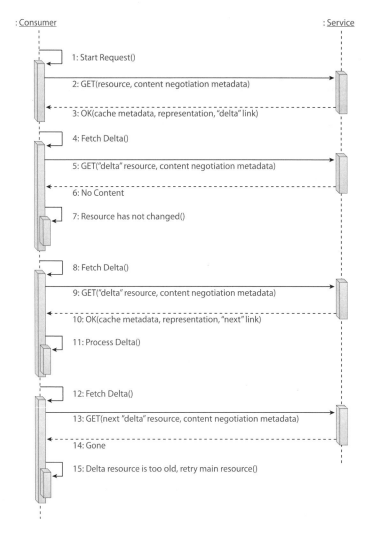

Figure 10.14

An example of the message interaction encompassed by the Delta complex method.

The requested delta resource can be in any one of the following states:

1. It can represent a set of one or more changes that have occurred to the main resource since the point in history that the delta resource identifier refers to. In this case, all changes in the history from the nominated point are returned along with a link to the new delta for the current point in the history buffer. This link will be found in the Link header with relation type Next.

2. It may not have a set of changes because no changes have occurred since its nominated point in the history buffer, in which case it can return the `204 No Content` response code to indicate that the service consumer is already up-to-date and can continue using the delta resource for its next retrieval.

3. Changes may have occurred, but the delta is now expired because the nominated point in history is now so old that the service has elected not to preserve the changes. In this situation, the resource can return a `410 Gone` code to indicate that the consumer has lost synchronization and should re-retrieve the main resource.

Delta resources use the same caching strategy as the main resource.

The service controls how many historical deltas it is prepared to accumulate based on how much time it expects consumers will take (on average) to get up-to-date, or in some cases where a full audit trail is maintained for other purposes the number of deltas can be indefinite. The amount of space required to keep this record is constant and predictable regardless of the number of consumers, leaving it up to each individual service consumer to keep track of where it is in the history buffer.

Async Method

This complex method provides pre-defined interactions for the successful and canceled exchange of asynchronous messages. It is useful for when a given request requires more time to execute than what the standard HTTP request timeouts allow.

Normally, if a request takes too long, the consumer message processing logic will time out or an intermediary will return a `504 Gateway Timeout` response code to the service consumer. The Async method provides a fallback mechanism for handling requests and returning responses that does not require the service consumer to maintain its HTTP connection open for the total duration of the request interaction.

As shown in Figure 10.15, the service consumer issues a request, but does so specifying a call-back resource identifier. If the service chooses to use this identifier, it responds with the `202 Accepted` response code, and may optionally return a resource identifier in the `Location` header to help it track the place of the asynchronous request in its processing queue. When the request has been fully processed, its result is delivered by the service, which then issues a PUT or POST request to the call-back address of the service consumer.

If the service consumer issues a DELETE request (as shown in Figure 10.16) while the Async request is still in the processing queue (and before a response is returned), a

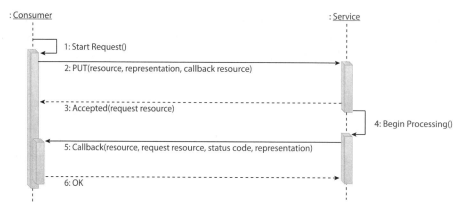

Figure 10.15

An asynchronous request interaction encompassed by the Async complex method.

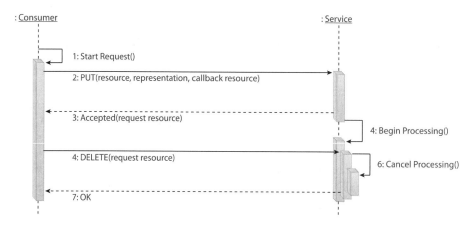

Figure 10.16

An asynchronous cancel interaction encompassed by the Async complex method.

separate pre-defined interaction is carried out to cancel the asynchronous request. In this case, no response is returned and the service cancels the processing of the request.

If the consumer cannot listen for call-back requests, it can use the asynchronous request identifier to periodically poll the service. Once the request has been successfully handled, it is possible to retrieve its result using the previously described Fetch method before deleting the asynchronous request state. Services that execute either interaction encompassed by this method must have a means of purging old asynchronous requests if service consumers are unavailable to pick up responses or otherwise "forget" to delete request resources.

Stateful Complex Methods

These next complex methods use REST as the basis of service design but incorporate interactions that intentionally breach the Stateless {395} constraint. Although the scenarios represented by these methods are relatively common in traditional enterprise application designs, this kind of communication is not considered native to the World Wide Web. The use of stateful complex methods can be warranted when we accept the reduction in scalability that comes with this design decision.

Trans Method

The Trans method essentially provides the interactions necessary to carry out a two-phase commit between one service consumer and one or more services (as per the application of the Atomic Transaction [432] pattern). Changes made within the transaction are guaranteed to either successfully propagate across all participating services, or all services are rolled back to their original states.

This type of complex method requires a "prepare" function for each participant before a final commit or rollback is carried out. Functionality of this sort is not natively supported by HTTP. Therefore, we need to introduce a custom PREP-PUT method (a variant of the PUT method), as shown in Figure 10.17.

In this example the PREP-PUT method is the equivalent of PUT, but it does not commit the PUT action. A different method name is used to ensure that if the service does not

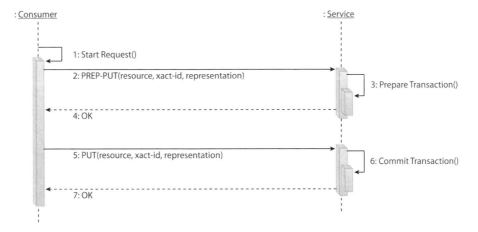

Figure 10.17
An example of a Trans complex method, using a custom primitive method called PREP-PUT.

understand how to participate in the Trans complex method, it then rejects the PREP-PUT method and allows the consumer to abort the transaction.

To carry out the logic behind a typical Trans complex method will usually require the involvement of a transaction controller to ensure that the commit and rollback functions are truly and reliably carried out with atomicity.

Alternative transaction models that have varying degrees of compliance with Stateless {395} are further explored in Chapter 12.

PubSub Method

A variety of publish-subscribe options are available once it is decided to intentionally breach the Stateless {395} constraint. As explained in the Event-Driven Messaging [465] pattern, these types of mechanisms are designed to support real-time interactions where a service consumer must act immediately when some pre-determined event at a given resource occurs. The Event-Driven Messaging [465] pattern is applied as an alternative to the repeated polling of the resource, which can negatively impact performance if the polling frequency is increased to detect changes with minimal delay.

There are various ways that this complex method can be designed. Figure 10.18 illustrates an approach that treats publish-subscribe messaging as a "cache-invalidation" mechanism.

This form of publish-subscribe interaction is considered "lightweight" because it does not require services to send out the actual changes to the subscribers. Instead, it informs them that a resource has changed by pushing out the resource identifier, and then reuses an existing, cacheable Fetch method as the service consumers pull the new representations of the changed resource.

The amount of state required to manage these subscriptions is bound to one fixed-sized record for each service consumer. If multiple invalidations queue up for a particular subscribed event, they can be folded together into a single notification. Regardless of whether the consumer receives one or multiple invalidation messages, it will still only need to invoke one Fetch method to bring itself up-to-date with the state of its resources each time it sees one or more new invalidation messages.

The PubSub method can be further adjusted to distribute subscription load and session state storage to different places around the network. This technique can be particularly effective within cloud-based environments that naturally provide multiple, distributed storage resources.

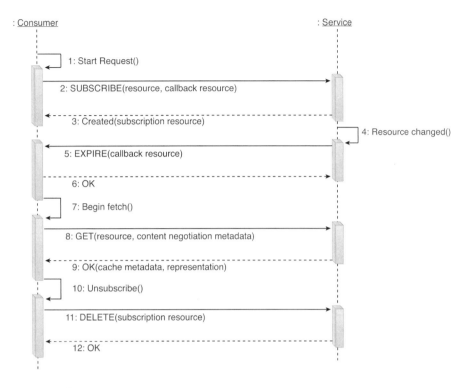

Figure 10.18

An example of a PubSub complex method based on cache invalidation. When the service determines that something has changed on one or more resources, it issues cache expiry notifications to its subscribers. Each subscriber can then use a Fetch complex method (or something equivalent) to bring the subscriber up-to-date with respect to the changes.

SUMMARY OF KEY POINTS

- When designing both the uniform contract and individual service contracts, we can consider creating complex methods as part of the functions offered by the contracts.

- Complex methods encompass the aggregation of multiple primitive HTTP methods or the repeated execution of a single primitive HTTP method, along with other functional features that are part of predefined message interactions.

- Complex methods are ideally standardized so that the interaction behavior is consistent across all services and consumers that use them.

- Both stateless and stateful complex methods can be designed, although the latter variation is not REST-compliant.

The MUA team responsible for service design encounters a number of requirements for accessing and updating resource state.

For example:

- One service consumer needs to atomically read the state of the resource, perform processing, and store the updated state back to the resource.

- Another service consumer needs to support concurrent user actions that modify the same resource. These actions update certain resource properties while others need to remain the same.

Allowing individual service consumers to contain different custom logic that performs these types of functions will inadvertently lead to problems and runtime exceptions when any two service consumers attempt updates to the same resource at the same time.

MUA architects conclude that the simplest way to avoid this is to introduce a new complex method that ensures that a resource is locked while being updated by a given consumer. Using the rules of optimistic locking, an approach commonly traditionally used with database updates, they are able to create a complex method that is stateless and takes advantage of existing standard features of the HTTP protocol. They name the method "OptLock" and write up an official description that is made part of the uniform contract profile:

OptLock Complex Method

If two separate service consumers attempt to update the state of a resource at the same time, their actions will clearly conflict with each other as the outcome depends on the order in which their requests reach the service. The OptLock method (Figure 10.19) addresses this problem by providing a means by which a service consumer can determine whether the state of a resource has changed since it was last read by the consumer before attempting an update.

Specifically, a consumer will first retrieve the current state associated with a resource identifier using the Fetch method. Along with the data the consumer receives an "ETag." ETag is a concept from HTTP that uniquely identifies the version of a resource

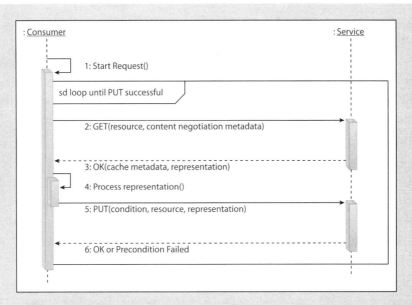

Figure 10.19
An example of an OptLock complex method.

in an opaque way. Whenever the resource changes state its ETag is guaranteed to be different. When the service consumer initiates a Store, it does so conditionally by requesting the service to only honor the Store interaction if the resource's ETag still matches the one that it had when fetched. This is done with the If-Match header. The service can use the ETag value in the condition to detect whether the resource state has been changed in the meantime.

The OptLock complex method does not introduce any new features to HTTP, but instead introduces new requirements for handling GET and PUT requests. Specifically, the GET request must return an ETag value and the PUT request must process the If-Match header. And, if the resource has changed, the service must further guarantee not to carry out the PUT request.

There are several techniques for computing ETags. Some compute a hash value out of the state information associated with the resource, some simply keep a "last modified" timestamp for each resource, and others track the version of the resource state explicitly.

The OptLock method may not scale effectively for high concurrent access to a particular resource. If consumer update requests are denied with an HTTP `409 Conflict` response code, the OptLock method prescribes how the consumer can recover by fetching a newer version of the resource over which they have to re-compute the change and retry the Store method. However, this may fail again due to a conflicting update request. Service consumers that interact with a resource in this way rely on that particular resource having relatively low rates of write access.

The OptLock complex method becomes available as part of the uniform contract and is implemented by several services. However, scenarios emerge where a multiple consumers attempt to modify the resource at the same time, causing regular exceptions and failed updates. These situations occur during peak usage times and because concurrent usage volume is expected to increase further, it is determined that a more efficient means of serializing updates to the resource needs to be established.

It is proposed that the OptLock complex method be changed to perform pessimistic locking instead, as per the following PesLock complex method description:

PesLock Complex Method

Pessimistic locking provides greater flexibility and certainty than optimistic locking. From a REST perspective, this comes at the cost of introducing stateful interactions and limiting concurrent access while the pessimistic lock is held.

As shown in Figure 10.20, the WebDAV extensions to HTTP provide locking primitives that can be used within a composition architecture that intentionally breaches the Stateless {395} constraint. One consumer may lock out others from accessing a resource, so care must be taken that appropriate access control policies are in place. Consumers can also fail while the lock is held, which means that locks must be able to time out independently of the consumers that register them.

This way, the service consumer would be able to lock the resource for as long as it takes to read the state, modify it, and write it back again. Although other service consumers would still encounter exceptions while attempting to update the resource at the same time as the consumer that has locked it, it is deemed preferable to the unpredictability of managing the resource as part of an optimistic locking model.

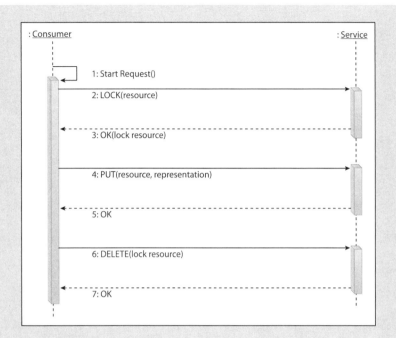

Figure 10.20
An example of a PesLock complex method.

This solution is not embraced by all of the MUA architects because retaining the lock on the resource requires that the Stateless {395} constraint be breached. It could further lead to the danger of stale locks starting to impact performance and scalability. In particular, unless proper measures are taken to ensure that only authorized consumers may lock a resource, this exposes the resources to denial of service attacks by malicious consumers that could lock out all other consumers.

After further discussion, a compromise is reached. The OptLock method will be attempted first. As a fallback, if the consumer tries three times and fails, it will attempt the stateful PesLock method to ensure it is able to complete the action.

Part IV

Service Composition with REST

Chapter 11: Fundamental Service Composition with REST

Chapter 12: Advanced Service Composition with REST

Chapter 13: Service Composition with REST Case Study

Chapter 11

Fundamental Service Composition with REST

11.1 Service Composition Terminology

11.2 Service Composition Design Influences

11.3 Composition Hierarchies and Layers

11.4 REST Service Composition Design Considerations

11.5 A Step-by-Step Service Activity

PRINCIPLES, PATTERNS, AND CONSTRAINTS REFERENCED IN THIS CHAPTER:

- Atomic Service Transaction [432]

- Cache {398}

- Capability Recomposition [441]

- Code-on-Demand {407}

- Compensating Service Transaction [443]

- Entity Abstraction [463]

- Layered System {404}

- Process Abstraction [486]

- Service Abstraction (414)

- Service Autonomy (417)

- Service Composability (422)

- Service Layers [504]

- Service Loose Coupling (413)

- Service Reusability (415)

- Service Statelessness (418)

- Standardized Service Contract (411)

- Stateless {395}

- Three-Layer Inventory [513]

- Uniform Contract {400}

- Utility Abstraction [517]

In order for REST to be an effective implementation medium for service orientation it must be utilized in support of the Service Composability (422) principle. The next two chapters explore how and to what extent REST relates to and can be leveraged for the creation of composition-based enterprise solutions.

With a constant eye on the compliance rules of the Stateless {395} constraint, these chapters document options for building service compositions that are both fully and partially compliant with REST requirements.

11.1 Service Composition Terminology

The following introductory section is provided to establish definitions for key service composition terminology. This content is comprised of a modified excerpt from Chapter 13 from the book *SOA Principles of Service Design*. For those of you familiar with this book, feel free to skip ahead to the *Service Composition Design Influences* section.

Compositions and Composition Instances

A service composition is typically associated with the automation of a business process. When defining the workflow logic of this process, various decision points are created to determine the flow of data and action in response to runtime variables and conditions. Therefore, it can be helpful to distinguish between a *static business process definition* (comprised of workflow logic) and a *business process instance* that represents what parts of the workflow logic actually occurred at runtime.

Similarly, service *compositions* are defined when required inter-capability interactions are mapped out to accommodate various scenarios in support of the business process workflow logic. A service *composition instance* represents what actually happens when an occurrence of the workflow logic is carried out by a series of service instances at runtime.

> **NOTE**
>
> For simplicity's sake, the term "service composition" can be used to refer to both a static composition definition and a composition instance, unless otherwise qualified.

Composition Members and Controllers

When taking part in compositions, services can fulfill different roles depending on how they are positioned within the overall composition configuration. As a *composition controller*, the service is located at the head of a composition hierarchy. This occurs when the service capability that is being executed contains and carries out logic that invokes capabilities in other services (Figure 11.1).

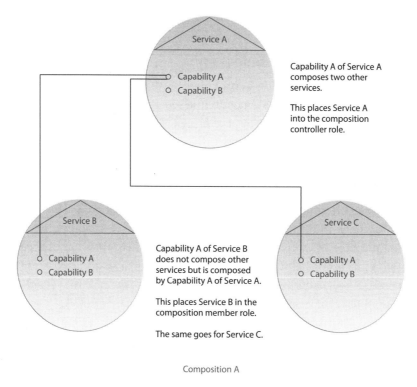

Composition A

Figure 11.1
Services assume composition roles based on how their individual capabilities participate within the composition.

A *composition member*, on the other hand, represents a service being composed by another. Again, as shown in Figure 11.1, it is the fact that the service's capability is being invoked by another service that places the service into this role.

A composition member may compose other compositions members, which can, in turn, compose others as well (Figure 11.2). Composition members that compose other services can be further qualified as *sub-controllers*.

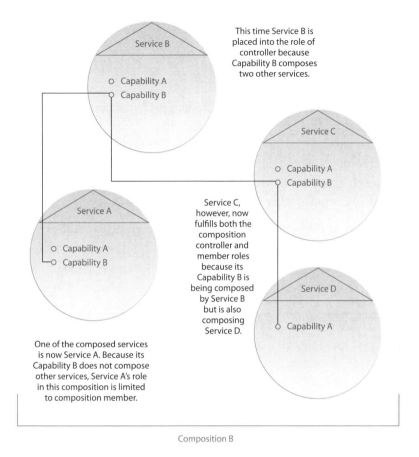

This time Service B is placed into the role of controller because Capability B composes two other services.

Service C, however, now fulfills both the composition controller and member roles because its Capability B is being composed by Service B but is also composing Service D.

One of the composed services is now Service A. Because its Capability B does not compose other services, Service A's role in this composition is limited to composition member.

Composition B

Figure 11.2

The same services from Composition A are reutilized as participants in a new composition. New capabilities are now involved, which change the service composition roles.

This terminology is important especially when working with business services. The controller role can just as easily be assumed by an entity service as it can by a task service. However, it is less common for a task service to be a sub-controller than it is for an entity service.

Service Compositions Are Actually Service Capability Compositions

The composition controller and member labels are used to represent the roles that services assume, depending on their position within a given service activity. It is important to continually remind ourselves that it is actually the individual service capabilities that are responsible for placing services into these roles.

Therefore, the capabilities themselves can be further qualified, as follows:

- *composition controller capability* (or just *controller capability*)

- *composition member capability*

When using these role classifications, it is also helpful to acknowledge that they may be temporary for services, but more likely permanent for capabilities. For example, if three of six capabilities within a service encapsulate logic that composes other services, then the service will only be classified a controller when one of those three capabilities is invoked. However, each of these three capabilities will always be controller capabilities for as long as they compose other services.

Regardless of the controller designation, this principle emphasizes the need for all service logic to be composable, which means that all six of the service's capabilities will ideally have been designed to carry out their capabilities as an effective part of larger compositions.

> **NOTE**
>
> When studying service composition architecture from a REST perspective, we can view it as controller resources composing member resources instead of controller capabilities composing member capabilities. These are two sides of the same coin because from a REST service contract design perspective, resources themselves are defined in terms of the service capabilities they participate in.

Designated Controllers

Services, in their entirety, can also be designed as *designated controllers*, which limits them to the controller role only. The classic example of a designated controller is a task service with just one capability used to kick off the automation of a business process that will involve the composition of multiple other services.

Collective Composability

Depending on the extent to which the Service Abstraction (414) principle is applied to a reusable service, when we incorporate one of its capabilities into a new composition, we may not be aware of the fact that it is acting as a composition controller. We will therefore place the same expectations on that service capability in terms of performance, reliability, and overall quality of service, as we would on any other.

However, underneath the covers, it is the collective measure of composability of all members involved in a composition that ultimately determines the quality of service offered by the controller of the composition. Furthermore, because Service Composability is comprised of and directly supported by other principles, it is their application that collectively determines the overall quality of a composition. For example, the individual levels of capability autonomy for each composition member can be combined to represent the levels of autonomy of a composition's controller capability, as illustrated in Figure 11.3.

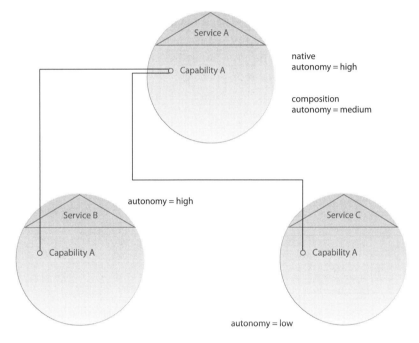

Figure 11.3

Even though Capability A's native autonomy is high, its overall autonomy (the autonomy of the composition it encapsulates) is lower due to the fact that the autonomy level of one of its composed service capabilities is low.

One can take this a step further and even equate the effectiveness of composition members with the success of SOA as a whole. As we will discuss shortly, the advent of the complex service composition is considered a key factor to leveraging the investment that goes into assembling an effective service inventory.

> ## NOTE
>
> A related architectural consideration is the concept of "composition autonomy," as described in the upcoming *Service Autonomy (417) and Composition Autonomy Loss* section and further explained in Chapter 10 of *SOA Principles of Service Design*.

Service Activities

Before we can model a composition, we need to establish a means of mapping the flow of data and processing through a composed environment. To accomplish this, we need to define a *service activity*—the mapping of an inter-service message path. A service activity is intentionally limited to representing interaction *with* and *between* services only—not with what occurs within the underlying service logic.

There are *primitive* and *complex* service activities, as illustrated in Figures 11.4 and 11.5. Depending on the level of Service Abstraction applied to a given controller capability, what may appear to be a primitive service activity may actually be a complex service activity. For example, Capability A in Figure 11.4 may be abstracting the complex composition illustrated in Figure 11.5.

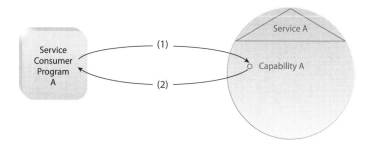

Figure 11.4

An example of a primitive service activity. The consumer program interacts with Capability A of Service A to carry out a simple point-to-point data exchange.

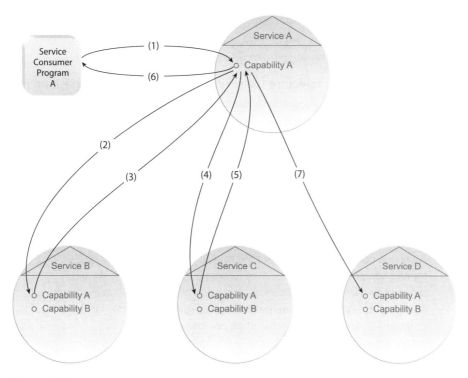

Figure 11.5
A complex service activity spanning a service composition. The numbered arrows represent the activity sequence.

Composition Initiators

The scope of a service composition does not always map to the corresponding service activity. We qualify a collection of services as being part of a composition through association with a well-defined business process. In other words, the functional scope of a service composition is determined by the business process it automates.

A service activity can (and often does) exceed this scope. If we draw a boundary around a set of coordinated services that collectively execute a business task, we usually end up with a composition controller and several composition members. A runtime component that exists outside of this boundary is usually represented by the service consumer program responsible for invoking the composition controller in order to kick off the service composition.

In this case, the service activity spans beyond the composition to include the program responsible for initiating the composition logic. When carrying out this role, the program can be referred to as the *composition initiator*.

A composition controller is therefore the service at the head of a composition and the one that typically embodies the parent functional context and scope by encapsulating the required business process logic. A composition initiator is generally not a composition controller; instead, it is a program that exists outside of the composition but fulfills this role by initiating the composition logic. In the previously displayed Figure 11.5, the composition initiator would be the Service Consumer A, whereas the composition controller is Service A.

NOTE

A service consumer can assume the roles of both composition initiator and composition controller if it exists as a program that contains the range of required composition logic but does not make itself available as a service. However, it is often desirable to reserve the "controller" label for programs to which service-orientation has been applied.

Point-to-Point Data Exchanges and Compositions

Continuing our discussion of composition scope, it is worthwhile to establish what extent of service activity constitutes a minimal service composition.

A simple interaction between a single service and its consumer can be referred to as a *point-to-point* exchange (a term that clearly originated from the world of integration architecture). Because this model (or architecture) is limited to a primitive service activity between two endpoints, we do not consider it a service composition.

The minimum scope of a service composition must encompass a complex service activity that spans two services plus the composition initiator. In other words, a consumer program that interacts with a service that does not invoke any other services is an example of the point-to-point model. In a scenario where the consumer program interacts with a service that invokes one or more additional services, a service composition is represented by all activity participants, excluding the composition initiator.

SUMMARY OF KEY POINTS

- Depending on the nature of the composition in which a service is participating, the service and its capabilities can assume composition controller and/or composition member roles.

- Services can be designated controllers if warranted by their underlying logic and their position within the service inventory.

- Service activities represent the message exchanges between services, not the activity that occurs within service boundaries.

- Composition initiators are programs that trigger a composition but reside outside of the composition boundary.

- To constitute a composition requires at least two services, one of which is then invoked by a composition initiator. A point-to-point model represents the scenario when only the initiator and one service are involved.

11.2 Service Composition Design Influences

Before we explore the details behind REST-based service compositions, let's first highlight constraints and principles that can shape service composition design. This will help establish an understanding as to why the marriage of REST and service-orientation results in distinct architectural characteristics and requirements.

Service-Orientation Principles and Composition Design

As explained earlier in this book, all service-orientation principles exist to support and enable composability as an inherent characteristic of software programs designed as services. The ultimate goal of applying service-orientation is that resultant services are as reusable and interoperable—via repeated composition—as possible. This is also the basis of the fundamental Capability Recomposition [441] pattern.

Let's take a brief look at how individual principles relate specifically to REST-based composition design.

Standardized Service Contract (411) and the Uniform Contract

A REST-compliant service composition requires that all service activities flow through the uniform contract. As a result, a uniform contract becomes an intrinsic part of service architectures and a centralized part of service composition architectures. This naturally applies an extent of Standardized Service Contract (411) in that uniform contract methods and media types can become inherently standard across a service inventory.

The *Design Principles and Constraints* section in Chapter 7 provided a list of examples to illustrate how and where, beyond the native standardization that comes with using a uniform contract, the Standardized Service Contract (411) principle can further be applied to more explicitly standardize various other elements of REST service contracts. All of these examples relate to and support service composition.

The upcoming sections in this chapter as well as sections within Chapter 12 introduce topics specific to REST-based service composition design. Many of these features need to be standardized in order for them to be effectively leveraged by a service inventory, without jeopardizing the intrinsic interoperability of its services.

For example:

- Support for synchronous and asynchronous message exchanges may need to carry over into how service capabilities are designed and what types of predictable response messages may need to be issued. This pertains especially to when service contracts are further equipped with capabilities that enable consumers to query the status of an on-going service activity. (See the *Synchronous and Asynchronous Service Compositions* section in this chapter.)

- The use of hypermedia and parameterized service capabilities may require standardization to ensure that service consumer logic is prepared to work with dynamic binding features, and to ensure such features do not unnecessarily complicate service composition architectures and runtime service activities. (See the *Binding Between Composition Participants* section in this chapter and the *Service Composition with Dynamic Binding and Logic Deferral* section in Chapter 12.)

- The use of complex methods needs to be strictly standardized so that consumers and services required to work with complex methods are pre-designed to do so in full compliance with the interaction behavior that is predefined within each such method. (See the *Complex Method Design* section in Chapter 10.)

- Though not explicitly expressed in REST service contracts, response codes require standardization, both with regards to how common success and exception codes are interpreted, as well as any codes that may be less explicit or that are customized. (See the *Designing and Standardizing HTTP Response Codes* section in Chapter 10.)

In whatever capacity Standardized Service Contract (411) is applied to aspects of a service inventory's uniform contract, the utmost care must be taken to avoid inadvertently inhibiting or negatively impacting multiple composition-based service-oriented solutions. The global effect of making changes to uniform contract features increases as the quantity of potentially affected services within the inventory grows.

Service Loose Coupling (413) and the Uniform Contract

A fundamental goal of service-oriented computing is that of increasing the agility of an organization. In order to enable a consistent level of responsiveness, enterprise solutions need to be flexible enough to be subjected to change on a regular basis, while imposing minimal impact and effort in response to change. Service Loose Coupling (413) supports this goal directly by advocating reduced dependencies between the programs that comprise a service-oriented solution. REST further advocates a reduction in coupling via its required use of a uniform contract.

When sufficiently standardized via Standardized Service Contract (411), the diligent application of Service Loose Coupling (413) together with the consistent use of a uniform contract and its features (such as hypermedia) can help significantly loosen dependencies between services, while requiring all services within a service inventory to remain coupled to the required (and standardized) use of overarching uniform contract features.

This principle can influence a variety of REST composition design considerations, including:

- The separation of logic into service layers based on common service models, such as task, entity, and utility services. While these services exist independently, many will provide capabilities that rely on the composition of other capabilities that reside in other services. (See the *Composition Hierarchies and Layers* section in this chapter.)

- The creative usage of hypermedia within REST service composition can lead to different forms of dynamic runtime functionality that reduce the extent of design-time coupling required by consumers and services. (See the *Denormalized Capabilities Across Normalized Services*, *Composition Deepening*, and *Dynamically Binding with Common Properties* sections in Chapter 12.)

- Dependencies formed on transaction coordinators and other components of both REST-friendly and non-REST-friendly cross-service transaction-based composition architectures. (See the *Cross-Service Transactions with REST* section in Chapter 12.)

- Dependencies formed on event managers and other components of event-driven messaging and publish-and-subscribe composition architectures. (See the *Event-Driven Interactions with REST* section in Chapter 12.)

The successful application of this principle increases the independence of each member of a REST service composition, allowing the moving parts of a solution to evolve more freely on an individual basis.

Service Abstraction (414) and Composition Information Hiding

As already established in Chapter 8, Service Abstraction (414) reduces the quantity of information present within service contracts to the minimum required for service consumers to invoke their required service capabilities. Service composition-related information that can be excluded from service contracts on the basis of this principle includes:

- Knowledge that individual composition members may be running on different implementation platforms.

- Information as to whether a given service capability may encapsulate logic that composes one or more other services.

- Details of algorithms and data structures used by the service logic.

- Service capabilities and associated resources that may be intentionally hidden or restricted from certain types of service consumers.

- Detailed quality-of-service information (such as the mean time to failure of hardware components, or the memory and computational resources available to the service).

- Resource information pertaining to service capabilities that support parameter-ized input and hypermedia.

The application of Service Abstraction (414) may result in the need to hide this type of information to help ensure the evolvability of service and consumer logic within the constraints imposed by the abstract service contract. This further supports Service Loose Coupling (413) and Uniform Contract {400} in creating sustainable service compositions that can remain responsive to change.

Service Reusability (415) for Repeatable Composition

Service Reusability (415) is central to the proposition of Service Composability (422). It is the principle that ensures there are logic and resources encapsulated by a REST service that allow for the repeatable composition of that service as part of different service compositions.

The separation of service logic into agnostic and non-agnostic service layers, as explained in the upcoming *Composition Hierarchies and Layers* section, represents a direct application of this principle in support of composition.

Service Autonomy (417) and Composition Autonomy Loss

As explained in Chapter 10 of *SOA Principles of Service Design*, a service naturally loses autonomy when it composes another service. This is because, as part of a function it is tasked to complete, the composing service is required to go outside of its physical boundary. As a result of this dependency, it loses control by deferring processing to other services. This reduces its autonomy. A consequence is that the higher we go in a service composition hierarchy, the more the potential loss of autonomy. To minimize the negative effects of this, it is important that all composition members be designed with as high individual autonomy as possible. Figure 11.6 further highlights how, with REST-based services, there is additional loss of autonomy pertaining to the required compliance of each service contract with the uniform contract.

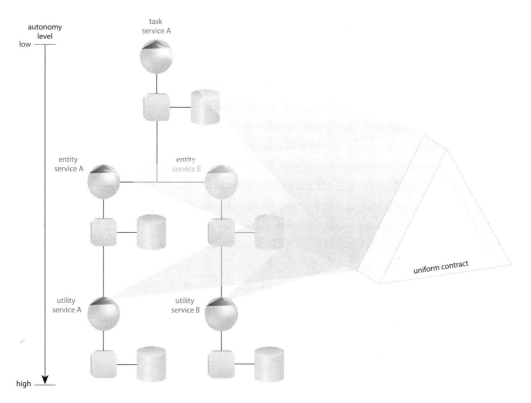

Figure 11.6

The higher we go in a typical service composition hierarchy, the greater the loss of autonomy due to the layers of dependency on services. Further, all REST service contracts are dependent on the required and standardized usage of the uniform contract, which typically imposes additional autonomy loss by limiting how service capabilities can be expressed to predefined methods and media types.

Service Statelessness (418) and Stateless {395}

The deferral of runtime state and the usage of various state management mechanisms are advocated by this principle in support of optimizing service composition architecture. When applied to REST-based compositions, the extent of this principle is further moderated by the Stateless {395} constraint.

We elaborate on these topics further in the upcoming *Stateless {395} and Stateful Compositions* section, as well as several sections within Chapter 12.

Service Composability (422) and Service-Orientation

The primary purpose of this overarching principle is to regulate the application of the other seven principles to ensure they are applied to an extent sufficient to make the service as effective of a composition participant as possible. When applied to REST-based service compositions, the objective of this principle does not change. Its focus is on leveraging the features and benefits of service-orientation and REST-style architecture in support of on-going, repeatable composition.

REST Constraints and Composition Design

Unlike with service-orientation, native composability is not a primary goal or priority of REST. Although REST architecture is distributed in nature and certainly accommodates message exchanges across multiple services at runtime, how these message exchanges can and cannot be carried out is closely regulated, but without regard as to how it affects composability. This is because REST is based on emulating the loose relationships between artifacts on the World Wide Web. When applying this architectural style to service compositions for enterprise business solutions, some natural tensions arise, the foremost of which pertains to state management.

Stateless {395} and Stateful Compositions

This constraint is often considered an inhibitor to the application of Service Composability (422), especially in support of creating more complex service compositions involving service activities that span multiple composition members. Several common interactions among enterprise applications are interpreted as being prohibited by this constraint.

Examples of interactions that may violate Stateless {395} include:

- cross-service transaction (such as those that emulate ACID transactions)
- event-driven interactions (such as publish-subscribe)

On the Web it is common not to have any real form of transaction between different services or between requests. Each request is handled as its own transaction that is independent of all other requests. In the enterprise it has become increasingly important to have a consistent means of performing cross-service transactions in order to carry out complex interactions with strong guarantees about their reliability.

When business automation requirements conflict with the rules of the Stateless {395} constraint, we are faced with two simple options:

- compromise on the business automation requirements to remain compliant with Stateless {395}
- violate Stateless {395} to fulfill the business automation requirements

In the former case we can attempt to explore alternatives that minimize the impact on the enterprise solution. With regards to the latter option, we must understand and plan for the consequences of violating Stateless {395}.

Cross-service transactions and event-driven interactions are covered in detail in Chapter 12, along with content that specifically highlights the relationship of REST-friendly and non-REST-friendly architectures with the Stateless {395} constraint.

Cache {398} and Layered System {404}

These two constraints introduce the notion of intermediaries that can exist between any given service and consumer pair. This can add design and governance complexity to service composition technology architectures, due to layers of processing that are part of the composition but exist separately from the services. We will only touch on these constraints in the next two chapters, as many of their considerations are more relevant at an infrastructure level.

Code-on-Demand {407} and Composition Logic Deferral

This optional constraint introduces potentially novel ways that logic can be distributed between services within a service composition, and even between the initiator of a service composition and the controller and members of that composition. Though various techniques exist, they are not common in enterprise solution design. This constraint is therefore also not covered in depth over the next two chapters, with the exception of the *Runtime Logic Deferral* section in Chapter 12.

Uniform Contract {400} and Composition Coupling

In terms of its impact on service composition design, Uniform Contract {400} is perhaps the most recognizable and influential of the REST constraints. This constraint transfers the coupling of service consumer logic from service-specific elements of individual service contracts onto the common elements of an overarching uniform technical interface. This shift augments the complexity of the architecture for an entire service inventory and any resultant service composition.

SUMMARY OF KEY POINTS

- Most service-orientation principles and REST constraints directly influence the composability potential of REST-based services.

- A common point of tension with complex service composition design is the application of Service Statelessness (418) and Stateless {395}.

11.3 Composition Hierarchies and Layers

As explained in previous chapters, service-oriented analysis and design approaches tend to naturally partition solution logic into logical service layers based on service models. Figure 11.7 illustrates how a complex REST-based service composition can be comprised of collections of entity and utility services that compose each other under the direction of parent composition logic encapsulated by a task service.

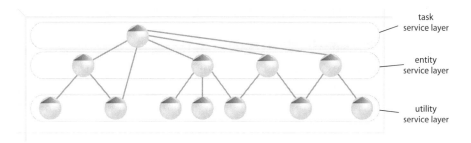

Figure 11.7
Tiers of services based on established service models form a service composition hierarchy.

Within such a hierarchy, service capabilities are invoked across task, entity, and utility layers that correspond to the following individual patterns:

- *Process Abstraction [486]* – This pattern establishes a logical layer comprised of non-agnostic task services, each of which contains business process and parent service composition logic. Task services are typically designated controllers that contain logic that is not reusable and subject to change at a faster rate than service based on agnostic service models.

- *Entity Abstraction [463]* – Entity services provide agnostic functionality that fits within the context of specific business entities (such as invoice, purchase order, etc.). This pattern represents the logical layer of entity services that generally contain the core reusable and business-centric logic and data within a service inventory. Reuse of entity services by different business processes (via different service compositions) is an essential foundation for achieving the goals of service-orientation.

- *Utility Abstraction [517]* – Utility services provide agnostic, non-business-centric logic to address common, low-level functions (such as logging, security, etc.). Also grouped in the utility layer are wrappers of legacy systems. Because utility services tend to end up toward the bottom of composition hierarchies, they can be designed with the highest degree of runtime autonomy.

Each of these patterns is based on the fundamental Service Layers [504] pattern and their combination into the three-tiered hierarchy shown in Figure 11.6 is considered an application of the Three-Layer Inventory [513] compound pattern.

Let's now take a closer look at common considerations that pertain to task services composing entity services and entity services composing each other. The composition of utility services is not explicitly covered as it does not raise any further, distinct design considerations beyond what is covered in the two upcoming sections.

Task Services Composing Entity Services

When a task service composes one or more entity services (Figure 11.8), the resulting interactions will generally create new entity resources or transition the state of existing entity resources. The long-lived nature of entity resources means that there are more state transitions and relatively fewer quick creation and destruction actions involved in their lifecycles.

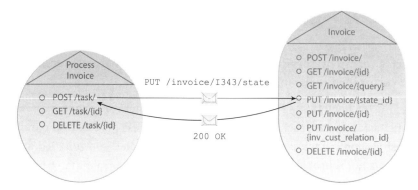

Figure 11.8
A task service will often be able to update the state of composition member resources synchronously.

Both task services and entity services may handle requests asynchronously. This can result in the need for the on-going execution of a particular service capability to be modeled as an independent resource so that the task service can continue to interact with it. More commonly, any on-going processes will be reflected in the state of an entity or sub-entity modeled at this level.

Entity services further do not typically form permanent parts of the state data managed by a task service. They will come and go as members of the resource state depending on how they are involved (or uninvolved) in the composition logic. Any interactions between the task service and the entity service that occur synchronously can generally be excluded from the state of the task's resource.

As with requests and responses at the task level, the body of each request or response at the entity level is generally either:

- a requested state for a resource or…
- the actual state of a resource.

This is part of the basic "representational state transfer" concept where most runtime functions transfer representations (snapshots) of the state of resources. If defining a resource for each significant set of properties and relationships proves too complex it is possible to reduce the number of resources needed to manipulate individual sets of entity properties and relationships by instead applying the PATCH method to a single top-level entity resource.

> **NOTE**
>
> Note that PATCH (like POST) is not idempotent, and needs to be combined with a technique such as optimistic locking, reliable messaging, or a general transaction approach to ensure it is executed at most once.
>
> Any composition that requires a series of requests to result in a consistent state within an entity service or between entity services will need to employ a transaction pattern such as Atomic Service Transaction [432] or Compensating Service Transaction [443].

Entity Services Composing Entity Services

It is relatively common for one entity service to compose another as part of a greater service composition. This requirement is usually a reflection of how different business entities relate to each other or form parent-child hierarchies.

At the task service level we witnessed how the message exchanges between composition controller and composition member services are typically short-lived, expiring soon after the composition member processing is completed. With cross-entity service interaction, durations of individual message exchanges and frequency of repeated message exchanges can be increased, depending on the nature and complexity of the business logic being executed.

As shown in Figure 11.9, an entity service capability that composes another entity service is likely to behave as if the composed service's resource is part of the state of its resource. Such relationships between "resources that compose other resources" can be long-lived.

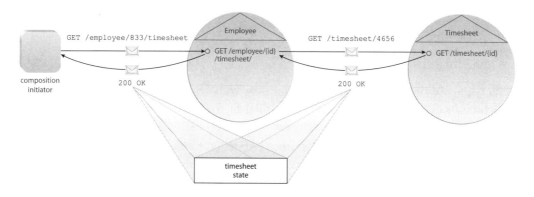

Figure 11.9

The employee resource for employee number 833 encapsulates logic that repeatedly composes not only the same Timesheet service capability, but also the same specific timesheet resource.

SUMMARY OF KEY POINTS

- REST services can be based on common task, entity, and utility service models.

- REST service compositions can establish common task, entity, and utility service layers.

- REST service composition based on common service layers raises distinct design considerations and often results in the formation of hierarchical composition architectures.

11.4 REST Service Composition Design Considerations

Building service compositions with REST introduces a series of distinct issues, challenges, and benefits that need to be understood in order to take advantage of what REST can offer and to avoid problems imposed by its limitations. The upcoming sections address some of the more fundamental areas, with additional issues and considerations covered in Chapter 12.

Synchronous and Asynchronous Service Compositions

Kicking off a service activity requires a software program to act as the composition initiator. This program (whether it is automated or human-driven) provides the input values necessary for a composition instance to be created and processed. With REST-based task services, the service capability being invoked will typically be based on a POST method.

Composition logic may need to be completed synchronously or asynchronously. When a consumer requests a service composition that is guaranteed to be executed synchronously, the interaction is a straightforward HTTP request and response message exchange. The consumer is able to wait for a response message that indicates either the successful completion of a task or an exception.

Asynchronous service activities will usually result in an immediate success response in the form of a 201 Created message, issued by the task service to the composition initiator. This message will include the identifier for a new resource that encapsulates the state of the on-going composition logic until it reaches a terminal state.

Figure 11.10 illustrates both synchronous and asynchronous message exchange scenarios.

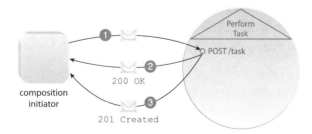

Figure 11.10

A composition initiator may have to deal with different types of responses from a task service. For example, the automation may complete synchronously (2) or may be accepted for asynchronous processing (3) with the task instance URL provided in the Link header.

Within REST service contracts we can model resources that demarcate state within the service. The initial POST request message received from the composition initiator can be seen as transferring the initial resource state to the task service. Similarly, the synchronous success and failure responses can be seen as transferring the final state of the resource back to the composition initiator. In the case of asynchronous interactions, the state is retained with the service between requests, and can be queried with a GET-based service capability or cancelled with a DELETE-based service capability, as shown in the extended contract displayed in Figure 11.11.

Figure 11.11

The Perform Task service from Figure 11.10, with additional service capabilities for state processing.

If the task service uses a `201 Created` response code to indicate asynchronous processing, then the resource identifier for the on-going state of the automation process will be present in the response message returned to the composition initiator. This allows the task service to not express the resource identifier as part of its service contract. Instead, it refers the composition initiator to this resource using a hyperlink.

The task service will need to keep the resource for the on-going composition execution up-to-date until the execution reaches a terminal state. The resource will be maintained as long as it is not deleted by the corresponding capability logic. The additional resources may need to be present within the service contract to facilitate other service capabilities that the composition initiator may need to invoke and that relate directly to the state.

Idempotent Service Activities

If a service capability is considered safe because it is idempotent, the service composition architecture needs to be designed to ensure that any other capabilities invoked as part of the service activity initiated by the idempotent capability are also idempotent.

Specifically, if the request method to a composition controller is a safe GET request or an idempotent PUT or DELETE, the composition controller must not break these guarantees when composing other service capabilities. The composition controller must not issue unsafe requests on behalf of the composition initiator in the case of a GET, and must only issue safe and idempotent requests on behalf of the composition initiator in the case of PUT and DELETE.

There are exceptions to this rule. Other requests are still allowed, under some circumstances, as long as they are not attributable to the composition initiator. For example, if a composition controller issues a POST of new records to a Logging utility service, the recording of the data by the Logging service is in no way attributable to the composition initiator; it is simply the result of internal processing within the composition controller.

> **NOTE**
>
> Because the POST message is not idempotent, a governance standard may need to be established within a service inventory that requires that asynchronous-capable task services use a complex method, similar to the Store method described in Chapter 10. This can ensure that any sort of "Start" capability as part of task services can be reliably executed at most once.

Lingering Composition State

Any composition instance may need to hang around for a period after the task has reached a terminal state. This is to allow the composition initiator to check on the state of the composition at a later time, if necessary.

For example, with some compositions, the final state may need to be archived for an extended period. In other cases, the final state can be purged relatively quickly after completion the composition logic. Services that do need to purge completed composition state will typically do so after a predetermined time, or earlier, if the composition initiator is available to issue a DELETE request once it has retrieved the terminal state.

Sometimes it is preferable to maintain the simple request/response pattern of interaction between the composition initiator and its task service by explicitly introducing an asynchronous message exchange that does not involve a dedicated resource. Under this model, the consumer would provide a "callback" resource identifier for the asynchronous response to be delivered to. This frees up the task service to forget old task instances quickly, in cases where the composition initiator can still be reached by the time the composition logic completes. (However, this can result in additional complexity if the composition initiator cannot be easily reached at that time.)

Binding Between Composition Participants

The binding of composition logic to specific composition member resource identifiers can occur at different times and for different reasons.

For example, the resource identifiers needed by the task service:

- may be known at design time and may be hard-coded into the task service logic.

- may be built up from known resource identifier templates

- may be known at configuration time, and may be incorporated into a configuration file or database

- may be found in response messages from other composition members

- may be passed to a task service capability by the composition initiator

Composition logic can depend directly on uniform contract methods and media types or it can embed part of the service contract into its message processing logic. If the service contract is abstracted so that resource identifier information is omitted, the resource identifiers can be "late bound" by being supplied to the composition logic at runtime.

As explained in the *REST Service Contracts and Late Binding* section from Chapter 6, we are able to reduce the coupling between services and consumers (including services acting as consumers) by reducing the need for logic to be designed to process specific parameters or even specific resource identifiers. By incorporating this aspect of REST service contract design within a service composition architecture, we can further leverage the resultant, inherent flexibility, not just between services, but across some or all composition participants.

However, the delayed knowledge of composition member resource identifiers can come at a price. Here are some common trade-offs:

- When services are designed to receive resource identifiers at runtime, they may leave themselves vulnerable to malicious consumers that intend to supply harmful resource identifier statements. With the same methods and media types being reused by services throughout the service inventory the level of design time checking of these interactions is reduced. Services that rely on late binding may need to be equipped with additional verification logic.

- When using late binding it can become more difficult to invoke some service capabilities. With early binding, any service capability can be invoked as long as the correct parameters are supplied. With late binding, the resource identifier being used is itself a primary parameter. In some cases, it may be necessary to query one or more resources in turn before a service consumer is able to discover the actual resource identifier it needs to invoke a given service capability.

- The requirement to discover a resource identifier before being able to use it can introduce additional runtime processing overhead. This may be especially impactful when having to query a service multiple times before discovering the correct resource identifier (as explained in the previous bullet item).

When resource identifiers are hard-coded within a task service or as part of a configuration file used by the task service, or when they are supplied by the composition initiator, they are less prone to the aforementioned concerns. However, when late binding is used between the composition controller and composition members, or between composition members, these design considerations need to be taken into account.

SUMMARY OF KEY POINTS

- REST-based service compositions can utilize synchronous or asynchronous message exchanges between composition initiator and composition controller.

- Idempotency often needs to be guaranteed across multiple service invocations within a given service activity.

- The advantages and disadvantages of late binding between composition participants need to be understood to design effective REST service composition architectures.

11.5 A Step-by-Step Service Activity

To get a better level of insight into how the participants of a REST service composition can interact, we'll provide a simple scenario that steps through the message exchanges required to automate the Purchase Ticket business process comprised of the following workflow:

1. Request to Purchase a Ticket

2. Verify the Requested Flight Details

3. Confirm a Seat on the Flight

4. Generate an Invoice

5. Create the Ticket

The remaining sections explore the details of the composition logic and resultant service activity carried out to automate this business process.

1. Request to Purchase a Ticket

We begin with the HTTP request message issued by a composition initiator to a Purchase Ticket task service:

```
POST http://purchase-ticket.example.com/purchase
Content-Type: application/vnd.com.example.ticket+xml
Accept: application/vnd.com.example.ticket+xml
<ticket>
 <customer href="http://customer.example.com/customer/88008"/>
 <agent href="http://agent.example.com/agent/internal"/>
 <flight href="http://flight.example.com/flight/XX88"/>
 <type href="http://ticket-type.example.com/type/SuperSaver"/>
</ticket>
```

Upon receiving the request message, the Purchase Ticket task service, acting as the composition controller, uses the supplied resource identifiers to invoke composition member capabilities based on the message content.

2. Verify the Requested Flight Details

The Purchase Ticket task service invokes the Customer service to retrieve data about the customer's default billing address, frequent flier program member identifier, and any other affiliations the customer may have, as well as special terms or restrictions that may exist in relation to the customer. Specifically, the following message exchange occurs.

a. The Purchase Ticket service issues: GET `http://flight.example.com/flight/`
    `XX88`

b. The Flight service responds with: `200 OK`, with the requested `application/`
    `vnd.com.example.flight+xml` content in the response message.

c. The Purchase Ticket service verifies the returned content.

3. Confirm a Seat on the Flight

Next, the Purchase Ticket service invokes the Ticket service to request details of the
ticket type and then proceeds to invoke the Flight service to modify the flight's reservation status.

a. The Purchase Ticket service creates a preliminary ticket resource with the Ticket
    entity service by issuing: POST `http://ticket.example.com/ticket`

b. The Ticket service responds with: `201 Created`, with a location URL of:
    `http://ticket.example.com/ticket/T1233223`

c. The Purchase Ticket service reads the hyperlink within the following Flight ser-
    vice's response message: `<SeatReservation href="http://flights.example.`
    `com/flight/XX88/seats"/>`

d. The Purchase Ticket service sends: POST `http://flight.example.com/`
    `flight/XX88/seats` with the ticket URL `http://ticket.example.com/ticket/`
    `T1233223` in the message body.

e. The Flight service adds the preliminary ticket to the set of existing reservations
    and responds with: `200 OK`

4. Generate an Invoice

The Purchase Ticket service now issues requests to the Customer, Agent, and Ticket
services to determine the invoice total, as well as the billing address and other details
necessary to create an invoice.

a. The Purchase Ticket service combines the aforementioned data into the body of a
    POST request to: `http://invoice.example.com/invoice`

b. The Invoice responds with: `201 Created`, and the location URL is set to:
    `http://invoice.example.com/invoice/INV134444`

5. Create the Ticket

As the ticket entity was already created in step 2, the Purchase Ticket service now sends a confirmation request to the Ticket service. It follows a "confirm" hyperlink and issues the appropriate following confirmation message:

```
PUT http://ticket.example.com/ticket/T1233223/confirmed
```

... with the `text/plain` body containing a value of "1".

Summary

In this example, the resource identifiers used by the task service came from a number of different sources:

- The initial request message included resource identifiers for customer, agent, flight, and ticket type resources.

- The resource identifiers needed to create new ticket and invoice entities were already known to the task service.

- Issuing a POST request to create new ticket and invoice entity resources returned the specific resource identifiers of those entities, as well as the resource identifier needed to confirm the ticket.

Only a portion of the resource identifiers used in the composition logic was known to the Purchase Ticket service prior to being invoked. This highlights the potential reduced coupling between composition controller and composition members in a REST service composition architecture. This reduction in coupling increases the flexibility for the composition to adapt to change with less impact.

> **NOTE**
>
> Chapter 13 is dedicated to providing a detailed case study example that demonstrates service composition scenarios based on services modeled and designed in Chapters 9 and 10.

Chapter 12

Advanced Service Composition
with REST

12.1 Service Compositions and Stateless {395}

12.2 Cross-Service Transactions with REST

12.3 Event-Driven Interactions with REST

12.4 Service Composition with Dynamic Binding and Logic Deferral

12.5 Service Composition Across Service Inventories

PRINCIPLES, PATTERNS, AND CONSTRAINTS REFERENCED IN THIS CHAPTER:

- Atomic Service Transaction [432]

- Canonical Schema [437]

- Code-on-Demand {407}

- Compensating Service Transaction [443]

- Contract Denormalization [448]

- Data Format Transformation [451]

- Data Model Transformation [452]

- Domain Inventory [458]

- Event-Driven Messaging [465]

- Inventory Endpoint [472]

- Logic Centralization [475]

- Protocol Bridging [488]

- Service Composability (422)

- Service Normalization [506]

- Service Statelessness {418}

- Stateful Services [511]

- Stateless {395}

- State Messaging [509]

- State Repository [510]

- Three-Layer Inventory [513]

The basis of service-orientation is to shape software programs into repeatedly composable IT assets with the full expectation that these services can be combined into a variety of composition architectures that can vary in size, depth, and complexity. REST does not directly address service composition beyond establishing client-server interactions that involve middleware tiers. When we explore the application of REST for the creation of multi-level, hierarchical service compositions, we need to understand how and where REST constraints and features can benefit and limit our design options. We further need to understand the pros and cons of selectively breaching REST constraints as a means of potentially overcoming some forms of limitations. With this understanding we can make educated decisions to leverage the parts of service-orientation and REST we need to best fulfill distinct business automation requirements.

This chapter reveals the tension between REST and common forms of non-REST-like runtime service activities and message interactions. With an emphasis on the Stateless {395} constraint, we take a look at different (REST-compliant and non-REST-compliant) approaches to cross-service transactions and event-driven message exchanges. We then move on to explore the use of hypermedia within multi-layer compositions to highlight areas in which dynamic binding can be utilized. The chapter concludes with some coverage of how REST can be used for cross-service inventory communication.

NOTE

This chapter does not contain a *Case Study Example* section. The case study content for Chapters 11 and 12 is provided separately in a detailed example that comprises Chapter 13.

Also note that several of the state-related terms used in this chapter are explained in Appendix F.

12.1 Service Compositions and Stateless {395}

The Stateless {395} constraint is generally viewed as an inhibitor to the application of Service Composability (422) because it prevents types of interactions between services that are common in distributed enterprise solution designs. Stateless {395} introduces these limitations to prevent service state from being locked for extended periods in order to avoid negatively impacting scalability and availability, as well as to avoid exceeding memory limitations.

Of the solution requirements impacted by this constraint, cross-service transactions are generally the hardest hit. In the upcoming sections we will briefly revisit state management in relation to Stateless {395} and Service Statelessness (418), after which (in the *Cross-Service Transactions with REST* section) we explain how transaction functionality compliant with Stateless {395} can be achieved and how REST-based (but not REST-compliant) transaction features can also be designed. The *Event-Driven Interactions with REST* section then further documents issues and limitations pertaining to Stateless {395} in relation to event-driven message exchange.

Composition Design with Service Statelessness (418)

A business process requires that a number of steps be completed before it reaches its final state. Let's briefly revisit the Purchase Ticket process from Chapter 11. The composition logic may dictate that available flights be queried, that a seat on a flight be put on hold, and that payment be provided to complete the purchase. While the task service is performing these functions, it must hold the state of the Purchase Ticket service activity in memory. When the service activity is idle for an extended period, it is not generally considered desirable to keep this state data in memory. Doing so limits the scalability of the services that comprise the solution that is based on the service composition automating the business process. The extent of the impact is proportional to the quantity of the state data and the duration it needs to be retained.

A composition's runtime service activity may need to be idle for any number of reasons, including:

- waiting on human user input
- waiting for a response message from another composition member
- waiting for a mandatory cooling off period to expire (such as when, after the purchase is completed, the human user is allowed to still roll back the transaction for a limited time)

Service Statelessness (418) advocates the deferral of state data using a state delegation mechanism to minimize the amount of state data that needs to be kept in memory during idle periods, a consideration particularly of relevance to the design of task services.

The following SOA design patterns support this principle via common forms of state delegation mechanisms:

- State Repository [510]

- Stateful Services [511]

- State Messaging [509]

As explained in Appendix F, there are different measures of statelessness that can be achieved within the logic encompassed by service capabilities. While Service Statelessness (418) advocates runtime state deferral, it does not mandate it, nor does it mandate the extent to which it should be implemented as part of a service composition architecture.

Composition Design with Stateless {395}

The REST view of state management does not focus on the composition of long-running automation logic; instead, it is concerned with single interactions between individual consumers and services. Stateless {395} is based on the premise that all messages are self-contained artifacts within a technology architecture. In other words, the state of the interaction is deferred away from the service layer to the message layer. The SOA design pattern most comparable to this type of messaging architecture is State Messaging [509].

Violations of this constraint imply that we are establishing a stateful session between a service and a consumer. Compliance with this constraint still allows services to store business state data, just not session state. A service must be designed to forget session state after issuing a response message back to a consumer. This is a firm requirement for the service composition architecture to be considered REST-compliant.

SUMMARY OF KEY POINTS

- Both service-orientation and REST promote the reduction of in-memory state data in support of increasing solution scalability.

- Service Statelessness (418) advocates runtime state deferral via a range of mechanisms and patterns.

- Stateless {395} requires the runtime deferral of session state via self-contained messages.

12.2 Cross-Service Transactions with REST

As soon as we introduce the concept of a Three-Layer Inventory [513] it is clear that many of our task services will need to compose multiple entity services in a typical complex service composition architecture. Many task services will need some form of transactional functionality to ensure that the state of entities in different entity services is able to remain consistent. This is a tricky objective when it comes to applying State-less {395}.

Depending on the interpretation of Stateless {395}, many types of established cross-service transaction architectures are considered prohibited. In addition to protecting the scalability of services, REST suggests that violations of this constraint can result in applications becoming unreliable when there are many cross-service transactions occurring at the same time.

Transaction-related problems can include:

- resource locks become exhausted or significantly limit concurrent access to a resource

- transactions time out, requiring that they be re-invoked

- the behavior of complex transactions can be unpredictable and may require consumers to wait an inordinately long time for completion

In on-premise environments these types of problems are typically solvable by upgrading the enterprise infrastructure and optimizing application designs. In cloud-based environments, these concerns can be even more effectively addressed by leasing on-demand cloud-based resources, as required.

This leads to the pivotal question:

Should we be trying to eliminate cross-service transactions or should we be trying to solve the problems that cross-service transactions can potentially introduce?

The answer, within the context of REST, lies in the distinct business requirements and goals behind the solutions, service inventories, and the IT enterprise itself. To help address this, the upcoming sections cover REST-friendly and not-so-REST-friendly alternatives to transactions using REST features.

REST-Friendly Atomic Service Transactions

By remaining compliant with Stateless {395}, we can develop a service composition architecture able to provide limited two phase commit capabilities for the creation of new resource state.

The basis of this model is as follows:

1. A service consumer makes a request to the service to create a new resource.

2. The service accepts the request and creates the resource, but leaves it in an inactive state.

3. The service provides instructions as to how to activate the new resource.

4. When the consumer has confirmed it is able to create as many new resources as required, it transitions each to an active state.

If a resource is never activated, it is timed out and destroyed autonomously by the service. Likewise, the consumer can cancel the resource creation explicitly if required. We'll call this transaction model *Store and Confirm*. It is usually necessary for this type of architecture to include a transaction coordinator service whose purpose is to ensure the consistent completion, timeout, or rollback of the transaction. However, this approach does not require initializing any transactional context as participating services remain unaware of the transaction.

It makes use of a simple protocol, structured in three phases:

- Phase 1: Initialization

- Phase 2: Reservation

- Phase 3: any one of Confirmation, Cancellation, or Timeout

Let's look at each phase, as well as each possible outcome for phase 3.

Phase 1: Initialize

The composition logic registers the Store and Confirm Transaction with a transaction coordinator service.

For example, the consumer sends the transaction coordinator:

```
POST http://xact-coordinator.example.com/store-and-confirm
```

...and the transaction coordinator returns back to the consumer:

```
201 Created
Location: http://xact-coordinator.example.com/store-and-confirm/110
```

The link to the transaction resource will be later used to keep track of which resources are involved in the transaction, and to collect the necessary information to perform the third phase.

Phase 2: Reserve

The composition logic executed by the composition controller interacts with the composition member resources. The new required entities are created but left in an intermediate, temporary state. This intermediate state is associated with a confirmation resource identifier generated by the composition member and forwarded by the composition controller to the transaction coordinator resource.

For example, the consumer sends to the service:

```
POST http://bookings.example.com/booking
```

The service replies with a link to the confirmation resource identifier, which can be included as metadata or extracted from the response payload:

```
201 Created
Location: http://bookings.example.com/booking/BRF134422
Link: http://bookings.example.com/
  booking/BRF134422/confirmed; rel="store-and-confirm"
```

The consumer then forwards the confirmation resource identifier to the transaction coordinator and associates it with the pending transaction:

```
POST http://xact-coordinator.example.com/store-and-confirm/110
Content-Type: text/uri-list
http://bookings.example.com/booking/BRF134422/confirmed
```

The transaction coordinator returns to the service:

```
200 OK
```

The booking will have been created, but it will be inactive at the end of the Reserve phase. The composition member service will await a confirmation or cancellation. The consumer proceeds to create other resources and keeps collecting the corresponding confirmation resource identifiers. They may forward them to the transaction coordinator as they are collected, or all together before entering the Confirm phase.

Phase 3A: Confirm

Once all required resources have been created in an inactive state, the set of confirmation resource identifiers gathered by the composition controller is sent to the transaction coordinator. The coordinator applies an idempotent PUT request on each confirmation resource identifier, thereby informing the composition members that the resource can now become active.

For example, the composition controller sends to the transaction coordinator:

```
PUT http://xact-coordinator.example.com/store-and-confirm/110
Content-Type: text/plain
Confirmed
```

…and the transaction coordinator invokes the resource confirmation identifiers of each participant service:

```
PUT http://bookings.example.com/booking/BRF134422/confirmed
Content-Type: text/plain
Confirmed
```

The service then replies to the transaction coordinator:

```
200 OK
```

…and, after collecting positive replies from all participants, the transaction coordinator correspondingly replies to the composition controller:

```
200 OK
```

Once all participants complete the confirmation step, the transaction coordinator informs the composition controller that the transaction has reached a consistent, confirmed state. Note that services are not permitted to reject this confirmation request. If they do, there will be no way to roll back other composition members who have already accepted the confirmation.

Phase 3B: Cancel

If it was not possible for all of the composition members to create the required resources, or if the consumer determined that it no longer wants to complete the transaction, then the transaction can be explicitly cancelled by transitioning the inactive resources to a cancelled state.

For example, the consumer sends to the transaction coordinator:

```
PUT http://xact-coordinator.example.com/store-and-confirm/110
Content-Type: text/plain
Cancelled
```

The transaction coordinator sends to the service:

```
PUT http://bookings.example.com/booking/BRF134422/confirmed
Content-Type: text/plain
Cancelled
```

The service then replies to the transaction coordinator:

```
200 OK
```

...and the transaction coordinator sends back to the consumer:

```
200 OK
```

Phase 3C: Timeout

The transaction coordinator may trigger a timeout to destroy the inactive resources if it determines that the composition controller has failed to complete the transaction. This condition could result in a long transaction being unable to complete, so timeout values should be chosen carefully. Likewise, individual participating services may unilaterally decide to destroy inactive resources if they do not receive a confirmation or cancellation request within a certain period of time.

An example of this protocol would be to extend the preceding booking scenario to also incorporate payment processing. In this case, the consumer's goal would be to create an invoice (using an Invoice service) at the same time as it creates the booking record. (The translation of this invoice into an actual payment is not covered by the following example.)

1. The consumer initializes the transaction with a POST request to the transaction coordinator.

2. The consumer sends a POST request to the bookings resource, which returns the booking resource identifier and the corresponding confirmed resource identifier.

3. The consumer sends a POST request to the invoices resource, returns the invoice resource identifier and the corresponding confirmed resource identifier.

4. The consumer forwards the confirmed resource identifiers to the transaction coordinator, together with the corresponding payloads.

5. The consumer either requests the transaction coordinator confirm or cancel the transaction.

6. The transaction coordinator carries out the confirmation or cancellation request.

This procedure ensures that the invoice is only created and confirmed if the booking is created and confirmed, and vice versa.

Compliance with Stateless {395}

So, is this truly a stateless transaction? The service is creating a new resource. This is a resource it would have created anyway if the request had been for an ordinary POST, so nothing extra is being done or allocated by making the initial state of the new resource inactive. Likewise, activating the resource is a stateless action because the consumer is simply changing the state of a resource that exists by following the hyperlink to the confirmed resource identifier. The combination of these stateless steps means that the overall interaction can also be considered stateless.

However, it is important to note that with this approach we still risk a level of statefulness if in creating the inactive resource it locked out some other operations, or if the inactive resource is deleted due to a timeout during the *Confirm* phase. Even in the preceding example, where an inactive booking reserves seats such that those seats are not available to other consumers, we arguably cross the border from stateless to stateful. In order to guarantee that the commit will be successful, the service may need to reserve other resources than simple storage capacity within its database. If so, the inactive resource may still prevent other transactions from completing until it is either activated or cancelled.

Any implicit locking associated with the inactive resource will result in lock contention between requests, and can potentially be considered a stateful use. If this approach is used to model a full two-phase commit, where the new resource is really a transaction that, when committed (or rolled back), ceases to exist, then this is state the service would not otherwise have allocated. This should then be considered session state because it is specific to a particular consumer. This is also true of any application of this model to modify state rather than create new state, because it is likely then being used to create an additional copy of the state for each participating consumer.

Additional Considerations

Note also, that because HTTP has no inherent must-understand semantics for headers, it may be necessary to define a special POST method with a prefix that indicates the consumer requires Store and Confirm functionality (such as SC-POST, for example), and therefore expects the response to include a hyperlink to the confirmed resource identifier. In general it's important to have a strategy for ensuring both the consumer and the service know that a Store and Confirm is being requested.

NOTE

The Store and Confirm transaction approach we just described is based on the Try-Cancel/Confirm pattern developed by Dr. Guy Pardon Atomikos.

REST-Friendly Compensating Service Transactions

The lock contention and state memory consumption demands of two-phase commit transactions can be too burdensome for an IT infrastructure when having to support long-running transactions. The standard pattern for addressing this is Compensating Service Transaction [443], whereby we sacrifice the atomicity of Atomic Service Transaction [432] by replacing the pessimistic PREPARE and COMMIT operations with an optimistic "do" action and an optional "undo" action. Because of their reduced level of locking between requests, compensating transactions have a natural alignment with Stateless {395}.

As with Store and Confirm, compensating transactions benefit from having a transaction coordinator in place.

The common phases are:

* Phase 1: Begin
* Phase 2: Do
* Phase 3: any one of Complete, Undo, Timeout

The following sections describe each phase.

Phase 1: Begin

This phase establishes a link with a transaction coordinator, which will collect information about the operations so that they can be consistently confirmed or undone. The transaction coordinator is needed to avoid a partly-committed, inconsistent transaction if the consumer were to fail partway through its execution.

For example, to initialize a new cross-service transaction, the consumer sends to the transaction coordinator:

```
POST http://xact-coordinator.example.com/compensating
```

The transaction coordinator then replies back to the consumer with a hyperlink to a transaction resource:

```
201 Created
Location: http://xact-coordinator.example.com/compensating/1004
```

Phase 2: Do

The consumer invokes the required service capability but (as opposed to the previously described Store-and-Confirm approach), it includes the transaction identifier in the request message. The service then processes the request as it would normally and generates resource identifiers pointing to the corresponding undo logic and optional confirm logic. It records this logic with the transaction coordinator by registering it together with the resource identifiers.

For example, the consumer sends to the service:

```
PUT http://invoice.example.com/invoice/INV024/paid
Link: <http://xact-coordinator.example.com/compensating/1004>;
rel="compensating-transaction"
Content-Type: text/plain
1
```

The service forwards to the transaction coordinator the undo or confirm links as metadata:

```
POST http://xact-coordinator.example.com/compensating/1004
Link: <http://invoice.example.com/set?resource=/invoice/INV024/
paid&value=0>, rel="undo"
```

The link will be followed by the transaction coordinator to undo the previous action and reset the state of the invoice resource to the initial unpaid state.

The transaction coordinator then issues to the service:

```
200 OK
```

...and the service responds to the consumer:

```
200 OK
```

Phase 3A: Complete

To conclude the transaction, the consumer sends to the transaction coordinator:

```
PUT http://xact-coordinator.example.com/compensating/1004
Content-Type: text/plain
Confirmed
```

Since there is no confirm link or action registered with the transaction coordinator, nothing else happens and the transaction coordinator returns to the consumer:

```
200 OK
```

Phase 3B: Undo

If something goes wrong, the consumer may wish to cancel the transaction. To do so, the consumer sends to the transaction coordinator:

```
PUT http://xact-coordinator.example.com/compensating/1004
Content-Type: text/plain
Cancelled
```

The transaction coordinator then executes the undo logic registered by the service:

```
PUT http://invoice.example.com/invoice/INV024/paid
Content-Type: text/plain
0
```

The service subsequently returns to the transaction coordinator:

```
200 OK
```

...and the transaction coordinator then responds to the consumer:

```
200 OK
```

Note that an alternative means of performing the Undo Action step is to carry it out within the composition logic itself. The consumer can be built to already know that a PUT of the old state back to the resource will reverse the transaction and to register this logic on the service's behalf. This approach allows a service that does not support registering its compensation logic natively to still be involved in a compensating transaction.

Whether the undo logic is registered by the service or defined within the service consumer it must not fail. If the logic was to raise an exception, the transaction would be left in an inconsistent state.

Phase 3C: Timeout

If the transaction coordinator does not receive a Confirm or Undo command within a reasonable period of time, it will execute the undo logic that was deferred to it and further reject any other interactions with the transaction. This returns the services to their original state.

The following sample steps update a General Ledger service at the same time as the Invoice service is updated. Here, the consumer's goal is to mark the invoice as "paid" and enter a transaction into the general ledger.

1. The consumer initiates the transaction.

2. The consumer sends a POST to the General Ledger service to create a new journal entry. The General Ledger service registers the undo resource identifier with the transaction coordinator to undo the creation of the journal entry.

3. The consumer sends a PUT request to the invoice's paid resource. The Invoice service registers the undo resource identifier with the transaction coordinator that will set the invoice back to a status of "unpaid."

4. The consumer then either requests that the transaction coordinator confirm or undo the transaction.

5. The Transaction coordinator executes the confirmation or undo action by invoking the corresponding confirm or undo logic, and then deleting the transaction.

These steps ensure that the invoice is only set to "paid" if the general ledger can be updated, and that the general ledger journal entry is voided if the invoice cannot be set to "paid." There might be a period where only one of the two changes is made, and participating services will return to a consistent state when the transaction is confirmed, undone, or times out.

Compliance with Stateless {395}

Compensating service transactions make use of undo operations either implemented by the service logic or by the composition logic. In our preceding example we made the service responsible for telling its consumer how to undo the action that was just requested. The composition logic can make requests to several services, and if it hits an exceptional condition, it can undo each of its previous requests.

Can we consider this a truly stateless transaction? In the preceding scenario, the Invoice and General Ledger services operated statelessly. The transaction coordinator was arguably pushing the boundaries of statelessness by having so much temporary transaction state deferred to it. That deferred undo logic could possibly be considered session state held by the transaction coordinator on behalf of the consumer session.

The undo logic is not allowed to fail in this type of transaction, or otherwise the transaction can fall into an inconsistent state. Guaranteeing that the undo option is available can require the transaction to consume resources within the service, such as needing to lock a resource to prevent further changes. This would have negative properties consistent with breaching the Stateless {395} constraint.

Additional Considerations

In some cases it may be appropriate for the composition controller to define the undo logic and defer it to the transaction coordinator rather than requiring that each service individually defer the logic. This can be particularly appropriate if undo steps require coordination between composition members consisting of an ordered sequence of undo steps.

As with the Store and Commit approach, it may be necessary to have a signaling mechanism between the service and consumer to ensure that both sides are aware that a compensating transaction is required and implemented. An entity service that fails to provide an undo link will break the transaction consistency model. For this reason it may be necessary to use special primitive method names that are only understood by services that support the transaction or to enforce a inventory-wide policy that the transaction always be supported. A supporting design standard could be to prefix all methods involved in the transaction with "CT-", such as: CT-POST, CT-PUT, and CT-DELETE.

Non-REST-Friendly Atomic Service Transactions

The variation of Atomic Service Transaction [432] we covered under the heading of Store and Confirm provides an atomic-style, Stateless {395} compliant (or near compliant) transaction model. However, it does introduce some limitations. When designing service composition architectures that use or are based on REST features, we have the option of intentionally breaching the Stateless {395} constraint to emulate a "real" atomic transaction.

The following example steps us through such a system. As with the preceding models, a reliable transaction coordinator is needed to ensure consistency. In addition, participating services themselves are required to hold transactions open for the duration of the composition.

The phases are:

- Phase 1: Initialize

- Phase 2: Do

- Phase 3: Prepare

- Phase 4: any one of Commit, Rollback, or Timeout

Let's step through a sample scenario that spans these phases individually.

Phase 1: Initialize

The service consumer initializes the transaction by creating a new transaction resource with the transaction coordinator.

For example, the consumer sends to the transaction coordinator:

```
POST http://xact-coordinator.example.com/atomic
```

...and the transaction coordinator returns back to the consumer:

```
201 Created
Location: http://xact-coordinator.example.com/atomic/1044
```

Phase 2: Do

The consumer sends a series of requests to the services it wishes to interact with. In each request it identifies the transaction that it wants the service to participate in. Each service begins a new local transaction with its database if it does not recognize the transaction identifier. Otherwise, the services reuse the existing local transaction within their databases. This ensures that both read and write actions occur within the context of the correct transaction, and that service state that has been accessed as part of the transaction is locked and will not be modified in conflicting ways by other consumers.

For example, the consumer sends to the service:

```
POST http://maintenance.example.com/aircraft/ACC223/log
Link: <http://xact-coordinator.example.com/atomic/1044>;
rel="atomic-transaction"
Content-Type: application/maintenance-log+xml
```

The service then sends to the transaction coordinator:

```
POST http://xact-coordinator.example.com/atomic/1044
Content-Type: text/uri-list
http://maintenance.example.com/xact/XACT987
```

The transaction coordinator returns to the service:

```
200 OK
```

...and the service responds back to the consumer with:

```
200 OK
```

In this example, the Maintenance service now has a transaction open that is associated with the transaction coordinator's transaction identifier. The underlying database transaction has further been given its own resource identifier that has been registered with the transaction coordinator.

Additional requests that relate to the same transaction resource will need to occur within the same database transaction, but they will not require additional interactions with the transaction coordinator. If the service has several redundant instances it may be necessary for these later requests to be directed back to the service instance that handled the first such request.

Phase 3: Prepare

The coordinator sends a request to each registered participant to prepare to commit. All participants should declare whether they are ready and willing to commit. If at least one participant responds negatively, then we proceed to the Rollback phase. If at least one participant fails to respond within a given time, then we move on to the Timeout phase. If all participants agree to commit, then the transaction continues with the Commit phase.

Phase 4A: Commit

The consumer sends to the transaction coordinator:

```
PUT http://xact-coordinator.example.com/atomic/1044
Content-Type: text/plain
Committed
```

The transaction coordinator issues to the service:

```
PUT http://maintenance.example.com/xact/XACT987
Content-Type: text/plain
Committed
```

The service then responds to the transaction coordinator with:

```
200 OK
```

…and the transaction coordinator finally replies to the consumer:

```
200 OK
```

Phase 4B: Rollback

The consumer sends to the transaction coordinator:

```
PUT http://xact-coordinator.example.com/atomic/1044
Content-Type: text/plain
Cancelled
```

The transaction coordinator forward to the service:

```
PUT http://maintenance.example.com/xact/XACT987
Content-Type: text/plain
Cancelled
```

The service replies to the transaction coordinator:

```
200 OK
```

The transaction coordinator finally responds back to the consumer with:

```
200 OK
```

Phase 4C: Timeout

If the consumer fails to complete the transaction, the transaction coordinator will automatically initiate a rollback of all service transactions to their pre-transaction state.

One possible scenario for this is if the update of an Aircraft Maintenance Log service happens at the same time as the update an Aircraft Maintenance Job service. In this situation, the consumer's goal is to add an entry to the log stating that a job is required, and to register the job as needing to be done.

1. The consumer creates the transaction via the transaction coordinator.

2. The consumer sends a POST request to the Aircraft Maintenance Log service, which begins a transaction and modifies its state within the transaction but does not commit that transaction. It stores a resource identifier for the transaction with the transaction coordinator.

3. The consumer sends a POST request to the Aircraft Maintenance Job service, which begins a transaction and modifies its state within the transaction. It also does not commit that transaction and proceeds to store a resource identifier for the transaction with the transaction coordinator.

4. The consumer requests the transaction coordinator service either commit or rollback the set of transactions.

5. The transaction coordinator issues a PUT request to both services, thus committing or rolling back the underlying database transactions.

Compliance with Stateless {395}

Although clearly not a stateless option because all participant services must explicitly lock access to their resources, this transaction model remains in compliance with other REST constraints. By intentionally violating the Stateless {395} constraint this type of transaction is most compliant with established ACID properties, although the described architecture is still based on a "race condition," where one service may commit slightly ahead of the other.

In the preceding example, participating services keep the transaction open between requests and require a series of requests to be issued to the same instance of a redundant service. The negative impacts of this can include increased lock contention, reduced performance, and increased resource utilization. These impacts can be offset by the benefits of near-ACID transaction semantics and a highly reliable, yet still comparatively simple transaction architecture.

Additional Considerations

In a multi-layer composition it is important that composition members apply the Atomic Service Transaction [432] pattern with members of their own composition. They can do this by using the same transaction identifier with their composition members that was used by their own composition controller.

As with the Store and Commit model, it may be necessary to have a signaling mechanism between the service and consumer to ensure that both sides are aware that an atomic transaction is required and implemented. An entity service that ignores the `atomic-transaction` Link header would automatically break the transaction consistency model.

For this reason, it may be necessary to use the same type of primitive method naming convention described in the *REST-Friendly Compensating Service Transactions* section.

SUMMARY OF KEY POINTS

- It is possible to architect a service composition that incorporates atomic service transactions in a REST-friendly manner through a Store and Confirm model.

- Similarly, REST-friendly compensating service transactions can be created via message interactions that issue Do and Undo commands.

- A REST-based atomic service transaction architecture can be created, leveraging REST features while intentionally breaching Stateless {395}.

12.3 Event-Driven Interactions with REST

A common form of asynchronous service composition is based on the event-driven architecture (EDA) and publish-and-subscribe models, whereby a service consumer can subscribe to events that occur within or in relation to a service. The upcoming sections explore how and where these types of messaging requirements can incorporate REST-based services.

Event-Driven Messaging [465]

Event-driven architectures typically rely on the use of a dedicated Event Manager service to facilitate notifications between services (that publish events available for subscription) and consumers (that act as the subscribers). Consumers use the Event Manager to register their interest in particular event types and services use the Event Manager to issue their event notifications (Figure 12.1).

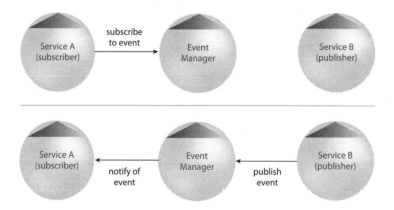

Figure 12.1
A service subscribes to an event via the Event Manager. When the event occurs later, the publisher service sends notifications to the Event Manager that forwards notifications to subscribed consumers.

Event-Driven Messaging [465] can be applied using REST features in a number of ways. For example, we could add a NOTIFY method to the uniform contract in order to inform both the Event Manager and subscribed consumers that a notification has occurred. A SUBSCRIBE method could also be created, or a POST request could be issued to the Event Manager resource to create a new subscription resource to register subscribers. A DELETE request to the subscription resource could correspondingly cancel the subscriber's interest. An example of this mapping into the Event Manager service contract can be seen in Figure 12.2.

An advantage to this approach is that it can establish some level of security control. For example, subscription requests can include a resource identifier that the Event Manager may be designed to automatically send notification messages to. If the method used to notify subscribers of new events was a POST or a PUT, a malicious subscriber could substitute its own notification capability with another service's vulnerable service capability and the Event Manager would blindly invoke that method. The use of the NOTIFY method for notification messages can prevent the Event Manager from accidentally triggering an unsafe service capability in this type of situation. We can define NOTIFY as being a safe method with no negative side-effects attributable to the caller.

Figure 12.2

A sample service contract for an Event Manager service.

This straightforward mapping approach does introduce some disadvantages. It may prevent media type negotiation from being supported, and tends to bypass the conventional service caching infrastructure by creating two lines of traffic for data exchange. The first is the usual GET requests that pass through the caching infrastructure and the second is the stream of notifications sent back to service consumers via the Event Manager.

The standard GET request in a typical uniform contract includes the ability to select between alternative media types for the response message. Therefore, without including GET into the mechanism, it becomes necessary for SUBSCRIBE to start to support this and other useful features of the GET method. In practice, in may be impossible to provide equivalent functionality to that of the primitive GET method.

To counter these problems it is possible to bring GET requests back into the message exchange pattern by ensuring that notification messages are as minimal as possible. If notification messages, as a rule, can be limited to identifying which resources have changed in which services, then consumers are able to complete the data transfer by communicating directly with those services.

Compliance with Stateless {395}

The challenge to remain stateless when applying Event-Driven Messaging [465] with REST is focused primarily on the state of subscriptions that are currently active, alongside the state of any active notifications associated with a particular event. An active

TCP connection or message queue related to a particular consumer can be seen as session state, which is what Stateless {395} disallows.

The aforementioned structure involving uniform contract methods already addresses this to an extent. By employing an explicit Event Manager service the publisher service can be kept relatively free of state. It does not need to deal directly with a large number of concurrent consumers. Instead, it delegates subscription responsibility to the Event Manager. The remaining state that is left with the publisher service is the state of any notifications currently being transferred to the Event Manager.

Within the Event Manager the active subscriptions walk a fine line between being counted as service state or session state. These subscriptions are intrinsic to the functional context of the Event Manager, so storing them between requests does not seem to pose a problem as long as a resource identifier is returned to consumers. This enables the subscribed consumers to continue to interact with and update the subscription.

However, the subscription is inherently tied to the notification resource identifier supplied by the subscriber as part of the subscription request. This resource identifier is further coupled to a particular consumer. With this identifier embedded within the subscription record, it is hard to argue that this is session state that has no dependency on any specific service consumer.

As we previously hinted, notifications can be pared back to only identifying which resources have changed in particular services. Taking this pared back approach to notifications has an additional advantage beyond ensuring that most data travels as part of GET requests. The benefit is that notifications can be idempotent. More specifically, a single notification to a consumer that a particular resource has changed is equivalent to two notifications that the resource has changed. If it has changed once, it has changed. If it has changed twice in the time it took to notify the consumer, then it has changed. Once, twice, or a hundred times the message to the consumer is the same: the resource has changed. This means that for a single subscription to a single resource the amount of storage space the Event Manager needs to allocate for notifications is constant. Multiple notifications can be folded into each other to become a single notification to the consumer. This approach significantly reduces the extent to which the Event Manager needs to remain stateful.

Message Polling

An alternative to Event-Driven Messaging [465] is message polling, the repeated use of a GET request to a resource by the subscriber. A regular message polling architecture can undesirably increase the latency of the consumer learning about an event by forcing the consumer to wait until the end of its next poll period before it issues the next request message and learns about a potential change. To combat the high latency problem the consumer may need to shorten its poll cycle and issue GET requests at a higher rate. In doing this the consumer issues more requests that consequently use up more network bandwidth and consume more of the publishing service's processing time.

The use of ETags is probably the most significant mitigation to polling because it can help bypass both processing and network bandwidth demands in exactly the case where Event-Driven Messaging [465] is most effective, namely where latency tolerances are tight but the actual rate of change for resources is low. Although a message still needs to be sent to the server to check whether the cached value is correct, it can be confirmed as correct while keeping the messaging overhead and the processing overhead low (Figure 12.3).

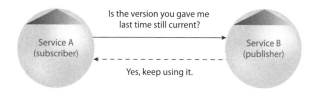

Figure 12.3
A sample interaction based on caching with ETags.

For example, the consumer sends to the service:

```
GET http://stock.example.com/stock/ABC/price
If-None-Match: "12345"
```

...and the service responds back to the consumer:

```
304 Not Modified
ETag: "12345"
```

When we are dealing with this polling scenario, the objective is sometimes not really to process a sequence of messages, but instead is to allow a composition controller to synchronize part of the state of a composition member. This way it can react to changes in the state. An approach that can be taken to minimize the impacts of staying synchronized with a large resource that changes relatively frequently is to use the Delta complex method described in Chapter 10. With this approach, we are not returning the whole resource state; just information about what has changed (Figure 12.4).

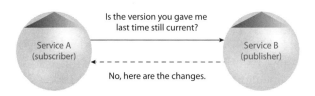

Figure 12.4

A sample interaction based on delta encoding.

For example, let's say that at 11:35 AM, the consumer sends to the service:

```
GET http://stock.example.com/stock/prices
```

The service responds with:

```
200 OK
Link: <http://stock.example.com/stock/prices?changed-since=11:35>;
rel="Delta"
Content-Type: ...
```

Then, at 11:38 AM, the consumer follows up with:

```
GET http://stock.example.com/stock/prices?changed-since=11:35
```

...and the service responds:

```
200 OK
Link: <http://stock.example.com/stock/prices?changed-since=11:38>;
rel="Next"
Content-Type: ...
```

A service can advertise its support for delta encoding by providing "Delta" hyperlinks from its resources. The next time the consumer wants to be updated with data (either due to a poll timeout or other trigger), it issues a request to the Delta resource instead of to the main resource it queried first. The service will respond with the set of changes, plus a new hyperlink to the next delta.

If no changes have occurred since the delta, then the service can respond with `204 No Content` to ensure that the consumer will keep using this delta resource until changes do occur. If the consumer ever finds itself out of sync with the queue of changes to such an extent that the service has destroyed the oldest changes, then the service will respond with `410 Gone`. In such a case, the consumer can always retrieve the main resource over again to get back in sync.

Having both the main resource and delta resources available means that many consumer failure modes can be overcome. A consumer that restarts or loses parts of its data then needs to issue a new request to the main resource to become correctly synchronized again with the resource state.

Compliance with Stateless {395}

Message polling can be considered a more REST-friendly means of enabling event-driven interactions when compared to Event-Driven Messaging [465]. Rather than employing an Event Manager service to keep a message queue for each consumer of the service, a polling solution does not require such queues. The service only has to deal with and allocate memory for each request as it receives it. When a request arrives, the service deals with that request, returns a response, and forgets about that consumer. This is in full compliance with Stateless {395} and only requires that the service allocate enough memory to process the current concurrent set of requests.

At some point, as the required latency for consumers to be notified about changes is reduced, the polling solution can become less feasible. If actual changes occur at a low rate and consumers need to know about these changes at a fast rate, then Event-Driven Messaging [465] offers significantly better performance. If the rate increases to such a degree that the service is effectively handling a concurrent request for each consumer all of the time, then Event-Driven Messaging [465] has clear scalability advantages. For this reason, some service inventories with low realtime tolerance requirements will need to apply Event-Driven Messaging [465], even if its implementation breaches Stateless {395}.

REST can mitigate scalability concerns introduced by polling in a number of ways, one of which is to simply not poll. If the consumer does not need to see events occur and just requires a check of the resource state, polling may not be necessary. Additionally, a cache can be used to respond on behalf of a service if it has a cached value that is known to be correct for a given period of time. Within that time any polls can be dealt with at reduced network bandwidth and processing cost. As previously demonstrated, more dynamic resources can use ETag headers in requests and responses to short-circuit service processing and message transfers if the data behind a cached response has not changed.

SUMMARY OF KEY POINTS

- Due to the subscription-related session state management requirements, it is challenging to apply Event-Driven Messaging [465] in a REST-friendly manner.

- Message polling provides an alternative means of achieving event-driven message behavior in closer compliance to Stateless {395}.

12.4 Service Composition with Dynamic Binding and Logic Deferral

In a normalized service inventory every service has its functional scope and every service capability a service it belongs to. For entity services this means that logic associated with a set of related entities can be grouped into one coarse-grained service or partitioned across more fine-grained services.

With hypermedia, we have a resource-centric means of navigating from one entity to its related entities, regardless of which service or services the entities are encapsulated within. This can blur the boundaries between services and service contracts when it comes to how we can design core service logic in relation to the processing of intra-service or cross-service resources.

Hyperlinks exchanged via hypermedia include the full identifier of the service that contains the entity-based resource. Using the parameter-based notation established in Chapter 6 and further discussed in Chapter 11, service contracts can be designed to accept entire resource identifiers as parameters. This service contract design option, together with the hypermedia feature-set, allows us to explore dynamic binding via various types of composition logic that leverage late binding.

This section also explores the application of Code-on-Demand {407} in relation to the dynamic runtime deferral of service logic.

Denormalized Capabilities Across Normalized Services

Applying Service Normalization [506] to avoid functional overlap is not always straight-forward when it comes to entity services. In Chapter 9 we learned how to model entity service candidates with functional boundaries representing respective entity-related processing. The expected result is a set of complementary entity services that can be composed together to perform processing in relation to their respective entity or entities.

So, where's the problem? Let's take, for example, an Employee service and a Timesheet service. Either service could provide capabilities for the retrieval of timesheet data associated with employees or vice versa (Figure 12.5). This type of commonality across services is not explicitly against any service-orientation principles or REST constraints. In fact, the Contract Denormalization [448] pattern advocates a given service contract offering redundant service capability functionality via different levels of capability granularity.

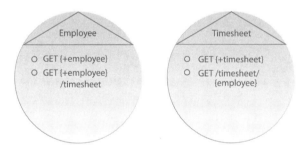

Figure 12.5
The Employee and Timesheet services, each with comparable service capabilities.

The reason this does not run contrary to Service Normalization [506] is because the logic being processed remains physically partitioned and requires composition. When we invoke the Employee service capability to retrieve employee timesheet data, the Employee service proceeds to compose the Timesheet service for the retrieval of this data (and, again, vice versa).

What's important about understanding how this relates specifically to REST service contract design is that with the use of parameter-based notation, comparable service capabilities are even more likely to surface throughout a service inventory. This is because, unlike other service mediums (such as SOAP-based Web services) where parameters are typically limited to data values, resource identifiers can point to anything. A resource can represent the data set of an entire entity, and it may not be desirable to share such coarse-grained resources across multiple services. It can lead to the types of configuration management and synchronization issues that the application of Service Normalization [506] is intended to avoid in the first place.

Figures 12.6, 12.7, and 12.8 provide alternative interactions that can be carried out by the Payroll Run task service to access timesheet data for a specific employee.

In this last step (Figure 12.8), the capability to retrieve the main employee resource clearly belongs within the Employee service's functional boundary. The capability to get a known timesheet correspondingly belongs to the Timesheet service. Both are highly agnostic and reusable capabilities that can be composed in many freeform ways by task services. The explicit capability to retrieve the timesheet for a given employee is replaced by a hypermedia link from the employee to the timesheet.

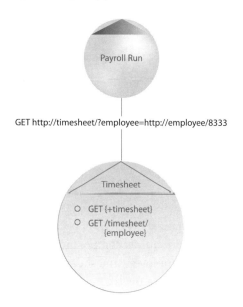

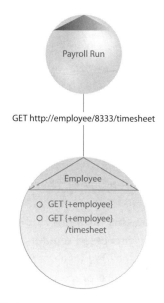

Figure 12.6

Option 1: The Payroll Run task service can invoke the GET /timesheet/{employee} capability from the Timesheet service to retrieve timesheet data based on the employee ID.

Figure 12.7

Option 2: The Payroll Run task service can invoke the GET {+employee}/timesheet capability from the Employee service to retrieve timesheet data based on the employee ID.

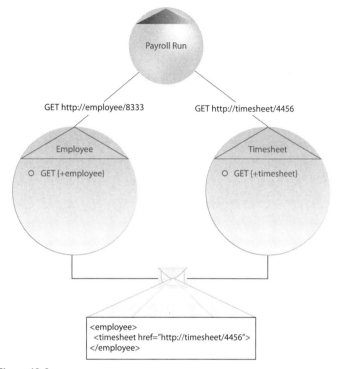

Figure 12.8

Option 3: The Payroll Run task service can use hypermedia to follow a two-step process:
First retrieve the employee record using the Employee service's GET {+employee}
capability, and then follow a timesheet hyperlink to retrieve the related Timesheet entity
service by invoking its GET {+timesheet} capability.

The composition logic within the task services remains straightforward as:

```
employee = Resource(employeeURL).GET(employee.class)
timesheet = Resource(employee.timesheetURL).GET(timesheet.class)
```

This design may also increase preformance. The commonly composed employee and
timesheet resources are more likely to already be present in caches than a less commonly used /timesheet{employee} or /employee/{id}/timesheet resource.

By replacing certain query resources with hyperlinks between existing entity resources
we create a flexible composition architecture that does not require specific query capabilities to be included in service contracts. This approach can come at the cost of discoverability because without the "get timesheet for employee" capability in the contract,
developers may not realize the capability exists within the hypermedia relationships.
To avoid redundant logic, it can be helpful to explicitly model these hidden capabilities,
as shown in Figure 12.9.

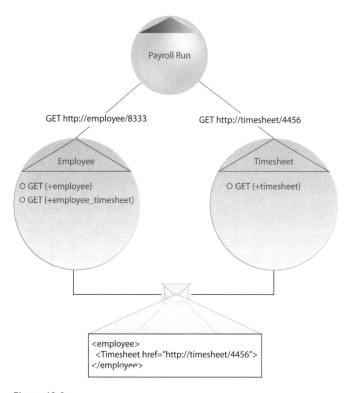

Figure 12.9

The addition of a `GET {+employee_timesheet}` capability to the
Employee service explicitly establishes the capability to retrieve an employee's
related timesheet resource. The consumer uses this capability by following the
timesheet hyperlink. The hyperlink actually refers to the timesheet resource in the
timesheet service, which will answer the request.

Composition Deepening

Just as it is possible for a task service to use hypermedia to discover a resource (and its
associated service) at runtime to further extend its composition logic, it is possible for
the task service to be the one forwarding resource identifiers to composition members
by providing hyperlinks in its request messages.

When a service consumer creates a request message, it can contain data provided by the
consumer or it can include an identifier to a source of that data. If the data set is large
and the consumer has no need for it, passing a "pointer" to the data can be significantly
more efficient than having the consumer generate the data and transmit it to the service.
With hypermedia and the uniform contract, all the service logic needs to be capable of is
issuing a valid GET request and processing the returned content (Figure 12.10).

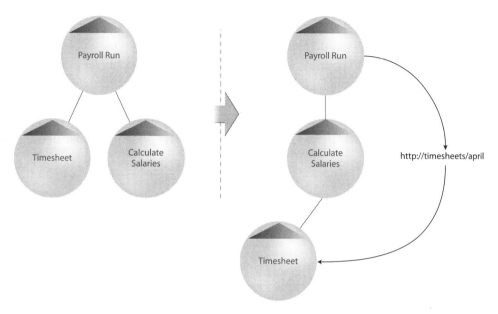

Figure 12.10

The Payroll Run task service was originally designed to query the timesheets of selected employees via the Timesheet service, and then provide this timesheet data as input to the Calculate Salaries service (left). It is redesigned to access the Calculate Salaries service to retrieve timesheet information, but Calculate Salaries doesn't know which service will provide the timesheet list and does not know what parameters might be present in the resource identifier.

The first Payroll Run task service (on the left side of Figure 12.10) requires that a large quantity of data be transferred from the Timesheet service, only to need this data be transferred again to the Calculate Salaries service. By intentionally "deepening" the composition architecture using hypermedia, the Payroll Run service does not have to see the timesheet data itself. It only needs to provide a reference to the list of timesheets that this particular calculation requires. All timesheet data is transferred directly from the Timesheet service to the Calculate Salaries service.

This example illustrates how hypermedia can be used to optimize service composition performance by reducing the number of unnecessary transfers of large data sets and documents between composition members. It is an approach that mimics concepts within functional programming, where the value of a variable is not evaluated until the last possible moment. The first service that sees the resource identifier does not actually need to retrieve the data; it is simply positioned as the final recipient of the data.

Composition deepening needs to be considered on a case-by-case basis. Under the different circumstances, it can certainly be misapplied, resulting in decreased performance and deeply nested composition hierarchies that are unnecessarily complex.

Dynamically Binding with Common Properties

Within a normalized service inventory it is not necessary for every sub-entity to be allocated its own service. For example, we don't need to have an entity service dedicated to business entities as common and granular as "address" or "name." As a result, these types of generic sub-entities tend to form common properties across multiple entity services. Figure 12.11 helps illustrate this by showing Customer, Partner, and Supplier entity services, each with a GET {+contact} capability that represents a construct of general contact data.

Figure 12.11
The Customer, Partner, and Supplier entity services.

When designing service compositions, there may be opportunities to leverage REST's dynamic binding features together with common service properties in order to streamline and reduce coupling between composition members. Due to their business context-neutral nature, utility services in particular can benefit from this approach. Therefore, we'll explore this topic through a scenario based on the use of a Label Printer utility service acting as the consumer of the aforementioned Customer, Partner, and Supplier entity services.

Figure 12.12 shows the Label Printer service positioned to invoke any or all three of the entity services, as part of a process to send printed mail to customers, suppliers, and/or partners. After the Label Printer service is invoked by another service, it needs to obtain address information in order to print its labels.

However, the designer of the Label Printer service did not want:

- the service's consumers to become coupled to knowledge of exactly which data the Label Printer service needs to obtain to send out the printed correspondence

- the Label Printer to contain processing logic specific to the entity services it may need to query to retrieve the contact information

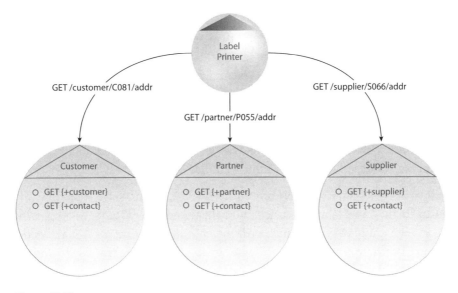

Figure 12.12

As an alternative to implementing service-specific logic to retrieve contact data from different entity services, the Label Printer service is designed with generic logic capable of dynamically binding to services.

Therefore, the Label Printer service is designed to:

- receive resource identifiers at runtime that indicate which entity services it needs to get contact information from

- use the received resource identifiers to late bind to the corresponding entity services

The Label Printer service's design has the following further characteristics:

- it assigns a standard media type for the address resources: `application/vcard+xml`

- it exposes a single `POST {+PrintSource}` service capability instead of a separate capability for each potential type of entity service it may need to access

The generic nature of the Label Printer's service logic requires that it be able to issue a GET request and process the `application/vcard+xml` response, similar to the following:

```
address = Resource(request.addressURL).GET(application/vcard+xml)
formattedAddress = format(address)
Resource(printerURL).POST(formattedAddress)
```

From a service invocation perspective, the Label Printer service only needs to know that there is a `GET {+contact}` service capability available for the entity service it is accessing. The internal logic required to parse out the required address details can rely on the standard uniform contract media type and related schema for contact information to be used across the entity services. If common constructs, such as address, have been successfully standardized via the application of Canonical Schema [437], then the Label Printer service will only need generic logic that is applicable to any entity service it may need to interact with. This will minimize the extent to which the Label Printer service will be coupled at design-time to the entity services.

However, if address constructs within entity service schemas are disparate and non-standardized, the Label Printer service will either need to have embedded parsing logic specific to each entity service (which will increase its coupling) or it may need to rely on intermediate data transformation logic. In the latter case, the Data Model Transformation [452] pattern may need to be applied to an intermediary utility service or service agent.

NOTE

In this type of composition architecture, it may also be worthwhile to explore the use of the Resource Descriptor Framework (RDF), combined with a service inventory-wide vocabulary for common properties and relationships, as one potential supertype for entities that is able to capture common properties and relationships across different entity types. For example, a Label Printer service that understands the generic RDF media type and the "contact" relationship would be able to navigate from any entity that uses RDF and that contains a "contact" relationship to its related contact resource.

Service Normalization [506] ensures that redundant logic is not implemented within the service inventory and that data relating to specific business entities is accessed via corresponding entity-based service contracts. Dynamic binding within a service inventory encourages us to look from the consumer perspective for capabilities, properties, and relationships that are equivalent from the perspective of the service consumer. With business-centric services, these opportunities will be limited, but utility services are often able to leverage similarities across business services.

Runtime Logic Deferral

It is relatively common practice to reside and execute service-specific logic within the boundary of the service implementation. This ensures that the logic only exists in one location from where it can be easily modified and upgraded. However, some services are accessed so frequently that this repeated usage can become a performance burden and can inhibit their scalability.

For example, a utility policy decision service may need to be consulted each time a service (to which the policy applies) processes a request message. Rather than involve the utility service in each interaction, we could embed the policy decision logic into each service instead. This may improve efficiency and reduce performance overhead, but it creates the predictable problem that denormalized replicas of the policy enforcement logic will subsequently become a potentially major maintenance challenge.

Code-on-Demand {407} operates between these two extremes. With this constraint, latency-sensitive logic can be executed redundantly by services throughout the service inventory, but they are designed to obtain this logic at runtime from a single, normalized service.

Going back to the example from the preceding *Composition Deepening* section, one additional means by which the Employee service could have returned timesheet data would have been to utilize Code-on-Demand {407} to require that the Payroll Run service execute logic of its choosing in order to complete the two-step composition (Figure 12.13).

Suitable logic for this type of runtime deferral tends to not change frequently, so cache directives can be associated with the logic that ensure services that compose it check for updates at an appropriate rate. By utilizing a combination of cache control directives (such as `max-age` and `ETag`), the service providing the shared logic is able to ensure that its consumers check for updates no more often than the pre-defined period. On the downside, this type of runtime functionality can introduce a security vulnerability whereby a malicious service can attempt to defer harmful logic to consumers designed to receive deferred logic at runtime.

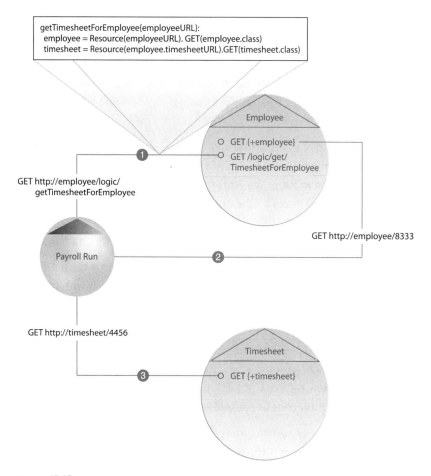

Figure 12.13

Instead of embedding logic for obtaining the timesheet for an employee itself, the Payroll Run service could obtain this logic from the Employee service at runtime using a Code-on-Demand {407} based mechanism.

SUMMARY OF KEY POINTS

- Adding capabilities to service contracts that would otherwise be "hidden" in hypermedia relationships between entities can improve service discoverability and increase governance control.

- Through the use of hypermedia we can pass resource identifiers at runtime, allowing for the virtual chaining of service capability interactions, referred to as composition deepening.

- Services can be designed to minimize coupling between consumers and composition members by leveraging dynamic binding across common service properties.

- By designing service logic based on Code-on-Demand {407}, we can have services obtain and execute at runtime latency-sensitive logic from a centralized service without compromising Logic Centralization [475].

12.5 Service Composition Across Service Inventories

When an IT enterprise proceeds with Domain Inventory [458], distinct service inventories naturally form large-scale "continents" of service logic and data. It is an accepted part of applying Domain Inventory [458] that integration channels will need to be established between domain service inventory boundaries in order to overcome their disparity.

Inventory Endpoint [472] with REST

A common approach to enabling required, cross-inventory integration logic is through the application of Inventory Endpoint [472], a pattern that establishes mediation services that are positioned as the point of entry for external (extra-inventory) contact and communication.

Inventory endpoint services typically house or utilize a range of transformation logic necessary to perform runtime translations between data models, data format, and other areas in which exchanged messages may be incompatible. This pattern is therefore closely associated with Data Model Transformation [452], Data Format Transformation [451], and Protocol Bridging [488]. In a REST-based service inventory, the inventory service needs to deal with both the current state of the uniform contracts, as well as the service contracts of related service inventories.

The Product Mediator service in Figure 12.14 acts as an inventory endpoint being composed by a task service that uses it to compare and select data from three different Product services, each of which is in a different service inventory. To accommodate this composition logic, the Product Mediator service repeats each of the common service capabilities as part of its own service contract and performs all necessary transformations between request methods, media types, and message content.

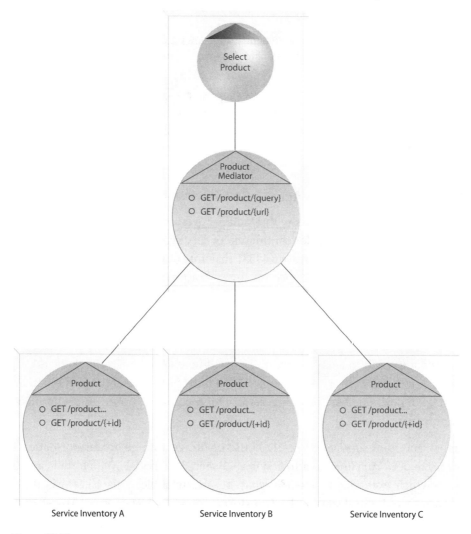

Figure 12.14

The Product Mediator service collects data from three different Product services across three service inventories to allow the Select Product task service to compare product data from different sources. This particular scenario is also applicable to B2B composition architectures.

The Product Mediator service has two capabilities:

- `GET /product{query}` – This capability issues a query to each of the Product services to locate products that have the properties required by the Select Product task service.

- `GET /product{url}` – The second capability provides detailed product data suitable for the Select Product task service to use to determine the best product to choose for its purchase order and to provide input to the composition initiator (not shown in Figure 12.14).

For example, the Select Product task service sends the following to the Product Mediator service:

```
GET http://product/product?query=paper,A4,80gsm
```

The Product Mediator service repeats the query to each Product service in their specific required formats:

```
GET http://domainA/product?query=paper,A4,80gsm
GET http://domainB/product?type=paper&size=A4&weight=80gsm
GET http://domainC/product?customer=
  example&type=paper&size=A4&weight=80gsm
```

The responses come back in their respective formats:

```
text/uri-list: http://supplierA/stationary/paper/A4/80gsm
application/vnd.supplierB.product+xml: <Product...
application/vnd.supplierC.product.xml: <product...
```

The Product Mediator service normalizes the returned data and rewrites any resource identifiers included in the responses. This rewriting ensures that any requests to resources from the other service inventories will be passed through the mediator service. Once the Select Product task service has determined which results are shortlisted, it requests more detailed data via the following message:

```
GET http://product/product?url=
  http://supplierA/stationary/paper/A4/80gsm
```

The rewritten resource identifier tells the Product Mediator service which Product service to contact again. The media type used by the Product service determines how the response message is transformed into a form suitable for local service consumption, with logic such as:

```
product =
Resource(request.url).GET(application/vnd.supplierA.product+xml,
application/vnd.supplierB.product+xml,
application/vnd.supplierC.product+xml)
if (product.type == application/vnd.domainA.product+xml)
   return transformA(product)
else if (product.type == application/vnd.domainB.product+xml)
   return transformB(product)
else if (product.type == application/vnd.domainC.product+xml)
   return transformC(product)
```

The governance burden associated with this type of application of Inventory Endpoint [472] is that the mediator logic needs to be authored and kept up-to-date with the individual service contracts of the Product services.

Dynamic Binding Between Service Inventories with Baseline Standardization

In cases where Service Normalization [506] is not possible, such as when we have two disparate domain service inventories, the scope for dynamic binding to solve interoperability problems is increased. In the preceding example there was already an extent of dynamic binding being demonstrated.

Instead of defining different service capabilities to retrieve product data from each of the Product services, the Product Mediator service reused the same capability and dynamically bound that capability to each Product service. To accomplish this, the Product Mediator service logic needed to selectively apply transformation logic.

The quantity of this transformation logic can further be reduced by having domain service inventories share standard media types and methods. This way, service consumers that use HTTP methods to access resources within their service inventories will not need any modification in order to issue requests to equivalent entity services in different service inventories. A GET or PUT request will usually indicate the same overall purpose in different REST-compliant service inventory architectures. If the media type used to convey data across inventory boundaries is also externally defined (and service inventories reuse the same externally defined media types), then consumers in one inventory will not need any modification to insert correct data into PUT requests and to understand the result of a GET request from services in another inventory.

For example, let's say that the Select Product task service sends the following message to the Product Mediator service:

```
GET http://product/product?query=paper,A4,80gsm
```

The Product Mediator service repeats the query to each Product service in a standard-ized format. If the query is different between service inventories, then the mediator logic will still pull the query apart and construct appropriate service-specific queries. But if the query itself is able to be standardized, then the mediator logic does not need to interpret or even understand the query format. It will be able to pass the query on verbatim each time, as follows:

```
GET http://domainA/product?query=paper,A4,80gsm
GET http://domainB/product?query=paper,A4,80gsm
GET http://domainC/product?query=paper,A4,80gsm
```

The response messages returned by the three Product services are in a standard format, although the product resource identifiers themselves do not need to share a common structure:

```
text/uri-list: http://domainA/stationary/paper/A4/80gsm
text/uri-list: http://domainB/paper;size=A4&weight=80gsm&sheets=1000
text/uri-list: http://domainC/product/PRD00134433
```

The Product Mediator service collates the returned data and, in this case, has no need to rewrite any resource identifiers. Instead it returns the hyperlinks from other Product services directly to its own consumers.

Once the Select Product task service has determined which results have been short-listed, the request for more detailed data is issued without needing any service-specific or inventory-specific logic:

```
productList = Resource(http://product/product?query=paper,A4,80gsm).
GET(text/uri-list)
for (i: productList)
  product = Resource(i).GET(application/product+xml)
  processProduct(product)
```

This logic being carried out in the `for` loop can occur directly, without the need for mediation because of the layers of standardization that exist between the different ser-vice inventories for this service capability. The method and media type have been stan-dardized (at least for interchange purposes) and the semantics of the GET {+product} capability are the same between the different inventories as well. This means that the Product Mediator service has little to do when this capability is invoked. The Product service responds with:

```
200 OK
Content-Type: application/product+xml
<Product...
```

If specific targeted methods and media types are standardized across service inventories, and similar capabilities are present within respective inventory services, then mediation logic can be reduced to the collation of data from the services being composed.

The layers of standardization we have been describing so far are native to REST architectures, which is why they are relatively easy to establish and standardize across REST-based service inventories. This is also why this level of standardization is considered "baseline."

Beyond these base layers is the challenge of standardizing actual schemas and media types for business entities. These tend to be designed specifically for the business context that each entity service will operate in, which is related to or derived from the overarching business context of the domain inventory itself. In these cases it may be feasible to only use a standard "interchange" media type alongside the native, custom types. Depending on the importance and nature of the integration, both native and the interchange type may tend to become increasingly aligned over time. But in some cases, they may actually grow further apart.

SUMMARY OF KEY POINTS

- The Inventory Endpoint [472] pattern can be applied with REST to establish services with mediator logic that facilitate communication between services within and outside a service inventory boundary.

- Hypermedia can be utilized to achieve dynamic binding across service inventory boundaries by leveraging baseline standardization common to service inventory architectures.

Chapter 13

Service Composition with REST Case Study

13.1 Revisiting the Confer Student Award Process

13.2 Application Submission and Task Service Invocation

13.3 Confer Student Award Service Composition Instance
(Pre-Review Service Activity View)

13.4 Review of Pending Applications and Task Service Invocation

MUA architects proceed with design efforts for a service composition architecture capable of automating the Confer Student Award business process from Chapters 9 and 10. Figure 13.1 shows the current scope of the planned service composition.

The contracts of individual composition member services have been refined since the first iteration. Some of the original service contracts have been further split to better group common service capabilities.

Specifically, the following changes have been made to the service composition from Chapter 10:

- Transcript-related data processing was separated from the Student entity service into a dedicated Student Transcript entity service. This new service keeps records of student classes and grades, along with other events of note, such as special awards and penalties.

- The original Document utility service was removed from the composition due to a review of business process logic during which it was determined that the automated printing of the conferral document was not necessary. As a result, both the Print Rejection Notice and Print Acceptance Notice actions are now carried out manually.

Another change to the overall service composition architecture is the inclusion of a cross-service transaction that encapsulates data updates made via the Conferral and Student services.

13.1 Revisiting the Confer Student Award Process

Provided in Figure 13.2 is the workflow diagram from Chapter 9 that describes the sequence of steps that comprise the Confer Student Award business process logic. In a nutshell, the student submits an application that is either verified or rejected. If verification succeeds, the application is approved and the award is conferred. If rejected, the student is notified.

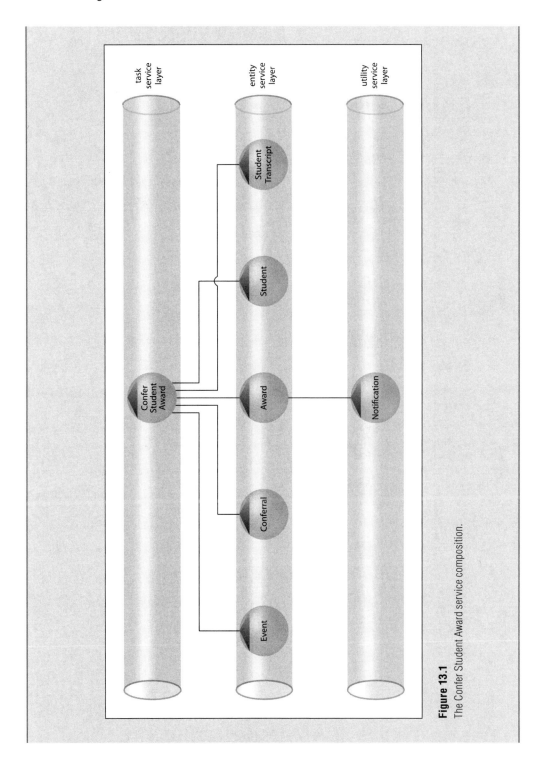

Figure 13.1

The Confer Student Award service composition.

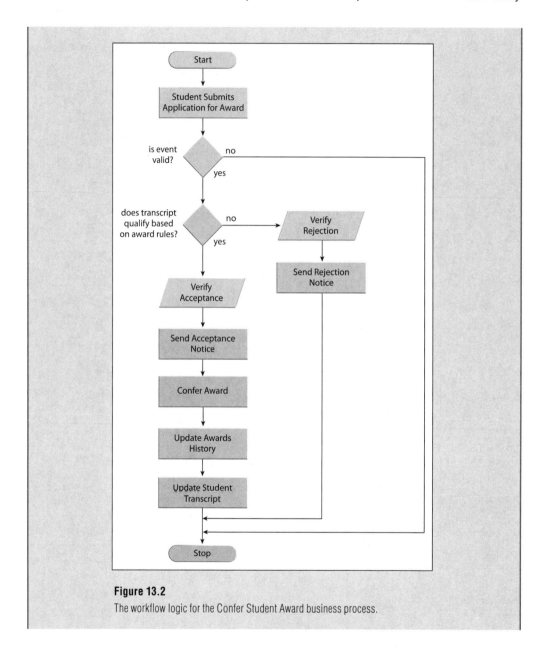

Figure 13.2
The workflow logic for the Confer Student Award business process.

Also provided here are the individual actions, listed in sequence and further formatted as per the following conventions:

- Actions bolded and colored red are mapped to message exchanges and upcoming step-by-step service activity description sections.

- Actions bolded and colored black are relevant to the described interactions, but are not explicitly mapped.

- Actions without formatting are not represented or not relevant to the described service activities.

This list of actions is labeled with a sequence of letters for easier reference in upcoming sections.

A. **Initiate Conferral Application**

B. **Get Event Details**

C. **Verify Event Details**

D. If Event is Invalid or Ineligible for Award, Cancel Process

E. **Get Award Details**

F. **Get Student Transcript**

G. **Verify Student Transcript Qualifies for Award Based on Award Conferral Rules**

H. If Student Transcript does not Qualify, Initiate Rejection

I. Manually Verify Rejection

J. Print Rejection Notice

K. Send Rejection Notice

L. **Manually Verify Acceptance**

M. Print Acceptance Notice

N. **Send Acceptance Notice**

O. **Confer Award**

P. **Record Award Conferral in Student Transcript**

Q. **Record Award Conferral in Awards Database**

R.   Print Hard Copy of Award Conferral Record

S.   File Hard Copy of Award Conferral Record

This business process logic is explored through a specific scenario that is documented across the following four sections:

- *Application Submission and Task Service Invocation* – A student submits an application for award conferral using a front-end interface. This results in an interaction between composition initiator and task service.

- *Confer Student Award Service Composition Instance (Pre-Review Service Activity View)* – An instance of the composition is initiated up until action L, a manual step that is performed by a human reviewer.

- *Review of Pending Applications and Task Service Invocation* – A human reviewer queries outstanding applications.

- *Confer Student Award Service Composition Instance (Post-Review Service Activity View)* – The reviewer selects the application to approve, and the instance of the composition is resumed (subsequent to action L).

Note that the completion of the composition represents the approval of the application and a successful award conferral. Several other service activity scenarios are possible.

13.2 Application Submission and Task Service Invocation

The Confer Student Award process begins with a composition initiator sending a request message to the Confer Student Award task service. The message identifies the student that submitted the application to claim an award, plus the award being requested (Figure 13.3):

```
POST http://confer-student-award.mua.edu/task
Content-Type: application/vnd.edu.mua.award-conferral+xml
<Conferral>
  <Student href="http://student.mua.edu.au/student/335810"/>
  <Award href="http://award.mua.edu.au/award/BS/CompSci"/>
  <Event href="http://event.mua.edu.au/
    event/main-graduation/2015"/>
</Conferral>
```

This request message is processed asynchronously, and the subsequent response to the composition initiator is as follows:

```
201 Created
Location: http://confer-student-award.mua.edu/task/3353
<Conferral>
  <Student href="http://student.mua.edu.au/student/335810"/>
  <Award href="http://award.mua.edu.au/award/BS/CompSci"/>
  <Event href="http://event.mua.edu.au/
    event/main-graduation/2015"/>
  <State href="http://confer-student-award.mua.edu/
    task/3353/state">Initial</State>
</Conferral>
```

The location resource is provided to the student in the form of a processing receipt. The human user (student) can enter the receipt ID in the Web-based front-end to check on the status of an application. Behind the scenes, this issues a GET request to

Figure 13.3

The Web-based front-end is used by the student to asynchronously initiate an instance of the Confer Student Award composition, as illustrated with the exchange of the POST /task and 201 Created request and response messages. While the service activity is on-going, the student can use the front-end to repeatedly request the award conferral application status via the GET /task {state} capability.

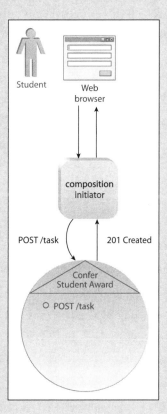

the location resource, resulting in application status data being returned, with any changes being represented by updates to the state element.

The states defined for Confer Student Award service composition include automatic acceptance and rejection states, both of which are manually confirmed by MUA staff. These manual steps help to safeguard the integrity of the process, and for the same reason, the automatic acceptance and rejection states are never made available directly to human users. These states, along with the Initial state, are reported as "Accepted for Processing."

13.3 Confer Student Award Service Composition Instance (Pre-Review Service Activity View)

After the Confer Student Award task service receives an application and confirms receipt with the composition initiator, an instance of the composition is officially initiated and service activity processing is underway. Figure 13.4 illustrates the processing steps that occur up until the point when manual verification (action I in the preceding list of process actions) is required.

Let's now detail the message exchange that occurs with each processing step.

Step 1: Composition Initiator to Confer Student Award Task Service (A)

This represents the request and response message exchange between the composition initiator and task service, described earlier in the *Application Submission and Task Service Invocation* section.

Step 2: Confer Student Award Task Service to Event Entity Service (B)

The Confer Student Award task service sends the following request message to retrieve event information via the Event service:

```
GET http://event.mua.edu.au/event/main-graduation/2015
Accept: application/vnd.edu.mua.event+rdf+xml
```

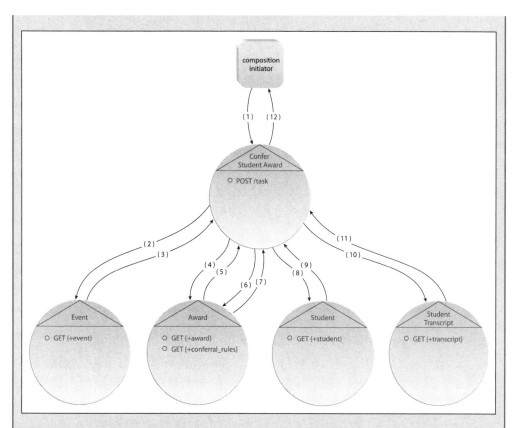

Figure 13.4
The composition processing steps leading up to manual acceptance or rejection of the application.

Step 3: Event Entity Service to Confer Student Award Task Service (B)

The Event service returns the requested event data, including supplemental calendar information, using a response message based on RDF:

```
200 OK
Content-Type: application/vnd.edu.mua.event+rdf+xml
<rdf:RDF xmlns:rdf="http://www.w3.org/1999/02/
  22-rdf-syntax-ns#"
  xmlns:mua="http://mua.edu/service-vocabulary#"
  xmlns:ical="http://www.w3.org/2002/12/cal#">
  <mua:Event rdf:about="http://event.mua.edu/graduation-2015">
    <ical:Vevent rdf:about=
      "http://event.mua.edu/graduation-2015/calendar">
```

```
    <ical:dtstart>2015-11-12</ical:dtstart>
    ...
  </ical:Vevent>
  <mua:description rdf:resource="http://event.mua.edu/
    graduation-2015/description"/>
  <mua:eventType>Graduation</mua:eventType>
  </mua:Event>
</rdf:RDF>
```

Step 4: Confer Student Award Task Service to Award Entity Service (E)

The Confer Student Award service requests data about the award for which the student is applying. It can also retrieve the corresponding conferral rules, but these aren't accessed as commonly as some other datasets, and are included in a sub-resource.

```
GET http://award.mua.edu/award/BS/CompSci
Accept: application/vnd.edu.mua.award+rdf+xml
```

Step 5: Award Entity Service to Confer Student Award Task Service (E)

The Award service responds back to the Confer Student Award service with the requested award data, as well as a link to the conferral rules resource.

```
200 OK
Content-Type: application/vnd.edu.mua.award+rdf+xml
<rdf:RDF xmlns:rdf="http://www.w3.org/1999/
  02/22-rdf-syntax-ns#"
  xmlns:mua="http://mua.edu/service-vocabulary#">
  <mua:Award rdf:about="http://event.mua.edu/award/BS/CompSci">
    <mua:conferralRules href=" http://event.mua.edu/award/
      BS/CompSci/rules"/>
    ...
  </mua:Award>
</rdf:RDF>
```

Step 6: Confer Student Award Task Service to Award Entity Service (E)

The Confer Student Award service re-invokes the Award service to request the conferral award data. It will need to execute this logic to determine whether the student transcript qualifies for the award. It requests JavaScript, as follows:

```
GET http://award.mua.edu/award/BS/CompSci/rules
Accept: application/javascript
```

Step 7: Award Entity Service to Confer Student Award Task Service (E)

The Award service returns the requested logic as JavaScript that can be executed by the Confer Student Award Service.

```
200 OK
Content-Type: application/javascript
function checkConferral()
{
  ...
}
```

Step 8: Confer Student Award Task Service to Student Entity Service (F)

The Confer Student Award service needs the student transcript, for which it issues a request to the Student entity service:

```
GET http://student.mua.edu/student/335810
Accept: application/vnd.edu.mua.student+rdf+xml
```

Step 9: Student Entity Service to Confer Student Award Task Service (F)

The Student service does not respond with the transcript data. Instead, it uses hypermedia to respond with the identifier of the student's transcript resource (highlighted in red):

```
200 OK
: Content-Type: application/vnd.edu.mua.student+rdf+xml
<rdf:RDF xmlns:rdf="http://www.w3.org/1999/
  02/22-rdf-syntax-ns#"
  xmlns:mua="http://mua.edu/service-vocabulary#">
  <mua:Student rdf:about="http://student.mua.edu/student/335810">
    <mua:studentTranscript href="http://student-
      transcript.mua.edu/transcript/335810"/>
    ...
  </muaAward>
</rdf:RDF>
```

Step 10: Confer Student Award Task Service to Student Transcript Entity Service (F)

The Confer Student Award Task Service uses the received identifier (highlighted in red) to access the Student Transcript Service and the corresponding transcript resource, as follows:

```
GET http://student-transcript.mua.edu/transcript/335810
Accept: application/vnd.edu.mua.student-transcript+rdf+xml
```

Step 11: Student Transcript Entity Service to Confer Student Award Task Service (F)

The Student Transcript service responds with the requested transcript data:

```
200 OK
Content-Type: application/vnd.edu.mua.student-transcript+rdf+xml
<rdf:RDF xmlns:rdf="http://www.w3.org/1999/
  02/22-rdf-syntax-ns#"
  xmlns:mua="http://mua.edu/service-vocabulary#">
  <mua:Student rdf:about="http://student.mua.edu/student/335810">
    <mua:classRecord>
      <mua:Subject href="http://subjects.mua.edu/CS300"/>
      <mua:GPA>5</mua:GPA>
    </mua:classRecord>
    ...
  </mua:Award>
</rdf:RDF>
```

Step 12: Confer Student Award Task Service to Composition Initiator

The Confer Student Award service responds with a confirmation back to the composition initiator that the composition instance has been created and is underway:

```
201 Created
```

Upon completion of these steps, the Confer Student Award task service has sufficient data to render an automatic verdict on the conferral request. It can confirm whether the requested event is valid, and can execute the award conferral rules on the transcript of the student to either accept or reject the conferral. The results of these verifications are presented to the MUA staff responsible for carrying out the manual verification steps represented by actions I and L.

13.4 Review of Pending Applications and Task Service Invocation

The preceding steps led to the student application being submitted and tentatively approved or rejected (based on the automated application of conferral rules), pending the review of a human MUA staff member.

This manual review does not happen on a regular basis. Staff members responsible for this review periodically use a separate Web-based form to determine how many (if any) pending applications are in the queue (Figure 13.5).

Figure 13.5

Staff responsible for manually reviewing award conferral applications are able to query which applications are pending review.

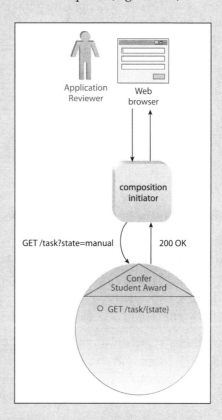

When issuing this query, the Confer Student Award's GET /task {state} capability is invoked, as follows:

```
GET http://confer-student-award/task?state=manual
Accept: application/vnd.edu.mua.award-conferral+xml
```

The task service responds with all application records that have a registered state of "manual," as shown here:

```
200 OK
Content-Type: application/vnd.edu.mua.award-conferral+xml
<Conferrals>
  <Conferral>
    <Student href="http://student.mua.edu.au/student/335810"/>
    <Award href="http://award.mua.edu.au/award/BS/CompSci"/>
    <Event href="http://event.mua.edu.au/event/\
      main-graduation/2015"/>
    <State href="http://confer-student-award.mua.edu/
      task/3353/state">manual</State>
    <Disposition href="http://confer-student-award.mua.edu/
      task/3353/state">accept</Disposition>
  </Conferral>
  ...
</Conferrals>
```

The reviewer is able to select any one of the listed, pending applications. This subsequently carries out the post-review service activity described next.

Confer Student Award Service Composition Instance (Post-Review Service Activity View)

Upon reviewing a pending application, the human reviewer confirms the tentative approval or rejection status. The service activity scenario depicted in Figure 13.6 and explained in the following step descriptions provides the detailed message exchanges carried out for an application approval.

After an award conferral is manually approved, a notification is sent to the student, and databases containing award and student transcript history need to be updated. To accomplish this, the Conferral and Student Transcript services are enlisted in a cross-service transaction.

As the staff member proceeds through the list of applications that need manual processing they will set the state to accepted or rejected. This occurs as a request to the related "state" resource within the Conferral Student Award service.

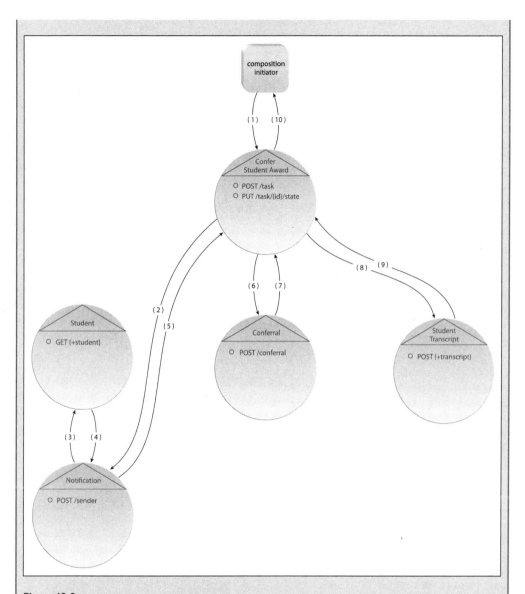

Figure 13.6
The composition processing steps carried out subsequent to a manual review and approval of the application.

Step 1: Composition Initiator to Confer Student Award Task Service (L)

The human reviewer approves an application via the front-end user interface, which subsequently issues a PUT request to the Confer Student Award task service that triggers the next phase of the service activity:

```
PUT http://confer-student-award.mua.edu/task/3353/state
Content-Type: text/plain
Accepted
```

Step 2: Confer Student Award Task Service to Notification Utility Service (N)

With the application having been accepted, the Confer Student Award service transfers the state of the application process to the Notification service via the following message:

```
POST http://notification.mua.edu/sender
Content-Type: application/vnd.edu.mua.award-conferral+xml
<Conferral>
  <Student href="http://student.mua.edu.au/student/335810"/>
  <Award href="http://award.mua.edu.au/award/BS/CompSci"/>
  <Event href="http://event.mua.edu.au/event/
    main-graduation/2015"/>
  <State href="http://confer-student-award.mua.edu/
    task/3353/state">accepted</State>
</Conferral>
```

Step 3: Notification Utility Service to Student Entity Service (N)

The Notification service invokes the Student service to obtain contact information needed to issue the notification.

```
GET http://student.mua.edu.au/student/335810
Accept: application/rdf+xml
```

Step 4: Student Entity Service to Notification Utility Service (N)

The Student service responds with the following:

```
200 OK
Content-Type: application/rdf+xml
```

```
<rdf:RDF xmlns:rdf="http://www.w3.org/1999/
  02/22-rdf-syntax-ns#"
  xmlns:mua="http://mua.edu/service-vocabulary#">
  <mua:Student rdf:about="http://student.mua.edu/student/335810">
    <mua:contact href="mailto:335810@student.mua.edu"/>
    ...
  </mua:Award>
</rdf:RDF>
```

Step 5: Notification Utility Service to Confer Student Award Task Service (N)

With the contact information in-hand, the Notification service sends an e-mail notifying the student on the application's approval. The Notification service then returns to the Confer Student Award Task Service the following acknowledgement:

```
200 OK
```

Intermediate Step: Confer Student Award Task Service to Transaction Coordinator (P, Q)

With the award conferral having been accepted, there is no point delaying the entry of this data into the necessary databases. The Confer Student Award service initiates a transaction that encompasses the Conferrals service and the Student Transcript service, as per the Compensating Service Transaction [443] pattern.

It begins by issuing the following to the transaction coordinator (not shown on Figure 13.6):

```
POST http://xact-coordinator.mua.edu/compensating
```

Intermediate Step: Transaction Coordinator to Confer Student Award Task Service (P, Q)

The transaction coordinator responds with the following:

```
201 Created
Location: http://xact-coordinator.mua.edu/compensating/3434
```

Step 6: Confer Student Award Task Service to Conferral Entity Service (P)

The Confer Student Award service transfers its conferral record to the Award Conferrals database via the Conferral entity service:

```
POST http://conferrals.mua.edu/conferral
Link: <http://xact-coordinator.mua.edu/compensating
  /3434>; rel="compensating-transaction"
Content-Type: application/vnd.edu.mua.award-conferral+xml
<Conferral>
  <Student href="http://student.mua.edu.au/student/335810"/>
  <Award href="http://award.mua.edu.au/award/BS/CompSci"/>
  <Event href="http://event.mua.edu.au/event/
    main-graduation/2015"/>
  <State href="http://confer-student-award.mua.edu/
    task/3353/state">accepted</State>
</Conferral>
```

Intermediate Step: Conferral Entity Service to Transaction Coordinator (P)

The Conferral service registers undo logic with the transaction controller, as follows:

```
POST http://xact-coordinator.mua.edu/compensating/3434
Content-Type: application/javascript
...
```

Intermediate Step: Transaction Coordinator to Conferral Entity Service

The transaction coordinator responds with the following acknowledgement:

```
200 OK
```

Step 7: Conferral Entity Service to Confer Student Award Task Service (Q)

The Conferrals service responds with the official long term storage location for the conferral record:

```
201 Created
Location: http://conferrals.mua.edu/
conferral/335810;2015;BC;CompSci;1
```

Step 8: Confer Student Award Task Service to Student Manuscript Entity Service (Q)

The Confer Student Award service transfers its conferral record to the Student Transcript service:

```
POST http://student-transcript.mua.edu/transcript/335810
Link: <http://xact-coordinator.mua.edu/
  compensating/3434>; rel="compensating-transaction"
Content-Type: application/vnd.edu.mua.award-conferral+xml
<Conferral href="http://conferrals.mua.edu/
  conferral/335810;2015;BC;CompSci;1">
  <Student href="http://student.mua.edu.au/student/335810"/>
  <Award href="http://award.mua.edu.au/award/BS/CompSci"/>
  <Event href="http://event.mua.edu.au/event/
    main-graduation/2015"/>
  <State href="http://confer-student-award.mua.edu/
    task/3353/state">accepted</State>
</Conferral>
```

Intermediate Step: Student Transcript Entity Service to Transaction Controller (Q)

The Student Transcript service registers its undo logic with the transaction controller:

```
POST http://xact-coordinator.mua.edu/compensating/3434
Content-Type: application/javascript
...
```

Intermediate Step: Transaction Controller to Student Transcript Entity Service (Q)

The transaction controller responds with:

```
200 OK
```

Step 9: Student Transcript Entity Service to Confer Student Award Task Service (Q)

The Student Transcript confirms the update to the transcript record with the following response message:

```
200 OK
```

Intermediate Step: Confer Student Award Task Service to Transaction Coordinator (P, Q)

The Confer Student Award service confirms the completion of the transaction by issuing the following to the Transaction Coordinator:

```
PUT http://xact-coordinator.mua.edu/compensating/3353
Content-Type: text/plain
Confirmed
```

Intermediate Step: Transaction Coordinator to Confer Student Award Task Service (P, Q)

The transaction controller confirms back that the transaction has been completed:

```
200 OK
```

Step 10: Confer Student Award Task Service to Composition Initiator

The Confer Student Award service confirms the state transition of the completion of the award conferral back to the composition initiator:

```
200 OK
```

Part V

Supplemental

Chapter 14: Design Patterns for SOA with REST

Chapter 15: Service Versioning with REST

Chapter 16: Uniform Contract Profiles

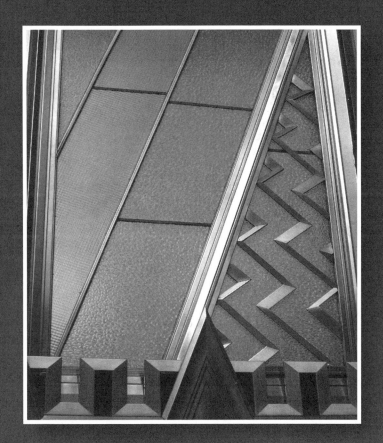

Chapter 14

Design Patterns for SOA with REST

14.1 Rest-Inspired SOA Design Patterns

14.2 Other Relevant SOA Design Patterns

PRINCIPLES, PATTERNS, AND CONSTRAINTS REFERENCED IN THIS CHAPTER:

- Canonical Expression [434]

- Client-Server {393}

- Compatible Change [442]

- Concurrent Contracts [445]

- Content Negotiation [446]

- Contract Centralization [447]

- Contract Denormalization [448]

- Decoupled Contract [455]

- Domain Inventory [458]

- Endpoint Redirection [460]

- Entity Linking [464]

- Idempotent Capability [470]

- Lightweight Endpoint [474]

- Reliable Messaging [491]

- Reusable Contract [492]

- Schema Centralization [494]

- Stateless {395}

- State Messaging [509]

- Uniform Contract [516]

- Validation Abstraction [518]

Design patterns are an effective and established means by which proven practices can be shared and used to address common design problems. Design patterns further provide a standardized notation for expressing architectural features and design decisions.

Appendix E in this book contains a master set of profiles for SOA design patterns. You will have noticed, throughout preceding chapters, numerous references to these pattern profile tables, via the delimited page number convention explained in Chapter 1.

Eighty-five of the design pattern profiles in Appendix E were originally documented in the *SOA Design Patterns* series title. The remaining seven design patterns are introduced to the SOA design patterns catalog, for the first time, by this book. As such, these new REST-inspired SOA design patterns follow the established format used for the SOA patterns catalog, and further identify relationships to existing design patterns and principles.

This supplemental chapter concludes with a section that provides summarized descriptions and commentary for key established SOA design patterns, several of which are related to the newly introduced REST-inspired patterns.

NOTE

The upcoming sections that discuss REST-inspired patterns provide content that supplements the pattern profile descriptions in Appendix E. Prior to reading each of these sections, be sure to first jump ahead to and read the corresponding pattern profile using the page number references that follow the pattern names.

14.1 REST-Inspired SOA Design Patterns

The following new design patterns are documented in this book:

- Content Negotiation [446]
- Endpoint Redirection [460]
- Entity Linking [464]
- Idempotent Capability [470]
- Lightweight Endpoint [474]
- Reusable Contract [492]
- Uniform Contract [516]

Note that the last pattern on the preceding list is a compound pattern, meaning that it is comprised of a set of other patterns.

As previously mentioned, you will find the official profile tables for these patterns amidst other SOA design patterns, all of which are organized alphabetically by pattern name in Appendix E.

Even though some of these new patterns were inspired and influenced by REST constraints, it is important to understand the intent behind most patterns is not to directly embody a constraint. Instead, these patterns should be viewed as a formal means of capturing successful and proven design elements that do not necessarily display any of the standard features of REST.

Each pattern can be applied individually and in combination with others without any requirement that it complies with REST architecture. Moreover, because these patterns are official parts of the SOA design pattern catalog, they have been authored specifically within the context of service-orientation.

UNDERSTANDING "ENDPOINTS"

You will notice the term "endpoint" used in a number of the upcoming design pattern descriptions and even as part of some pattern names. An endpoint (or service endpoint) is a generic term used to represent the point of access for a given service. It is most commonly equated to a service capability. With REST an endpoint does not represent the method of the uniform contract, but instead corresponds to the combination of a method, a resource identifier, and possibly a media type (which, taken as a whole, are the REST equivalent of a service capability) or just the resource identifier or the resource itself. As such, this term does not have a specific definition the way other terms introduced in Part I of this book have. It is an intentionally vague term along the lines of "artifact" or "component." The reason the "endpoint" term is used as part of design pattern descriptions is to keep the pattern intentionally abstract. That way, it can be explored as a technology-neutral design solution applicable to a range of architecture styles or platforms (REST-based and otherwise). Keeping design pattern descriptions at this abstract level is common practice.

Content Negotiation [446]

Although a basic function provided by HTTP, the mechanics of this pattern can be applied using other technologies. For example, custom SOAP message headers can be created to emulate the same behavior. Content Negotiation [446] allows a single capability to deal with different types of consumers based on the metadata they supply in requests. Two common uses for Content Negotiation [446] are to enable services to support multiple devices (as illustrated in Figure 14.1) and to support different versions of service consumers.

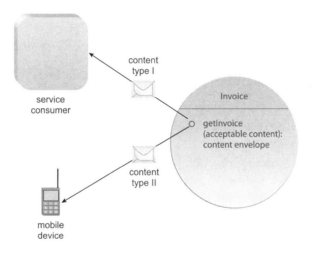

Figure 14.1

The service contract accepts and returns different types of content to accommodate the needs of different service consumers. Incorporating content negotiation into a reusable service contract allows a service to be compatible with old and new consumers and to accommodate other variations without introducing new service capabilities to the contract.

The envelope combining a media type identifier, a block of data, and associated metadata elements is called a *representation* in REST. This generic container continues to be reused both for old and new media types, as they are introduced to the service inventory. Representations permit generic components that do not need to interact with the data itself to deal with it opaquely. For example, caches can be introduced within the service inventory without needing to be aware of the specific media types in use and will continue to work as the media types for the service inventory evolve over time.

Related Patterns

- Compatible Change [442]

- Concurrent Contracts [445]

- Lightweight Endpoint [474]

- Schema Centralization [494]

Related Service-Oriented Computing Goals

- Increased Organizational Agility

- Reduced IT Burden

Endpoint Redirection [460]

Redirection is a natural part of Web architecture that can be leveraged to allow for the evolution of Web-based resources without compromising consumer programs designed to access those resources (Figure 14.2). The simple but effective feature of redirection is captured by the Endpoint Redirection [460] pattern as a technique that can be applied to service composition design. The assumption is that even when a service endpoint

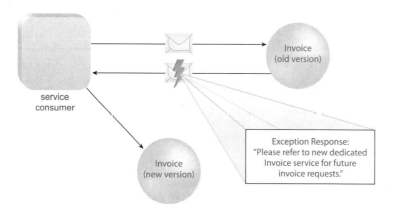

Figure 14.2

Consumers that access stale service endpoints do not have to be upgraded as they can be simply redirected to the updated service endpoint. Redirection built into service contracts along with predefined redirection rules built into service consumers allow service capabilities to evolve without needing to immediately upgrade service consumers that still hold stale references.

becomes stale, a placeholder service remains active in the old resource location so that out-of-date consumers can be informed about the new endpoint as they attempt to inter-act with the old one.

Related Patterns

- Lightweight Endpoint [474]

Related Service-Oriented Computing Goals

- Increased Organizational Agility

- Reduced IT Burden

Entity Linking [464]

The application of this pattern enables the runtime communication of entity relation-ships via links provided by the service to the service consumer in response messages (Figure 14.3). Inspired by the HTTP feature-set and the use of hyperlinks, Entity Link-ing [464] can help reduce consumer-to-service coupling while increasing entity rela-tionship intelligence available at runtime.

The roots of this pattern lie in the concept known as *resource linking*, whereby a uniform contract enables service consumers to access resources without required foreknowledge of their existence. Each provided link can introduce supplementary business context information and can identify the resource and provide a machine-readable means of describing the business entity to which the link is referring. Let's revisit Figure 14.3 to demonstrate. A link from Invoice 2 to Customer 1 will not simply inform the Invoice Printer that a customer exists, but also that Customer 1 is the purchaser of items listed in Invoice 2. It does this by stating the type of the link and any other required metadata to correctly interpret the business context.

The link could be expressed in XML as follows:

```
<Invoice>
  <link rel="purchaser" href="http://customer/cust01"/>
  ...
</Invoice>
```

Example 14.1

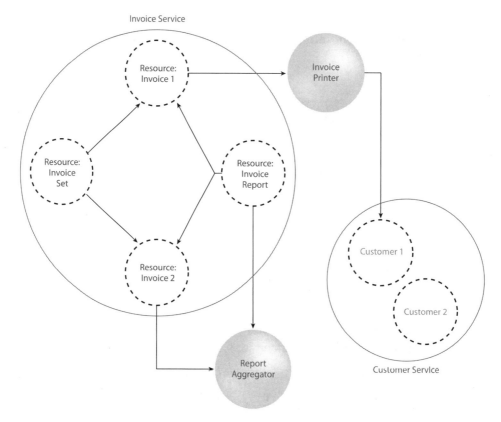

Figure 14.3

Services that expose identifiers of related entities to service consumers are able to be used in a wider variety of compositions. In this example, related business entities are discovered by following links between resources. The Report Aggregator service is able to look up any invoice fields that it might require and is not limited to a predefined set within the standard report. The Invoice Printer service is able to then cross-reference invoice and customer records in order to print mailing labels.

The Invoice Printer service expects that following the link by issuing a GET request will return the correct customer record for use on the invoice's mailing label. This expectation is derived from the media type's definition of the link (as interpreted by the developer who wrote the Invoice Printer service logic).

The freedom to link to a resource in any service allows the application of Entity Linking [464] to overcome service denormalization that may occur in some service inventories, and to further avoid other barriers introduced by crossing functional or business context boundaries. For example, the invoice can refer to a customer resource in a service maintained by another department or business. Different invoices in the same service could refer to customers in different Customer services. It is even possible for each invoice to refer to a canonical resource provided by the customer through services they operate themselves. The Invoice Printer service (acting as a service consumer) is decoupled from the detail of which service it accesses through the uniform contract.

Related Patterns

- Lightweight Endpoint [474]

- Reusable Contract [492]

- Uniform Contract [516]

Related Service-Oriented Computing Goals

- Increased Intrinsic Interoperability

- Increased Business and Technology Alignment

- Increased ROI

- Increased Organizational Agility

- Reduced IT Burden

Idempotent Capability [470]

Idempotency is an important concept within Web architectures and messaging frameworks in general. The value of this pattern is that it brings the rule of idempotency to the service contract level by building in a level of communications reliability between consumer and service without requiring that they share a persistent connection. As shown in Figure 14.4, services may be required to offer idempotent capabilities alongside non-idempotent capabilities.

Related Patterns

- Reliable Messaging [491]

- Reusable Contract [492]

- Uniform Contract [516]

Related Service-Oriented Computing Goals

- Increased Organizational Agility

- Reduced IT Burden

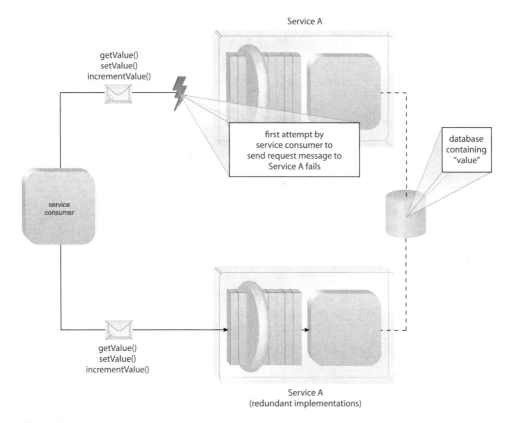

Figure 14.4

The `getValue()` and `setValue()` capabilities can be safely retried because they are idempotent. The `incrementValue()` capability is not idempotent and must not be retried unless each request is associated with a unique identifier. Such an identifier would need to be incorporated into the service's session state and must be synchronized between service instances alongside changes to the value.

Lightweight Endpoint [474]

This pattern is inspired by a resource-centric view of business entities and artifacts involved in business automation or that relate to business automation requirements (Figure 14.5). These are the same types of artifacts that form the basis of entity services.

The Lightweight Endpoint [474] pattern is derived from Contract Denormalization [448], which encourages service capability overlap when it can be justified. Lightweight Endpoint [474] can also be considered a specialized application of Contract Denormalization [448] in that it is focused on specific business entities.

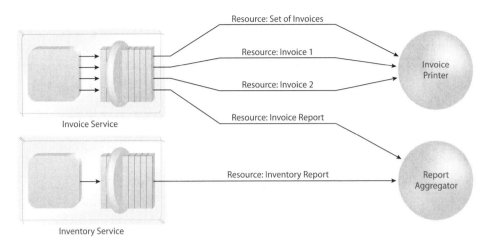

Figure 14.5
In this example, fine-grained resources (lightweight endpoints) provide varying levels of access to parts of individual business entities.

This pattern complements Reusable Contract [492] because business-centric resources naturally provide business contexts for use in conjunction with a (business context-free) reusable contract providing abstract functions.

Related Patterns

- Contract Denormalization [448]

- Concurrent Contract [445]

- Reusable Contract [492]

- Uniform Contract [516]

Related Service-Oriented Computing Goals

- Increased Intrinsic Interoperability

- Increased Business and Technology Alignment

- Increased ROI

- Increased Organizational Agility

- Reduced IT Burden

Reusable Contract [492]

This important pattern represents the foundation of a uniform contract and perhaps the core of REST style architecture. By establishing a centralized technical contract that is shared by services, we shift the underlying technology architecture in a very distinct manner (Figure 14.6). You'll see this pattern pop up again in the Uniform Contract [516] compound pattern description.

Related Patterns

- Canonical Expression [434]

- Decoupled Contract [455]

- Lightweight Endpoint [474]

- Uniform Contract [516]

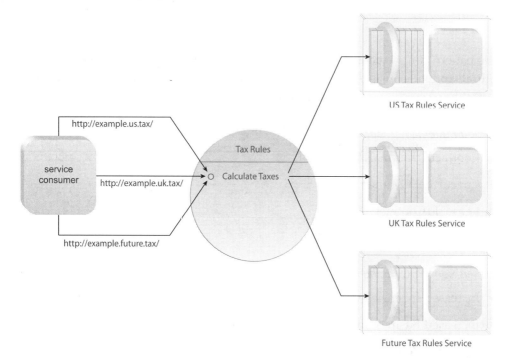

Figure 14.6

With REST, the emphasis is on applying this pattern in a highly generic manner so that its functions do not impose any business context. This example contrasts this approach by demonstrating how a reusable contract can introduce an overarching business context of Tax Rules. The function exposed by the reusable contract further specifies this context as Calculate Taxes. The resulting service capabilities inherit this context and combine it with their own identifiers. The result is three service capabilities that can be read as "calculate taxes for the US," "calculate taxes for the UK," and "calculate taxes for a future jurisdiction."

Related Service-Oriented Computing Goals

- Increased Intrinsic Interoperability

- Increased Business and Technology Alignment

- Increased ROI

- Increased Organizational Agility

- Reduced IT Burden

Uniform Contract [516]

Uniform contracts are highly abstract and general. As explained throughout previous chapters, they are a core part of REST service architecture, relying on generic methods, such as GET and PUT (Figure 14.7), which are combined with media types in order to maximize the applicability and reuse of the contract.

Also included, when this pattern is applied via HTTP, are standardized headers and response codes used as part of the protocol and media types.

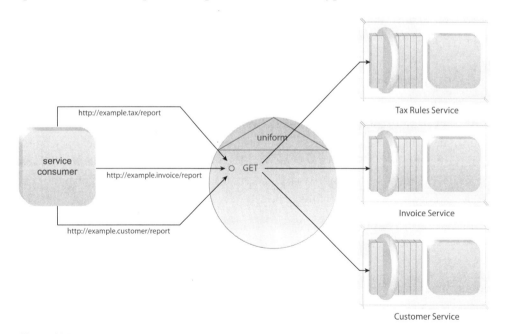

Figure 14.7

A uniform contract may necessitate that services expose multiple lightweight endpoints in order to provide enough context to ascribe meaning to uniform method invocations. In this case, the service capabilities can be read as "Get the tax report," "Get the invoice report," and "Get the customers report." Each of these capabilities can return information in documents compliant with the same report media type.

14.2 Other Relevant SOA Design Patterns

This section briefly covers some key SOA design patterns in order to highlight their relevance to REST and to further supplement the coverage of other SOA design patterns detailed in previous chapters. Several of these particular patterns were listed as being related to the previously described REST-inspired design patterns.

Contract Centralization [447]

The Contract Centralization [447] pattern seeks to reduce coupling between service consumer and service implementations by requiring a service to be accessed only via its published contract. Consumers that access service capabilities through back-door mechanisms, such as shared databases or private APIs, introduce implicit coupling that is difficult to manage and control, and quickly becomes unsustainable. Limiting and "centralizing" access to the service contract avoids negative forms of implementation coupling.

Positioning a uniform contract within a service inventory naturally applies this pattern to all services within the inventory boundary, but additional standardization effort may be required to ensure its on-going use. As explained in the Client-Server {393} profile, this pattern has further relevance to supporting this constraint.

Contract Denormalization [448]

Contract Denormalization [448] encourages service designers to expose capabilities at multiple levels of granularity for use by different service consumers. One service consumer may want a whole invoice or a list of invoices, while another may only need to access the customer details of a given invoice. By providing capabilities at varying levels of granularity, a service contract can reduce processing and network performance overhead associated with capability invocation.

The Lightweight Endpoint [474] pattern can be viewed as a specialized variation of Contract Denormalization [448].

Domain Inventory [458]

Domain Inventory [458] is a fallback pattern used when the services of an enterprise cannot be successfully incorporated into a single centrally-governed service inventory. This pattern suggests that while not ideal, it is acceptable, and in many cases inevitable, that different domains or organizational groups manage individual service inventories independently. Service compositions that cross over multiple service inventories will then likely require integration to resolve disparities (such as the use of different media types to exchange the same kind of data).

This is an extremely important pattern to understand when defining the scope of operation for a uniform contract and the boundary of its supporting REST architecture. Using this pattern we can effectively establish and govern multiple independent uniform contracts within a single IT enterprise.

Schema Centralization [494]

Individual service contracts that express capabilities that process similar documents or types of data can each define their own schema, resulting in mismatched data models representing the same data. Schema Centralization [494] requires the extraction of a single, standardized data model into a centralized schema that is shared by services required to work with that data.

This pattern is important for harmonization between REST and service-orientation, because it merges the media type architecture element with the service-oriented architectural model. Combining Schema Centralization [494] and Content Negotiation [447] can result in a flexible data exchange architecture that can accommodate standardization and schema versioning.

State Messaging [509]

The State Messaging [509] pattern can improve the scalability of services by deferring session state data to the messaging layer. Each time a request message is received by the service it can read the session state present in the message, process the request, modify its own service state, and modify the session state that was present in the message. When its processing is completed the service returns the modified session state back to the service consumer. Instead of a service needing to maintain a specific session state record for each active service consumer, the service is able to return that record back to the service consumer. The service consumer only needs to keep track of its own state.

State Messaging [509] provides a fundamental mechanism that supports the application of the Stateless {395} constraint, in that each request message from a service consumer corresponds to a response message from the service, and that the response message follows this pattern by returning all session state back to the service consumer.

Validation Abstraction [518]

It initially seems useful, when defining contracts, to impose a range of automatic validity checks on requests to be embedded in the contract as they pass through a service's message processing logic. However, excessive validation constraints can harm the reuse of a service contract over time and may require that new contracts or contract revisions be devised and published more often. The Validation Abstraction [518] pattern suggests that validation logic be carefully abstracted to avoid including constraints that are likely to change in the future.

This pattern takes on special significance with REST, as there is greater emphasis on ensuring that media types and related schemas, as members of an overarching uniform contract, are highly generic and reusable.

Chapter 15

Service Versioning with REST

15.1 Versioning Basics

15.2 Version Identifiers

> **NOTE**
>
> The following chapter contains fragments of content that originated in Chapter 21 from the book *Web Service Contract Design and Versioning for SOA*. This content is primarily comprised of general versioning topics and has been further augmented and expanded upon in support with REST-specific versioning content.

After a service contract is deployed, consumer programs will naturally begin forming dependencies on it. When we are subsequently forced to make changes to the contract, we need to figure out:

- whether the changes will negatively impact existing (and potentially future) service consumers

- how changes that will and will not impact consumers should be implemented and communicated

These issues result in the need for versioning. Anytime you introduce the concept of versioning into an SOA project, a number of questions will likely be raised.

For example:

- What exactly constitutes a new version of a service contract? What's the difference between a major and minor version?

- What do the parts of a version number indicate?

- Will the new version of the contract still work with existing consumers that were designed for the old contract version?

- Will the current version of the contract work with new consumers that may have different data exchange requirements?

- What is the best way to add changes to existing contracts while minimizing the impact on consumers?

These types of questions are amplified when changes occur at a uniform contract level because they impact multiple service contracts. And, at any given point in time, multiple services and consumers within the service inventory may be implemented to different versions of these uniform contract elements.

This chapter addresses these and other topics, and further provides a set of options for solving common versioning problems. The upcoming section begins by covering some basic concepts and terminology.

15.1 Versioning Basics

In services-based distributed computing, services and their consumers are deployed as independently executing software programs with potentially different release schedules and requirements. They are able to communicate because they are both implemented according to the same technical contract or interface. In a REST architecture, the service implements its contract, which in turn complies with a uniform contract. The consumer sends messages that comply with the service contract and uniform contract, and understands the responses sent by the service (again, via the uniform contract).

When a contract changes within a software program the logic that depends on that contract is usually modified at the same time. However, it is not always possible for a shared service with multiple service consumers to be modified and deployed in synch with all of its consumers at the same time. This leads to consumers and services often having different views of the contract. As a result, we might end up with a newly-upgraded service handling requests from legacy consumers that have not yet been brought up-to-date. Depending on the release schedules, we may even end up with consumers that have been updated to the latest contract version trying to interact with a legacy version of the service that has not yet been upgraded.

When taking a uniform contract into consideration, we have additional versioning requirements that need to be planned for. For example, a service consumer might be updated to work with a new version of a service contract, but may still be using a legacy version of a media type. Or, a service consumer might be built to use new uniform contract methods that the service may not yet support. Much of this can be addressed by taking forwards and backwards-compatibility into account when designing contract content. In this chapter we cover forwards and backwards compatibility separately for service contracts and uniform contracts.

REST Service Contract Compatibility

A new version of a service contract that continues to support consumer programs designed to work with the old (or legacy) version, is considered *backwards-compatible*. From a design perspective, this means that the new contract has not changed in such a way that it impacts existing consumer programs that are already using the contract. Each of the old service capabilities are still present and continue to support the old combinations of method, resource identifier, and media types.

A backwards-compatible change to a REST-compliant service contract can include:

- Adding new service capabilities with new resource identifiers that were not previously available.

- Adding new service capabilities using existing resource identifiers, but with new methods.

- Adding new supported media types to existing service capabilities using existing methods and resource identifiers that can be selected using Content Negotiation [446].

- Changing resource identifiers in use by an existing service capability, and using Endpoint Redirection [460] to direct legacy consumers to the new resource identifiers.

In each of these cases existing service consumers can invoke old methods on old resources using old media types that continue to work as they previously did, as shown here:

```
POST /orders(application/vnd.com.actioncon.po+xml)
GET /orders/{id}:
  application/vnd.com/actioncon.po+xml, text/html
PUT /orders/{id}(application/vnd.com/actioncon.po+xml)
GET /orders/{id}/items: text/uri-list
GET /orders/{id}/status: text/plain
PUT /orders/{id}/status(text/plain)
DELETE /orders/{order-id}
GET /orders/{id}/invoice
Redirect to http://invoice/invoice/{invoice-id}
```

Example 15.1

The red text highlights changes that have been made to the REST service contract. These changes are considered backwards-compatible because they do not impact existing service consumers.

Here are some more specific examples of backwards-compatible changes:

- The addition of a new capability that introduces a new GET method on a new set of resource identifiers that will not be invoked by old consumers.

- The addition of a new PUT-based capability that requests the transitioning of the status of a purchase order. This introduces a new supported method for a set of existing resource identifiers, and will also not be invoked by old consumers.

- The addition of a new media type for the existing GET-based service capability which allows the purchase order data to be returned in a human-readable form. The use of Content Negotiation [446] ensures that consumers that continue to require the machine-readable format are still accommodated by the service contract, as long as a service inventory-wide design standard is in place that requires all service consumers to include an `Accept` header in their request messages.

- The application of Logic Centralization [475] to the service inventory so that all invoices are now required to be served solely by a centralized Invoice service. The legacy invoice retrieval capability on the Purchase Order service is replaced with a redirection that continues to support legacy service consumers.

When a REST service contract is designed in such a manner that it can support a range of future consumer programs, it is considered to have an extent of *forwards-compatibility*. This means that the contract can essentially accommodate how some consumer requirements may evolve over time. Forwards-compatibility is primarily a concern addressed at the uniform contract level. Within individual REST service contracts, parameterized service capabilities and the use of hypermedia can potentially enable an extent of forwards-compatibility by enabling the service contract to support a broader range of input and output values.

Compatible and Incompatible Changes

When we make a change to a service contract that does not negatively affect existing consumers, then the change itself is considered a *compatible change*. For the purpose of this chapter, we can consider the term "compatible change" as referring to backwards-compatibility by default.

If a change to a contract makes that contract no longer compatible with existing consumers, then it is considered to have received an *incompatible change*. These are the types of changes that impose the most versioning challenges.

Incompatible changes to a REST service contract can include:

- Removing an old service capability.

- Removing support for an old media type for a given service capability.

- Changing the resource identifiers for an existing service capability without applying Endpoint Redirection [460].

Backwards-incompatible changes can also be introduced by sending response messages to legacy consumers that they do not understand.

One way of alleviating the impact of incompatible changes is to equip services with logic that returns an appropriate response message to a consumer that attempts to invoke a capability or feature that is no longer supported by the service. In HTTP, the typical response for this situation is either `404 Not Found` for a resource identifier that is no longer available, or `405 Method Not Allowed` if a method is no longer supported for an existing resource identifier.

The term "incompatible change" can be substituted with "backwards-incompatible change." When referring to incompatible changes that affect forwards-compatibility, the term can further be qualified as "forwards-incompatible change."

Uniform Contract Method Compatibility

When we consider the compatibility of methods we need to look at all of the aspects of the method, including its headers and response codes. Let's take a closer look at these aspects in relation to backwards and forwards-compatibility.

Backwards-compatible changes can be made to the uniform contract method by:

- Introducing new uniform contract methods that legacy service consumers will not use.

- Introducing new optional headers in request messages that legacy service consumers do not need to supply.

- Introducing new response codes or "must understand" response headers that are only used if the consumer has signaled in its request message that it is able to understand them; for example, a new response code that is used solely in conjunction with a corresponding new method or header.

- Introducing new headers in response messages that do not need to be supported, as long as a service inventory-wide standard exists for consumers to ignore response headers they do not understand

Backwards-incompatible changes include:

- Introducing new mandatory headers in request messages that are not supplied by legacy service consumers.

- Sending new response codes or "must understand" response headers to legacy service consumers.

Example 15.2 demonstrates a simple compatible change when a custom SUBSCRIBE method is added to the uniform contract for a service inventory. Corresponding standard fallback logic will be invoked when a service does not understand SUBSCRIBE to periodically issue a GET request, instead. The new method will include new associated headers and link relations that allow the service to notify the consumers when a resource changes. New response codes may also be defined to be backwards-compatible if they are only returned in a response message to the new method.

```
GET
PUT
DELETE
POST
SUBSCRIBE
```

Example 15.2

The addition of a new method added to a service inventory's uniform contract can be backwards-compatible.

Uniform Contract Media Type Compatibility

Compatible changes to a media type include:

- The addition of new optional XML elements and attributes or equivalent structures that do not need to be understood by their recipient, as long as a service inventory-wide design standard exists allowing services to ignore elements and attributes that are not understood

- Changes to a schema that impact the validation logic associated with the media type, if the validation logic is centralized (such as in a utility service) and can be easily upgraded.

Incompatible changes to a media type include:

- The addition of new mandatory XML elements and attributes (or equivalent structures) that are not supplied by legacy services and consumers.

- The addition of new optional XML elements and attributes (or equivalent structures) that must be understood by their recipient.

- Changes to a schema that impact the validation logic associated with the media type when the validation logic is implemented redundantly in both service and consumer.

Example 15.3 demonstrates the introduction of a new optional XML element to an existing media type. This change will be compatible only if legacy services and service consumers are able to use validation logic that accommodates the new element, if the new element does not have "must understand" semantics, and if the legacy services and consumers ignore the new content when it is supplied.

```
Media type = application/vnd.com.actioncon.po+xml
<xsd:schema xmlns:xsd="http://www.w3.org/2001/XMLSchema"
  targetNamespace="http://actioncon.com/schema/po"
  xmlns="http://actioncon.com/schema/po">
  <xsd:element name="LineItem" type="LineItemType"/>
  <xsd:complexType name="LineItemType">
    <xsd:sequence>
      <xsd:element name="productID" type="xsd:string"/>
      <xsd:element name="productName" type="xsd:string"/>
      <xsd:element name="available" type="xsd:boolean"
        minOccurs="0"/>
    </xsd:sequence>
  </xsd:complexType>
</xsd:schema>
```

Example 15.3

The addition of the optional `available` element to the `LineItemType` complex type has no impact on legacy services and consumers that produce this type because they are not required to provide this element in their messages, provided legacy services and consumers can also safely ignore the additional information if a document that contains the `available` element is supplied to them.

Changes to validation logic can sometimes be avoided by altering the validation constraint granularity. Schemas can be authored in a way that enforces minimal actual validation to maximize the opportunity for later versions of the schema to make compatible changes. This is the basis of the Validation Abstraction [518] pattern. However, when it comes to versioning, such an approach can lead to a tradeoff between supporting backwards-compatibility and performing adequate validation of input data. Service inventories that implement validation logic redundantly across multiple services and consumers add a maintenance burden that can force architects to choose between backwards-compatibility and strict validation logic.

With REST, it is possible to use Code-on-Demand {407} to normalize the definition of the logic and to then decentralize its execution. This technique allows the validation logic that would be embedded into each service and each consumer to become dynamic to support new versions of the schema as they are introduced. In the simplest case this can amount to a service that is given the responsibility to maintain the current XML schema version for each media type. The services and consumers that need to validate documents against the media type can do so by obtaining a copy of the XML schema and executing the validation logic themselves.

This approach can ensure that documents are validated strictly against the most current schema for that media type, even if they were not designed specifically for that schema version. It is important that such services ignore elements and attributes that they do not understand in validated documents. This allows compatible changes to be made to subsequent versions of the media type schema.

When we have control over how we choose to design a new version of a media type, compatibility is generally attainable. However, mandatory changes (such as those imposed by laws or regulations) can often force us to break backwards-compatibility. When incompatible changes are required to a media type it can be preferable to create a new media type with a new identifier rather than modifying the existing media type. This allows services and consumers to remain compatible with one another through Content Negotiation [446], as follows:

- Legacy service consumers generate the legacy media type in request messages and request the legacy media type in response messages.

- Legacy services reject the current version as input and return the legacy version in response messages.

- Updated services support both the legacy media type and the current media type for as long as it takes to upgrade all of the related service consumers.

- Updated service consumers continue to be able to supply the legacy media type in request messages and process it in response messages until the service that uses the legacy type has been upgraded.

This type of approach avoids cases where service compositions suddenly stop working due to the incompatible changes and further facilitates the incremental rollout of new media types.

NOTE

When XML schemas are used with REST services, the scope of compatible changes that are possible is often tied to the increase or reduction of the quantity or granularity of validation logic expressed in the schema definition. Therefore, let's briefly recap the meaning of the term "validation constraint granularity" (first introduced in Chapter 4) in relation to a type definition.

Note the red and bolded parts in the following example:

```
<xsd:element name="LineItem" type="LineItemType"/>
<xsd:complexType name="LineItemType">
  <xsd:sequence>
    <xsd:element name="productID" type="xsd:string"/>
    <xsd:element name="productName" type="xsd:string"/>
    <xsd:any minOccurs="0" maxOccurs="unbounded"
      namespace="##any" processContents="lax"/>
  </xsd:sequence>
  <xsd:anyAttribute namespace="##any"/>
</xsd:complexType>
```

Example 15.4

A complexType construct containing fine and coarse-grained validation constraints.

As indicated by the red text, there are elements with specific names and data types that represent parts of the message definition with a *fine* level of validation constraint granularity. All of the message instances (the actual XML documents that will be created based on this structure) must conform to these validation constraints in order to be considered valid (which is why these are considered the absolute "minimum" constraints).

The bolded text shows the element and attribute wildcards also contained by this complex type. These represent parts of the message definition with an extremely *coarse* level of constraint granularity in that messages do not need to comply to these parts of the message definition at all. These wildcards act as possible "extension points" where new content can be added without becoming inconsistent with the existing validation logic provided by the schema. If redundant validation logic is allowed, then the validation logic that is coarser-grained can increase the possible scope of compatible change. If the validation logic is centralized, then it can be upgraded more easily and finer-grained validation logic can be applied.

Media Types and Forwards-compatibility

The fact that we can apply Content Negotiation [446] at runtime makes forwards compatibility somewhat of a built-in feature of a uniform contract. When it comes to a media type's schema design, one way of adding an extent of flexibility into the schema definition is to use wildcards, as shown here:

```
<xsd:schema xmlns:xsd="http://www.w3.org/2001/XMLSchema"
   targetNamespace="http://actioncon.com/schema/po"
   xmlns="http://actioncon.com/schema/po">
   <xsd:element name="LineItem" type="LineItemType"/>
   <xsd:complexType name="LineItemType">
     <xsd:sequence>
       <xsd:element name="productID" type="xsd:string"/>
       <xsd:element name="productName" type="xsd:string"/>
       <xsd:any namespace="##any" processContents="lax"
          minOccurs="0" maxOccurs="unbounded"/>
     </xsd:sequence>
     <xsd:anyAttribute namespace="##any"/>
   </xsd:complexType>
</xsd:schema>
```

Example 15.5

The xsd:any and xsd:anyAttribute elements are added to allow for a range of unknown elements and data to be accepted by the service contract. In other words, the schema is being designed in advance to accommodate unforeseen changes in the future.

It is important to understand that building these types of extension points into service contracts for forwards-compatibility by no means eliminates the need to consider compatibility issues when making contract changes. New data can only be added to schemas in a forwards compatible manner if it is genuinely safe for processors to ignore. Furthermore, a forwards compatible service contract will often not be able to process all message content; it's simply designed to accept a wider range of data unknown at the time of its design.

SUMMARY OF KEY POINTS

- Service contracts enable backwards-compatibility by continuing to support service capabilities with existing methods, resource identifiers, and media types.

- Uniform contract methods support backwards-compatibility by only activating new features when the consumer has indicated it can support them.

- Media types support backwards-compatible changes by adding new optional fields that do not need to be understood and keeping validation logic centralized or abstracted. An extent of forwards-compatibility can be supported through the use of Content Negotiation [446] and schema language features, such as wildcards.

15.2 Version Identifiers

One of the most fundamental design patterns related to service contract design is Version Identification [519]. It essentially advocates that version numbers should be clearly expressed, not just at the contract level, but right down to the versions of the schemas that underlie the message definitions. The first step to establishing an effective versioning strategy is to decide on a means by which versions themselves are identified and represented within service contracts.

Versions are almost always communicated with version numbers. The most common format is a decimal, followed by a period and then another decimal, as shown here:

```
version="2.0"
```

Sometimes, you will see additional period + decimal pairs that lead to more detailed version numbers like this:

```
version="2.0.1.1"
```

The typical meaning associated with these numbers is the measure or significance of the change. Incrementing the first decimal generally indicates a major version change (or upgrade) in the software, whereas decimals after the first period usually represent various levels of minor version changes.

From a compatibility perspective, we can associate additional meaning to these numbers. Specifically, the following convention has emerged in the industry:

- A minor version is expected to be backwards-compatible with other minor versions associated with a major version. For example, version 5.2 of a program should be fully backwards-compatible with versions 5.0 and 5.1.

- A major version is generally expected to break backwards-compatibility with programs that belong to other major versions. This means that program version 5.0 is not expected to be backwards-compatible with version 4.0.

> **NOTE**
>
> A third "patch" version number is also sometimes used to express changes that are both forwards-compatible and backwards-compatible. Typically these versions are intended to clarify the schema only, or to fix problems with the schema that were discovered once it was deployed. For example, version 5.2.1 is expected to be fully compatible with version 5.2.0, but may be added for clarification purposes.

This convention of indicating compatibility through major and minor version numbers is referred to as the *compatibility guarantee*. Another approach, known as "amount of work," uses version numbers to communicate the effort that has gone into the change. A minor version increase indicates a modest effort, and a major version increase predictably represents a lot of work.

These two conventions can be combined and often are. The result is often that version numbers continue to communicate compatibility as explained earlier, but they sometimes increment by several digits, depending on the amount of effort that went into each version.

Using Version Identifiers

Regardless of the version identifier numbering system that is used, there will be various options for how and where this system can be applied. Web service contracts that use a WSDL definition as the primary technical document to represent the scope of the service and its capabilities can include an overall service version number within the definition code. REST services, however, may have no such base technical interface definition. We are therefore required to rely more upon the documented symbol notation as a means of communicating the service's functional context, its capabilities and, if we also choose to, its version.

There is no established industry standard for expressing versioning information for REST service contracts. This means, as with a versioning identifier system, we need to select a convention that works best for our IT enterprise. Figure 15.1 provides an example of such a convention.

Figure 15.1

A sample extension to the REST service contract notation in which the version number is displayed on the bottom of the chorded circle symbol.

Once we get into the actual technical documents that are used by and in conjunction with REST service contracts we can explore various syntax options for expressing version numbers.

For example, the declaration statement that begins an XML document can contain a number that expresses the version of the XML specification being used:

```
<?xml version="1.0"?>
```

That same `version` attribute can be used with the root `xsd:schema` element, as follows:

```
<xsd:schema version="2.0" ...>
```

You can further create a custom variation of this attribute by assigning it to any element you define (in which case you are not required to name the attribute "version").

```
<LineItem version="2.0">
```

An alternative custom approach is to embed the major version number into a namespace or media type identifier, as shown here:

```
<LineItem xmlns="http://actioncon.com/schema/po/v2">
```

or

```
application/vnd.com.actioncon.po.v2+xml
```

Including a major version number or some other means of communicating an incompatible change into the media type identifier allows services to use the Content Negotiation [446] pattern to distinguish and select between different major versions of the same media type.

Note that it has become a common convention to use date values in namespaces when versioning XML schemas, as follows:

```
<LineItem xmlns="http://actioncon.com/schema/po/2010/09">
```

In this case, it is the date of the change that acts as the major version identifier. Regardless of which type of version identifier you choose, it is important to consider Canonical Versioning [439] which dictates that the expression of version information must be standardized across all service contracts within the boundary of a service inventory. In larger environments, this will often require a central authority that can guarantee the linearity, consistency, and description quality of version information.

> **NOTE**
>
> Of course you may also be required to work with third-party schema definitions that may already have implemented their own versioning conventions. In this case, the extent to which Canonical Versioning [439] can be applied will be limited.

Version Identifiers and the Uniform Contract

Each part of the uniform contract is specified and versioned independently from the others. Changing any one does not generally require another to be updated or versioned. Likewise, changing any part of a uniform contract does not generally require that we change the version numbers of dependent REST service contracts.

With a uniform contract we further have the opportunity to use industry specification identifiers as an alternative to custom version identifiers, as follows:

- The version number or specification of the resource identifier syntax (as per the "Request for Comments 6986 - Uniform Resource Identifier (URI): Generic Syntax" specification).

- The version number or specification of the collection of HTTP methods, response codes, and other interaction protocol details (as per the "Request for Comments 2616 - Hypertext Transfer Protocol - HTTP/1.1" specification).

- The version number or individual specifications for legal media types (for example, the "Request for Comments 4287 - The Atom Syndication Format" specification).

SUMMARY OF KEY POINTS

- Version numbers are commonly expressed with a decimal followed by one or more decimals and/or periods. The first decimal typically represents a major version number, whereas the following decimal(s) represent minor version numbers.

- A minor version is usually expected to be backwards-compatible, whereas a major version is not.

- There are various parts of a REST service contract and a uniform contract that can be versioned separately and independently.

- The standardization of versioning within a service inventory is required to ensure the interoperability goals of service-orientation.

NOTE

One aspect of service versioning not covered in this chapter is the retirement of services and service capabilities. SOA design patterns, such as Termination Notification [512], can be used to address common concerns. However, with REST in particular, the use of hypermedia and late binding (as described in Chapters 6, 11, and 12) can introduce new and distinct challenges. For example, with service compositions that incorporate dynamic binding, it can be relatively easy to lose track of which services are being composed and when. Because there is no concrete mapping of how consumers are invoking service capabilities, it can be difficult to know whether a particular service or service capability can safely be retired. The use of modern governance and management tools can alleviate this by providing runtime monitoring metrics used to track actual service and capability usage.

Chapter 16

Uniform Contract Profiles

16.1 Uniform Contract Profile Template

16.2 REST Service Profile Considerations

16.3 Case Study Example

In Chapter 15 from the book *SOA Principles of Service Design* we introduced the service profile as a standardized, living definition used to document the characteristics of a service, from its inception through to its implementation and on-going evolution. The service profile is typically owned by the service custodian, a role assumed by an individual or group responsible for the service's implementation, usage, maintenance, and infrastructure.

With a REST-based service inventory, we require an equivalent profile for the uniform contract. This profile is owned and maintained by whichever group is responsible for overseeing the service inventory as a whole. Standardized uniform contract profiles are especially important when multiple domain service inventories exist or are being planned within an enterprise.

> **NOTE**
>
> With a few customizations, a REST-based service can be as effectively documented using the established service profile template as any other type of service. We briefly highlight recommendations for augmenting conventional service profiles for REST services in the *REST Service Profile Considerations* section.

16.1 Uniform Contract Profile Template

As with the service profile, the uniform contract profile is also a template-based document used to capture not only the methods and media types supported by the uniform contract, but also a range of properties and descriptions that help clearly communicate its scope and required usage.

Each uniform contract profile will contain a number of sections and fields for separately evolving facets, as well as references to relevant technical specifications. These sections and fields are organized into the following parts:

- one uniform-level structure
- one or more method profile structures
- one or more media type profile structures

This uniform-level structure establishes the global properties of the uniform contract. It is then further supplemented by method and media type profile structures, each of which provides a separate profile for an individual uniform method or media type.

Uniform-Level Structure

- *Uniform Contract Name* – Uniform contracts don't usually have a technical name; however, it can be helpful to assign practical labels, especially in environments with multiple service inventories.

- *Purpose Description (Short)* – A concise explanation of the uniform contract's overall purpose and functional context.

- *Purpose Description (Detailed)* – A detailed explanation of the uniform contract's overall purpose and functional context, and its relationship to any other related uniform contracts.

- *Service Inventory* – The service inventory associated with this uniform contract. In the less common circumstance where a single uniform contract is used in multiple service inventories, then each service inventory would be listed here.

- *Industry Standards* – A master list of the official industry standards used for defining methods, media types, and any other applicable parts of the uniform contract.

- *Methods* – The list of (primitive and complex) methods exposed by the uniform contract.

- *Media Types* – The list of media types supported by the uniform contract.

- *Version* – The current version number of the uniform contract. Depending on the version control system in use, version numbers may only be applicable to methods and media types.

- *Status* – The development status of the uniform contract (or uniform contract version) is expressed in this field using standard terms identifying a project lifecycle stage, such as "analysis," "design." This status field may also be applied individually to methods and media types.

- *Custodian* – Details on how to reach the official uniform contract custodian or owner, as well as others that contributed to this documentation.

Method Profile Structure

- *Method Name* – For primitive methods, standard pre-defined method names are used (such as GET and POST). For complex methods, the custom method names are used (such as Fetch and Store).

- *Purpose Description (Short)* – A concise explanation of the method's overall purpose and functional context (similar to the short uniform contract description).

- *Purpose Description (Detailed)* – A detailed explanation of the method including an explanation of how this method differs from others, justifications for any breaches of REST constraints, and guidance for when to use this method.

- *Logic Description* – A step-by-step description of the method's logic and likely message exchanges between service and consumer. For complex methods, this field explains the involvement of the previously listed primitive methods, as well as other forms of logic that services or consumers that use this method must comply with (such as redirection or the delivery of specific message content).

- *Input/Output* – This field contains a description of the input and output of the method, including headers and generic message content but excluding media types. It can be helpful to describe these in plain English during the uniform contract modeling phase.

- *Response Code Handling* – A set of pre-defined response codes the service method may issue, along with pre-defined behaviors that may be required by the consumer. This field is primarily relevant to support complex method interactions and may be excluded from primitive method profiles.

- *Primitive Methods* – This field is only used for complex methods. The list of primitive methods invoked by the complex method logic are listed and described for reference purposes.

- *Required Intermediaries* – Portions of a method's processing logic can be delegated to an intermediary proxy or gateway, in which case the relevant service agents are listed in this field. For example, caching or policy enforcement may be performed by an intermediary or perhaps the coordination of a transaction (for a complex method) may require a controller agent.

- *QoS Requirements* – This field captures any specific quality-of-service requirements associated with the method.

- *Keywords* – It can be helpful to associate keywords with the method to improve its discoverability, especially when using search facilities with front-end tools. Keywords can be used to express the method's purpose and properties, such as "stateful" or "transactional." Keywords used with uniform contract and REST service profiles must be based on the same parent vocabulary.

- *Version* – Depending on the versioning system in place, methods themselves may be versioned with a number, which may be included at runtime in a header.

- *Status* – The same lifecycle identifiers used for the uniform contract can be applied to the status of individual methods. However, this field can also be used to earmark methods that were identified during the modeling stage but for which no specific delivery date exists.

- *Custodian* – More often than not, the custodian of the uniform contract will be the custodian of the related methods. However, there may be exceptions, especially with complex methods.

Media Type Profile Structure

- *Media Type Name* – This is usually the official identifier used to reference the media type. The identifier syntax can follow the Internet media type naming conventions when used in conjunction with HTTP, or another form of identifier (such as a URL) when used with other types of methods. However, plain English terms (such as "XML" or "JSON") can be further used as an alias for ease of communication.

- *Purpose Description (Short)* – A concise explanation of the media type's overall purpose and functional context (similar to the short uniform contract description).

- *Purpose Description (Detailed)* – A detailed explanation of the media type including references to prior sources that the media type may be based on, along with justification of the new type, and descriptions as to how this media type may differ from related types.

- *Schema Description* – A step-by-step description of the type of information defined for the media type and the way in which the information is to be produced, validated, and consumed as part of various scenarios. References to external schema may be used.

- *Keywords* – Often the same keywords that apply to the uniform contract can be carried over to the media type. But it is not uncommon for additional keywords to be added to individual media types so as to better classify their purpose or properties. Keywords for uniform contract and media types should originate from the same parent vocabulary.

- *Version* – Media types will commonly have their own version, distinct from the version number of the uniform contract. If backwards-incompatible changes have been made since the last revision the major version number is likely to appear within the media type identifier (as per guidelines provided in Chapter 15). Otherwise, the previous media type identifier may be reused and the version number included as part of the content of documents compliant with the media type.

- *Status* – The same lifecycle identifiers used for the uniform contract can be applied to the status of individual media types. However, this field can also be used to earmark media types that were identified during the modeling stage but for which no specific delivery date exists, and can indicate an earlier or later stage in the project lifecycle than other parts of the uniform contract.

- *Custodian* – A media type may have a different custodian from the uniform contract, especially when it is determined that the media type and its associated schema need to be maintained by an expert in the specific field from which the schema vocabulary was drawn.

> **NOTE**
>
> We have described the uniform contract profile in terms of the uniform-level structure, the method structure, and the media type structure. In some cases we can consider using different or additional structures as part of a uniform contract profile.
>
> For example:
>
> - *Response Code Structure* – Describes an individual response code that is common to multiple methods.
>
> - *Header Structure* – Describes a request or response header that is common to multiple methods.

- *Link Relation Type Structure* – Describes a global vocabulary of link relation type (similar to the IETF's Link Relation Type registry), that can be reused between different media types or as part of headers to describe relationships between resources.

- *Canonical Vocabulary Structure* – Describes a consistent business vocabulary to be used across multiple media types.

- *Canonical Schema Structure* – Describes a standardized data representation or schema to be used across multiple media types.

16.2 REST Service Profile Considerations

REST services introduce new considerations for what service profiles need to encompass. Specifically, the following common fields should be included as part of REST service profiles:

- the set of resource identifiers for each service capability

- the uniform contract method used by each service capability

- alternative representations supported by a service capability (for both input and output)

- anticipated response codes

The service profile needs to document aspects of a REST service that may not be publically available. For example, REST service contracts may not publish all of the resources available at runtime. Some resources may be kept private and only made known to service consumers through hyperlinks that the service logic itself hands out.

Resource identifiers are typically published in the form of URI templates that include variable parts. In many cases the URI template can be based on the form {+*uri*}, where the entire structure of the resource identifier is optimized out of the contract. This minimizes undesirable coupling of service consumer logic to precise resource identifier structures, while still allowing capabilities to be effectively invoked through late binding of resource identifiers.

Table 16.1 contains some sample content that demonstrates how REST service capabilities can be documented in a service profile.

Method	Resource Identifier Set (replace {parameters} with identifier values as per RFC 6570)	Alternative Representations (including media types)	Documentation and Exceptions
GET	`/{manufacturer}` `/{model}` or `{+board}`	`application/` `vnd.com.example.` `board-model+xml`	Retrieve description of the specified board. Exception Response: `404 Not Found`
GET	`/{ticker-symbol}` `/LastTradePrice`	`application/` `vnd.com.example.` `currency+xml`	Retrieve last trade for ticker-symbol. Exception Response: `204 No Trades Today`
GET	`/hello` `/{firstname}`	`text/html`	Returns a greeting with first name included.
GET	`/{auction-id}` `/CurrentPrice`	`text/float+plain`	Returns the price of the auction-id auction. Exception Responses: `404 Not Found` or `204 Not Started`
POST	`/{auction-id}/Bids`	`application/` `vnd.com.bid+xml`	Enter a new bid in the auction identified by auction-id. Exception Responses: `404 Not Found` or `204 Not Started` or `409 Closed`

Table 16.1

An example of service capability documentation that can be part of a service profile for a REST service.

16.3 CASE STUDY EXAMPLE

MUA architects initially determined that they would use HTTP methods and a combination of internally defined and externally defined media types. They published descriptions of the initial versions of the media types and supplied references to the media type specifications upon request.

They quickly found development teams coming to them with a number of problems:

- It wasn't clear which services the uniform contract should apply to.

- Media types were being developed, but their specifications were difficult for developers to find and it was difficult to determine the current version for each type

- When new media types needed to be defined there was redundant effort being expended searching for existing media types and underlying schemas were being missed or ignored

- HTTP methods were being implemented inconsistently. Services were being written that ignored most request headers and only returned the response headers needed to make their test programs work, and so didn't support important features. Consumers were not dealing with all of the exceptional conditions they needed to deal with, or were requiring the core consumer logic to perform complex exception recovery handling.

The MUA team took a number of steps to resolve these problems:

- They created a uniform contract profile to document the scope, status, and intent of the uniform contract and to capture related, trusted sources.

- They established an HTTP Adoption Group responsible for coordinating policy on how HTTP methods can be used (complex methods in particular), as well as to publish related standards and address concerns from project teams, as they arise.

- The HTTP Adoption Group defined baseline standards for handling GET, PUT, DELETE, and other requests and for handling exceptional conditions. These standards were further codified in the Fetch and Store complex methods. For example, service contracts would no longer refer to GET and PUT, but instead to the MUA Fetch and Store methods that impose extra MUA policy requirements on processing. This also had the effect of simplifying service contract definitions.

- They developed a catalog of relevant industry media types, as well as upcoming media types they predict will be relevant.

Having a centralized place to find current methods and media types improved development efficiency and reduced developer confusion significantly. A standardization process was put in place to qualify HTTP libraries used by consumers and services to ensure they had all required features available in a form that allowed for efficient development activities. Additionally, checks against MUA policy were included in service qualification testing activities.

From this foundation, the MUA team authors the MUAUC uniform contract profile, as shown in the remaining tables in this chapter. With this detailed profile document, the team is now able to start thinking more deeply about interactions that will be required for complex service compositions.

Uniform-Level Structure: MUAUC

Uniform Contract Name	MUA Uniform Contract (MUAUC)
Purpose Description (Short)	To define the uniform contract for services in the MUA service inventory.
Purpose Description (Detailed)	To define the uniform contract used by all services, in the MUA service inventory, that have been identified as participating in the REST program. To document externally used methods and media types that MUA services and service consumers need to interact with, and to define complex methods that comply with all relevant MUA policies and standards.
Service Inventory	MUA service inventory
Industry Standards	The following sources will be used preferentially for methods and media types, and for underlying schema to develop new media types where required: • HTTP/1.1 (as defined in RFC 2616 and related specifications) • IANA Media Type Registry • The Common Education Data Standards (v 2.0)

Methods	Fetch*, Store*, GET, PUT, POST *Sample structures for these methods are included in this case study example.*
Media Types	<ul><li>`text/plain`</li><li>`application/xhtml+xml`</li><li>`application/vnd.edu.mua.invoice+xml`</li><li>`Student Record*`</li><li>`Book List*`</li></ul> *These media types are still under development and have yet to be assigned an Internet Media Type identifier. They may be replaced with an externally-defined type if a suitable existing media type is found.
Keywords	HTTP, Education
Status	Proposed
Custodian	MUA HTTP Adoption Team

Table 16.2
The MUA uniform contract profile, uniform-level contract structure.

Method Profile Structure: Fetch

Method Name	Fetch
Purpose Definition (Short)	Efficiently and reliably perform data retrievals.
Purpose Description (Detailed)	Retrieve data in a manner consistent with MUA policy, with all required features supported by service and consumer. The service provides all necessary information to the consumer for it to continue operating regardless of service failure modes, and the consumer is capable of dealing with all exception-type responses.

continues

Logic Description	1. The consumer sends a GET request to the service.
	2. The service processes the request according to GET semantics and service contract semantics, including support for headers noted in the Input/Output field of this profile.
	3. The consumer message processing logic processes the normal or exception response, and recovers automatically for response codes (in Table 16.4). Other responses are returned to the core consumer logic as exceptions
	Note: Services must support the HEAD method for all Fetch URLs.
Input/Output	The consumer's GET request must contain the following information:
	• The list of acceptable media types in its `Accept` header.
	• The ETag of its cached response (if any) in its `If-None-Match` header or timestamp of its cached response in its `If-Modified-Since` header
	• Evidence of identity (when challenged) in its `Authorization` and/or `Proxy-Authorization` headers, but only if a secure connection has been established to the party requesting authentication
	The service must process the following request headers if supplied:
	• `Accept`
	• `If-None-Match`
	• `If-Modified-Since`
	• `Authorization`
	The service must return valid content for the following headers:
	• `Content-Type`
	• `ETag`
	• `Last-Modified`
	• `Cache-Control`
	• `Vary`

Primitive Methods	GET, HEAD
Required Intermediaries	n/a
QoS Requirements	All responses must begin transmission within 40 seconds of the GET request being sent, and must complete within 300 seconds.
Keywords	Compound, HTTP, Safe, Idempotent
Version	1.0
Status	Proposed—The new policy decisions for this complex method have been defined but not yet implemented for services or consumers within the MUA service inventory.
Custodian	MUA HTTP Adoption Group

Table 16.3
The MUA Fetch method profile.

Response Code Handling for GET Methods in Fetch Method

`200 OK`	Return content supplied in response.
`204 No Content`	Return null content.
`304 Not Modified` `412 Precondition Failed`	Return cached content.

`301 Moved Permanently`
`302 Found`
`303 See Other`
`305 Use Proxy`
`307 Temporary Redirect`
	Follow redirection as per RFC2 616 for at least five redirections, but the consumer must maintain a list of recent redirections to avoid following a redirection loop.

continues

`401 Unauthorized`
 	
`407 Proxy Authentication Required`
	Retry request with requested credentials information to complete any security negotiation for Basic and SPENGO authentication mechanisms only if communication is over a secure connection.

`408 Request Timeout` `504 Gateway Timeout` (or a TCP connection was lost before the response was completely returned)	Retry immediately, with up to a limit of 5 retries.
`503 Service Unavailable` (or a connection cannot be established with the service or proxy)	The consumer should try all available IP addresses for the service or proxy and consider the service to be unavailable if none are responsive. It should continue retrying at a period of once per 30 seconds or at the rate specified by the Retry-After header for three further attempts.

Table 16.4
Response code handling for the MUA Fetch method.

Method Profile Structure: Store

Method Name	Store
Purpose Definition (Short)	Reliably store data received from a consumer.
Purpose Description (Detailed)	Replace the nominated state with the supplied data in a manner consistent with MUA policy, with all required features supported by service and consumer. The service provides all necessary data to the consumer for it to continue operating regardless of service failure modes, and the consumer is capable of dealing with all exceptional responses. This method is capable of storing data (indicated by the PUT primitive method, or a "deleted" state (indicated by the DELETE primitive method).

Logic Description	1. The consumer sends a PUT or DELETE request to the service. 2. The service processes the request based on PUT or DELETE semantics and service contract semantics, including support for headers noted in the Input/Output field of this profile. 3. The consumer message processing logic processes the normal or exception response, and recovers automatically for response codes (in Table 16.6) without requiring the core consumer logic to be aware of the processing. Other responses are to be returned to the core consumer logic as exceptions.
Input/Output	The consumer's PUT or DELETE request must contain the following information: • The data being supplied (if the request is PUT). • The format of the supplied data in its `Content-Type` header (if the request is PUT). • Evidence of identity (when challenged) in its `Authorization` and/or `Proxy-Authorization` headers. The service must be capable of processing the following headers: • Content-Type • Authorization
Primitive Methods	PUT, DELETE.
Required Intermediaries	n/a
QoS Requirements	All responses must begin transmission within 40 seconds of the PUT or DELETE request being sent, and must complete within 60 seconds.
Keywords	Compound, HTTP, Idempotent
Version	1.0

continues

Status	Proposed—The new policy decisions for this compound method have been defined but not yet implemented for services or consumers within the MUA service inventory.
Custodian	MUA HTTP Adoption Group

Table 16.5
The MUA Store method profile.

Response Code Handling for PUT and DELETE Methods in Store Method

Code	Processing
`200 OK`	The request completed successfully
`404 Not Found` `410 Gone`	The request completed successfully (for DELETE requests only)

`301 Moved Permanently`
`302 Found`
`303 See Other`
`305 Use Proxy`
`307 Temporary Redirect`
	Follow redirection for at least five redirections, but the consumer must maintain a list of recent redirections to avoid following a redirection loop.
	
	Note that MUA policy contradicts RFC 2616 in this case, which only permits GET requests to be redirected without human interaction.

`401 Unauthorized` `407 Proxy Authentication Required`	Retry request with requested credentials information to complete any security negotiation for Basic and SPENGO authentication mechanisms only if communication is over a secure connection.
`408 Request Timeout` `504 Gateway Timeout` (or a TCP connection was lost before the response was completely returned)	Retry immediately, up to a limit of 5 retries.

`415 Unsupported Media Type`	If this response includes an `Accept` header the consumer must format the information according to one of the service's supported media types if any are supported by the consumer
`503 Service Unavailable` (or a connection cannot be established with the service or proxy)	The consumer should try all available IP addresses for the service or proxy and consider the service to be unavailable if none are responsive. It should continue retrying at a period of once per 30 seconds or at the rate specified by the `Retry-After` header for three further attempts.

Table 16.6
Response code handling for the MUA Store method.

Method Profile Structure: GET

Method Name	GET
Purpose Description	Retrieve data.
Purpose Description (Detailed)	Retrieve data with support for content negotiation, caching, and other standard HTTP features.
Logic Description	A single GET request is made by the consumer to the desired URL, and the service returns a normal or exceptional response. All behavior is compliant with RFC 2616.
Input/Output	Returns the requested data or an exception response code.
Required Intermediaries	n/a
QoS Requirements	n/a
Keywords	Primitive, HTTP, Safe, Idempotent

continues

Version	1.1, RFC 2616
Status	Private—This method is only made available to published complex methods.
Custodian	MUA HTTP Adoption Group

Table 16.7
The HTTP GET method profile.

Method Profile Structure: PUT

Method Name	PUT
Purpose Description	Store data.
Purpose Description (Detailed)	Replace the nominated state with the supplied data.
Logic Description	A single PUT request is made by the consumer to the desired URL, and the service returns a normal or exception response code. All behavior is compliant with RFC 2616.
Input/Output	Accepts the request data as input.
Required Intermediaries	n/a
QoS Requirements	n/a
Keywords	Primitive, HTTP, Idempotent
Version	1.1, RFC 2616
Status	Private—This method is only made available to published complex methods.
Custodian	MUA HTTP Adoption Group

Table 16.8
The HTTP PUT method profile.

Media Type Profile Structure:
Invoice (`application/vnd.edu.mua.invoice+xml`)

Media Type Name	Invoice (`application/vnd.edu.mua.invoice+xml`)
Purpose Description (Short)	To capture invoice data.
Purpose Description (Detailed)	To capture invoice data both in paid and unpaid states, to facilitate payment of the invoice, and to facilitate updates to the invoice state in response to various conditions.
Schema Description	To maximize its applicability to multiple use cases the invoice schema allows for zero or more invoices to be defined. Each invoice includes: • Supplier reference (anyURI) • Customer reference (anyURI) • Payment terms (string) • Due date (date) • State (paid or unpaid) • Items, each listing the item part number, Part Description, Quantity, Price • Payments, a list of payments related to the invoice • Link to State resource • Link to input new payments Schema location: `http://schema.mua.com/application/vnd.com.mua.invoice+xml`
Keywords	XML, Invoice
Version	1.0
Status	Draft Standard (in use by multiple interoperable services)
Custodian	Internal, Finance

Table 16.9
The Invoice media type profile.

Part VI

Appendices

Appendix A: Case Study Conclusion

Appendix B: Industry Standards Supporting the Web

Appendix C: REST Constraints Reference

Appendix D: Service-Orientation Principles Reference

Appendix E: SOA Design Patterns Reference

Appendix F: State Concepts and Types

Appendix G: The Annotated SOA Manifesto

Appendix H: Additional Resources

Appendix A

Case Study Conclusion

The MUA project team completes multiple iterations of the service-oriented analysis process, during which the service inventory's uniform contract is further refined. By the time they move on to subsequent service-oriented design processes, they have defined a set of uniform methods and set of uniform media types that have incrementally become better aligned to service contracts and the overall business automation needs of MUA.

Their uniform contract methods are mostly derived from the HTTP specification, but a small number of custom primitive methods and related complex methods have been introduced to support specific types of message exchanges that are not widely used on the Web, and for which no industry standards exist. The uniform contract does contain a few media types that are defined by external bodies. MUA settled on using these external standards to encode primitive data types, such as strings and numbers, as well as human-readable data. They use an externally-defined media type to capture the properties and relationships of most entities to allow utility services to reliably extract properties and relationships that are common to multiple entity types.

Despite this level of media type standardization, most media types are still internally defined. This provides those that oversee the service inventory the freedom to model entities in a way that is relevant to the MUA enterprise and its partner schools. Only at a few key integration points (in support of partner schools and some suppliers), is there the need for complex entity media types to be standardized separately from the MUA service inventory. Where these integration points do exist the internally-defined types have tended to align to the corresponding media types. When this has occurred it has produced an increased intrinsic level of interoperability between MUA services and those found in external service inventories that share the common media types. Primitive methods are openly reused between service inventories due to their common origin in the HTTP specification.

A modest percentage of message exchange interactions within the service inventory are not compliant with the Stateless {395} constraint. This is understood by the architects who added extra memory and other infrastructure to compensate for any loss in scalability. Those same architects further document these and other cases where REST constraints are intentionally breached, along with explanations for each exception.

Genuine reuse of media types has stabilized at around the 70% mark. The remaining media types have so far turned out to be too specialized for reuse. Of the 70% that are being reused, 40% are in use by less than three services. These reuse levels impact the degree to which dynamic binding within service compositions is possible. Many utility services compose entity services and occasionally task services by retrieving additional data from resources identified in their requests. This has reduced the need for consumers of the utility services to know exactly what information the utility services need to perform their function. It has further enabled the utility services to obtain that data directly for themselves. The few media types that are reused by most services facilitate this type of composition with the result of lowering coupling requirements between utility and entity services.

As part of establishing a governance framework, the MUA team established a formal process for reviewing service contracts for compliance with the uniform contract as well as REST constraints and service-orientation principles. The standards enforced by this contract further govern the use of late binding, allowing resource identifier information to be stripped out of service contracts, when appropriate. Processes are also in place for maintaining the uniform contract by handling requests to modify, add, or remove uniform contract elements.

Overall, the MUA project team achieved several of the goals that were first defined when it had decided to adopt SOA to improve legacy integration and enhance user experience. The centralized governance framework that was established helped successfully deliver the SFN service that introduced a new dimension of functionality and features for students to better connect with each other. This first service delivery project further assisted MUA with collecting better quality information about student preferences, and helped set the stage for the many additional service delivery projects currently being planned.

Finally, KioskEtc's goal to broaden accessibility to its stores was realized via the Stores REST service that allowed customers with mobile devices to search and locate various information about individual store locations.

There is further case study content pertaining to MUA in the book *Service-Oriented Infrastructure: On-Premise and in the Cloud*, where a series of REST-related infrastructure topics are covered. Figure A.1 displays a diagram from this book that provides a logical view that hints at how the MUA infrastructure evolves in support of new requirements.

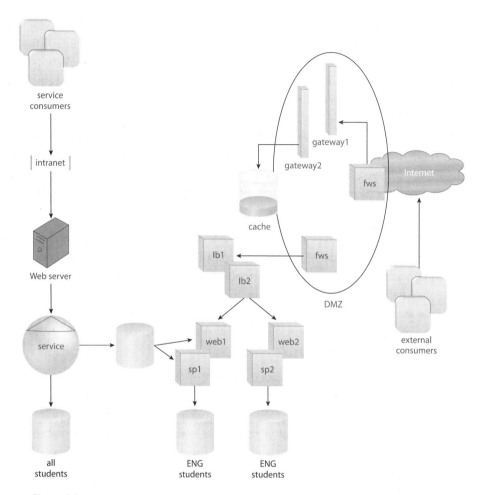

service
consumers

| intranet |

Web server

service

all
students

cache

gateway1

gateway2

fws

Internet

lb1

lb2

fws

DMZ

web1

web2

sp1

sp2

ENG
students

ENG
students

external
consumers

Figure A.1

Appendix B

Industry Standards Supporting the Web

The Internet Engineering Taskforce (IETF)

The World Wide Web Consortium

Other Web Standards

In a REST-style architecture the application protocol is defined by the uniform contract. The three constituent standards of the Web's application layer are the Uniform Resource Identifier (URI), Hypertext Transfer Protocol (HTTP), and Internet Media Types (MIME).

These facets are defined separately to each other, allowing the specifications to be modified on independent release schedules, combined with other specifications as part of the Web, or used in contexts outside of the Web.

HTTP forms the Web's application layer and is usually built on top of the Transmission Control Protocol (TCP) and often on top of the Transport Layer Security (TLS) protocol, also known as Secure Sockets Layer (SSL). These protocols, in turn, are built on various versions of the Internet Protocol (IP), and on top of a variety of Link Layer protocols.

The pre-defined set of Internet media types contains an array of schemas that can be used to encode data in ways that are interpretable by a range of arbitrary recipients. Some of the media types are based on the Extensible Markup Language (XML), while others may be based on the older Standard Generalized Markup Language (SGML), JavaScript Object Notation (JSON), or on various binary foundations.

The URI specification supports both application protocol and media type specifications. This syntax allows resources to be identified using a generic container that can be used to directly exchange messages with the service that owns each resource.

The Internet Engineering Taskforce (IETF)

The Internet Engineering Taskforce (IETF) is the primary body behind the Internet. It is responsible for specifications governing application protocols, such as HTTP, transports, routing, security, real-time communications, operational management, and several others.

The IETF standardization process is a combination of bottom-up development and top-down control mechanisms. Anyone may pen an Internet draft, on any topic they choose. These drafts expire within six months, and must generally be adopted by a working group to achieve a Request for Comments (RFC) status. When a working group has chosen to promote a specific draft, it is subjected to a review by the Internet Engineering Steering Group (IESG) who may seek to further revise the specification before it is adopted or rejected.

The Internet Assigned Numbers Authority (IANA) group controls the allocation of numbers and identifiers for small registries. For example, the set of identifiers for media types on the Internet is governed by the IANA. The assignment of TCP port numbers is also a responsibility of this group. The IANA provides registries of important identifiers that can act as a quick reference into applicable standards and can avoid identifier clashes from occurring. A separate body, known as the RFC editor, is responsible for assigning identifiers to standards themselves, as they move out of draft phase and become RFCs.

Key standards governed by the IETF include:

- HyperText Transfer Protocol (HTTP) – http://www.ietf.org/rfc/rfc2616
- Uniform Resource Identifier (URI) – http://www.ietf.org/rfc/rfc3986
- Atom Syndication Format – http://www.ietf.org/rfc/rfc4287
- Transmission Control Protocol (TCP) – http://www.ietf.org/rfc/rfc793

Additional media types are registered by the IANA:

http://www.iana.org/assignments/media-types/

The World Wide Web Consortium

The World Wide Web Consortium (W3C) began as an organization designed to feed specifications into the IETF for formal standardization. The W3C has a particular focus on the Web and governs standards for HTML, XML, XML Schema, Semantic Web, SOAP-based Web Services, and a range of others.

Each member organization has a seat on the Advisory Committee and can access member-only information and make member submissions. Members may participate in working, interest, and coordination groups, in workshops and symposia, or on the W3C (management) team as W3C fellows. The W3C team provides technical leadership and organizes and manages W3C activities. The Advisory Board provides ongoing guidance to the team on issues of strategy, management, legal matters, process, and conflict resolution. The Technical Architecture Group (TAG) documents and builds consensus around principles of Web architecture and interpreting and clarifying these principles where necessary. It resolves issues involving general Web architecture, and helps coordinate cross-technology architecture developments inside and outside the W3C.

Although the ongoing work is carried on via private lists by working members, the significant milestones and drafts are published in public lists and made available to the public at large. The general public may participate in mailing lists and workshops, comment on upcoming standards, or may be invited as experts in working groups.

> http://www.w3.org/2005/10/Process-20051014/

Other Web Standards

The industry standards below are also worth noting:

JavaScript Object Notation (JSON)

> http://www.json.org/

JavaScript, ECMA International

> http://www.ecma-international.org/memento/TC39.htm

Appendix C

REST Constraints Reference

This appendix provides profile tables for the five constraints that were introduced in Chapter 5. Each constraint that is referenced in this book is suffixed with the page number of its corresponding profile table in this appendix.

Every profile table contains the following sections:

- *Short Definition* – A concise, single-statement definition that establishes the fundamental purpose of the constraint.

- *Long Definition* – A longer description of the constraint that provides more detail as to what it is intended to accomplish.

- *Application* – A list of common steps and requirements for applying the constraint.

- *Impacts* – A list of positive and negative impacts that can result from the application of the constraint.

- *Relationship to REST* – A brief explanation of how the constraint can relate to other constraints and overall REST architecture.

- *Related REST Goals* – A list of REST design goals that are related to and relevant to the application of this constraint. (The design goals were covered in Chapter 5 and are also known as design properties.)

- *Related Service-Orientation Principles* – A list of service-orientation principles related to the constraint.

- *Related SOA Patterns* – A list of SOA design patterns related to the constraint (including REST-inspired design patterns introduced in Appendix F).

Each profile table is followed by a *Related Excerpts from Fielding's Dissertation* section that provides relevant excerpts from Roy Fielding's *Architectural Styles and the Design of Network-based Software Architectures* for reference purposes.

Note that the upcoming constraint profiles have been authored using language and terminology compatible with this book. You may notice different terminology being used in the aforementioned excerpts. For example, Fielding's references to interface or uniform interface correspond to the term uniform contract in this book. This and other vocabulary differences are explained in Chapters 5 and 6.

Client-Server	
Short Definition	Solution logic is separated into consumer and service logic that share a technical contract.
Long Definition	Business automation logic is organized into a solution comprised of units of consumer and service logic. Service consumers actively invoke service capabilities by sending messages that comply with a published technical service contract. Services passively wait to process request messages and respond to their receipt in compliance with the technical contract.
Application	• Solution logic must undergo a process whereby it is subjected to the separation of concerns. This partitions the logic into units that address defined concerns. These units of logic are composed to form the solution at runtime. • The consumer's required knowledge about a service and the service's required knowledge of its consumers are limited to the contents of the shared technical contract.
Impacts	• Service logic can become more scalable and reusable because it is freed from having to implement consumer-specific logic. • Service and consumer logic are simplified due to respective information hiding. • Service and consumer implementations can be evolved independently in ways that do not require alterations to the shared contract. • Interactions between services and consumers that circumvent the shared technical contract are prohibited, potentially resulting in lost opportunities to optimize the solution architecture.
Relationship to REST	This is a foundational constraint that defines the separation between service, consumer, and the technical contract they share. All of the other constraints reference these artifacts and so build upon this constraint.
Related REST Goals	Modifiability, Scalability
Related Service-Orientation Principles	Service Loose Coupling (413), Service Abstraction (414)
Related SOA Patterns	Capability Composition [440], Contract Centralization [447], Decoupled Contract [455], Functional Decomposition [469]

Related Excerpts from Fielding's Dissertation

"A client is a triggering process; a server is a reactive process. Clients make requests that trigger reactions from servers. Thus, a client initiates activity at times of its choosing; it often then delays until its request has been serviced. On the other hand, a server waits for requests to be made and then reacts to them. A server is usually a non-terminating process and often provides service to more than one client."

"Separation of concerns is the principle behind the client-server constraints. A proper separation of functionality should simplify the server component in order to improve scalability. ...The separation also allows the two types of components to evolve independently, provided that the interface doesn't change."

NOTE

This definition was authored primarily from the perspective of applying the constraint on the Web, separating Web Server from a client-side consumer, such as a Web Browser. The definition does not directly make reference to a technical contract, but the goals for the Client-Server constraint do refer to the equivalent "interface." It is made clear that the purpose of this constraint is to allow service and consumer to evolve independently, and to simplify their respective implementations via a separation of concerns.

Note also that the first paragraph is a quote from the dissertation that cites: "Paradigms for process interaction in distributed programs" by G. Andrews, ACM Computing Surveys, 23(1), Mar. 1991.

Stateless	
Short Definition	Services remain stateless between request/response message exchanges with service consumers.
Long Definition	The communication between a service and a consumer is regulated so that the consumer provides all data necessary for the service to understand each consumer request. Between requests, the service is not permitted to retain any state data specific to its interaction with the consumer instance, allowing it to exist in a stateless condition. Instead, session state is deferred to the consumer at the end of each request.
Application	• Consumer logic must be designed to preserve state data between requests and to issue request messages containing state data. • The request message must contain all of the state data necessary for the service to process the request, and the service must be able to "forget" the state data upon issuing the response without compromising the overall interaction. • Because the service is only involved in the automation of a solution when a consumer is actively making a request to it, in-between requests the service is "at rest," and therefore using no CPU, memory, or network resources on behalf of the consumer. • The service cannot be required to store data specific to a run-time instance of a service consumer. However, the service is still allowed to store data that is related to its own functional context.

continues

Impacts	• Making consumers responsible for preserving state data alleviates the service from having to store and replicate potentially volatile data that is only relevant to the individual consumer program.
	• Deferring session state to consumers between requests frees up service memory resources, allowing the service to scale with the number of concurrent requests, rather than with the total number of concurrent consumers.
	• Messages can be understood by the service without the need to have inspected earlier messages. This can simplify service logic design and further reduce the complexity of debugging.
	• The requirement to repeatedly transmit potentially redundant state data can increase network traffic and processing overhead.
	• Reliability of state data can be both positively and negatively impacted: Service instance failures can be dealt with gracefully because the service does not retain state, but failure of the service consumer can result in a loss of state data.
Relationship to REST	While this constraint builds upon Client-Server {393}, it helps enable Cache {398} and Layered System {404}.
Related REST Goals	Modifiability, Scalability, Performance (negative), Visibility, Reliability
Related Service-Orientation Principles	Service Statelessness (418)
Related SOA Patterns	State Messaging [509]

Related Excerpts from Fielding's Dissertation

"The client-stateless-server style derives from client-server with the additional constraint that no session state is allowed on the server component. Each request from client to server must contain all of the information necessary to understand the request, and cannot take advantage of any stored context on the server. Session state is kept entirely on the client."

"These constraints [Client-Server, Stateless] improve the properties of visibility, reliability, and scalability. Visibility is improved because a monitoring system does not have to look beyond a single request datum in order to determine the full nature of the request. Reliability is improved because it eases the task of recovering from partial failures. Scalability is improved because not having to store state between requests allows the server component to quickly free resources and further simplifies implementation."

"The disadvantage of client-stateless-server is that it may decrease network performance by increasing the repetitive data (per-interaction overhead) sent in a series of requests, since that data cannot be left on the server in a shared context."

Cache	
Short Definition	Service consumers can cache and reuse response message data.
Long Definition	The data provided by a prior response message can be temporarily stored and reused by the service consumer for later request messages.
Application	• Services must be designed to produce accurate cache control metadata and return it in response messages. Response messages are marked as cacheable or non-cacheable, either with explicit message metadata or as part of the contract definition.
	• An optional consumer-side or intermediary cache repository enables the consumer to reuse cacheable response data for later request messages.
	• Request messages must be comparable to determine whether or not they are equivalent.
	• Contracts must either include explicit statements about the cacheability of responses, or must allow for cache control metadata to be included in responses.
Impacts	• Runtime efficiency is improved by eliminating the need for duplicate response messages to be transmitted and processed.
	• The cache provides a robust and simple mechanism to perform "lazy replication" of service state data to its consumers.
	• Some forms of cached data can become stale and outdated if not regularly checked and updated.
Relationship to REST	A number of established techniques for pushing data out to consumers are disallowed by the application of Client-Server {393} and Stateless {395}. The Cache constraint provides a mechanism that is permitted by other constraints and one that results in a simple and robust architecture for reusing and optimizing the distribution of data.
Related REST Goals	Performance, Scalability, Reliability (Negative)
Related Service-Orientation Principles	n/a
Related SOA Patterns	Messaging Metadata [477]

Related Excerpts from Fielding's Dissertation

"The client-cache-stateless-server style derives from the client-stateless-server and cache styles via the addition of cache components. A cache acts as a mediator between client and server in which the responses to prior requests can, if they are considered cacheable, be reused in response to later requests that are equivalent and likely to result in a response identical to that in the cache if the request were to be forwarded to the server."

"Caching provides slightly less improvement than the replicated repository style in terms of user-perceived performance, since more requests will miss the cache and only recently accessed data will be available for disconnected operation. On the other hand, caching is much easier to implement, doesn't require as much processing and storage, and is more efficient because data is transmitted only when it is requested. The cache style becomes network-based when it is combined with a client-stateless-server style."

"The advantage of adding cache components is that they have the potential to partially or completely eliminate some interactions, improving efficiency and user-perceived performance."

Uniform Contract	
Short Definition	Service consumers and services share a common, overarching, generic technical contract.
Long Definition	Consumers access service capabilities via methods, media types, and a common resource identifier syntax that are standardized across many consumers and services. Service capabilities provide access to resources that can further provide links to other resources.
Application	• A uniform contract with generic and reusable methods, media types, and resource identifier syntax is established for a collection of consumers and services. • Consumer message processing logic is designed to be tightly coupled to the uniform contract. • Consumer message processing logic is designed to be decoupled or loosely coupled to service-specific capabilities and resources. • Resources can further provide links to other resources that the service consumer can "discover" and optionally access, dynamically at runtime.
Impacts	• The application of this constraint results in baseline standardization of technical interface characteristics across all services within the scope of application. This level of standardization can foster interoperability across all affected services. • Standardization resulting from Uniform Contract can include canonical schemas associated with media types. The common use of such schemas can further improve the extent of intrinsic interoperability. • By limiting coupling to the uniform contract and leveraging dynamic binding, consumers and services can achieve reduced levels of overall coupling requirements. • It can be difficult to identify and entirely rely on built-in uniform contract semantics for machine-to-machine interactions that need to be reusable by multiple services and their consumers. • Request and response messages based on uniform methods and media types may contain more information than is strictly required for a particular interaction. The transfer of redundant data can increase performance overhead.

Relationship to REST	The Uniform Contract constraint builds upon Client-Server {393} to support reuse and composition of consumers and services.
Related REST Goals	Simplicity, Modifiability, Performance (negative), Visibility
Related Service-Orientation Principles	Standardized Service Contract (411), Service Loose Coupling (413), Service Abstraction (414)
Related SOA Patterns	Decoupled Contract [455]

Related Excerpts from Fielding's Dissertation

"REST provides a hybrid of [traditional client-server style sending a fixed format image to the recipient, mobile object style encapsulating the data with a rendering engine and sending both to the client, and sending the raw data to the recipient along with metadata that describes the type so the recipient can choose its own rendering engine] options by focusing on a shared understanding of data types with metadata, but limiting the scope of what is revealed to a standardized interface. REST components communicate by transferring a representation of a resource in a format matching one of an evolving set of standard data types, selected dynamically based on the capabilities or desires of the recipient and the nature of the resource. Whether the representation is in the same format as the raw source, or is derived from the source, remains hidden behind the interface."

"The key abstraction of information in REST is a resource. Any information that can be named can be a resource: a document or image, a temporal service (e.g. "today's weather in Los Angeles"), a collection of other resources, a non-virtual object (e.g. a person), and so on. In other words, any concept that might be the target of an author's hypertext reference must fit within the definition of a resource. A resource is a conceptual mapping to a set of entities, not the entity that corresponds to the mapping at any particular point in time."

"REST components perform actions on a resource by using a representation to capture the current or intended state of that resource and transferring that representation between components. A representation is a sequence of bytes, plus representation metadata to describe those bytes. Other commonly used but less precise names for a representation include: document, file, and HTTP message entity, instance, or variant."

"... a given representation may indicate the current state of the requested resource, the desired state for the requested resource, or the value of some other resource, such as a representation of the input data within a client's query form, or a representation of some error condition for a response. For example, remote authoring of a resource requires that the author send a representation to the server, thus establishing a value for that resource that can be retrieved by later requests. If the value set of a resource at a given time consists of multiple representations, content negotiation may be used to select the best representation for inclusion in a given message."

"REST enables intermediate processing by constraining messages to be self-descriptive: interaction is stateless between requests, standard methods and media types are used to indicate semantics and exchange information, and responses explicitly indicate cacheability."

"Restricting the interface allows independently developed [services and consumers] to be arranged at will to form new applications. It also simplifies the task of understanding how a given [service or consumer] works."

"A disadvantage of the uniform interface is that it may reduce network performance if the data needs to be converted to or from its natural format."

"By applying the software engineering principle of generality to the component interface, the overall system architecture is simplified and the visibility of interactions is improved. Implementations are decoupled from the services they provide, which encourages independent evolvability. The trade-off, though, is that a uniform interface degrades efficiency, since information is transferred in a standardized form rather than one which is specific to an application's needs. The REST interface is designed to be efficient for large-grain hypermedia data transfer, optimizing for the common case of the Web, but resulting in an interface that is not optimal for other forms of architectural interaction."

Layered System

Short Definition	A solution can be comprised of multiple architectural layers.
Long Definition	A solution is defined in terms of architectural layers, where no one layer can see past the next. Layers can be comprised of consumers and services with published contracts or event-driven middleware components (intermediaries) that establish processing layers between consumers and services. In either case, logic within a given solution layer cannot have knowledge beyond the immediate layers above or below it (within the solution hierarchy).
Application	• Consumers are designed to invoke services without knowledge of what other services those services may also invoke. • Intermediaries are added to perform runtime message processing without knowledge of how those messages may be further processed beyond the next layer of processing. • The solution architecture is designed to allow new middleware layers to be added or old middleware layers to be removed without changing the technical contract between services and consumers. • Request and response messages must not reveal which layer the message comes from to their recipients.
Impacts	• At the consumer/service level, this constraint ensures an extent of information hiding, which naturally reduces consumer-to-service coupling. • At the middleware component level, this constraint advocates the use of cross-cutting agents capable of performing generic, utility-centric functions on messages exchanged by consumers and services. • These types of architectural layers can provide a flexible means of evolving a solution architecture and/or its underlying infrastructure while minimizing the impact on the solution logic itself. • The increased separation and distribution of moving parts performing solution logic processing can negatively impact the overall performance overhead (especially when middleware components are being reused by multiple solutions). • By limiting knowledge of the entire solution architecture to consumer designers, opportunities for optimizing the runtime performance of a solution can be lost.

Relationship to REST	The middleware components commonly introduced by the application of this constraint can directly support or enable Uniform Contract {400}, Cache {398}, and Stateless {395}.
Related REST Goals	Modifiability, Scalability, Performance (negative), Simplicity, Visibility
Related Service-Orientation Principles	Service Loose Coupling (413), Service Abstraction (414)
Related SOA Patterns	Capability Composition [440], Service Agent [495], Service Layers [504]

Related Excerpts from Fielding's Dissertation

"A layered system is organized hierarchically, each layer providing services to the layer above it and using services of the layer below it. Although layered system is considered a "pure" style, its use within network-based systems is limited to its combination with the client-server style to provide layered-client-server.

... Layered-client-server adds proxy and gateway components to the client-server style. A proxy acts as a shared server for one or more client components, taking requests and forwarding them, with possible translation, to server components. A gateway component appears to be a normal server to clients or proxies that request its services, but is in fact forwarding those requests, with possible translation, to its "inner-layer" servers. These additional mediator components can be added in multiple layers to add features like load balancing and security checking to the system.

... the layered system style allows an architecture to be composed of hierarchical layers by constraining component behavior such that each component cannot "see" beyond the immediate layer with which they are interacting. By restricting knowledge of the system to a single layer, we place a bound on the overall system complexity and promote substrate independence.

Layered systems reduce coupling across multiple layers by hiding the inner layers from all except the adjacent outer layer, thus improving evolvability and reusability. Examples include the processing of layered communication protocols, such as the TCP/IP and OSI protocol stacks, and hardware interface libraries. The primary disadvantage of layered systems is that they add overhead and latency to the processing of data, reducing user-perceived performance.

... LCS is also a solution to managing identity in a large scale distributed system, where complete knowledge of all servers would be prohibitively expensive. Instead, servers are organized in layers such that rarely used services are handled by intermediaries rather than directly by each client.

... Layers can be used to encapsulate legacy services and to protect new services from legacy clients, simplifying components by moving infrequently used functionality to a shared intermediary. Intermediaries can also be used to improve system scalability by enabling load balancing of services across multiple networks and processors."

Code-on-Demand	
Short Definition	Service consumers support the execution of deferred service logic.
Long Definition	Service consumer architectures include an execution environment for logic provided by a service. This deferred logic can be used to extend the functionality of the consumer, or to temporarily specialize it for a particular purpose.
Application	• Service consumers are designed to process logic offloaded to them by services at runtime. • Services make explicit decisions as to whether they will execute logic themselves or defer the execution of that logic to their consumers.
Impacts	• Features can be dynamically added to consumers without the need for them to be formally upgraded. • Services are able to avoid becoming execution bottlenecks by deferring logic to consumers rather than executing the logic themselves. • The required execution environments for consumers to process service logic can introduce security vulnerabilities.
Relationship to REST	n/a
Related REST Goals	Modifiability, Scalability, Performance, Visibility (negative), Simplicity (negative)
Related Service-Orientation Principles	n/a
Related SOA Patterns	n/a

Related Excerpts from Fielding's Dissertation

"In the code-on-demand style, a client component has access to a set of resources, but not the know-how on how to process them. It sends a request to a remote server for the code representing that know-how, receives that code, and executes it locally."

"REST allows client functionality to be extended by downloading and executing code in the form of applets or scripts. This simplifies clients by reducing the number of features required to be pre-implemented. Allowing features to be downloaded after deployment improves system extensibility. However, it also reduces visibility, and thus is only an optional constraint within REST."

"The advantages of code-on-demand include the ability to add features to a deployed client, which provides for improved extensibility and configurability, and better user-perceived performance and efficiency when the code can adapt its actions to the client's environment and interact with the user locally rather than through remote interactions. Simplicity is reduced due to the need to manage the evaluation environment, but that may be compensated in some cases as a result of simplifying the client's static functionality. Scalability of the server is improved, since it can off-load work to the client that would otherwise have consumed its resources. Like remote evaluation, the most significant limitation is the lack of visibility due to the server sending code instead of simple data. Lack of visibility leads to obvious deployment problems if the client cannot trust the servers."

Appendix D

Service-Orientation Principles
Reference

This appendix provides profile tables for the eight design principles that are documented in *SOA Principles of Service Design*, a title that is part of this book series. Each principle that is referenced in this book is suffixed with the page number of its corresponding profile table in this appendix.

Every profile table contains the following sections:

- *Short Definition* – A concise, single-statement definition that establishes the fundamental purpose of the principle.

- *Long Definition* – A longer description of the principle that provides more detail as to what it is intended to accomplish.

- *Goals* – A list of specific design goals that are expected from the application of the principle. Essentially, this list provides the ultimate results of the principle's realization.

- *Design Characteristics* – A list of specific design characteristics that can be realized via the application of the principle. This provides some insight as to how the principle ends up shaping the service.

- *Implementation Requirements* – A list of common prerequisites for effectively applying the design principle. These can range from technology to organizational requirements.

Note that these tables provide only summarized content from the original publication. Information about service-orientation principles is also published online at SOAPrinciples.com and ServiceOrientation.com.

Standardized Service Contract	
Short Definition	*"Services share standardized contracts."*
Long Definition	*"Services within the same service inventory are in compliance with the same contract design standards."*
Goals	• To enable services with a meaningful level of natural interoperability within the boundary of a service inventory. This reduces the need for data transformation because consistent data models are used for information exchange. • To allow the purpose and capabilities of services to be more easily and intuitively understood. The consistency with which service functionality is expressed through service contracts increases interpretability and the overall predictability of service endpoints throughout a service inventory. Note that these goals are further supported by other service-orientation principles as well.
Design Characteristics	• A service contract (comprised of a technical interface or one or more service description documents) is provided with the service. • The service contract is standardized through the application of design standards.
Implementation Requirements	The fact that contracts need to be standardized can introduce significant implementation requirements to organizations that do not have a history of using standards. For example: • Design standards and conventions need to ideally be in place prior to the delivery of any service in order to ensure adequately scoped standardization. (For those organizations that have already produced ad-hoc Web services, retro-fitting strategies may need to be employed.) • Formal processes need to be introduced to ensure that services are modeled and designed consistently, incorporating accepted design principles, conventions, and standards.

- Because achieving standardized service contracts generally requires a "contract first" approach to service-oriented design, the full application of this principle will often demand the use of development tools capable of importing a customized service contract without imposing changes.

- Appropriate skill-sets are required to carry out the modeling and design processes with the chosen tools. When working with Web services, the need for a high level of proficiency with XML schema and WSDL languages is practically unavoidable. WS-Policy expertise may also be required.

These and other requirements can add up to a noticeable transition effort that goes well beyond technology adoption.

Table D.1
A profile for the Standardized Service Contract principle.

Service Loose Coupling	
Short Definition	*"Services are loosely coupled."*
Long Definition	*"Service contracts impose low consumer coupling requirements and are themselves decoupled from their surrounding environment."*
Goals	By consistently fostering reduced coupling within and between services we are working toward a state where service contracts increase independence from their implementations and services are increasingly independent from each other. This promotes an environment in which services and their consumers can be adaptively evolved over time with minimal impact on each other.
Design Characteristics	• The existence of a service contract that is ideally decoupled from technology and implementation details. • A functional service context that is not dependent on outside logic. • Minimal consumer coupling requirements.
Implementation Requirements	• Loosely coupled services are typically required to perform more runtime processing than if they were more tightly coupled. As a result, data exchange in general can consume more runtime resources, especially during concurrent access and high usage scenarios. • To achieve the right balance of coupling, while also supporting the other service-orientation principles that affect contract design, requires increased service contract design proficiency.

Table D.2
A profile for the Service Loose Coupling principle.

Service Abstraction	
Short Definition	*"Non-essential service information is abstracted."*
Long Definition	*"Service contracts only contain essential information and information about services is limited to what is published in service contracts."*
Goals	Many of the other principles emphasize the need to publish *more* information in the service contract. The primary role of this principle is to keep the quantity and detail of contract content concise and balanced and prevent unnecessary access to additional service details.
Design Characteristics	• Services consistently abstract specific information about technology, logic, and function away from the outside world (the world outside of the service boundary). • Services have contracts that concisely define interaction requirements and constraints and other required service meta details. • Outside of what is documented in the service contract, information about a service is controlled or altogether hidden within a particular environment.
Implementation Requirements	The primary prerequisite to achieving the appropriate level of abstraction for each service is the level of service contract design skill applied.
Web Service Region of Influence	The *Region of Influence* part of this profile has been moved to the *Types of Meta Abstraction* section (in the book *SOA Principles of Service Design*) where a separate Web service figure is provided for each form of abstraction.

Table D.3

A profile for the Service Abstraction principle.

Service Reusability	
Short Definition	*"Services are reusable."*
Long Definition	*"Services contain and express agnostic logic and can be positioned as reusable enterprise resources."*
Goals	The goals behind Service Reusability are tied directly to some of the most strategic objectives of service-oriented computing: • To allow for service logic to be repeatedly leveraged over time so as to achieve an increasingly high return on the initial investment of delivering the service. • To increase business agility on an organizational level by enabling the rapid fulfillment of future business automation requirements through wide-scale service composition. • To enable the realization of agnostic service models. • To enable the creation of service inventories with a high percentage of agnostic services.
Design Characteristics	• *The service is defined by an agnostic functional context*—The logic encapsulated by the service is associated with a context that is sufficiently agnostic to any one usage scenario so as to be considered reusable. • *The service logic is highly generic* The logic encapsulated by the service is sufficiently generic, allowing it to facilitate numerous usage scenarios by different types of service consumers. • *The service has a generic and extensible contract*—The service contract is flexible enough to process a range of input and output messages. • *The service logic can be accessed concurrently*—Services are designed to facilitate simultaneous access by multiple consumer programs.

Implementation Requirements	From an implementation perspective, Service Reusability can be the most demanding of the principles we've covered so far. Below are common requirements for creating reusable services and supporting their long-term existence: • A scalable runtime hosting environment capable of high-to-extreme concurrent service usage. Once a service inventory is relatively mature, reusable services will find themselves in an increasingly large number of compositions. • A solid version control system to properly evolve contracts representing reusable services. • Service analysts and designers with a high degree of subject matter expertise who can ensure that the service boundary and contract accurately represent the service's reusable functional context. • A high level of service development and commercial software development expertise so as to structure the underlying logic into generic and potentially decomposable components and routines. These and other requirements place an emphasis on the appropriate staffing of the service delivery team, as well as the importance of a powerful and scalable hosting environment and supporting infrastructure.

Table D.4

A profile for the Service Reusability principle.

Service Autonomy	
Short Definition	*"Services are autonomous."*
Long Definition	*"Services exercise a high level of control over their underlying runtime execution environment."*
Goals	• To increase a service's runtime reliability, performance, and predictability, especially when being reused and composed. • To increase the amount of control a service has over its runtime environment. By pursuing autonomous design and runtime environments, we are essentially aiming to increase post-implementation control over the service and the service's control over its own execution environment.
Design Characteristics	• Services have a contract that expresses a well-defined functional boundary that should not overlap with other services. • Services are deployed in an environment over which they exercise a great deal (and preferably an exclusive level) of control. • Service instances are hosted by an environment that accommodates high concurrency for scalability purposes.
Implementation Requirements	• A high level of control over how service logic is designed and developed. Depending on the level of autonomy being sought, this may also involve control over the supporting data models. • A distributable deployment environment, so as to allow the service to be moved, isolated, or composed as required. • An infrastructure capable of supporting desired autonomy levels.

Table D.5

A profile for the Service Autonomy principle.

Service Statelessness	
Short Definition	*"Services minimize statefulness."*
Long Definition	*"Services minimize resource consumption by deferring the management of state information when necessary."*
Goals	• To increase service scalability. • To support the design of agnostic service logic and improve the potential for service reuse.
Design Characteristics	What makes this somewhat of a unique principle is the fact that it is promoting a condition of the service that is temporary in nature. Depending on the service model and state deferral approach used, different types of design characteristics can be implemented. Some examples include: • Highly business process-agnostic logic so that the service is not designed to retain state information for any specific parent business process. • Less constrained service contracts so as to allow for the receipt and transmission of a wider range of state data at runtime. • Increased amounts of interpretive programming routines capable of parsing a range of state information delivered by messages and responding to a range of corresponding action requests.
Implementation Requirements	Although state deferral can reduce the overall consumption of memory and system resources, services designed with statelessness considerations can also introduce some performance demands associated with the runtime retrieval and interpretation of deferred state data. Here is a short checklist of common requirements that can be used to assess the support of stateless service designs by vendor technologies and target deployment locations: • The runtime environment should allow for a service to transition from an idle state to an active processing state in a highly efficient manner.

- Enterprise-level or high-performance XML parsers and hardware accelerators (and SOAP processors) should be provided to allow services implemented as Web services to more efficiently parse larger message payloads with less performance constraints.

- The use of attachments may need to be supported by Web services to allow for messages to include bodies of payload data that do not undergo interface-level validation or translation to local formats.

The nature of the implementation support required by the average stateless service in an environment will depend on the state deferral approach used within the service-oriented architecture.

Table D.6
A profile for the Service Statelessness principle.

Service Discoverability	
Short Definition	*"Services are discoverable."*
Long Definition	*"Services are supplemented with communicative meta data by which they can be effectively discovered and interpreted."*
Goals	• Services are positioned as highly discoverable resources within the enterprise. • The purpose and capabilities of each service are clearly expressed so that they can be interpreted by humans and software programs. Achieving these goals requires foresight and a solid understanding of the nature of the service itself. Depending on the type of service model being designed, realizing this principle may require both business and technical expertise.
Design Characteristics	• Service contracts are equipped with appropriate meta data that will be correctly referenced when discovery queries are issued. • Service contracts are further outfitted with additional meta information that clearly communicates their purpose and capabilities to humans. • If a service registry exists, registry records are populated with the same attention to meta information as just described. • If a service registry does not exist, service profile documents are authored to supplement the service contract and to form the basis for future registry records. (See Chapter 15 in *SOA Principles of Service Design* for more details about service profiles.)

Implementation Requirements	• The existence of design standards that govern the meta information used to make service contracts discoverable and interpretable, as well as guidelines for how and when service contracts should be further supplemented with annotations.
	• The existence of design standards that establish a consistent means of recording service meta information outside of the contract. This information is either collected in a supplemental document in preparation for a service registry, or it is placed in the registry itself.
	You may have noticed the absence of a service registry on the list of implementation requirements. As previously established, the goal of this principle is to implement design characteristics within the service, not within the architecture.

Table D.7

A profile for the Service Discoverability principle.

Service Composability	
Short Definition	*"Services are composable."*
Long Definition	*"Services are effective composition participants, regardless of the size and complexity of the composition."*
Goals	When discussing the goals of Service Composability, pretty much all of the goals of Service Reusability (415) apply. This is because service composition often turns out to be a form of service reuse. In fact, you may recall that one of the objectives we listed for the Service Reusability (415) principle was to enable wide-scale service composition. However, above and beyond simply attaining reuse, service composition provides the medium through which we can achieve what is often classified as the ultimate goal of service-oriented computing. By establishing an enterprise comprised of solution logic represented by an inventory of highly reusable services, we provide the means for a large extent of future business automation requirements to be fulfilled through…you guessed it: service composition.
Design Characteristics for Composition Member Capabilities	Ideally, every service capability (especially those providing reusable logic) is considered a potential composition member. This essentially means that the design characteristics already established by the Service Reusability (415) principle are equally relevant to building effective composition members. Additionally, there are two further characteristics emphasized by this principle: • The service needs to possess a highly efficient execution environment. More so than being able to manage concurrency, the efficiency with which composition members perform their individual processing should be highly tuned. • The service contract needs to be flexible so that it can facilitate different types of data exchange requirements for similar functions. This typically relates to the ability of the contract to exchange the same type of data at different levels of granularity. The manner in which these qualities go beyond mere reuse has to do primarily with the service being capable of optimizing its runtime processing responsibilities in support of multiple, simultaneous compositions.

Design Characteristics for Composition Controller Capabilities	Composition members will often also need to act as controllers or sub-controllers within different composition configurations. However, services designed as designated controllers are generally alleviated from many of the high-performance demands placed on composition members.

These types of services therefore have their own set of design characteristics:

- The logic encapsulated by a designated controller will almost always be limited to a single business task. Typically, the task service model is used, resulting in the common characteristics of that model being applied to this type of service.

- While designated controllers may be reusable, service reuse is not usually a primary design consideration. Therefore, the design characteristics fostered by Service Reusability (415) are considered and applied where appropriate, but with less of the usual rigor applied to agnostic services.

- Statelessness is not always as strictly emphasized on designated controllers as with composition members. Depending on the state deferral options available by the surrounding architecture, designated controllers may sometimes need to be designed to remain fully stateful while the underlying composition members carry out their respective parts of the overall task.

Of course, any capability acting as a controller can become a member of a larger composition, which brings the previously listed composition member design characteristics into account as well. |

Table D.8
A profile for the Service Composability principle.

Appendix E

SOA Design Patterns Reference

This appendix provides profile tables for the 85 patterns that are documented in *SOA Design Patterns* plus the following new REST-inspired patterns introduced in this book:

- Content Negotiation [446]

- Endpoint Redirection [460]

- Entity Linking [464]

- Idempotent Capability [470]

- Lightweight Endpoint [474]

- Reusable Contract [492]

- Uniform Contract [516]

As shown in this list, each pattern that is referenced in this book is suffixed with the page number of its corresponding profile table in this appendix.

Every profile table contains the following sections:

- *Requirement* – A requirement is a concise, single-sentence statement that presents the fundamental requirement addressed by the pattern in the form of a question. Every pattern description begins with this statement.

- *Icon* – Each pattern description is accompanied by an icon image that acts as a visual identifier. The icons are displayed together with the requirement statements in each pattern profile as well as on the inside book cover.

- *Problem* – The issue causing a problem and the effects of the problem. It is this problem for which the pattern is expected to provide a solution.

- *Solution* – This represents the design solution proposed by the pattern to solve the problem and fulfill the requirement.

- *Application* – This part is dedicated to describing how the pattern can be applied. It can include guidelines, implementation details, and sometimes even a suggested process.

- *Impacts* – This section highlights common consequences, costs, and requirements associated with the application of a pattern and may also provide alternatives that can be considered.

- *Principles* – References to related service-orientation principles.

- *Architecture* – References to related SOA architecture types.

Note that these tables provide only summarized content from the original publication. All pattern profile tables in this book are also published online at SOAPatterns.org.

Agnostic Capability

By Thomas Erl

How can multi-purpose service logic be made effectively consumable and composable?

Problem	Service capabilities derived from specific concerns may not be useful to multiple service consumers, thereby reducing the reusability potential of the agnostic service.
Solution	Agnostic service logic is partitioned into a set of well-defined capabilities that address common concerns not specific to any one problem. Through subsequent analysis, the agnostic context of capabilities is further refined.
Application	Service capabilities are defined and iteratively refined through proven analysis and modeling processes.
Impacts	The definition of each service capability requires extra up-front analysis and design effort.
Principles	Standardized Service Contract (411), Service Reusability (415), Service Composability (422)
Architecture	Service

Agnostic Context

By Thomas Erl

How can multi-purpose service logic be positioned as an effective enterprise resource?

Problem	Multi-purpose logic grouped together with single purpose logic results in programs with little or no reuse potential that introduce waste and redundancy into an enterprise.
Solution	Isolate logic that is not specific to one purpose into separate services with distinct agnostic contexts.
Application	Agnostic service contexts are defined by carrying out service-oriented analysis and service modeling processes.
Impacts	This pattern positions reusable solution logic at an enterprise level, potentially bringing with it increased design complexity and enterprise governance issues.
Principles	Service Reusability (415)
Architecture	Service

Agnostic Sub-Controller

By Thomas Erl

How can agnostic, cross-entity composition logic be separated, reused, and governed independently?

Problem	Service compositions are generally configured specific to a parent task, inhibiting reuse potential that may exist within a subset of the composition logic.
Solution	Reusable, cross-entity composition logic is abstracted or made accessible via an agnostic sub-controller capability, allowing that subset of the parent composition logic to be recomposed independently.
Application	A new agnostic service is created or a task service is appended with an agnostic sub-controller capability.
Impacts	The addition of a cross-entity, agnostic service can increase the size and complexity of compositions and the abstraction of agnostic cross-entity logic can violate modeling and design standards established by Service Layers [504].
Principles	Service Reusability (415), Service Composability (422)
Architecture	Composition, Service

Asynchronous Queuing

By Mark Little, Thomas Rischbeck, Arnaud Simon

How can a service and its consumers accommodate isolated failures and avoid unnecessarily locking resources?

Problem	When a service capability requires that consumers interact with it synchronously, it can inhibit performance and compromise reliability.
Solution	A service can exchange messages with its consumers via an intermediary buffer, allowing service and consumers to process messages independently by remaining temporally decoupled.
Application	Queuing technology needs to be incorporated into the surrounding architecture, and back-up stores may also be required.
Impacts	There may be no acknowledgement of successful message delivery, and atomic transactions may not be possible.
Principles	Standardized Service Contract (411), Service Loose Coupling (413), Service Statelessness (418)
Architecture	Inventory, Composition

Atomic Service Transaction

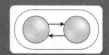

By Thomas Erl

How can a transaction with rollback capability be propagated across messaging-based services?

Problem	When runtime activities that span multiple services fail, the parent business task is incomplete and actions performed and changes made up to that point may compromise the integrity of the underlying solution and architecture.
Solution	Runtime service activities can be wrapped in a transaction with rollback feature that resets all actions and changes if the parent business task cannot be successfully completed.
Application	A transaction management system is made part of the inventory architecture and then used by those service compositions that require rollback features.
Impacts	Transacted service activities can consume more memory because of the requirement for each service to preserve its original state until it is notified to rollback or commit its changes.
Principles	Service Statelessness (418)
Architecture	Inventory, Composition

Brokered Authentication

By Jason Hogg, Don Smith, Fred Chong, Tom Hollander, Wojtek Kozaczynski, Larry Brader, Nelly Delgado, Dwayne Taylor, Lonnie Wall, Paul Slater, Sajjad Nasir Imran, Pablo Cibraro, Ward Cunningham

How can a service efficiently verify consumer credentials if the consumer and service do not trust each other or if the consumer requires access to multiple services?

Problem	Requiring the use of Direct Authentication [456] can be impractical or even impossible when consumers and services do not trust each other or when consumers are required to access multiple services as part of the same runtime activity.
Solution	An authentication broker with a centralized identity store assumes the responsibility for authenticating the consumer and issuing a token that the consumer can use to access the service.
Application	An authentication broker product introduced into the inventory architecture carries out the intermediary authentication and issuance of temporary credentials using technologies such as X.509 certificates or Kerberos, SAML, or SecPAL tokens.
Impacts	This pattern can establish a potential single point of failure and a central breach point that, if compromised, could jeopardize an entire service inventory.
Principles	Service Composability (422)
Architecture	Inventory, Composition, Service

Canonical Expression

By Thomas Erl

How can service contracts be consistently understood and interpreted?

Problem	Service contracts may express similar capabilities in different ways, leading to inconsistency and risking misinterpretation.
Solution	Service contracts are standardized using naming conventions.
Application	Naming conventions are applied to service contracts as part of formal analysis and design processes.
Impacts	The use of global naming conventions introduces enterprise-wide standards that need to be consistently used and enforced.
Principles	Standardized Service Contract (411), Service Discoverability (420)
Architecture	Enterprise, Inventory, Service

Canonical Protocol

By Thomas Erl

How can services be designed to avoid protocol bridging?

Problem	Services that support different communication technologies compromise interoperability, limit the quantity of potential consumers, and introduce the need for undesirable protocol bridging measures.
Solution	The architecture establishes a single communications technology as the sole or primary medium by which services can interact.
Application	The communication protocols (including protocol versions) used within a service inventory boundary are standardized for all services.
Impacts	An inventory architecture in which communication protocols are standardized is subject to any limitations imposed by the communications technology.
Principles	Standardized Service Contract (411)
Architecture	Inventory, Service

Canonical Resources

By Thomas Erl

How can unnecessary infrastructure resource disparity be avoided?

Problem	Service implementations can unnecessarily introduce disparate infrastructure resources, thereby bloating the enterprise and resulting in increased governance burden.
Solution	The supporting infrastructure and architecture can be equipped with common resources and extensions that can be repeatedly utilized by different services.
Application	Enterprise design standards are defined to formalize the required use of standardized architectural resources.
Impacts	If this pattern leads to too much dependency on shared infrastructure resources, it can decrease the autonomy and mobility of services.
Principles	Service Autonomy (417)
Architecture	Enterprise, Inventory

Canonical Schema

By Thomas Erl

How can services be designed to avoid data model transformation?

Problem	Services with disparate models for similar data impose transformation requirements that increase development effort, design complexity, and runtime performance overhead.
Solution	Data models for common information sets are standardized across service contracts within an inventory boundary.
Application	Design standards are applied to schemas used by service contracts as part of a formal design process.
Impacts	Maintaining the standardization of contract schemas can introduce significant governance effort and cultural challenges.
Principles	Standardized Service Contract (411)
Architecture	Inventory, Service

Canonical Schema Bus

By Clemens Utschig-Utschig, Berthold Maier, Bernd Trops, Hajo Normann, Torsten Winterberg, Thomas Erl

While Enterprise Service Bus [462] provides a range of messaging-centric functions that help establish connectivity between different services and between services and resources they are required to encapsulate, it does not inherently enforce or advocate standardization.

Building upon the platform established by Enterprise Service Bus [462], this pattern positions entry points into the logic, data, and functions offered via the service bus environment as independently standardized service contracts.

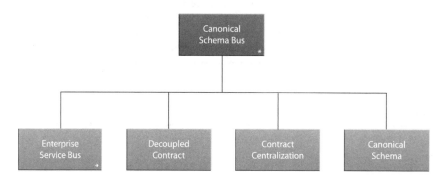

Canonical Schema Bus is comprised of the co-existent application of Enterprise Service Bus [462], Decoupled Contract [455], Contract Centralization [447], and Canonical Schema [437].

Canonical Versioning

By Thomas Erl

How can service contracts within the same service inventory be versioned with minimal impact?

Problem	Service contracts within the same service inventory that are versioned differently will cause numerous interoperability and governance problems.
Solution	Service contract versioning rules and the expression of version information are standardized within a service inventory boundary.
Application	Governance and design standards are required to ensure consistent versioning of service contracts within the inventory boundary.
Impacts	The creation and enforcement of the required versioning standards introduce new governance demands.
Principles	Standardized Service Contract (411)
Architecture	Service, Inventory

Capability Composition

By Thomas Erl

How can a service capability solve a problem that requires logic outside of the service boundary?

Problem	A capability may not be able to fulfill its processing requirements without adding logic that resides outside of its service's functional context, thereby compromising the integrity of the service context and risking service denormalization.
Solution	When requiring access to logic that falls outside of a service's boundary, capability logic within the service is designed to compose one or more capabilities in other services.
Application	The functionality encapsulated by a capability includes logic that can invoke other capabilities from other services.
Impacts	Carrying out composition logic requires external invocation, which adds performance overhead and decreases service autonomy.
Principles	All
Architecture	Inventory, Composition, Service

Capability Recomposition

By Thomas Erl

How can the same capability be used to help solve multiple problems?

Problem	Using agnostic service logic to only solve a single problem is wasteful and does not leverage the logic's reuse potential.
Solution	Agnostic service capabilities can be designed to be repeatedly invoked in support of multiple compositions that solve multiple problems.
Application	Effective recomposition requires the coordinated, successful, and repeated application of several additional patterns.
Impacts	Repeated service composition demands existing and persistent standardization and governance.
Principles	All
Architecture	Inventory, Composition, Service

Compatible Change

By David Orchard, Chris Riley

How can a service contract be modified without impacting consumers?

Problem	Changing an already-published service contract can impact and invalidate existing consumer programs.
Solution	Some changes to the service contract can be backwards-compatible, thereby avoiding negative consumer impacts.
Application	Service contract changes can be accommodated via extension or by the loosening of existing constraints or by applying Concurrent Contracts [445].
Impacts	Compatible changes still introduce versioning governance effort, and the technique of loosening constraints can lead to vague contract designs.
Principles	Standardized Service Contract (411), Service Loose Coupling (413)
Architecture	Service

Compensating Service Transaction

By Clemens Utschig-Utschig, Berthold Maier, Bernd Trops, Hajo Normann, Torsten Winterberg, Brian Loesgen, Mark Little

How can composition runtime exceptions be consistently accommodated without requiring services to lock resources?

Problem	Whereas uncontrolled runtime exceptions can jeopardize a service composition, wrapping the composition in an atomic transaction can tie up too many resources, thereby negatively affecting performance and scalability.
Solution	Compensating routines are introduced, allowing runtime exceptions to be resolved with the opportunity for reduced resource locking and memory consumption.
Application	Compensation logic is pre-defined and implemented as part of the parent composition controller logic or via individual "undo" service capabilities.
Impacts	Unlike atomic transactions that are governed by specific rules, the use of compensation logic is open-ended and can vary in its actual effectiveness.
Principles	Service Loose Coupling (413)
Architecture	Inventory, Composition

Composition Autonomy

By Thomas Erl

How can compositions be implemented to minimize loss of autonomy?

Problem	Composition controller services naturally lose autonomy when delegating processing tasks to composed services, some of which may be shared across multiple compositions.
Solution	All composition participants can be isolated to maximize the autonomy of the composition as a whole.
Application	The agnostic member services of a composition are redundantly implemented in an isolated environment together with the task service.
Impacts	Increasing autonomy on a composition level results in increased infrastructure costs and government responsibilities.
Principles	Service Autonomy (417), Service Reusability (415), Service Composability (422)
Architecture	Composition

Concurrent Contracts

By Thomas Erl

How can a service facilitate multi-consumer coupling requirements and abstraction concerns at the same time?

Problem	A service's contract may not be suitable for or applicable to all potential service consumers.
Solution	Multiple contracts can be created for a single service, each targeted at a specific type of consumer.
Application	This pattern is ideally applied together with Service Façade [501] to support new contracts as required.
Impacts	Each new contract can effectively add a new service endpoint to an inventory, thereby increasing corresponding governance effort.
Principles	Standardized Service Contract (411), Service Loose Coupling (413), Service Reusability (415)
Architecture	Service

Content Negotiation

By Raj Balasubramanian, David Booth, Thomas Erl

How can a service capability accommodate service consumers with different data format or representation requirements?

Problem	Different service consumers may have differing requirements for how data provided by a given service capability needs to be formatted or represented.
Solution	Allow the service capability to support alternative formats and representations by providing a means by which consumer and service can "negotiate" data characteristics at runtime.
Application	The pattern is most commonly applied via HTTP media types that can define the format and/or representation of message data. The media type of the data is decoupled from the data itself, allowing the service to support a range of media types. The consumer provides metadata in each request message to identify preferred and supported media types. The service attempts to accommodate preferences, but can also return the data in other supported media types when issuing the response message.
Impacts	Fewer service capabilities are needed to accommodate variation in service consumer requirements. Services are able to support old and new service consumer versions concurrently using the same service capabilities. The complexity of cache implementations is increased, and requires that caching metadata indicate what metadata input to each request may affect which representation will be returned. Requesting metadata that is not abstract enough can introduce consumer to service implementation coupling.
Principles	Standardized Service Contract, (411) Service Loose Coupling (413)
Architecture	Composition, Service

Contract Centralization

By Thomas Erl

How can direct consumer-to-implementation coupling be avoided?

Problem	Consumer programs can be designed to access underlying service resources using different entry points, resulting in different forms of implementation dependencies that inhibit the service from evolving in response to change.
Solution	Access to service logic is limited to the service contract, forcing consumers to avoid implementation coupling.
Application	This pattern is realized through formal enterprise design standards and the targeted application of the Service Abstraction (414) design principle.
Impacts	Forcing consumer programs to access service capabilities and resources via a central contract can impose performance overhead and requires on-going standardization effort.
Principles	Standardized Service Contract (411), Service Loose Coupling (413), Service Abstraction (414)
Architecture	Composition, Service

Contract Denormalization
By Thomas Erl

How can a service contract facilitate consumer programs with differing data exchange requirements?

Problem	Services with strictly normalized contracts can impose unnecessary functional and performance demands on some consumer programs.
Solution	Service contracts can include a measured extent of denormalization, allowing multiple capabilities to redundantly express core functions in different ways for different types of consumer programs.
Application	The service contract is carefully extended with additional capabilities that provide functional variations of a primary capability.
Impacts	Overuse of this pattern on the same contract can dramatically increase its size, making it difficult to interpret and unwieldy to govern.
Principles	Standardized Service Contract (411), Service Loose Coupling (413)
Architecture	Service

Cross-Domain Utility Layer
By Thomas Erl

How can redundant utility logic be avoided across domain service inventories?

Problem	While domain service inventories may be required for independent business governance, they can impose unnecessary redundancy within utility service layers.
Solution	A common utility service layer can be established, spanning two or more domain service inventories.
Application	A common set of utility services needs to be defined and standardized in coordination with service inventory owners.
Impacts	Increased effort is required to coordinate and govern a cross-inventory utility service layer.
Principles	Service Reusability (415), Service Composability (422)
Architecture	Enterprise, Inventory

Data Confidentiality

By Jason Hogg, Don Smith, Fred Chong, Tom Hollander, Wojtek Kozaczynski, Larry Brader, Nelly Delgado, Dwayne Taylor, Lonnie Wall, Paul Slater, Sajjad Nasir Imran, Pablo Cibraro, Ward Cunningham

How can data within a message be protected so that it is not disclosed to unintended recipients while in transit?

Problem	Within service compositions, data is often required to pass through one or more intermediaries. Point-to-point security protocols, such as those frequently used at the transport-layer, may allow messages containing sensitive information to be intercepted and viewed by such intermediaries.
Solution	The message contents are encrypted independently from the transport, ensuring that only intended recipients can access the protected data.
Application	A symmetric or asymmetric encryption and decryption algorithm, such as those specified in the XML-Encryption standard, is applied at the message level.
Impacts	This pattern may add runtime performance overhead associated with the required encryption and decryption of message data. The management of keys can further add to governance burden.
Principles	Service Composability (422)
Architecture	Inventory, Composition, Service

Data Format Transformation

By Mark Little, Thomas Rischbeck, Arnaud Simon

How can services interact with programs that communicate with different data formats?

Problem	A service may be incompatible with resources it needs to access due to data format disparity. Furthermore, a service consumer that communicates using a data format different from a target service will be incompatible and therefore unable to invoke the service.
Solution	Intermediary data format transformation logic needs to be introduced in order to dynamically translate one data format into another.
Application	This necessary transformation logic is incorporated by adding internal service logic, service agents, or a dedicated transformation service.
Impacts	The use of data format transformation logic inevitably adds development effort, design complexity, and performance overhead.
Principles	Standardized Service Contract (411), Service Loose Coupling (413)
Architecture	Inventory, Composition, Service

Data Model Transformation

By Thomas Erl

How can services interoperate when using different data models for the same type of data?

Problem	Services may use incompatible schemas to represent the same data, hindering service interaction and composition.
Solution	A data transformation technology can be incorporated to convert data between disparate schema structures.
Application	Mapping logic needs to be developed and deployed so that data compliant to one data model can be dynamically converted to comply to a different data model.
Impacts	Data model transformation introduces development effort, design complexity, and runtime performance overhead, and overuse of this pattern can seriously inhibit service recomposition potential.
Principles	Standardized Service Contract (411), Service Reusability (415), Service Composability (422)
Architecture	Inventory, Composition

Data Origin Authentication

By Jason Hogg, Don Smith, Fred Chong, Tom Hollander, Wojtek Kozaczynski, Larry Brader, Nelly Delgado, Dwayne Taylor, Lonnie Wall, Paul Slater, Sajjad Nasir Imran, Pablo Cibraro, Ward Cunningham

How can a service verify that a message originates from a known sender and that the message has not been tampered with in transit?

Problem	The intermediary processing layers generally required by service compositions can expose sensitive data when security is limited to point-to-point protocols, such as those used with transport-layer security.
Solution	A message can be digitally signed so that the recipient services can verify that it originated from the expected consumer and that it has not been tampered with during transit.
Application	A digital signature algorithm is applied to the message to provide "proof of origin," allowing sensitive message contents to be protected from tampering. This technology must be supported by both consumer and service.
Impacts	Use of cryptographic techniques can add to performance requirements and the choice of digital signing algorithm can affect the level of security actually achieved.
Principles	Service Composability (422)
Architecture	Composition

Decomposed Capability

By Thomas Erl

How can a service be designed to minimize the chances of capability logic deconstruction?

Problem	The decomposition of a service subsequent to its implementation can require the deconstruction of logic within capabilities, which can be disruptive and make the preservation of a service contract problematic.
Solution	Services prone to future decomposition can be equipped with a series of granular capabilities that more easily facilitate decomposition.
Application	Additional service modeling is carried out to define granular, more easily distributed capabilities.
Impacts	Until the service is eventually decomposed, it may be represented by a bloated contract that stays with it as long as proxy capabilities are supported.
Principles	Standardized Service Contract (411), Service Abstraction (414)
Architecture	Service

Decoupled Contract
By Thomas Erl

How can a service express its capabilities independently of its implementation?

Problem	For a service to be positioned as an effective enterprise resource, it must be equipped with a technical contract that exists independently from its implementation yet still in alignment with other services.
Solution	The service contract is physically decoupled from its implementation.
Application	A service's technical interface is physically separated and subject to relevant service-orientation design principles.
Impacts	Service functionality is limited to the feature-set of the decoupled contract medium.
Principles	Standardized Service Contract (411), Service Loose Coupling (413)
Architecture	Service

Direct Authentication

By Jason Hogg, Don Smith, Fred Chong, Tom Hollander, Wojtek Kozaczynski,
Larry Brader, Nelly Delgado, Dwayne Taylor, Lonnie Wall, Paul Slater,
Sajjad Nasir Imran, Pablo Cibraro, Ward Cunningham

How can a service verify the credentials provided by a consumer?

Problem	Some of the capabilities offered by a service may be intended for specific groups of consumers or may involve the transmission of sensitive data. Attackers that access this data could use it to compromise the service or the IT enterprise itself.
Solution	Service capabilities require that consumers provide credentials that can be authenticated against an identity store.
Application	The service implementation is provided access to an identity store, allowing it to authenticate the consumer directly.
Impacts	Consumers must provide credentials compatible with the service's authentication logic. This pattern may lead to multiple identity stores, resulting in extra governance burden.
Principles	Service Composability (422)
Architecture	Composition, Service

Distributed Capability
By Thomas Erl

How can a service preserve its functional context while also fulfilling special capability processing requirements?

Problem	A capability that belongs within a service may have unique processing requirements that cannot be accommodated by the default service implementation, but separating capability logic from the service will compromise the integrity of the service context.
Solution	The underlying service logic is distributed, thereby allowing the implementation logic for a capability with unique processing requirements to be physically separated, while continuing to be represented by the same service contract.
Application	The logic is moved and intermediary processing is added to act as a liaison between the moved logic and the main service logic.
Impacts	The distribution of a capability's logic leads to performance overhead associated with remote communication and the need for new intermediate processing.
Principles	Standardized Service Contract (411), Service Autonomy (417)
Architecture	Service

Domain Inventory

By Thomas Erl

How can services be delivered to maximize recomposition when enterprise-wide standardization is not possible?

Problem	Establishing a single enterprise service inventory may be unmanageable for some enterprises, and attempts to do so may jeopardize the success of an SOA adoption as a whole.
Solution	Services can be grouped into manageable, domain-specific service inventories, each of which can be independently standardized, governed, and owned.
Application	Inventory domain boundaries need to be carefully established.
Impacts	Standardization disparity between domain service inventories imposes transformation requirements and reduces the overall benefit potential of the SOA adoption.
Principles	Standardized Service Contract (411), Service Abstraction (414), Service Composability (422)
Architecture	Enterprise, Inventory

Dual Protocols

By Thomas Erl

How can a service inventory overcome the limitations of its canonical protocol while still remaining standardized?

Problem	Canonical Protocol [435] requires that all services conform to the use of the same communications technology; however, a single protocol may not be able to accommodate all service requirements, thereby introducing limitations.
Solution	The service inventory architecture is designed to support services based on primary and secondary protocols.
Application	Primary and secondary service levels are created and collectively represent the service endpoint layer. All services are subject to standard service-orientation design considerations and specific guidelines are followed to minimize the impact of not following Canonical Protocol [435].
Impacts	This pattern can lead to a convoluted inventory architecture, increased governance effort and expense, and (when poorly applied) an unhealthy dependence on Protocol Bridging [488]. Because the endpoint layer is semi-federated, the quantity of potential consumers and reuse opportunities is decreased.
Principles	Standardized Service Contract (411), Service Loose Coupling (413), Service Abstraction (414), Service Autonomy (417), Service Composability (422)
Architecture	Inventory, Service

Endpoint Redirection

By Raj Balasubramanian, David Booth, Thomas Erl

How can consumers of a specific service endpoint adapt when the service endpoint changes or is removed?

Problem	Service endpoint identifiers include information that can change over time. It may not be possible to replace all references to an out-of-date endpoint, which can lead to the service consumer being unable to further interact with the service endpoint.
Solution	Automatically redirect service consumers that attempt to access out-of-date service endpoints to the current service endpoints.
Application	Include endpoint redirection as a feature of the service contract. When a service consumer attempts to invoke a stale service capability, return a redirection response. The service consumer follows the redirection instructions and retries the request on the new service capability.
	Redirections can be temporary or permanent. Permanent redirections are automatically recorded in the service consumer's configuration data to avoid subsequent requests to stale service capabilities.
	For services relying on resource identifiers to express capabilities, changes to identifiers amount to a change to the runtime-discovered service contract. Redirection is able to facilitate these changes.
Impacts	The service consumer needs to be developed with the logic required to process the redirection instructions.
	Explicit upgrades may be avoided entirely if permanent redirections are used. However, this can lead to wasteful runtime processing of repeated redirections that can be avoided by upgrading the service consumers.
	Returning redirection information to the consumer requires consumers to determine in advance how much to trust a redirection response. A service that has been compromised from a security perspective may cause the consumer to permanently change its identifiers to point to an invalid or malicious service. A misconfigured service can lead to similar disruption. Care may also need to be taken in order to avoid infinite redirection loops.
Principles	Service Loose Coupling (413)
Architecture	Composition, Service

Enterprise Inventory

By Thomas Erl

How can services be delivered to maximize recomposition?

Problem	Delivering services independently via different project teams across an enterprise establishes a constant risk of producing inconsistent service and architecture implementations, compromising recomposition opportunities.
Solution	Services for multiple solutions can be designed for delivery within a standardized, enterprise-wide inventory architecture wherein they can be freely and repeatedly recomposed.
Application	The enterprise service inventory is ideally modeled in advance, and enterprise-wide standards are applied to services delivered by different project teams.
Impacts	Significant upfront analysis is required to define an enterprise inventory blueprint and numerous organizational impacts result from the subsequent governance requirements.
Principles	Standardized Service Contract (411), Service Abstraction (414), Service Composability (422)
Architecture	Enterprise, Inventory

Enterprise Service Bus
By Thomas Erl, Mark Little, Thomas Rischbeck, Arnaud Simon

An enterprise service bus represents an environment designed to foster sophisticated interconnectivity between services. It establishes an intermediate layer of processing that can help overcome common problems associated with reliability, scalability, and communications disparity.

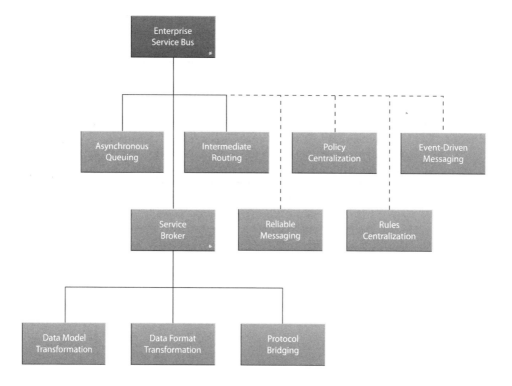

Enterprise Service Bus is fundamentally comprised of the co-existent application of Asynchronous Queuing [431], Intermediate Routing [471], and Service Broker [496], and can be further extended via Reliable Messaging [491], Policy Centralization [485], Rules Centralization [493], and Event-Driven Messaging [465].

Entity Abstraction

By Thomas Erl

How can agnostic business logic be separated, reused, and governed independently?

Problem	Bundling both process-agnostic and process-specific business logic into the same service eventually results in the creation of redundant agnostic business logic across multiple services.
Solution	An agnostic business service layer can be established, dedicated to services that base their functional context on existing business entities.
Application	Entity service contexts are derived from business entity models and then establish a logical layer that is modeled during the analysis phase.
Impacts	The core, business-centric nature of the services introduced by this pattern require extra modeling and design attention and their governance requirements can impose dramatic organizational changes.
Principles	Service Loose Coupling (413), Service Abstraction (414), Service Reusability (415), Service Composability (422)
Architecture	Inventory, Composition, Service

Entity Linking

By Raj Balasubramanian, David Booth, Thomas Erl

How can services expose the inherent relationships between business entities in order to support loosely-coupled composition?

Problem	Business entities have natural relationships, yet entity services are commonly designed autonomously with no indication of these relationships. Service consumers acting as composition controllers are commonly required to have entity linking logic hard-coded in order to work with entity relationships. This limits the composition controller to any additional links that may become relevant and further adds a governance burden to ensure that hard-coded entity linking logic is kept in synch with the business.
Solution	Services inform their consumers about the existence of related entities as part of the consumer's interactions with the services.
Application	Links are included in relevant response messages from the service. Service consumers are able to navigate from entity to entity by following these links, and accumulate further business knowledge along the way. This allows service consumers with little up-front entity linking logic to correctly compose entity services based on their relationships.
Impacts	Resource identifiers representing business entities need to remain relatively stable over the lifespan of the business entities they identify. Once an identifier is known it can be referred to in the future again by the same service consumers. Links can be difficult to define if identifiers for business entities are specific to the services that own them. The application of Lightweight Endpoint [474] can help achieve a uniform syntax for linked identifiers. Links are not valuable if the service consumer is unable to access information about the linked entity. Therefore, the further application of Reusable Contract [492] can ensure that service consumers are able to interact with linked entities.
Principles	Service Reusability (415), Service Abstraction (414), Service Composability (422)
Architecture	Inventory, Service

Event-Driven Messaging

By Mark Little, Thomas Rischbeck, Arnaud Simon

How can service consumers be automatically notified of runtime service events?

Problem	Events that occur within the functional boundary encapsulated by a service may be of relevance to service consumers, but without resorting to inefficient polling-based interaction, the consumer has no way of learning about these events.
Solution	The consumer establishes itself as a subscriber of the service. The service, in turn, automatically issues notifications of relevant events to this and any of its subscribers.
Application	A messaging framework is implemented capable of supporting the publish-and-subscribe MEP and associated complex event processing and tracking.
Impacts	Event-driven message exchanges cannot easily be incorporated as part of Atomic Service Transaction [432], and publisher/subscriber availability issues can arise.
Principles	Standardized Service Contract (411), Service Loose Coupling (413), Service Autonomy (417)
Architecture	Inventory, Composition

Exception Shielding

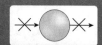

By Jason Hogg, Don Smith, Fred Chong, Tom Hollander, Wojtek
Kozaczynski, Larry Brader, Nelly Delgado, Dwayne Taylor, Lonnie Wall,
Paul Slater, Sajjad Nasir Imran, Pablo Cibraro, Ward Cunningham

*How can a service prevent the disclosure of information about its internal
implementation when an exception occurs?*

Problem	Unfiltered exception data output by a service may contain internal implementation details that can compromise the security of the service and its surrounding environment.
Solution	Potentially unsafe exception data is "sanitized" by replacing it with exception data that is safe by design before it is made available to consumers.
Application	This pattern can be applied at design time by reviewing and altering source code or at runtime by adding dynamic sanitization routines.
Impacts	Sanitized exception information can make the tracking of errors more difficult due to the lack of detail provided to consumers.
Principles	Service Abstraction (414)
Architecture	Service

Federated Endpoint Layer
By Thomas Erl

Federation is an important concept in service-oriented computing. It represents the desired state of the external, consumer-facing perspective of a service inventory, as expressed by the collective contracts of all the inventory's services.

The more federated and unified this collection of contracts (endpoints) is, the more easily and effectively the services can be repeatedly consumed and leveraged.

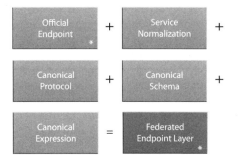

The joint application of Official Endpoint [481], Service Normalization [506], Canonical Protocol [435], Canonical Schema [437], and Canonical Expression [434] results in Federated Endpoint Layer.

File Gateway
By Satadru Roy

How can service logic interact with legacy systems that can only share information by exchanging files?

Problem	Data records contained in flat files produced by a legacy system need to be processed individually by service logic, but legacy systems are not capable of directly invoking services. Conversely, service logic may need to produce information for the legacy system, but building file creation and transfer functionality into the service can result in an inflexible design.
Solution	Intermediary two-way file processing logic is positioned between the legacy system and the service.
Application	For inbound data the file gateway processing logic can detect file drops and leverage available broker features to perform Data Model Transformation [452] and Data Format Transformation [451]. On the outbound side, this logic intercepts information produced by services and packages them (with possible transformation) into new or existing files for consumption by the legacy system.
Impacts	The type of logic provided by this pattern is unsuitable when immediate replies are required by either service or legacy system. Deployment and governance of two-way file processing logic can further add to operational complexity and may require specialized administration skills.
Principles	Service Loose Coupling (413)
Architecture	Service

Functional Decomposition
By Thomas Erl

*How can a large business problem be solved without having
to build a standalone body of solution logic?*

Problem	To solve a large, complex business problem a corresponding amount of solution logic needs to be created, resulting in a self-contained application with traditional governance and reusability constraints.
Solution	The large business problem can be broken down into a set of smaller, related problems, allowing the required solution logic to also be decomposed into a corresponding set of smaller, related solution logic units.
Application	Depending on the nature of the large problem, a service-oriented analysis process can be created to cleanly deconstruct it into smaller problems.
Impacts	The ownership of multiple smaller programs can result in increased design complexity and governance challenges.
Principles	n/a
Architecture	Service

Idempotent Capability

By Cesare Pautasso, Herbjörn Wilhelmsen

How can a service capability safely accept multiple copies of the same message to handle communication failure?

Problem	Network and server hardware failure can lead to lost messages, resulting in cases where a service consumer receives no response to its request. Attempts to reissue the request message can lead to unpredictable or undesirable behavior when the service capability inadvertently receives multiple copies of the same request message.
Solution	Design service capabilities with idempotent logic that enables them to safely accept repeated message exchanges.
Application	Idempotency guarantees that repeated invocations of a service capability are safe and will have no negative effect.
	Idempotent capabilities are generally limited to read-only data retrieval and queries. For capabilities that do request changes to service state, their logic is generally based on "set," "put" or "delete" actions that have a post-condition that does not depend on the original state of the service.
	The design of an idempotent capability can include the use of a unique identifier with each request so that repeated requests (with the same identifier value) that have already been processed will be discarded or ignored by the service capability, rather than being processed again.
Impacts	The use of a unique identifier to define an idempotent capability requires session state to be reliably recorded by the service and preserved across server hardware failures. This can harm the scalability of the service, and may be further complicated if redundant service implementations are operating at different sites that experience network failures.
	Not all service capabilities can be idempotent. Potentially unsafe capabilities include those that need to perform "increment," "reverse" or "escalate" transition functions, where the post-execution condition is dependent upon the original state of the service.
Principles	Standardized Service Contract (411), Service Statelessness (418), Service Composability (422)
Architecture	Inventory, Composition, Service

Intermediate Routing

By Mark Little, Thomas Rischbeck, Arnaud Simon

How can dynamic runtime factors affect the path of a message?

Problem	The larger and more complex a service composition is, the more difficult it is to anticipate and design for all possible runtime scenarios in advance, especially with asynchronous, messaging-based communication.
Solution	Message paths can be dynamically determined through the use of intermediary routing logic.
Application	Various types of intermediary routing logic can be incorporated to create message paths based on message content or runtime factors.
Impacts	Dynamically determining a message path adds layers of processing logic and correspondingly can increase performance overhead. Also the use of multiple routing logic can result in overly complex service activities.
Principles	Service Loose Coupling (413), Service Reusability (415), Service Composability (422)
Architecture	Composition

Inventory Endpoint

By Thomas Erl

How can a service inventory be shielded from external access while still offering service capabilities to external consumers?

Problem	A group of services delivered for a specific inventory may provide capabilities that are useful to services outside of that inventory. However, for security and governance reasons, it may not be desirable to expose all services or all service capabilities to external consumers.
Solution	Abstract the relevant capabilities into an endpoint service that acts as a the official inventory entry point dedicated to a specific set of external consumers.
Application	The endpoint service can expose a contract with the same capabilities as its underlying services, but augmented with policies or other characteristics to accommodate external consumer interaction requirements.
Impacts	Endpoint services can increase the governance freedom of underlying services but can also increase governance effort by introducing redundant service logic and contracts into an inventory.
Principles	Standardized Service Contract (411), Service Loose Coupling (413), Service Abstraction (414)
Architecture	Inventory

Legacy Wrapper
By Thomas Erl, Satadru Roy

How can wrapper services with non-standard contracts be prevented from spreading indirect consumer-to-implementation coupling?

Problem	Wrapper services required to encapsulate legacy logic are often forced to introduce a non-standard service contract with high technology coupling requirements, resulting in a proliferation of implementation coupling throughout all service consumer programs.
Solution	The non-standard wrapper service can be replaced by or further wrapped with a standardized service contract that extracts, encapsulates, and possibly eliminates legacy technical details from the contract.
Application	A custom service contract and required service logic need to be developed to represent the proprietary legacy interface.
Impacts	The introduction of an additional service adds a layer of processing and associated performance overhead.
Principles	Standardized Service Contract (411), Service Loose Coupling (413), Service Abstraction (414)
Architecture	Service

Lightweight Endpoint

By Raj Balasubramanian, Benjamin Carlyle, Thomas Erl, Cesare Pautasso

How can lightweight units of business logic be positioned as effective reusable enterprise resources?

Problem	A service consumer that requires access to business entity information (such as data about an invoice) needs to maintain two identifiers: one for the service and another for the invoice itself. The business entity identifier may be unique only within the scope of the service contract, and the service consumer may be limited to using unnecessarily coarse-grained service capabilities pre-defined as part of the published service contract. This can result in wasteful data exchange and consumer-side processing.
Solution	Expose data and functionality associated with business entities as a series of granular, lightweight endpoints. Allow consumers to target those endpoints in order to optimize data exchange and consumer-side processing.
Application	A service contract needs to expose service capabilities that offer a range of functional granularity. Each of these "lightweight" capabilities is associated with a business entity.
Impacts	Finer-grained service capabilities can result in verbose resource identifiers that may impose a greater governance burden.
	Applying this pattern can lead to resource overlap in order for multiple service capabilities to offer access at multiple levels of granularity. For example, an invoice and properties of the invoice can be exposed as separate resources, even though they refer to a common set of underlying data or functionality.
	Greater effort may be required when applying Service Façade [501], when the facade relates functionality associated with granular resources to core service logic.
Principles	Standardized Service Contract (411), Service Loose Coupling (413), Service Abstraction (414), Service Composability (422)
Architecture	Inventory, Service

Logic Centralization
By Thomas Erl

How can the misuse of redundant service logic be avoided?

Problem	If agnostic services are not consistently reused, redundant functionality can be delivered in other services, resulting in problems associated with inventory denormalization and service ownership and governance.
Solution	Access to reusable functionality is limited to official agnostic services.
Application	Agnostic services need to be properly designed and governed, and their use must be enforced via enterprise standards.
Impacts	Organizational issues reminiscent of past reuse projects can raise obstacles to applying this pattern.
Principles	Service Reusability (415), Service Composability (422)
Architecture	Inventory, Composition, Service

Message Screening

By Jason Hogg, Don Smith, Fred Chong, Tom Hollander ,Wojtek
Kozaczynski, Larry Brader, Nelly Delgado, Dwayne Taylor, Lonnie Wall,
Paul Slater, Sajjad Nasir Imran, Pablo Cibraro, Ward Cunningham

How can a service be protected from malformed or malicious input?

Problem	An attacker can transmit messages with malicious or malformed content to a service, resulting in undesirable behavior.
Solution	The service is equipped or supplemented with special screening routines that assume that all input data is harmful until proven otherwise.
Application	When a service receives a message, it makes a number of checks to screen message content for harmful data.
Impacts	Extra runtime processing is required with each message exchange, and the screening logic requires additional, specialized routines to process binary message content, such as attachments. It may also not be possible to check for all possible forms of harmful content.
Principles	Standardized Service Contract (411)
Architecture	Service

Messaging Metadata

By Thomas Erl

How can services be designed to process activity-specific data at runtime?

Problem	Because messaging does not rely on a persistent connection between service and consumer, it is challenging for a service to gain access to the state data associated with an overall runtime activity.
Solution	Message contents can be supplemented with activity-specific metadata that can be interpreted and processed separately at runtime.
Application	This pattern requires a messaging framework that supports message headers or properties.
Impacts	The interpretation and processing of messaging metadata adds to runtime performance overhead and increases service activity design complexity.
Principles	Service Loose Coupling (413), Service Statelessness (418)
Architecture	Composition

Metadata Centralization

By Thomas Erl

How can service metadata be centrally published and governed?

Problem	Project teams, especially in larger enterprises, run the constant risk of building functionality that already exists or is already in development, resulting in wasted effort, service logic redundancy, and service inventory denormalization.
Solution	Service metadata can be centrally published in a service registry so as to provide a formal means of service registration and discovery.
Application	A private service registry needs to be positioned as a central part of an inventory architecture supported by formal processes for registration and discovery.
Impacts	The service registry product needs to be adequately mature and reliable, and its required use and maintenance needs to be incorporated into all service delivery and governance processes and methodologies.
Principles	Service Discoverability (420)
Architecture	Enterprise, Inventory

Multi-Channel Endpoint

By Satadru Roy

How can legacy logic fragmented and duplicated for different delivery channels be centrally consolidated?

Problem	Legacy systems custom-built for specific delivery channels (mobile phone, desktop, kiosk, etc.) result in redundancy and application silos when multiple channels need to be supported, thereby making these systems burdensome to govern and difficult to federate.
Solution	An intermediary service is designed to encapsulate channel-specific legacy systems and expose a single standardized contract for multiple channel-specific consumers.
Application	The service established by this pattern will require significant processing and workflow logic to support multiple channels while also coordinating interaction with multiple backend legacy systems.
Impacts	The endpoint processing logic established by this pattern often introduces the need for infrastructure upgrades and orchestration-capable middleware and may turn into a performance bottleneck.
Principles	Service Loose Coupling (413), Service Reusability (415)
Architecture	Service

Non-Agnostic Context

By Thomas Erl

How can single-purpose service logic be positioned as an effective enterprise resource?

Problem	Non-agnostic logic that is not service-oriented can inhibit the effectiveness of service compositions that utilize agnostic services.
Solution	Non-agnostic solution logic suitable for service encapsulation can be located within services that reside as official members of a service inventory.
Application	A single-purpose functional service context is defined.
Impacts	Although they are not expected to provide reuse potential, non-agnostic services are still subject to the rigor of service-orientation.
Principles	Standardized Service Contract (411), Service Composability (422)
Architecture	Service

Official Endpoint
By Thomas Erl

As important as it is to clearly differentiate Logic Centralization [475] from Contract Centralization [447], it is equally important to understand how these two fundamental patterns can and should be used together.

Applying these two patterns to the same service realizes the Official Endpoint [481] compound pattern. The repeated application of Official Endpoint [481] supports the goal of establishing a federated layer of service endpoints, which is why this compound pattern is also a part of Federated Endpoint Layer [467].

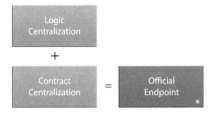

The joint application of Logic Centralization [475] and Contract Centralization [447] results in Official Endpoint.

Orchestration
By Thomas Erl, Brian Loesgen

An orchestration platform is dedicated to the effective maintenance and execution of parent business process logic. Modern-day orchestration environments are especially expected to support sophisticated and complex service composition logic that can result in long-running runtime activities.

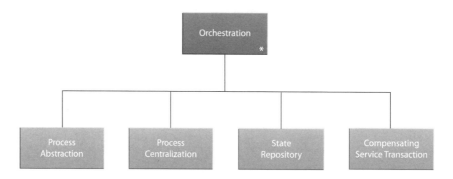

Orchestration is fundamentally comprised of the co-existent application of Process Abstraction [486], State Repository [510], Process Centralization [485], and Compensating Service Transaction [443], and can be further extended via Atomic Service Transaction [432], Rules Centralization [493], and Data Model Transformation [452].

Partial State Deferral
By Thomas Erl

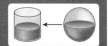

How can services be designed to optimize resource consumption while still remaining stateful?

Problem	Service capabilities may be required to store and manage large amounts of state data, resulting in increased memory consumption and reduced scalability.
Solution	Even when services are required to remain stateful, a subset of their state data can be temporarily deferred.
Application	Various state management deferral options exist, depending on the surrounding architecture.
Impacts	Partial state management deferral can add to design complexity and bind a service to the architecture.
Principles	Service Statelessness (418)
Architecture	Inventory, Service

Partial Validation
By David Orchard, Chris Riley

How can unnecessary data validation be avoided?

Problem	The generic capabilities provided by agnostic services sometimes result in service contracts that impose unnecessary data and validation upon consumer programs.
Solution	A consumer program can be designed to only validate the relevant subset of the data and ignore the remainder.
Application	The application of this pattern is specific to the technology used for the consumer implementation. For example, with Web services, XPath can be used to filter out unnecessary data prior to validation.
Impacts	Extra design-time effort is required and the additional runtime data filtering-related logic can reduce the processing gains of avoiding unnecessary validation.
Principles	Standardized Service Contract (411), Service Loose Coupling (413)
Architecture	Composition

Policy Centralization
By Thomas Erl

How can policies be normalized and consistently enforced across multiple services?

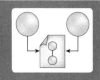

Problem	Policies that apply to multiple services can introduce redundancy and inconsistency within service logic and contracts.
Solution	Global or domain-specific policies can be isolated and applied to multiple services.
Application	Up-front analysis effort specific to defining and establishing reusable policies is recommended, and an appropriate policy enforcement framework is required.
Impacts	Policy frameworks can introduce performance overhead and may impose dependencies on proprietary technologies. There is also the risk of conflict between centralized and service-specific policies.
Principles	Standardized Service Contracts (411), Service Loose Coupling (413), Service Abstraction (414)
Architecture	Inventory, Service

486   Appendix E: SOA Design Patterns Reference

Process Abstraction

By Thomas Erl

How can non-agnostic process logic be separated and governed independently?

Problem	Grouping task-centric logic together with task-agnostic logic hinders the governance of the task-specific logic and the reuse of the agnostic logic.
Solution	A dedicated parent business process service layer is established to support governance independence and the positioning of task services as potential enterprise resources.
Application	Business process logic is typically filtered out after utility and entity services have been defined, allowing for the definition of task services that comprise this layer.
Impacts	In addition to the modeling and design considerations associated with creating task services, abstracting parent business process logic establishes an inherent dependency on carrying out that logic via the composition of other services.
Principles	Service Loose Coupling (413), Service Abstraction (414), Service Composability (422)
Architecture	Inventory, Composition, Service

Process Centralization
By Thomas Erl

How can abstracted business process logic be centrally governed?

Problem	When business process logic is distributed across independent service implementations, it can be problematic to extend and evolve.
Solution	Logic representing numerous business processes can be deployed and governed from a central location.
Application	Middleware platforms generally provide the necessary orchestration technologies to apply this pattern.
Impacts	Significant infrastructure and architectural changes are imposed when the required middleware is introduced.
Principles	Service Autonomy (417), Service Statelessness (418), Service Composability (422)
Architecture	Inventory, Composition

Protocol Bridging

By Mark Little, Thomas Rischbeck, Arnaud Simon

How can a service exchange data with consumers that use different communication protocols?

Problem	Services using different communication protocols or different versions of the same protocol cannot exchange data.
Solution	Bridging logic is introduced to enable communication between different communication protocols by dynamically converting one protocol to another at runtime.
Application	Instead of connecting directly to each other, consumer programs and services connect to a broker, which provides bridging logic that carries out the protocol conversion.
Impacts	Significant performance overhead can be imposed by bridging technologies, and their use can limit or eliminate the ability to incorporate reliability and transaction features.
Principles	Standardized Service Contract (411), Service Composability (422)
Architecture	Inventory, Composition

Proxy Capability

By Thomas Erl

How can a service subject to decomposition continue to support consumers affected by the decomposition?

Problem	If an established service needs to be decomposed into multiple services, its contract and its existing consumers can be impacted.
Solution	The original service contract is preserved, even if underlying capability logic is separated, by turning the established capability definition into a proxy.
Application	Façade logic needs to be introduced to relay requests and responses between the proxy and newly located capabilities.
Impacts	The practical solution provided by this pattern results in a measure of service denormalization.
Principles	Service Loose Coupling (413)
Architecture	Service

Redundant Implementation
By Thomas Erl

How can the reliability and availability of a service be increased?

Problem	A service that is being actively reused introduces a potential single point of failure that may jeopardize the reliability of all compositions in which it participates if an unexpected error condition occurs.
Solution	Reusable services can be deployed via redundant implementations or with failover support.
Application	The same service implementation is redundantly deployed or supported by infrastructure with redundancy features.
Impacts	Extra governance effort is required to keep all redundant implementations in synch.
Principles	Service Autonomy (417)
Architecture	Service

Reliable Messaging

By Mark Little, Thomas Rischbeck, Arnaud Simon

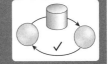

How can services communicate reliably when implemented in an unreliable environment?

Problem	Service communication cannot be guaranteed when using unreliable messaging protocols or when dependent on an otherwise unreliable environment.
Solution	An intermediate reliability mechanism is introduced into the inventory architecture, ensuring that message delivery is guaranteed.
Application	Middleware, service agents, and data stores are deployed to track message deliveries, manage the issuance of acknowledgements, and persist messages during failure conditions.
Impacts	Using a reliability framework adds processing overhead that can affect service activity performance. It also increases composition design complexity and may not be compatible with Atomic Service Transaction [432].
Principles	Service Composability (422)
Architecture	Inventory, Composition

Reusable Contract

By Raj Balasubramanian, Benjamin Carlyle, Thomas Erl, Cesare Pautasso

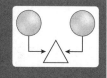

How can service consumers compose services without having to couple themselves to service-specific contracts?

Problem	To access a service capability of a service with a service-specific contract, the service consumer must be designed to couple itself to the service contract. When the service contract changes, the service consumer may no longer be functional. To access a new version of the service contract, or to access other service contracts in order to compose other services, the service consumer must be subjected to additional development cycles, thereby incurring time, effort, and expense.
Solution	Limit tight coupling to a common, reusable technical contract that is shared by multiple services. The technical contract provides only generic, high-level functions that are less likely to be impacted when service logic changes.
Application	A reusable service contract can provide abstract and agnostic data exchange methods, none of which are related to a specific business function. Methods within a reusable contract are typically focused on types of data rather than on the business context of the data.
	The set of methods of the reusable contract is complemented by service-specific resource identifiers and media types to apply the context established by reusable methods to individual service capabilities.
	HTTP provides a reusable contract via generic methods, such as GET, PUT, and DELETE, that allow consumer programs to access Web-based resources by further providing resource identifiers. The combination of the resource identifier and the HTTP method and media type can comprise a service-specific capability.
	A reusable contract can also be created using a centralized WSDL definition, as long as the operations defined are sufficiently generic.
Impacts	Sharing the same contract across services increases the importance of getting the contract right, both initially, and over the contract's lifetime.
	The reusable contract may still need to change if new services with new high-level functional requirements are introduced into the service inventory.
	The reusable contract can lack sufficient metadata to effectively enable a service to be discovered. Service-specific metadata may need to be maintained separately from the reusable contract definition to ensure that service consumers are able to select the correct service capability with which to interact.
Principles	Standardized Service Contract (411), Service Loose Coupling (413), Service Abstraction (414), Service Discoverability (420), Service Composability (422)
Architecture	Inventory, Composition, Service

Rules Centralization
By Thomas Erl

How can business rules be abstracted and centrally governed?

Problem	The same business rules may apply across different business services, leading to redundancy and governance challenges.
Solution	The storage and management of business rules are positioned within a dedicated architectural extension from where they can be centrally accessed and maintained.
Application	The use of a business rules management system or engine is employed and accessed via system agents or a dedicated service.
Impacts	Services are subjected to increased performance overhead, risk, and architectural dependency.
Principles	Service Reusability (415)
Architecture	Inventory

Schema Centralization

By Thomas Erl

How can service contracts be designed to avoid redundant data representation?

Problem	Different service contracts often need to express capabilities that process similar business documents or data sets, resulting in redundant schema content that is difficult to govern.
Solution	Select schemas that exist as physically separate parts of the service contract are shared across multiple contracts.
Application	Up-front analysis effort is required to establish a schema layer independent of and in support of the service layer.
Impacts	Governance of shared schemas becomes increasingly important as multiple services can form dependencies on the same schema definitions.
Principles	Standardized Service Contract (411), Service Loose Coupling (413)
Architecture	Inventory, Service

Service Agent

By Thomas Erl

How can event-driven logic be separated and governed independently?

Problem	Service compositions can become large and inefficient, especially when required to invoke granular capabilities across multiple services.
Solution	Event-driven logic can be deferred to event-driven programs that don't require explicit invocation, thereby reducing the size and performance strain of service compositions.
Application	Service agents can be designed to automatically respond to predefined conditions without invocation via a published contract.
Impacts	The complexity of composition logic increases when it is distributed across services, and event-driven agents and reliance on service agents can further tie an inventory architecture to proprietary vendor technology.
Principles	Service Loose Coupling (413), Service Reusability (415)
Architecture	Inventory, Composition

Service Broker

By Mark Little, Thomas Rischbeck, Arnaud Simon

Although all of the Service Broker patterns are used only out of necessity, establishing an environment capable of handling the three most common transformation requirements can add a great deal of flexibility to a service-oriented architecture implementation, and also has the added bonus of being able to perform more than one transformation function at the same time.

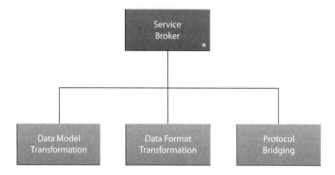

Service Broker is comprised of the co-existent application of Data Model Transformation [452], Data Format Transformation [451], and Protocol Bridging [488].

Related Patterns in Other Catalogs

Broker (Buschmann, Henney, Schmidt, Meunier, Rohnert, Sommerland, Stal)

Related Service-Oriented Computing Goals

Increased Intrinsic Interoperability, Increased Vendor Diversification Options, Reduced IT Burden

Service Callback

By Anish Karmarkar

How can a service communicate asynchronously with its consumers?

Problem	When a service needs to respond to a consumer request through the issuance of multiple messages or when service message processing requires a large amount of time, it is often not possible to communicate synchronously.
Solution	A service can require that consumers communicate with it asynchronously and provide a callback address to which the service can send response messages.
Application	A callback address generation and message correlation mechanism needs to be incorporated into the messaging framework and the overall inventory architecture.
Impacts	Asynchronous communication can introduce reliability concerns and can further require that surrounding infrastructure be upgraded to fully support the necessary callback correlation.
Principles	Standardized Service Contract (411), Service Loose Coupling (413), Service Composability (422)
Architecture	Inventory, Service, Composition

Service Data Replication

By Thomas Erl

How can service autonomy be preserved when services require access to shared data sources?

Problem	Service logic can be deployed in isolation to increase service autonomy, but services continue to lose autonomy when requiring access to shared data sources.
Solution	Services can have their own dedicated databases with replication to shared data sources.
Application	An additional database needs to be provided for the service and one or more replication channels need to be enabled between it and the shared data sources.
Impacts	This pattern results in additional infrastructure cost and demands, and an excess of replication channels can be difficult to manage.
Principles	Service Autonomy (417)
Architecture	Inventory, Service

Service Decomposition
By Thomas Erl

How can the granularity of a service be increased subsequent to its implementation?

Problem	Overly coarse-grained services can inhibit optimal composition design.
Solution	An already implemented coarse-grained service can be decomposed into two or more fine-grained services.
Application	The underlying service logic is restructured, and new service contracts are established. This pattern will likely require Proxy Capability [489] to preserve the integrity of the original coarse-grained service contract.
Impacts	An increase in fine-grained services naturally leads to larger, more complex service composition designs.
Principles	Service Loose Coupling (413), Service Composability (422)
Architecture	Service

Service Encapsulation
By Thomas Erl

How can solution logic be made available as a resource of the enterprise?

Problem	Solution logic designed for a single application environment is typically limited in its potential to interoperate with or be leveraged by other parts of an enterprise.
Solution	Solution logic can be encapsulated by a service so that it is positioned as an enterprise resource capable of functioning beyond the boundary for which it is initially delivered.
Application	Solution logic suitable for service encapsulation needs to be identified.
Impacts	Service-encapsulated solution logic is subject to additional design and governance considerations.
Principles	n/a
Architecture	Service

Service Façade

By Thomas Erl

How can a service accommodate changes to its contract or implementation while allowing the core service logic to evolve independently?

Problem	The coupling of the core service logic to contracts and implementation resources can inhibit its evolution and negatively impact service consumers.
Solution	A service façade component is used to abstract a part of the service architecture with negative coupling potential.
Application	A separate façade component is incorporated into the service design.
Impacts	The addition of the façade component introduces design effort and performance overhead.
Principles	Standardized Service Contract (411), Service Loose Coupling (413)
Architecture	Service

Service Grid

By David Chappell

How can deferred service state data be scaled and kept fault-tolerant?

Problem	State data deferred via State Repository or Stateful Services can be subject to performance bottlenecks and failure, especially when exposed to high-usage volumes.
Solution	State data is deferred to a collection of stateful system services that form a grid that provides high scalability and fault tolerance through memory replication and redundancy and supporting infrastructure.
Application	Grid technology is introduced into the enterprise or inventory architecture.
Impacts	This pattern can require a significant infrastructure upgrade and can correspondingly increase governance burden.
Principles	Service Statelessness (418)
Architecture	Enterprise, Inventory, Service

Service Instance Routing

By Anish Karmarkar

How can consumers contact and interact with service instances without the need for proprietary processing logic?

Problem	When required to repeatedly access a specific stateful service instance, consumers must rely on custom logic that more tightly couples them to the service.
Solution	The service provides an instance identifier along with its destination information in a standardized format that shields the consumer from having to resort to custom logic.
Application	The service is still required to provide custom logic to generate and manage instance identifiers, and both service and consumer require a common messaging infrastructure.
Impacts	This pattern can introduce the need for significant infrastructure upgrades and when misused can further lead to overly stateful messaging activities that can violate the Service Statelessness (418) principle.
Principles	Service Loose Coupling (413), Service Statelessness (418), Service Composability (422)
Architecture	Inventory, Composition, Service

Service Layers
By Thomas Erl

How can the services in an inventory be organized based on functional commonality?

Problem	Arbitrarily defining services delivered and governed by different project teams can lead to design inconsistency and inadvertent functional redundancy across a service inventory.
Solution	The inventory is structured into two or more logical service layers, each of which is responsible for abstracting logic based on a common functional type.
Application	Service models are chosen and then form the basis for service layers that establish modeling and design standards.
Impacts	The common costs and impacts associated with design standards and up-front analysis need to be accepted.
Principles	Service Reusability (415), Service Composability (422)
Architecture	Inventory, Service

Service Messaging

By Thomas Erl

How can services interoperate without forming persistent, tightly coupled connections?

Problem	Services that depend on traditional remote communication protocols impose the need for persistent connections and tightly coupled data exchanges, increasing consumer dependencies and limiting service reuse potential.
Solution	Services can be designed to interact via a messaging-based technology, which removes the need for persistent connections and reduces coupling requirements.
Application	A messaging framework needs to be established, and services need to be designed to use it.
Impacts	Messaging technology brings with it QoS concerns such as reliable delivery, security, performance, and transactions.
Principles	Standardized Service Contract (411), Service Loose Coupling (413)
Architecture	Inventory, Composition, Service

Service Normalization

By Thomas Erl

How can a service inventory avoid redundant service logic?

Problem	When delivering services as part of a service inventory, there is a constant risk that services will be created with overlapping functional boundaries, making it difficult to enable wide-spread reuse.
Solution	The service inventory needs to be designed with an emphasis on service boundary alignment.
Application	Functional service boundaries are modeled as part of a formal analysis process and persist throughout inventory design and governance.
Impacts	Ensuring that service boundaries are and remain well-aligned introduces extra up-front analysis and on-going governance effort.
Principles	Service Autonomy (417)
Architecture	Inventory, Service

Service Perimeter Guard

By Jason Hogg, Don Smith, Fred Chong, Tom Hollander, Wojtek Kozaczynski,
Larry Brader, Nelly Delgado, Dwayne Taylor, Lonnie Wall, Paul Slater,
Sajjad Nasir Imran, Pablo Cibraro, Ward Cunningham

How can services that run in a private network be made available to external consumers without exposing internal resources?

Problem	External consumers that require access to one or more services in a private network can attack the service or use it to gain access to internal resources.
Solution	An intermediate service is established at the perimeter of the private network as a secure contact point for any external consumers that need to interact with internal services.
Application	The service is deployed in a perimeter network and is designed to work with existing firewall technologies so as to establish a secure bridging mechanism between external and internal networks.
Impacts	A perimeter service adds complexity and performance overhead as it establishes an intermediary processing layer for all external-to-internal communication.
Principles	Service Loose Coupling (413), Service Abstraction (414)
Architecture	Service

Service Refactoring
By Thomas Erl

How can a service be evolved without impacting existing consumers?

Problem	The logic or implementation technology of a service may become outdated or inadequate over time, but the service has become too entrenched to be replaced.
Solution	The service contract is preserved to maintain existing consumer dependencies, but the underlying service logic and/or implementation are refactored.
Application	Service logic and implementation technology are gradually improved or upgraded but must undergo additional testing.
Impacts	This pattern introduces governance effort as well as risk associated with potentially negative side-effects introduced by new logic or technology.
Principles	Standardized Service Contract (411), Service Loose Coupling (413), Service Abstraction (414)
Architecture	Service

State Messaging
By Anish Karmarkar

How can a service remain stateless while participating in stateful interactions?

Problem	When services are required to maintain state information in memory between message exchanges with consumers, their scalability can be comprised, and they can become a performance burden on the surrounding infrastructure.
Solution	Instead of retaining the state data in memory, its storage is temporarily delegated to messages.
Application	Depending on how this pattern is applied, both services and consumers may need to be designed to process message-based state data.
Impacts	This pattern may not be suitable for all forms of state data, and should messages be lost, any state information they carried may be lost as well.
Principles	Standardized Service Contract (411), Service Statelessness (418), Service Composability (422)
Architecture	Composition, Service

State Repository

By Thomas Erl

How can service state data be persisted for extended periods without consuming service runtime resources?

Problem	Large amounts of state data cached to support the activity within a running service composition can consume too much memory, especially for long-running activities, thereby decreasing scalability.
Solution	State data can be temporarily written to and then later retrieved from a dedicated state repository.
Application	A shared or dedicated repository is made available as part of the inventory or service architecture.
Impacts	The addition of required write and read functionality increases the service design complexity and can negatively affect performance.
Principles	Service Statelessness (418)
Architecture	Inventory, Service

Stateful Services
By Thomas Erl

How can service state data be persisted and managed without consuming service runtime resources?

Problem	State data associated with a particular service activity can impose a great deal of runtime state management responsibility upon service compositions, thereby reducing their scalability.
Solution	State data is managed and stored by intentionally stateful utility services.
Application	Stateful utility services provide in-memory state data storage and/or can maintain service activity context data.
Impacts	If not properly implemented, stateful utility services can become a performance bottleneck.
Principles	Service Statelessness (418)
Architecture	Inventory, Service

Termination Notification

By David Orchard, Chris Riley

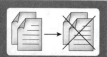

How can the scheduled expiry of a service contract be communicated to consumer programs?

Problem	Consumer programs may be unaware of when a service or a service contract version is scheduled for retirement, thereby risking runtime failure.
Solution	Service contracts can be designed to express termination information for programmatic and human consumption.
Application	Service contracts can be extended with ignorable policy assertions or supplemented with human-readable annotations.
Impacts	The syntax and conventions used to express termination information must be understood by service consumers in order for this information to be effectively used.
Principles	Standardized Service Contract (411)
Architecture	Composition, Service

Three-Layer Inventory
By Thomas Erl

This compound pattern is simply comprised of the combined application of the three service layer patterns. Three-Layer Inventory exists because the combined application of these three patterns results in common layers of abstraction that have been proven to complement and support each other by establishing services with flexible variations of agnostic and non-agnostic functional contexts.

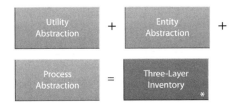

The joint application of Utility Abstraction [517], Entity Abstraction [463], and Process Abstraction [486] results in Three-Layer Inventory.

Trusted Subsystem

By Jason Hogg, Don Smith, Fred Chong, Tom Hollander, Wojtek
Kozaczynski, Larry Brader, Nelly Delgado, Dwayne Taylor, Lonnie Wall,
Paul Slater, Sajjad Nasir Imran, Pablo Cibraro, Ward Cunningham

*How can a consumer be prevented from circumventing a service
and directly accessing its resources?*

Problem	A consumer that accesses backend resources of a service directly can compromise the integrity of the resources and can further lead to undesirable forms of implementation coupling.
Solution	The service is designed to use its own credentials for authentication and authorization with backend resources on behalf of consumers.
Application	Depending on the nature of the underlying resources, various design options and security technologies can be applied.
Impacts	If this type of service is compromised by attackers or unauthorized consumers, it can be exploited to gain access to a wide range of downstream resources.
Principles	Service Loose Coupling (413)
Architecture	Service

UI Mediator

**By Clemens Utschig-Utschig, Berthold Maier,
Bernd Trops, Hajo Normann, Torsten Winterberg**

*How can a service-oriented solution provide a consistent,
interactive user experience?*

Problem	Because the behavior of individual services can vary depending on their design, runtime usage, and the workload required to carry out a given capability, the consistency with which a service-oriented solution can respond to requests originating from a user-interface can fluctuate, leading to a poor user experience.
Solution	Establish mediator logic solely responsible for ensuring timely interaction and feedback with user-interfaces and presentation logic.
Application	A utility mediator service or service agent is positioned as the initial recipient of messages originating from the user-interface. This mediation logic responds in a timely and consistent manner regardless of the behavior of the underling solution.
Impacts	The mediator logic establishes an additional layer of processing that can add to the required runtime processing.
Principles	Service Loose Coupling (413)
Architecture	Composition

Uniform Contract
By Raj Balasubramanian, Benjamin Carlyle, Cesare Pautasso

Uniform Contract is a compound pattern comprised of the combined application of Reusable Contract [492], Lightweight Endpoint [474], and Entity Linking [464].

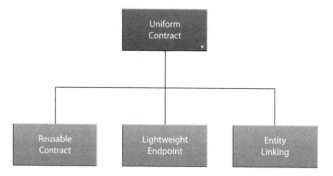

Uniform Contract is considered a specialized variation of Reusable Contract [492] that is applied to all services within a given boundary (usually a service inventory). This compound pattern further requires that service functions are broken down to related individual resources, as per Lightweight Endpoint [474]. It further enables links from one resource to another. Links are followed by service consumers to invoke the capabilities of each resource without foreknowledge of the service that exposes them, as per Entity Linking [464].

Utility Abstraction
By Thomas Erl

How can common non-business centric logic be separated, reused, and independently governed?

Problem	When non-business centric processing logic is packaged together with business-specific logic, it results in the redundant implementation of common utility functions across different services.
Solution	A service layer dedicated to utility processing is established, providing reusable utility services for use by other services in the inventory.
Application	The utility service model is incorporated into analysis and design processes in support of utility logic abstraction, and further steps are taken to define balanced service contexts.
Impacts	When utility logic is distributed across multiple services it can increase the size, complexity, and performance demands of compositions.
Principles	Service Loose Coupling (413), Service Abstraction (414), Service Reusability (415), Service Composability (422)
Architecture	Inventory, Composition, Service

Validation Abstraction

By Thomas Erl

How can service contracts be designed to more easily adapt to validation logic changes?

Problem	Service contracts that contain detailed validation constraints become more easily invalidated when the rules behind those constraints change.
Solution	Granular validation logic and rules can be abstracted away from the service contract, thereby decreasing constraint granularity and increasing the contract's potential longevity.
Application	Abstracted validation logic and rules need to be moved to the underlying service logic, a different service, a service agent, or elsewhere.
Impacts	This pattern can somewhat decentralize validation logic and can also complicate schema standardization.
Principles	Standardized Service Contract (411), Service Loose Coupling (413), Service Abstraction (414)
Architecture	Service

Version Identification

By David Orchard, Chris Riley

How can consumers be made aware of service contract version information?

Problem	When an already-published service contract is changed, unaware consumers will miss the opportunity to leverage the change or may be negatively impacted by the change.
Solution	Versioning information pertaining to compatible and incompatible changes can be expressed as part of the service contract, both for communication and enforcement purposes.
Application	With Web service contracts, version numbers can be incorporated into namespace values and as annotations.
Impacts	This pattern may require that version information be expressed with a proprietary vocabulary that needs to be understood by consumer designers in advance.
Principles	Standardized Service Contract (411)
Architecture	Service

Appendix F

State Concepts and Types

State Management Explained

Types of State

Measuring Service Statelessness

State Management Explained

State management represents a dimension of solution design that can vary from platform to platform. Therefore, we'll take the time to explicitly define its meaning in relation to service-orientation.

State Management in Abstract

State refers to the general condition of something. A car that is moving is in a state of motion, whereas a car that is not moving is in a stationary state (Figure F.1). In business automation, it is understood that a software program can also have and transition through different states, usually because of its involvement in a runtime activity.

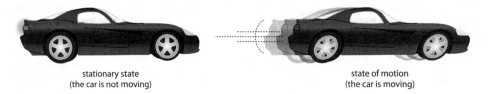

stationary state
(the car is not moving)

state of motion
(the car is moving)

Figure F.1
The states of a car can be represented by two very fundamental categories.

Each state can be represented and described by data that typically has a lifespan equivalent to the duration at which the program remains active for a given task or purpose. As a result, all variations of state information tend to be temporary in nature. Therefore, *state management* can be considered the management of temporary, activity-specific data.

The following types of state conditions and data can exist:

- active and passive states

- stateful and stateless conditions

- context, session, and business state data

- context data and context rules

Each of these is explained individually in the *Types of State* section later in this chapter. Also note that throughout diagrams in books in this series, state data is represented by the "liquid" shown within artifacts (Figure F.2). In books with color diagrams, this liquid is colored orange.

Figure F.2
Service and repository symbols can be used to illustrate how state data (orange) can transition through various temporary containers at runtime.

Origins of State Management

State information is required to do just about anything meaningful with software programs because data about an activity is fundamental to runtime processing.

Older, two-tier client-server solutions made state management a natural part of the primary solution components. The client user-interface would often retain large amounts of activity-specific data in memory for extended periods (Figure F.3). This was not considered a problem because each client program was deployed on a dedicated computer, intended for use by a single user.

In traditional distributed computing models, application processing logic shifted from the client workstation to the middle tier. As a result, a server-side program was now required to manage interaction with multiple client programs, each with their own individual state information processing requirements (Figure F.4).

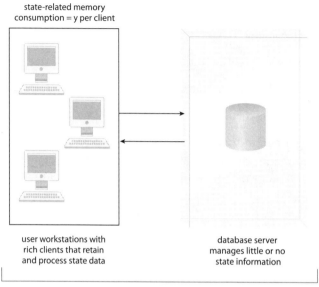

state-related memory
consumption = y per client

user workstations with
rich clients that retain
and process state data

database server
manages little or no
state information

two-tier Application A

Figure F.3
Typical one-sided division of state management responsibilities in a typical
two-tier client-server architecture.

When actively processing or retaining state information, a program is constantly consuming a base amount of memory and CPU cycles. A server-side program accessed concurrently by multiple clients can rapidly and significantly increase this amount (Figure F.5).

Because runtime usage scenarios are not always predictable and because hardware budgets are not always flexible, the risk of a concurrently accessed server-side program becoming a performance bottleneck is very real. Although state data processing requirements are not always the primary cause of system memory consumption, they contribute significantly.

In response to this problem, variations of distributed architectures were formed to alleviate components from state management responsibilities by providing *state delegation* and *state deferral* options. A common architectural extension that supported state deferral was centered around alternative state storage. A dedicated database (or a set of dedicated tables within an existing database) could be used by components to write and then later retrieve state data (Figure F.6).

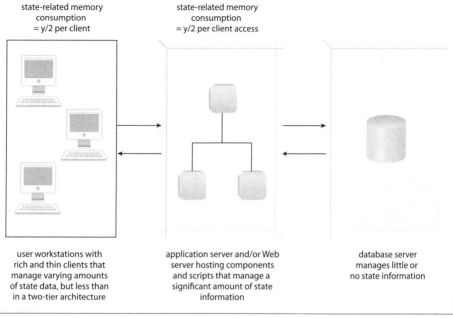

Figure F.4
Note that the "y/2" value is arbitrary. In most contemporary Web-based solutions the clients are relatively thin (browser-based), requiring the server-side components to manage a higher percentage of state data.

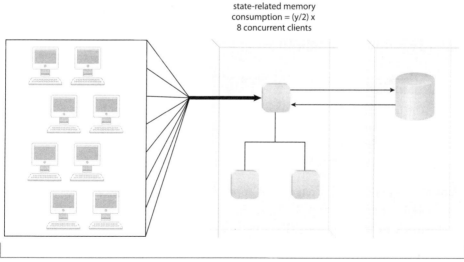

Figure F.5
Multiple clients concurrently accessing the same application component. Some enterprise solutions have thousands of clients that can raise concurrent access numbers into the hundreds.

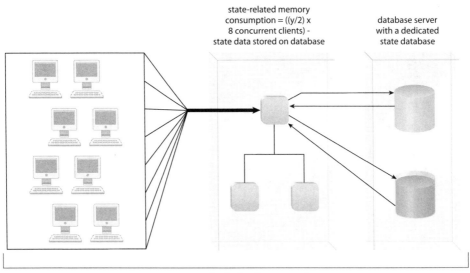

state-related memory
consumption = ((y/2) x
8 concurrent clients) -
state data stored on database

database server
with a dedicated
state database

Application A

Figure F.6

A separate database positioned as a state management deferral extension of the architecture (the orange area represents state data). Note that databases utilized in this role are often located on the application server alongside components.

Often these databases were physically located on the same application server as the components (as opposed to a separate database server) to reduce the performance impact caused by remote data access. In-memory databases were also used to further optimize data access by avoiding disk access.

NOTE

The use of databases for state deferral is documented in more detail in the *Measuring Service Statelessness* section in Chapter 11 of *SOA Principles of Service Design*.

To date, a variety of state management approaches have been developed. Middleware, for example, has become a popular state processing deferral option. It establishes a central, self-sufficient, and intentionally stateful part of the infrastructure that can be leveraged by other solutions within the enterprise. As explained in the *Messaging as a State Deferral Option* section in Chapter 11 from *SOA Principles of Service Design*, the deferral of state data to the messaging layer is another viable option, and one that is a focal point of REST-style architecture.

Deferral vs. Delegation

The temporary relocation of state information is referred to as state deferral because the intention is usually to retrieve the information at some later point. We are therefore postponing (deferring) the responsibility of managing the state data. To accomplish state management deferral we temporarily delegate this responsibility to another part of the architecture (such as a database). Therefore, we achieve state management deferral through temporary and periodic state management delegation.

Note that in this book we collectively refer to the process of state management delegation and deferral as state deferral.

Types of State

There are different state values and different types of state information. While state management is a common part of just about any program and platform, the manner in which state types and data are described and labeled can vary (Figure F.7). Let's cover some fundamentals to establish terminology referenced throughout this book.

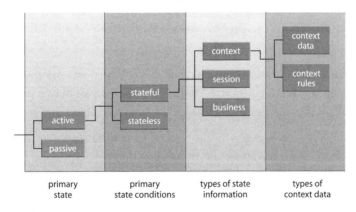

Figure F.7
Most services transition through all of these states and conditions and are required to work with at least some form of session or context information.

Active and Passive

As we established in the *State Management in Abstract* section earlier, a software program can transition through different states in its lifetime. Our example described two basic states a car was capable of having: in motion and stationary. A software program—or, in this case a service—can also have two comparable, primary states:

- active

- passive

The first represents the service being invoked or executed and therefore entering an active state. The latter refers to the period during which the service is not in use and therefore exists in a passive or "non-activate" state.

Stateless and Stateful

During the design stage of a service, we are very interested in what will happen when the service is active. We are so interested, in fact, that we have additional states to represent specific types of active conditions. In relation to our discussion of state management, there are two primary conditions:

- stateless

- stateful

These terms are used to identify the active or runtime condition of a service as it relates to the processing required to carry out a specific task. When automating a particular task, the service is required to process data specific to that task. We can refer to this information as *state* data.

A service can be active but may not be engaged in the processing of state data. In this idle condition, the service is considered to be *stateless*. As you may have guessed, a service that is actively processing or retaining state data is classified as being *stateful*.

A classic example of statelessness is the use of the HTTP protocol. When a browser requests a Web page from a Web server, the Web server responds by delivering the content and then returning to a stateless condition wherein it retains no further memory of the browser or the request (unless programmed otherwise).

Session and Context Data

The data a service processes when stateful can also vary. Many terms have been used to classify different types of state data, but we'll settle on the following:

- session data

- context data

- business data

Session data typically represents information associated with retaining a connection made between a program and its client program (or client user). This connection may or may not be an actual physical connection. For example, if you access a Web site with your browser, it may be programmed to establish a unique session identifier to correlate future interaction with the browser and other parts of the site. This value is then passed between the browser and the Web site with each subsequent exchange.

In service compositions, the execution of a business task can take the shape of a runtime activity that spans multiple services. In this case, the state information that is passed between them (if any) goes beyond session-type information, in that it pertains to more than just keeping track of the session. This type of activity-specific information is what we refer to as *context data*.

Associated with context data is the actual logic used to process it. Usually this logic is tied to the workflow rules that govern the processing of the activity. We therefore make a further distinction between context data and *context rules*. Both context data and context rules are commonly centralized within middleware, namely the type of transaction coordinator referenced in the *Cross-Service Transactions with REST* section in Chapter 12.

```
<Header>
   <wsc:CoordinationContext>
     <wsu:Identifier>
       http://www.soabooks.com/ids/process/23532
     </wsu:Identifier>
     <wsu:Expires>
       2010-04-23T24:00:00.000
     </wsu:Expires>
     <wsc:CoordinationType>
       http://schemas.xmlsoap.org/ws/2003/09/wsat
     </wsc:CoordinationType>
     ...
   </wsc:CoordinationContext>
</Header>
```

Example F.1

The WS-Coordination specification provides a context management framework that can represent context data and context rules in standardized headers. In this example, the `CoordinationType` element establishes that WS-AtomicTransaction protocols (rules) are in use.

Finally, *business data* represents information that is relevant to the business task ⟨ rently executing. This typically refers to persistent data retrieved from a repos The classic example is a set of data records returned by a database query. It required to store this information in memory for data sharing or future reference purposes within the lifespan of a service activity.

Unlike the other forms of state information we covered, business data is typically transported within the message body as part of the message payload. It therefore is not data that actually represents or expresses the state of the service or the activity; however, the need for it to be temporarily persisted by the service can require that the service remain stateful.

There are other forms of state information you will encounter or perhaps even create yourself when designing services. The types we described in this section are common to most service processing requirements.

Measuring Service Statelessness

Using the state types and data we just established, we can define common categories to measure the level of a service capability's statelessness during its participation in a runtime activity. It is then the collective levels of the capabilities that determine the extent of a service's overall statelessness (Figure F.8).

Figure F.8

As with most service-orientation design characteristics, measures of statelessness can exist at different levels within different service capabilities. REST-compliance does not allow anything other than the full deferral of session state.

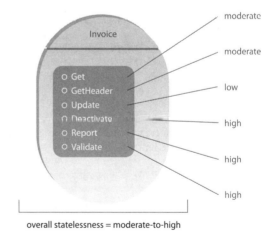

overall statelessness = moderate-to-high

Chapter 11 in *SOA Principles of Service* Design describes the following categories that can be used to label a service or any one of its capabilities in order to communicate its level of statelessness:

- Non-Deferred State Management (low-to-no statelessness)

- Partially Deferred Memory (reduced statefulness)

- Partial Architectural State Management Deferral (moderate statelessness)

- Full Architectural State Management Deferral (high statelessness)

- Internally Deferred State Management (high statelessness)

The examples that supplement these sections are all based on the use of a database as the means of state management deferral, which is why they are not included in this appendix. When associated with REST, the most relevant category is that of Full Architectural State Management Deferral, whereby service capabilities are designed to maximize statelessness by off-loading state data whenever possible (Figure F.9).

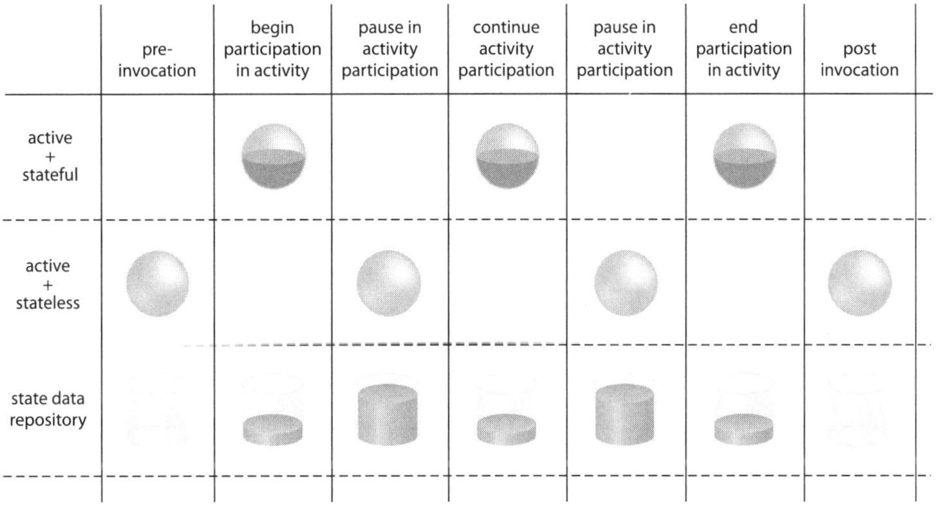

Figure F.9

The service with fully deferred state management maximizes its opportunities to exist in a stateless condition. Even when stateful, it defers state data when possible. Within a REST architecture, the state data repository would be substituted for the message layer for the deferral of session state data.

Appendix G

The Annotated SOA Manifesto

The SOA Manifesto was authored and announced during the 2nd Annual International SOA Symposium in Rotterdam by a working group comprised of 17 experts and thought leaders from different organizations.

The original SOA Manifesto is published at www.soa-manifesto.org. You are encouraged to visit this site and enter your name on the *Become a Signatory* form to show your support for the values and principles declared in the manifesto.

Subsequent to the announcement of the SOA Manifesto, Thomas Erl authored an annotated version that supplements individual statements from the original manifesto with additional commentary and insights. The Annotated SOA Manifesto is published at www.soa-manifesto.com and has been further provided as a supplementary resource in this appendix.

The Annotated SOA Manifesto

Commentary and Insights about the SOA Manifesto from Thomas Erl

Service-orientation is a paradigm that frames what you do. Service-oriented architecture (SOA) is a type of architecture that results from applying service-orientation.

From the beginning it was understood that this was to be a manifesto about two distinct yet closely related topics: the service-oriented architectural model and service-orientation, the paradigm through which the architecture is defined. The format of this manifesto was modeled after the Agile Manifesto, which limits content to concise statements that express ambitions, values, and guiding principles for realizing those ambitions and values. Such a manifesto is not a specification, a reference model, or even a white paper, and without an option to provide actual definitions, we decided to add this preamble in order to clarify how and why these terms are referenced in other parts of the manifesto document.

We have been applying service-orientation...

The service-orientation paradigm is best viewed as a method or an approach for realizing a specific target state that is further defined by a set of strategic goals and benefits. When we apply service-orientation, we shape software programs and technology architecture in support of realizing this target state. This is what qualifies technology architecture as being service-oriented.

...to help organizations consistently deliver sustainable business value, with increased agility and cost effectiveness...

This continuation of the preamble highlights some of the most prominent and commonly expected strategic benefits of service-oriented computing. Understanding these benefits helps shed some light on the aforementioned target state we intend to realize as a result of applying service-orientation.

Agility at a business level is comparable to an organization's responsiveness. The more easily and effectively an organization can respond to business change, the more efficient and successful it will be at adapting to the impacts of the change (and further leverage whatever benefits the change may bring about).

Service-orientation positions services as IT assets that are expected to provide repeated value over time that far exceeds the initial investment required for their delivery. Cost-effectiveness relates primarily to this expected return on investment. In many ways, an increase in cost-effectiveness goes hand-in-hand with an increase in agility; if there is more opportunity to reuse existing services, then there is generally less expense required to build new solutions.

"Sustainable" business value refers to the long-term goals of service-orientation to establish software programs as services with the inherent flexibility to be continually composed into new solution configurations and evolved to accommodate ever-changing business requirements.

...in line with changing business needs.

These last six words of the preamble are key to understanding the underlying philosophy of service-oriented computing. The need to accommodate business change on an on-going basis is foundational to service-orientation and considered a fundamental over-arching strategic goal.

Through our work we have come to prioritize:

The upcoming statements establish a core set of values, each of which is expressed as a prioritization over something that is also considered of value. The intent of this value system is to address the hard choices that need to be made on a regular basis in order for the strategic goals and benefits of service-oriented computing to be consistently realized.

Business value over technical strategy

As stated previously, the need to accommodate business change is an overarching strategic goal. Therefore, the foundational quality of service-oriented architecture and of any software programs, solutions, and eco-systems that result from the adoption of service-orientation is that they are business-driven. It is not about technology determining the direction of the business, it is about the business vision dictating the utilization of technology.

This priority can have a profound ripple effect within the regions of an IT enterprise. It introduces changes to just about all parts of IT delivery lifecycles, from how we plan for and fund automation solutions, to how we build and govern them. All other values and principles in the manifesto, in one way or another, support the realization of this value.

Strategic goals over project-specific benefits

Historically, many IT projects focused solely on building applications designed specifically to automate business process requirements that were current at that time. This fulfilled immediate (tactical) needs, but as more of these single-purpose applications were delivered, it resulted in an IT enterprise filled with islands of logic and data referred to as application "silos." As new business requirements would emerge, either new silos were created or integration channels between silos were established. As yet more business change arose, integration channels had to be augmented, even more silos had to be created, and soon the IT enterprise landscape became convoluted and increasingly burdensome, expensive, and slow to evolve.

In many ways, service-orientation emerged in response to these problems. It is a paradigm that provides an alternative to project-specific, silo-based, and integrated application development by adamantly prioritizing the attainment of long-term, strategic business goals. The target state advocated by service-orientation does not have traditional application silos. And even when legacy resources and application silos exist in environments where service-orientation is adopted, the target state is one where they are harmonized to whatever extent feasible.

Intrinsic interoperability over custom integration

For software programs to share data they need to be interoperable. If software programs are not designed to be compatible, they will likely not be interoperable. To enable interoperability between incompatible software programs requires that they be integrated. Integration is therefore the effort required to achieve interoperability between disparate software programs.

Although often necessary, customized integration can be expensive and time consuming and can lead to fragile architectures that are burdensome to evolve. One of the goals of service-orientation is to minimize the need for customized integration by shaping software programs (within a given domain) so that they are natively compatible. This is a quality referred to as intrinsic interoperability. The service-orientation paradigm encompasses a set of specific design principles that are geared toward establishing intrinsic interoperability on several levels.

Intrinsic interoperability, as a characteristic of software programs that reside within a given domain, is key to realizing strategic benefits, such as increased cost-effectiveness and agility.

Shared services over specific-purpose implementations

As just explained, service-orientation establishes a design approach comprised of a set of design principles. When applied to a meaningful extent, these principles shape a software program into a unit of service-oriented logic that can be legitimately referred to as a service.

Services are equipped with concrete characteristics (such as those that enable intrinsic interoperability) that directly support the previously described target state. One of these characteristics is the encapsulation of multi-purpose logic that can be shared and reused in support of the automation of different business processes.

A shared service establishes itself as an IT asset that can provide repeated business value while decreasing the expense and effort to deliver new automation solutions. While there is value in traditional, single-purpose applications that solve tactical business requirements, the use of shared services provides greater value in realizing strategic goals of service-oriented computing (which again include an increase in cost-effectiveness and agility).

Flexibility over optimization

This is perhaps the broadest of the value prioritization statements and is best viewed as a guiding philosophy for how to better prioritize various considerations when delivering and evolving individual services and inventories of services.

Optimization primarily refers to the fulfillment of tactical gains by tuning a given application design or expediting its delivery to meet immediate needs. There is nothing undesirable about this, except that it can lead to the aforementioned silo-based environments when not properly prioritized in relation to fostering flexibility.

For example, the characteristic of flexibility goes beyond the ability for services to effectively (and intrinsically) share data. To be truly responsive to ever-changing business requirements, services must also be flexible in how they can be combined and aggregated into composite solutions. Unlike traditional distributed applications that often were relatively static despite the fact that they were componentized, service compositions need to be designed with a level of inherent flexibility that allows for constant augmentation. This means that when an existing business process changes or when a new business process is introduced, we need to be able to add, remove, and extend services within the composition architecture with minimal (integration) effort. This is why service composability is one of the key service-orientation design principles.

Evolutionary refinement over pursuit of initial perfection

There is a common point of confusion when it comes to the term "agility" in relation to service-orientation. Some design approaches advocate the rapid delivery of software programs for immediate gains. This can be considered "tactical agility," as the focus is on tactical, short-term benefit. Service-orientation advocates the attainment of agility on an organizational or business level with the intention of empowering the organization, as a whole, to be responsive to change. This form of organizational agility can also be referred to as "strategic agility" because the emphasis is on longevity in that, with every software program we deliver, we want to work toward a target state that fosters agility with long-term strategic value.

For an IT enterprise to enable organizational agility, it must evolve in tandem with the business. We generally cannot predict how a business will need to evolve over time and therefore we cannot initially build the perfect services. At the same time, there is usually a wealth of knowledge that already exists within an organization's existing business intelligence that can be harvested during the analysis and modeling stages of SOA projects.

This information, together with service-orientation principles and proven methodologies, can help us identify and define a set of services that capture how the business exists and operates today while being sufficiently flexible to adapt to how the business changes over time.

That is, while we value the items on the right, we value the items on the left more.

By studying how these values are prioritized, we gain insight into what distinguishes service-orientation from other paradigms. This type of insight can benefit IT practitioners in several ways. For example, it can help establish fundamental criteria that we can use to determine how compatible service-orientation is for a given organization or IT enterprise. It can further help determine the extent to which service-orientation can or should be adopted.

An appreciation of the core values can also help us understand how challenging it may be to successfully carry out SOA projects within certain environments. For example, several of these prioritizations may clash head-on with established beliefs and preferences. In such a case, the benefits of service-orientation need to be weighed against the effort and impact their adoption may have (not just on technology, but also on the organization and IT culture).

The upcoming guiding principles were provided to help address many of these types of challenges.

We follow these principles:

So far, the manifesto has established an overall vision as well as a set of core values associated with the vision. The remainder of the declaration is comprised of a set of principles that are provided as guidance for adhering to the values and realizing the vision.

It's important to keep in mind that these are guiding principles specific to this manifesto. There is a separate set of established design principles that comprise the service-orientation design paradigm and there are many more documented practices and patterns specific to service-orientation and service-oriented architecture.

Respect the social and power structure of the organization.

One of the most common SOA pitfalls is approaching adoption as a technology-centric initiative. Doing so almost always leads to failure because we are simply not prepared for the inevitable organizational impacts.

The adoption of service-orientation is about transforming the way we automate business. However, regardless of what plans we may have for making this transformation effort happen, we must always begin with an understanding and an appreciation of the organization, its structure, its goals, and its culture.

The adoption of service-orientation is very much a human experience. It requires support from those in authority and then asks that an IT culture adopt a strategic, community-centric mindset. We must fully acknowledge and plan for this level of organizational change in order to receive the necessary long-term commitments required to achieve the target state of service-orientation.

These types of considerations not only help us determine how to best proceed with an SOA initiative, they further assist us in defining the most appropriate scope and approach for adoption.

Recognize that SOA ultimately demands change on many levels.

There's a saying that goes: "Success is being prepared for opportunity." Perhaps the number one lesson learned from SOA projects carried out so far is that we must fully comprehend and then plan and prepare for the volume and range of change that is brought about as a result of adopting service-orientation. Here are some examples.

Service-orientation changes how we build automation solutions by positioning software programs as IT assets with long-term, repeatable business value. An upfront investment is required to create an environment comprised of such assets and an on-going commitment is required to maintain and leverage their value. So, right out of the gate, changes are required to how we fund, measure, and maintain systems within the IT enterprise.

Furthermore, because service-orientation introduces services that are positioned as resources of the enterprise, there will be changes in how we own different parts of systems and regulate their design and usage, not to mention changes to the infrastructure required to guarantee continuous scalability and reliability.

The scope of SOA adoption can vary. Keep efforts manageable and within meaningful boundaries.

A common myth has been that in order to realize the strategic goals of service-oriented computing, service-orientation must be adopted on an enterprise-wide basis. This means establishing and enforcing design and industry standards across the IT enterprise so as to create an enterprise-wide inventory of intrinsically interoperable services. While there is nothing wrong with this ideal, it is not a realistic goal for many organizations, especially those with larger IT enterprises.

The most appropriate scope for any given SOA adoption effort needs to be determined as a result of planning and analysis in conjunction with pragmatic considerations, such as the aforementioned impacts on organizational structures, areas of authority, and cultural changes that are brought about.

These types of factors help us determine a scope of adoption that is manageable. But for any adoption effort to result in an environment that progresses the IT enterprise toward the desired strategic target state, the scope must also be meaningful. In other words, it must be meaningfully cross-silo so that collections of services can be delivered in relation to each other within a pre-defined boundary. In other words, we want to create "continents of services," not the dreaded "islands of services."

This concept of building independently owned and governed service inventories within domains of the same IT enterprise reduces many of the risks that are commonly attributed to "big-bang" SOA projects and furthermore mitigates the impact of both organizational and technological changes (because the impact is limited to a segmented and managed scope). It is also an approach that allows for phased adoption where one domain service inventory can be established at a time.

Products and standards alone will neither give you SOA nor apply the service-orientation paradigm for you.

This principle addresses two separate but very much related myths. The first is that you can buy your way into SOA with modern technology products, and the second is the assumption that the adoption of industry standards (such as XML, WSDL, SCA, etc.) will naturally result in service-oriented technology architecture.

The vendor and industry standards communities have been credited with building modern service technology innovation upon non-proprietary frameworks and platforms. Everything from service virtualization to cloud computing and grid computing has helped advance the potential for building sophisticated and complex service-oriented solutions. However, none of these technologies are exclusive to SOA. You can just as easily build silo-based systems in the cloud as you can on your own private servers.

There is no such thing as "SOA in a box" because in order to achieve service-oriented technology architecture, service-orientation needs to be successfully applied; this, in turn, requires that everything we design and build be driven by the unique direction, vision, and requirements of the business.

SOA can be realized through a variety of technologies and standards.

Service-orientation is a technology-neutral and vendor-neutral paradigm. Service-oriented architecture is a technology-neutral and vendor neutral architectural model. Service-oriented computing can be viewed as a specialized form of distributed computing. Service-oriented solutions can therefore be built using just about any technologies and industry standards suitable for distributed computing.

While some technologies (especially those based on industry standards) can increase the potential of applying some service-orientation design principles, it is really the potential to fulfill business requirements that ultimately determines the most suitable choice of technologies and industry standards.

Establish a uniform set of enterprise standards and policies based on industry, de facto, and community standards.

Industry standards represent non-proprietary technology specifications that help establish, among other things, consistent baseline characteristics (such as transport, interface, message format, etc.) of technology architecture. However, the use of industry standards alone does not guarantee that services will be intrinsically interoperable.

For two software programs to be fully compatible, additional conventions (such as data models and policies) need to be adhered to. This is why IT enterprises must establish and enforce design standards. Failure to properly standardize and regulate the standardization of services within a given domain will begin to tear at the fabric of interoperability upon which the realization of many strategic benefits relies.

This principle not only advocates the use of enterprise design standards, it also reminds us that, whenever possible and feasible, custom design standards should be based upon and incorporate standards already in use by the industry and the community in general.

Pursue uniformity on the outside while allowing diversity on the inside.

Federation can be defined as the unification of a set of disparate entities. While allowing each entity to be independently governed on the inside, all agree to adhere to a common, unified front.

A fundamental part of service-oriented architecture is the introduction of a federated endpoint layer that abstracts service implementation details while publishing a set of endpoints that represent individual services within a given domain in a unified manner. Accomplishing this generally involves achieving unity based on a combination of industry and design standards. The consistency of this unity across services is key to realizing intrinsic interoperability.

A federated endpoint layer further helps increase opportunities to explore vendor-diversity options. For example, one service may need to be built upon a completely different platform than another. As long as these services maintain compatible endpoints, the governance of their respective implementations can remain independent. This not only highlights that services can be built using different implementation mediums (such as EJB, .NET, SOAP, REST, etc.), it also emphasizes that different intermediary platforms and technologies can be utilized together, as required.

Note that this type of diversity comes with a price. This principle does not advocate diversification itself—it simply recommends that we allow diversification when justified, so that "best-of-breed" technologies and platforms can be leveraged to maximize business requirements fulfillment.

Identify services through collaboration with business and technology stakeholders.

In order for technology solutions to be business-driven, the technology must be in synch with the business. Therefore, another goal of service-oriented computing is to align technology and business. The stage at which this alignment is initially accomplished is during the analysis and modeling processes that usually precede actual service development and delivery.

The critical ingredient to carrying out service-oriented analysis is to have both business and technology experts working hand-in-hand to identify and define candidate services. For example, business experts can help accurately define functional contexts pertaining to business-centric services, while technology experts can provide pragmatic input to ensure that the granularity and definition of conceptual services remains realistic in relation to their eventual implementation environments.

Maximize service usage by considering the current and future scope of utilization.

The extent of a given SOA project may be enterprise-wide or it may be limited to a domain of the enterprise. Whatever the scope, a pre-defined boundary is established to encompass an inventory of services that need to be conceptually modeled before they can be developed. By modeling multiple services in relation to each other we essentially establish a blueprint of the services we will eventually be building. This modeling exercise is critical when attempting to identify and define services that can be shared by different solutions.

There are various methodologies and approaches that can be used to carry out service-oriented analysis stages. However, a common thread among all of them is that the functional boundaries of services be normalized to avoid redundancy. Even then, normalized services do not necessarily make for highly reusable services. Other factors come into play, such as service granularity, autonomy, state management, scalability, composability, and the extent to which service logic is sufficiently generic so that it can be effectively reused.

These types of considerations guided by business and technology expertise provide the opportunity to define services that capture current utilization requirements while having the flexibility to adapt to future change.

Verify that services satisfy business requirements and goals.

As with anything, services can be misused. When growing and managing a portfolio of services, their usage and effectiveness at fulfilling business requirements need to be verified and measured. Modern tools provide various means of monitoring service usage, but there are intangibles that also need to be taken into consideration to ensure that services are not just used because they are available, but to verify that they are truly fulfilling business needs and meeting expectations.

This is especially true with shared services that shoulder multiple dependencies. Not only do shared services require adequate infrastructure to guarantee scalability and reliability for all of the solutions that reuse them, they also need to be designed and extended with great care to ensure their functional contexts are never skewed.

Evolve services and their organization in response to real use.

This guiding principle ties directly back to the "Evolutionary refinement over pursuit of initial perfection" value statement, as well as the overall goal of maintaining an alignment of business and technology.

We can never expect to rely on guesswork when it comes to determining service granularity, the range of functions that services need to perform, or how services will need to be organized into compositions. Based on whatever extent of analysis we are able to initially perform, a given service will be assigned a defined functional context and will contain one or more functional capabilities that likely involve it in one or more service compositions.

As real world business requirements and circumstances change, the service may need to be augmented, extended, refactored, or perhaps even replaced. Service-orientation design principles build native flexibility into service architectures so that, as software programs, services are resilient and adaptive to change and to being changed in response to real world usage.

Separate the different aspects of a system that change at different rates.

What makes monolithic and silo-based systems inflexible is that change can have a significant impact on their existing usage. This is why it is often easier to create new silo-based applications rather then augment or extend existing ones.

The rationale behind the separation of concerns (a commonly known software engineering theory) is that a larger problem can be more effectively solved when decomposed into a set of smaller problems or concerns. When applying service-orientation to the separation of concerns, we build corresponding units of solution logic that solve individual concerns, thereby allowing us to aggregate the units to solve the larger problem in addition to giving us the opportunity to aggregate them into different configurations in order to solve other problems.

Besides fostering service reusability, this approach introduces numerous layers of abstraction that help shield service-comprised systems from the impacts of change. This form of abstraction can exist at different levels. For example, if legacy resources encapsulated by one service need to be replaced, the impact of that change can be mitigated as long as the service is able to retain its original endpoint and functional behavior.

Another example is the separation of agnostic from non-agnostic logic. The former type of logic has high reuse potential if it is multi-purpose and less likely to change. Non-agnostic logic, on the other hand, typically represents the single-purpose parts of parent business process logic, which are often more volatile. Separating these respective logic types into different service layers further introduces abstraction that enables service reusability while shielding services, and any solutions that utilize them, from the impacts of change.

Reduce implicit dependencies and publish all external dependencies to increase robustness and reduce the impact of change.

One of the most well-known service-orientation design principles is that of service loose coupling. How a service architecture is internally structured and how services relate to programs that consume them (which can include other services) all comes down to dependencies that are formed on individually moving parts that are part of the service architecture.

Layers of abstraction help ease evolutionary change by localizing the impacts of the change to controlled regions. For example, within service architectures, service facades can be used to abstract parts of the implementation in order to minimize the reach of implementation dependencies.

On the other hand, published technical service contracts need to disclose the dependencies that service consumers must form in order to interact with services. By reducing internal dependencies that can affect these technical contracts when change does occur, we avoid proliferating the impact of those changes upon dependent service consumers.

At every level of abstraction, organize each service around a cohesive and manageable unit of functionality.

Each service requires a well-defined functional context that determines what logic does and does not belong within the service's functional boundary. Determining the scope and granularity of these functional service boundaries is one of the most critical responsibilities during the service delivery lifecycle.

Services with coarse functional granularity may be too inflexible to be effective, especially if they are expected to be reusable. On the other hand, overly fine grained services may tax an infrastructure in that service compositions will need to consist of increased quantities of composition members.

Determining the right balance of functional scope and granularity requires a combination of business and technology expertise, and further requires an understanding of how services within a given boundary relate to each other.

Many of the guiding principles described in this manifesto will help in making this determination in support of positioning each service as an IT asset capable of furthering an IT enterprise toward that target state whereby the strategic benefits of service-oriented computing are realized.

Ultimately, though, it will always be the attainment of real world business value that dictates, from conception to delivery to repeated usage, the evolutionary path of any unit of service-oriented functionality.

—Thomas Erl (November 22, 2009)
www.soa-manifesto.com

Appendix H

Additional Resources

www.whatisrest.com

Bibliography and References

Resources

This appendix provides a bibliography of publications that were researched for the authoring of this book, as well as a series of supplemental online resources related to REST and SOA.

www.whatisrest.com

This Web site contains excerpts from this book and related content to provide a concise overview of REST architecture and constraints. Be sure to use this online resource as a quick reference for definitions and explanations of fundamental topics pertaining to REST.

Bibliography and References

The following is a list of books, papers, articles, and other bodies of work that provided valuable input in support of this book:

Rosa Alarcón, Erik Wilde, "Linking Data from RESTful Services," Prof. of the 3rd Workshop on Linked Data on the Web at WWW 2010, Raleigh, NC, April 2010.

Subbu Allamaraju, *RESTful Web Services Cookbook: Solutions for Improving Scalability and Simplicity*, O'Reilly, 2010

Mike Amundsen, *Building Hypermedia APIs with HTML5 and Node*, O'Reilly, 2011

Daniele Bonetta, Achille Peternier, Cesare Pautasso, Walter Binder, S: "A Scripting Language for High-Performance RESTful Web Services," 17th ACM SIGPLAN Symposium on Principles and Practice of Parallel Programming (PPoPP 2012), New Orleans, LA, USA, February 2012

Bill Burke, *RESTful Java*, O'Reilly, 2009

David Chou, John deVadoss, Thomas Erl, Nitin Gandhi, Hanu Kommalapati, Brian Loesgen, Christoph Schittko, Herbjorn Wilhelmsen, Mickey Williams, *SOA with .NET & Windows Azure: Realizing Service-Orientation with the Microsoft Platform*, Prentice Hall

Gero Decker, Alexander Lüders, Hagen Overdick, Kai Schlichting, Mathias Weske, "RESTful Petri Net Execution," WS-FM 2008: 73-87

Justin R. Erenkrantz, Michael M. Gorlick, Girish Suryanarayana, Richard N. Taylor, "From representations to computations: the evolution of web architectures," ESEC/SIGSOFT FSE 2007: 255-264

Thomas Erl, *Service-Oriented Architecture: A Field Guide to Integrating XML and Web Services*, Prentice Hall, 2004

Thomas Erl, *Service-Oriented Architecture: Concepts, Technology & Design*, Prentice Hall, 2005

Thomas Erl, *SOA Design Patterns*, Prentice Hall, 2009

Thomas Erl, *SOA Principles of Service Design*, Prentice Hall, 2007

Thomas Erl, Anish Karmarkar, Priscilla Walmsley, Hugo Haas, Umit Yalcinalp, Canyang Kevin Liu, David Orchard, Andre Tost, James Pasley, *Web Service Contract Design & Versioning for SOA*, Prentice Hall, 2008

Roy Fielding, "Architectural Styles and the Design of Network-based Software Architectures," PhD Thesis, University of California, Irvine, 2000

Roy T. Fielding, Richard N. Taylor, "Principled design of the modern Web architecture," ACM Trans. Internet Techn. 2(2): 115-150 (2002)

Jon Flanders, *RESTful .NET: Build and Consume RESTful Web Services with .NET 3.5*, O'Reilly, 2008

Ian T. Foster, Savas Parastatidis, Paul Watson, Mark McKeown, "How Do I Model State? Let Me Count the Ways," ACM Queue 7(2): 54-55 (2009)

Martin Fowler, Richardson Maturity Model, "Steps toward the glory of REST," martinfowler.com/articles/richardsonMaturityModel.html

Dominique Guinard, Vlad Trifa, Friedemann Mattern and Erik Wilde, "From the Internet of Things to the Web of Things: Resource-oriented Architecture and Best Practices, In: Architecting the Internet of Things," p. 97-129, Springer 2011

Andreas Heil, Johannes Meinecke, Martin Gaedke, "Components for Growing the RESTful Enterprise," MobIS 2008

Rohit Khare, Richard N. Taylor, "Extending the Representational State Transfer (REST) Architectural Style for Decentralized Systems," ICSE 2004: 428-437

Reto Krummenacher, Martin Hepp, Axel Polleres, Christoph Bussler, Dieter Fensel, "WWW or What Is Wrong with Web Services," Proc. of the Third IEEE European Conference on Web Services (ECOWS'05), pp.235-243, 2005

Janne Kuuskeri and Tuomas Turto, "On Actors and the REST," Proc. of the 10th International Conference on Web Engineering (ICWE 2010), Vienna, Austria, p. 144-157, Springer LNCS 6189, 2010

Ken Laskey, Philippe Le Hégaret, Eric Newcomer (eds.) Proc. of the W3C Workshop on "Web of Services for Enterprise Computing," Bedford, MA, February 2007

Erik Meijer, "Server side web scripting in Haskell," J. Funct. Program. 10(1): 1-18 (2000)

Savas Parastatidis, Ian Robinson, Jim Webber, *REST in Practice: Hypermedia and Systems Architecture*, O'Reilly, 2010

Cesare Pautasso, "BPEL for REST," Proc. of the 6th International Conference on Business Process Management (BPM 2008), Milan, Italy, September 2008.

Cesare Pautasso, "Composing RESTful Services with JOpera," In: Proc. of the International Conference on Software Composition (SC2009), July 2009, Zurich, Switzerland.

Cesare Pautasso, Erik Wilde, Alexandros Marinos, Proceedings of the First International Workshop on RESTful Design (WS-REST 2010), Raleigh, North Carolina, USA, April 26, 2010 ACM 2010

Cesare Pautasso, Erik Wilde, Rosa Alarcon, Proceedings of the Second International Workshop on RESTful Design (WS-REST 2011), Hyderabad, India, March 28, 2011, ACM 2011

Cesare Pautasso, "RESTful Web Service Composition with BPEL for REST, Data & Knowledge Engineering," Volume 68, Issue 9, September 2009, Pages 851-866, doi:10.1016/j.datak.2009.02.016.

Cesare Pautasso, Olaf Zimmermann, Frank Leymann, "RESTful Web Services vs. Big Web Services: Making the Right Architectural Decision," Proc. of the 17th International World Wide Web Conference (WWW2008), Beijing, China, April 2008

Cesare Pautasso, Erik Wilde, "Why is the Web Loosely Coupled? A Multi-Faceted Metric for Service Design," Proc. of the 18th International World Wide Web Conference (WWW2009), Madrid, Spain, April 2009.

Amir Reza Razavi, Alexandros Marinos, Sotiris Moschoyiannis, Paul J. Krause: RESTful Transactions Supported by the Isolation Theorems. Proc. of the 9th International Conference on Web Engineering 2009, San Sebastian, Spain, p. 394-409, Springer LNCS 5648, 2009

Hassan Reza, David Van Gilst, "A Framework for Testing RESTful Web Services," ITNG 2010: 216-221

Leonard Richardson, Sam Ruby, *RESTful Web Services*, O'Reilly, May 2007

Florian Rosenberg, Francisco Curbera, Matthew J. Duftler, Rania Khalaf, "Composing RESTful Services and Collaborative Workflows: A Lightweight Approach. IEEE Internet Computing," 12(5): 24-31 (2008)

Alessandro Sivieri, Gianpaolo Cugola and Carlo Ghezzi, "Computational REST Meets Erlang," Proc. of the 49th International Conference on Objects, Models, Components, Patterns (TOOLS 2011), Zurich, Switzerland, June 28-30, Springer LNCS 6705, p. 244-259, 2011

Richard N. Taylor, Nenad Medvidovic, Eric M. Dashofy, *Software Architecture: Foundations, Theory and Practice*, John-Wiley, January 2009

Stevan Tilkov, "HTTP und REST," dpunkt Verlag, 2009, rest-http.info

Erik Wilde, Cesare Pautasso (eds.), *REST: From Research to Practice*, Springer, 2011, ws-rest.org/book

Resources

Following is a list of resource Web sites that provide supplementary content for books in this series. If you'd like to be automatically notified of new book releases, new supplementary content for this title, or key changes to these Web sites, send a blank e-mail to notify@arcitura.com.

www.servicetechbooks.com

The official site of the *Prentice Hall Service Technology Series from Thomas Erl*. Numerous resources are provided, including sample chapters from available books and updates and corrections.

www.soaschool.com, www.cloudschool.com

These two educational sites describe the vast curricula dedicated to SOA and Cloud Computing. Books from the *Prentice Hall Service Technology Series from Thomas Erl* are official parts of these programs.

www.servicetechmag.com

The *Service Technology Magazine* (formerly the *SOA Magazine*) is a regular publication provided by Arcitura Education Inc. and Prentice Hall and is officially associated with *The Prentice Hall Service Technology Series from Thomas Erl*. The *Service Technology Magazine* is dedicated to publishing specialized articles, case studies, and papers by industry experts and professionals.

www.soaglossary.com

A master glossary for all books in the *The Prentice Hall Service Technology Series from Thomas Erl* is hosted by this site. This site is constantly growing as new titles are developed and released.

www.servicetechspecs.com

This Web site establishes a convenient central portal to industry standards and specifications covered or referenced by titles in this book series.

www.soapatterns.org, www.cloudpatterns.org

The official sites for the master SOA and cloud computing design patterns catalogs. These sites allow for the online submission and community review of candidate patterns proposed for inclusion in the master patterns catalogs.

www.serviceorientation.com, www.soaprinciples.com, www.whatissoa.com

These sites provide papers, book excerpts, and various content dedicated to describing and defining the service-orientation paradigm, associated principles, and the service-oriented technology architectural model.

www.servicetechsymposium.com

This is the official site for the international conference series dedicated to SOA, Cloud Computing, and Service Technology. These events are held throughout the world and frequently feature authors from the *Prentice Hall Service Technology Series from Thomas Erl*.

About the Authors

Thomas Erl

Thomas Erl is a best-selling IT author and the world's top-selling SOA author. His books encompass topics ranging from cloud computing, semantic Web technology, and SOA. He is the series editor of the *Prentice Hall Service Technology Series from Thomas Erl*, as well as the editor of the *Service Technology Magazine*. With more than 160,000 copies in print world-wide, his published books have become international bestsellers and have been formally endorsed by senior members of major IT organizations, such as IBM, Microsoft, Oracle, Intel, Accenture, IEEE, MITRE, SAP, CISCO, and HP. As the founder of Arcitura Education Inc., Thomas has overseen the development of curricula for the internationally recognized SOASchool.com SOA Certified Professional (SOACP) and CloudSchool.com Cloud Certified Professional (CCP) accreditation programs, which have established a series of formal, vendor-neutral industry certifications. Thomas has toured over 20 countries as a speaker and instructor for public and private events and regularly participates in SOA, Cloud + Service Technology Symposium, and Gartner conferences. More than 100 articles and interviews by Thomas have been published in numerous publications, including *The Wall Street Journal* and *CIO Magazine.*

Benjamin Carlyle

Benjamin is a founding developer of the Invensys Rail "SystematICS" services framework, and has worked for many years as a software developer, software architect, and systems engineer on railway projects worldwide. He has focused on integrating REST and services technologies since around 2004. His work is referenced in several books on Restful Web services and on microformats, he has presented at the International SOA Symposium, and has served on the technical committee for international workshops on RESTful Design. He is credited with helping inspire the RESTlet framework for Java, and coined the term "REST Triangle" to describe the structure of a REST uniform contract. He has a deep understanding of both the theory and practice of REST and related styles as well as broader software and systems architecture topics.

Cesare Pautasso

Cesare Pautasso is an assistant professor at the Faculty of Informatics at the University of Lugano, Switzerland. Previously he was a researcher at the IBM Zurich Research Lab and a senior researcher at ETH Zurich, where he also completed his graduate studies with a Ph.D. in 2004. His teaching, research, and consulting activities both in academia and in industry cover advanced topics related to Software Architecture, Service Oriented Computing, and emerging RESTful Web services technologies. His research group focuses on building experimental systems to explore the intersection between the REST architectural style and model-driven software composition techniques, business process management, and liquid, self-organizing service-oriented architectures. He is an active member of IEEE and ACM, where he has participated in more than 100 international conference/workshop program committees. He has started the series of International Workshops on RESTful Design (WS-REST) at the WWW conference and was the general chair of the 9th IEEE European Conference on Web Services (ECOWS 2011). He regularly referees for Swiss, EU, and international funding agencies.

Raj Balasubramanian

Raj Balasubramanian is a senior technologist from the Business Process Optimization (BPO) team within IBM Software Group focused on delivering SOA/BPM/Cloud solution across industries. Depending on the needs of the customer he has played the role of an enterprise architect, system architect, or solution architect to deliver on the engagement at hand. Prior to the focus on BPO, he was a lead portal architect delivering portal solutions to medium and large enterprise as part of the Lotus brand. He has published numerous articles on IBM DeveloperWorks and speaks at industry conferences on a variety of topics. His interests are in distributed systems, applying Web constructs to solution design, and using formal models and analytics to reason about large systems. Raj is also pursuing a Ph.D. in ECE at University of Texas at Austin where he is applying machine learning and data mining techniques to networked data from social Web to human travel. His official profile is on http://raj.balasubramanians.com, which links to his various personas.

About the Pattern Co-Contributors

The following individuals contributed to the authoring of SOA design patterns introduced in this book.

David Booth, Ph.D.

David Booth is based outside of Boston and currently works as a contractor for Cleveland Clinic where he is a Software Architect working on their SemanticDB project, which applies semantic Web technology to clinical research. Until 2009 David worked for HP, having joined when HP acquired Bluestone Software. He was a W3C Fellow from HP from 2002 to 2005 and remains an avid advocate of the Web, Web architecture, Semantic Web technology, and the use of http URIs as universal identifiers. More about David Booth is published at www.dbooth.org.

Herbjörn Wilhelmsen

Herbjörn Wilhelmsen is based in Stockholm, Sweden, and works as an Enterprise Architect at TUI Nordic—and also finds time to do public speaking, writing, teaching, and consulting. His main focus areas are service-oriented architecture (SOA), cloud computing, and enterprise architecture.

Herbjörn has many years of industry experience working as a developer, development manager, architect, and teacher. He has worked with clients in several fields of operations such as telecommunications, marketing, the payment industry, healthcare, public services, and tourism. Herbjörn is co-author of the *SOA with .NET & Windows Azure* book and is currently co-authoring the *Service-Oriented Infrastructure: On-Premise and in the Cloud* book. Both titles are part of the *Prentice Hall Service Technology Series from Thomas Erl*. Herbjörn has written several articles on SOA and cloud computing, most notably for *The SOA Magazine* and *MSDN Magazine*. Herbjörn is a frequent speaker at architecture and development conferences and blogs at herbjorn.wordpress.com.

About the Foreword
Contributor

Stefan Tilkov

Stefan Tilkov is a co-founder and principal consultant at innoQ, a technology consulting company with offices in Germany and Switzerland. He has been involved in the design of large-scale, distributed systems for almost two decades, using a variety of technologies and tools ranging from C++ and CORBA over J2EE/Java EE and Web Services to REST and Ruby on Rails. He has authored numerous articles and a book (*REST und HTTP*, German) and is a frequent speaker at conferences around the world.

Index

Symbols

+ (plus) symbol notation, 88

A

active message processing, 27
active state, 527-528
Agnostic Capability design pattern, 428
Agnostic Context design pattern, 429
agnostic logic, 42
agnostic service candidates, identifying, 155-172
Agnostic Sub-Controller design pattern, 430
Annotated SOA Manifesto, 39, 49, 534-546
application layer, Web standards for, 388
architectural goals. *See* design goals
architectural properties, 52
Architectural Styles and the Design of Network-based Software Architectures (Fielding), 392
Asynchronous Queuing design pattern, 431
asynchronous service compositions, synchronous versus, 253-254
Async method, 219-220

Atomic Service Transaction design pattern, 221, 251, 272, 432
atomic service transactions
    non-REST-friendly, 276-281
    REST-friendly, 267-272

B

backwards-compatibility
    REST service contracts, 346-349
    uniform contract media types, 350-353
    uniform contract methods, 349-350
baseline standardization, dynamic binding with, 302-304
bindings
    between composition participants, 255-257
    dynamic binding, 288-299
Brokered Authentication design pattern, 433
Building Hypermedia APIs with HTML5 and Node, 4
business data, 529-530
business models, defining, 132
business process automation, step-by-step example, 258-260

business processes
    decomposing, 152-172
    filtering, 154-172
business process instance, 233

C

Cache constraint, 55, 98, 145
    composition design and, 248
    Fielding dissertation related
        excerpts, 399
    profile, 398
    standardizing, 202-203
Canonical Expression design pattern,
    199, 434
Canonical Protocol design pattern, 435
Canonical Resources design pattern, 436
Canonical Schema Bus compound
    pattern, 438
Canonical Schema design pattern, 188,
    296, 437
canonical schema in uniform contract
    profile template, 367
Canonical Versioning design pattern,
    358, 439
canonical vocabulary in uniform
    contract profile template, 367
capabilities, service composition
    capabilities, 235-236
Capability Composition design
    pattern, 440
capability granularity, 45
Capability Recomposition design
    pattern, 441
case study examples
    KioskEtc Co.
        background, 18-20
        conclusion, 384-385
        REST services, 90-92

Midwest University Association
    (MUA)
        aligning SOA and REST design
            goals, 116-124
        background, 14-18
        complex method design, 224-227
        conclusion, 384-385
        REST constraints and design
            goals, 63-64
        REST service contract design,
            205-210
        REST service modeling process,
            152-172
        service composition with REST,
            306-324
        SOA infrastructure planning, 50
        uniform contract profile,
            369-379
CCP (Cloud Certified Professional), 11
centralization of REST services, 146-147
chapters, described, 4-8
chorded circle symbol, 25
client-server architectures, origins of
    state management, 523-526
Client-Server constraint, 53, 99, 101-102
    Fielding dissertation related
        excerpts, 394
    profile, 393
cloud computing, defined, 40
CloudSchool.com Cloud Certified
    Professional (CCP), 11
coarse-grained granularity, 45
Code-On-Demand constraint, 57, 100,
    102, 351
    composition logic deferral, 248
    Fielding dissertation related
        excerpts, 408
    profile, 407
    runtime logic deferral, 297-299

collective composability, 236-238

color grey in text convention, 14

color red in text convention, 8

common properties, dynamic binding with, 294-296

compatibility. *See also* versioning

    REST service contracts, 346-349

    uniform contract media types, 350-354

    uniform contract methods, 349-350

compatibility guarantee, 356

Compatible Change design pattern, 442

compatible changes

    REST service contracts, 348-349

    uniform contract media types, 350

Compensating Service Transaction design pattern, 251, 272, 443

compensating service transactions, REST-friendly, 272-276

complex methods, design considerations, 211-223

    case study example, 224-227

    stateful complex methods, 221-223

    stateless complex methods, 214-220

complex service activities, 239

components, defined, 39

Composition Autonomy design pattern, 444

composition controller capability, 236

composition controllers, defined, 234-238

composition deepening, 292-293

composition initiators, defined, 239-240

composition instances, defined, 233

composition member capability, 236

composition members, defined, 234-238

compositions

    across service inventories, 299-304

    autonomy loss, 245

composition deepening, 292-293

cross-service transactions. *See* cross-service transactions

defined, 27-28, 233

design considerations

    REST constraints and, 247-248

    REST service compositions, 253-257

    service-orientation principles and, 241-247

    Service Statelessness design principle, 264-265

    Stateless constraint, 265

with dynamic binding and logic deferral, 288-299

hierarchies and layers, 249-252

identifying candidates, 167-172

initiators, 239-240

members and controllers, 234-238

minimum scope, 240

repeatable compositions, 245

REST service compositions

    design considerations, 253-257

    step-by-step example, 258-260

Stateless constraint and, 263-265

compound patterns. *See also* design patterns

    Canonical Schema Bus, 438

    Enterprise Service Bus, 462

    Federated Endpoint Layer, 467

    Official Endpoint, 481

    Orchestration, 482

    Service Broker, 496

    Three-Layer Inventory, 167, 250, 513

    Uniform Contract, 339, 516

Concurrent Contracts design pattern, 445

configurability, 61-64

constraint granularity, 45

constraints (REST), 8-9, 52
　Cache, 55, 145
　　Fielding dissertation related
　　　excerpts, 399
　　profile, 398
　case study example, 63-64
　Client-Server, 53
　　Fielding dissertation related
　　　excerpts, 394
　　profile, 393
　Code-on-Demand, 57
　　Fielding dissertation related
　　　excerpts, 408
　　profile, 407
　　runtime logic deferral, 297-299
　common conflicts with SOA design
　　principles, 114-115
　defined, 52
　designing and standardizing,
　　201-204
　Layered System, 56-57, 145
　　Fielding dissertation related
　　　excerpts, 406
　　profile, 404-405
　Service Abstraction design principle
　　and, 107-109
　Service Autonomy design principle
　　and, 110-111
　Service Composability design
　　principle and, 114
　service composition design and,
　　247-248
　Service Discoverability design
　　principle and, 113
　Service Loose Coupling design
　　principle and, 105-107
　Service Reusability design principle
　　and, 109-110
　Service Statelessness design
　　principle, 111-112, 246

　Standardized Service Contract
　　design principle and, 104-105
　Stateless, 54, 145, 246
　　composition design, 265
　　cross-service transactions,
　　　266-281
　　Event-Driven Messaging design
　　　pattern and, 283-284
　　Fielding dissertation related
　　　excerpts, 397
　　message polling and, 287-288
　　profile, 395-396
　　service compositions and,
　　　263-265
　Uniform Contract, 55-56, 59-60, 62,
　　98-102, 145, 184
　　breaking, 115
　　composition coupling and, 248
　　Fielding dissertation related
　　　excerpts, 402-403
　　profile, 400-401
　　REST service inventory modeling
　　　and, 141-147
　　Service Abstraction design
　　　principle and, 108
　　Standardized Service Contract
　　　design principle and, 104-105
　　standardizing, 203
　uniform contract modeling and,
　　144-145
Content Negotiation design pattern,
　106-107, 331-332, 348, 352, 354,
　357, 446
context data, 529
context rules, 529
Contract Centralization design pattern,
　98, 340, 447
Contract Denormalization design
　pattern, 289, 336, 340, 448

Cross-Domain Utility Layer design
  pattern, 449
cross-service transactions, 266-281
    non-REST-friendly atomic service
        transactions, 276-281
    REST-friendly atomic service
        transactions, 267-272
    REST-friendly compensating service
        transactions, 272-276
customizing
    HTTP headers, 177-179
    HTTP response codes, 184-186
    media types, 186-188
    methods, 175-177

D

Data Confidentiality design pattern, 450
Data Format Transformation design
  pattern, 299, 451
data granularity, 45
Data Model Transformation design
  pattern, 296, 299, 452
Data Origin Authentication design
  pattern, 453
Decomposed Capability design
  pattern, 454
Decoupled Contract design pattern, 455
decoupling resource consumption, 60
deferral (state), 524, 527
delegation (state), 524, 527
Delta method, 217-219
denormalized service capabilities,
    Service Normalization design
    principle and, 289
designated controllers, 236
design considerations
    for complex methods, 211-223
        case study example, 224-227

    *stateful complex methods,
        221-223*
    *stateless complex methods,
        214-220*
for REST service compositions,
    253-257
    bindings, 255-257
    idempotency, 254-255
    lingering composition state, 255
    *synchronous versus asynchronous
        compositions, 253-254*
for REST service contracts, 191-204
    by service model, 191-193
    case study example, 205-210
    resource identifiers, 194-201
    REST constraints, 201-204
for service compositions
    REST constraints and, 247-248
    *service-orientation principles
        and, 241-247*
    *Service Statelessness design
        principle, 264-265*
    Stateless constraint, 265
for uniform contracts, 175-190
    HTTP headers, 177-179
    HTTP response codes, 179-186
    media types, 186-188
    media type schemas, 188-190
    methods, 175-177
design constraints. *See* constraints (REST)
design goals, 9, 52
    case study example, 63-64
    common to SOA and REST, 103-104
    REST, 58
        case study example, 116-124
        modifiability, 61
        performance, 58-59
        portability, 62

relationship with SOA design
    goals, 95-97, 97-104
reliability, 62
scalability, 59-60
simplicity, 60
visibility, 61-62
service-oriented computing
    increased business and
        technology alignment, 100
    increased federation, 98-99
    increased intrinsic
        interoperability, 97-98
    increased organizational agility,
        102
    increased ROI, 100-101
    increased vendor diversity
        options, 99-100
    list of, 33
    reduced IT burden, 102-103
    relationship with REST design
        goals, 95-97, 97-104
design patterns, 8-9, 329. *See*
also **compound patterns**
    Agnostic Capability, 428
    Agnostic Context, 429
    Agnostic Sub-Controller, 430
    Asynchronous Queuing, 431
    Atomic Service Transaction, 221,
        251, 272, 432
    Brokered Authentication, 433
    Canonical Expression, 199, 434
    Canonical Protocol, 435
    Canonical Resources, 436
    Canonical Schema, 188, 296, 437
    Canonical Versioning, 358, 439
    Capability Composition, 440
    Capability Recomposition, 441
    Code-on-Demand, 351
    Compatible Change, 442

Compensating Service Transaction,
    251, 272, 443
Composition Autonomy, 444
Concurrent Contracts, 445
Content Negotiation, 106-107,
    331-332, 348, 352, 354, 357, 446
Contract Centralization, 98,
    340, 447
Contract Denormalization, 289, 336,
    340, 448
Cross-Domain Utility Layer, 449
Data Confidentiality, 450
Data Format Transformation,
    299, 451
Data Model Transformation, 296,
    299, 452
Data Origin Authentication, 453
Decomposed Capability, 454
Decoupled Contract, 455
    defined, 46
Direct Authentication, 456
Distributed Capability, 457
Domain Inventory, 141, 299,
    340-341, 458
Dual Protocols, 459
Endpoint Redirection, 106-107,
    332-333, 460
    endpoints in, 330
Enterprise Inventory, 141, 461
Entity Abstraction, 167, 249, 463
Entity Linking, 333-335, 464
Event-Driven Messaging, 111, 222,
    282-284, 287, 465
Exception Shielding, 466
File Gateway, 468
Functional Decomposition, 469
Idempotent Capability, 217, 335, 470
Intermediate Routing, 471
Inventory Endpoint, 299-302, 472

Layered System, 111
Legacy Wrapper, 193, 473
Lightweight Endpoint, 106,
    336-337, 474
Logic Centralization, 110, 146, 156,
    192, 348, 475
Message Screening, 476
Messaging Metadata, 477
Metadata Centralization, 478
Multi-Channel Endpoint, 479
Non-Agnostic Context, 480
Partial State Deferral, 483
Partial Validation, 484
Policy Centralization, 485
Process Abstraction, 167, 249, 486
Process Centralization, 487
Protocol Bridging, 299, 488
Proxy Capability, 489
Redundant Implementation, 490
Reliable Messaging, 491
REST-inspired SOA design patterns,
    list of, 329
Reusable Contract, 107, 337,
    338-339, 492
Rules Centralization, 493
Schema Centralization, 98, 341, 494
Service Agent, 27, 495
Service Callback, 497
Service Data Replication, 498
Service Decomposition, 499
Service Encapsulation, 500
Service Façade, 501
Service Grid, 502
Service Instance Routing, 503
Service Layers, 250, 504
Service Messaging, 505
Service Normalization, 146, 156,
    289, 296, 506
Service Perimeter Guard, 507

Service Refactoring, 508
Stateful Services, 265, 511
State Messaging, 112, 265, 341, 509
State Repository, 265, 510
Termination Notification, 359, 512
Trusted Subsystem, 514
UI Mediator, 515
Utility Abstraction, 167, 249, 517
Validation Abstraction, 189, 342,
    351, 518
Version Identification, 355, 519
www.soapatterns.org Web site, 552
design principles, 8-9
common conflicts with REST
    constraints, 114-115
Service Abstraction, 35, 213, 236
        profile, 414
        REST constraints and, 107-109
Service Autonomy, 35
        composition autonomy loss, 245
        profile, 417
        REST constraints and, 110-111
Service Composability, 37, 263
        profile, 422-423
        REST constraints and, 114
        service-orientation and, 246-247
Service Discoverability, 37, 137, 194
        profile, 420-421
        REST constraints and, 113
Service Loose Coupling, 35,
    194, 200
        profile, 413
        REST constraints and, 105-107
        uniform contract and, 243-244
Service Reusability, 35, 101
        profile, 415-416
        repeatable composition, 245
        REST constraints and, 109-110

Service Statelessness, 35
    composition design, 264-265
    profile, 418-419
    REST constraints and, 111-112
    Stateless constraint and, 246
Standardized Service Contract, 35,
    44, 137
    profile, 411-412
    REST constraints and, 104-105
    uniform contract and, 242-243
Direct Authentication design
    pattern, 456
Distributed Capability design
    pattern, 457
diversity of vendors, 99-100
Domain Inventory design pattern, 141,
    299, 340-341, 458
domain service inventory, defined, 42
Dual Protocols design pattern, 459
dynamic binding, 288-299
    with baseline standardization,
        302-304
    with common properties, 294-296

E

Endpoint Redirection design pattern,
    106-107, 332-333, 460
endpoints in design patterns, 330
Enterprise Inventory design pattern,
    141, 461
Enterprise Service Bus compound
    pattern, 462
entities, resources versus, 149-150
Entity Abstraction design pattern, 167,
    249, 463
Entity Linking design pattern,
    333-335, 464

entity services
    common properties, dynamic
        binding with, 294-296
    composing entity services, 251-252
    defined, 41
    design considerations for REST
        service contracts, 192-193
    task services composing, 250-251
ETags, 285
Event-Driven Messaging design pattern,
    111, 222, 282-284, 287, 465
evolvability, 61-64
Exception Shielding design pattern, 466
extensibility, 61-64

F

Federated Endpoint Layer compound
    pattern, 467
federation, 98-99
Fetch method, 214-215
Fielding, Roy, 392
File Gateway design pattern, 468
filtering business processes, 154-172
fine-grained granularity, 45
forwards-compatibility, 354
    REST service contracts, 348
    uniform contract media types, 354
    uniform contract methods, 349-350
functional abstraction, 108
Functional Decomposition design
    pattern, 469

G

glossary Web site, 3, 10, 49, 552
goals. *See* design goals
granularity
    levels, defined, 45
    REST service modeling, 148
    validation constraint granularity, 353

H

header structure in uniform contract profile template, 366

hierarchies for service compositions, 249-252

HTTP (Hypertext Transfer Protocol), 72, 388

> headers, designing and standardizing, 177-179
>
> messaging, SOAP messaging versus, 81-82
>
> methods. *See* methods
>
> response codes
>> *customizing, 184-186*
>> *designing and standardizing, 179-186*
>> *list of, 180-183*

HTTP: The Definitive Guide, 4

hypermedia, role in REST services, 83-87

Hypertext Transfer Protocol. *See* HTTP (Hypertext Transfer Protocol)

I

IANA (Internet Assigned Numbers Authority), 389

Idempotent Capability design pattern, 217, 335, 470

idempotent REST service capabilities, 254-255

IETF (Internet Engineering Taskforce), 388-389

implementation mediums for services, 39

incompatible changes

> REST service contracts, 348-349
>
> uniform contract media types, 350

Interface (Uniform Contract) constraint, 55-56, 59

Intermediate Routing design pattern, 471

Internet Assigned Numbers Authority (IANA), 389

Internet Engineering Taskforce (IETF), 388-389

Internet Media Types (MIME), 388

interoperability, 97-98

inventories. *See* service inventory

Inventory Endpoint design pattern, 299-302, 472

IT resources, defined, 41

J–K

JavaScript, ECMA International Web site, 390

JSON (JavaScript Object Notation), 390

KioskEtc Co. case study. *See* case study examples, KioskEtc Co.

L

late binding, REST service contracts and, 87-89

Layered System constraint, 56-57, 60, 98-102, 111, 145

> composition design and, 248
>
> Fielding dissertation related excerpts, 406
>
> profile, 404-405
>
> standardizing, 204

Legacy Wrapper design pattern, 193, 473

Lightweight Endpoint design pattern, 106, 336-337, 474

lingering composition state, 255

linking, 83-87

link relation type structure in uniform contract profile template, 367

Logic Centralization design pattern, 110, 146, 156, 192, 348, 475

logic deferral, 288-299

> at runtime, 297-299

M

mainstream SOA methodology
  (MSOAM), 129
major versions, 356
measuring statelessness, 530-531
media type profile structure in uniform
  contract profile template, 365-367
media types, 68, 73-74
    compatibility, 350-354
    designing, 186-188
    schemas for, designing, 188-190
    standardization, 144
message-level security, 179
message polling, 285-288
Message Screening design pattern, 476
messaging
    Event-Driven Messaging design
      pattern, 282-284
    HTTP versus SOAP messaging,
      81-82
    message polling, 285-288
Messaging Metadata design pattern, 477
Metadata Centralization design
  pattern, 478
method profile structure, in uniform
  contract profile template, 364-365
methods, 68, 71-72
    associating service capabilities with,
      163-172
    compatibility, 349-350
    complex methods, design
      considerations, 211-223
    designing and standardizing,
      175-177
    primitive methods, 212
    standardization, 144
Midwest University Association (MUA)
  case study. *See* case study examples,
  Midwest University Association (MUA)
MIME (Internet Media Types), 388

minor versions, 355
modifiability (REST design goal), 61
MSOAM (mainstream SOA
  methodology), 129
Multi-Channel Endpoint design
  pattern, 479

N

Non-Agnostic Context design
  pattern, 480
non-agnostic logic, 42
non-REST-friendly atomic service
  transactions, 276-281
non-REST service contracts
    custom service contract example,
      77-79
    REST service contracts versus,
      77-83
normalization of REST services, 146-147
notifications. *See* messaging
notification service for this book series,
  11, 551
NOTIFY method, 283

O–P

Official Endpoint compound
  pattern, 481
Orchestration compound pattern, 182
organizational agility, 102

Partial State Deferral design pattern, 483
Partial Validation design pattern, 484
passive message processing, 27
passive state, 527-528
PATCH method, , 176
patch versions, 356
patterns. *See* design patterns
performance (REST design goal), 58-59
plus (+) symbol notation, 88
point-to-point data exchanges, 240
Policy Centralization design pattern, 485

portability (REST design goal), 62
Prentice Hall Service Technology Series from Thomas Erl, 551
primitive methods, 212
primitive service activities, 238
principles. *See* design principles
Process Abstraction design pattern, 167, 249, 486
Process Centralization design pattern, 487
process-specific logic, identifying, 160-172
profiles
    service profiles, REST and, 367-379
    uniform contract profile template, 362-367
        case study example, 369-379
        media type profile structure, 365-367
        method profile structure, 364-365
        uniform-level structure, 363
programmatic logic abstraction, 108
Protocol Bridging design pattern, 299, 488
protocol mechanisms (HTTP), 72
Proxy Capability design pattern, 489
PubSub method, 222-223

Q–R

quality of service abstraction, 108
queries in resource identifiers, 198

RDF (Resource Descriptor Framework), 296
recommended reading, 3-4, 548-552
red in text, 8
Redundant Implementation design pattern, 490
reliability (REST design goal), 62

Reliable Messaging design pattern, 491
repeatable compositions, 245
representations, 331
Resource Descriptor Framework (RDF), 296
resource identifiers
    design considerations for REST service contracts, 194-201
    syntax, 68, 69-71
resource linking, 333
resource queries, URI templates and, 86-87
resources
    associating service capabilities with, 163-172
    entities versus, 149-150
    identifying, 161-172
response codes (HTTP)
    customizing, 184-186
    designing and standardizing, 179-186
    list of, 180-183
response code structure in uniform contract profile template, 366
REST
    design goals, 58
        common with service-oriented computing, 103-104
        modifiability, 61
        performance, 58-59
        portability, 62
        relationship with SOA design goals, 95-104
        reliability, 62
        scalability, 59-60
        simplicity, 60
        visibility, 61-62
    design patterns, list of, 329

dynamic binding
    with baseline standardization,
      302-304
    with common properties,
      294-296
    and logic deferral, 288-299
    Event-Driven Messaging design
      pattern and, 282-284
    HTTP versus SOAP messaging,
      81-82
    hypermedia, role of, 83-87
    Inventory Endpoint design pattern
      and, 299-302
    message polling and, 285-288
    service capabilities, 75-77
    service composition with, case study
      example, 306-324
    service modeling, 147-151
      granularity, 148
      process for, 150-172
      resources versus entities, 149-150
    service profiles and, 367-379
    uniform contracts. *See also* Uniform
      Contract constraint
      elements of, 68-69
      media types, 73-74
      methods, 71-72
      resource identifier syntax, 69-71
REST constraints, 8-9, 52
    Cache, 55, 145
      Fielding dissertation related
        excerpts, 399
      profile, 398
    case study example, 63-64
    Client-Server, 53
      Fielding dissertation related
        excerpts, 394
      profile, 393

Code-on-Demand, 57
    Fielding dissertation related
      excerpts, 408
    profile, 407
    runtime logic deferral, 297-299
common conflicts with SOA design
    principles, 114-115
defined, 52
designing and standardizing,
    201-204
Layered System, 56-57, 145
    Fielding dissertation related
      excerpts, 406
    profile, 404-405
Service Abstraction design principle
    and, 107-109
Service Autonomy design principle
    and, 110-111
Service Composability design
    principle and, 114
service composition design and,
    247-248
Service Discoverability design
    principle and, 113
Service Loose Coupling design
    principle and, 105-107
Service Reusability design principle
    and, 109-110
Service Statelessness design
    principle, 111-112, 246
Standardized Service Contract
    design principle and, 104-105
Stateless, 54, 145, 246
    composition design, 265
    cross-service transactions,
      266-281
    Event-Driven Messaging design
      pattern and, 283-284

Fielding dissertation related excerpts, 397

message polling and, 287-288

profile, 395-396

service compositions and, 263-265

Uniform Contract, 55-56, 59-60, 62, 98-102, 145, 184

breaking, 115

composition coupling and, 248

Fielding dissertation related excerpts, 402-403

profile, 400-401

REST service inventory modeling and, 141-147

Service Abstraction design principle and, 108

Standardized Service Contract design principle and, 104-105

standardizing, 203

uniform contract modeling and, 144-145

REST-friendly atomic service transactions, 267-272

REST-friendly compensating service transactions, 272-276

RESTful .NET, 4

RESTful Web Services: Web Services for the Real World, 4

Restlet in Action: Developing RESTful Web APIs in Java, 4

REST requirements for SOA projects, 129-130

REST service compositions

design considerations, 253-257

bindings, 255-257

idempotency, 254-255

lingering composition state, 255

synchronous versus asynchronous compositions, 253-254

step-by-step example, 258-260

REST service contracts, 75-77

design considerations, 191-204

by service model, 191-193

case study example, 205-210

for resource identifiers, 194-201

for REST constraints, 201-204

late binding, 87-89

non-REST service contracts versus, 77-83

uniform contracts, 79-80

version identifiers, 356-358

with WSDL, 82-83

REST service inventory modeling, uniform contract modeling and, 141-147

REST services

case study example, 90-92

centralization, 146-147

normalization, 146-147

SOA and, 29-30

REST triangle, 68

retirement of services, 359

return on investment (ROI), 100-101

reusability, 61-64

Reusable Contract design pattern, 107, 337-339, 492

ROI (return on investment), 100-101

Rules Centralization design pattern, 493

runtime logic deferral, 297-299

S

scalability (REST design goal), 59-60

scaling

down, 59

in, 59

out, 59

up, 59

Schema Centralization design pattern, 98, 341, 494

schemas
>for media types, designing, 188-190
>service-specific XML schemas, 189-190

scope of service compositions, 240

security, message-level, 179

Service Abstraction design principle, 35, 213, 236
>profile, 414
>REST constraints and, 107-109

service activities, defined, 238

Service Agent design pattern, 27, 495

service agents, defined, 27

Service Autonomy design principle, 35
>composition autonomy loss, 245
>profile, 417
>REST constraints and, 110-111

Service Broker compound pattern, 496

Service Callback design pattern, 497

service candidate, defined, 44

service capabilities
>associating with resources and methods, 163-172
>defined, 26
>denormalized service capabilities, Service Normalization design principle and, 289
>REST, 75-77

Service Composability design principle, 37, 263
>profile, 422-423
>REST constraints and, 114
>service-orientation and, 246-247

service composition with REST, case study example, 306-324

service composition instances, defined, 233

service compositions
>across service inventories, 299-304
>autonomy loss, 245

composition deepening, 292-293
cross-service transactions. *See* cross-service transactions
defined, 27-28, 233
design considerations
>*REST constraints and, 247-248*
>*REST service compositions, 253-257*
>*service-orientation principles and, 241-247*
>*Service Statelessness design principle, 264-265*
>*Stateless constraint, 265*
with dynamic binding and logic deferral, 288-299
hierarchies and layers, 249-252
identifying candidates, 167-172
initiators, 239-240
members and controllers, 234-238
minimum scope, 240
repeatable compositions, 245
REST service compositions
>*design considerations, 253-257*
>*step-by-step example, 258-260*
Stateless constraint and, 263-265

service consumers, defined, 26

service contracts
>defined, 24-25, 44-45
>non-REST custom service contracts example, 77-79
>REST, 75-77
>>*design considerations, 191-204*
>>*late binding, 87-89*
>>*non-REST service contracts versus, 77-83*
>>*uniform contracts, 79-80*
>>*with WSDL, 82-83*
>in service-oriented design phase, 135

versioning
    compatibility, 346-349
    explained, 346
    need for, 345
    version identifiers, 355-359
Service Data Replication design
    pattern, 498
Service Decomposition design
    pattern, 499
Service Discoverability design principle,
    37, 137, 194
        profile, 420-421
        REST constraints and, 113
service discovery, 137
Service Encapsulation design
    pattern, 500
Service Façade design pattern, 501
service granularity, 45
Service Grid design pattern, 502
Service Instance Routing design
    pattern, 503
service inventory
        blueprints, 42, 132
        defined, 42
        dynamic binding with baseline
            standardization, 302-304
        service compositions across, 299-304
service inventory analysis, 131-132
        REST service inventory modeling,
            uniform contract modeling and,
            141-147
service inventory blueprints, 42, 132
Service Layers design pattern, 250, 504
Service Loose Coupling design principle,
    35, 194, 200
        profile, 413
        REST constraints and, 105-107
        uniform contract and, 243-244
Service Messaging design pattern, 505

service modeling, 133-134
        REST service modeling, 147-151
            granularity, 148
            process for, 150-172
            resources versus entities, 149-150
service models
        defined, 41-42
        design considerations for REST
            service contracts, 191-193
service names for resource identifiers,
    195-196
Service Normalization design pattern,
    146, 156, 289, 296, 506
service-orientation, defined, 34-37. *See
    also* design principles
service-orientation principles,
    composition design and, 241-247
service-oriented analysis, 133-134
*Service-Oriented Architecture: Concepts,
    Technology, and Design*, 49
service-oriented architecture. *See* SOA
    (service-oriented architecture)
service-oriented computing
        defined, 33
        design goals
            common with REST, 103-104
            *increased business and technology
                alignment, 100*
            increased federation, 98-99
            *increased intrinsic interoperability,
                97-98*
            *increased organizational
                agility, 102*
            increased ROI, 100-101
            *increased vendor diversity options,
                99-100*
            list of, 33
            reduced IT burden, 102-103
            *relationship with REST design
                goals, 95-104*

service-oriented design, 135

Service-Oriented Infrastructure: On Premise and in the Cloud, 4, 385

Service Perimeter Guard design pattern, 507

service portfolio, defined, 43-44

service profiles, 362
    defined, 46
    REST and, 367-379

Service Refactoring design pattern, 508

service-related granularity, defined, 45

Service Reusability design principle, 35, 101
    profile, 415, 416
    repeatable composition, 245
    REST constraints and, 109-110

services
    defined, 24, 39-40
    implementation mediums, 39
    REST and, 29-30
    retirement of, 359
    SOA and, 29

service-specific XML schemas, 189-190

Service Statelessness design principle, 35
    composition design, 264-265
    profile, 418-419
    REST constraints and, 111-112
    Stateless constraint and, 246

Service Technology Magazine, 10, 552

service versioning, 138

session data, 529

simplicity (REST design goal), 60

smoothing out, 60

SOA (service-oriented architecture)
    defined, 37-38
    REST services and, 29-30
    services and, 29

SOACP (SOA Certified Professional), 11

SOA Design Patterns, 3, 49, 329

SOA Governance: Governing Shared Services On-Premise and in the Cloud, 49

SOA Manifesto, 38, 534-546

SOAP messaging, HTTP messaging versus, 81-82

SOA Principles of Service Design, 3, 49, 108, 233

SOA projects
    REST requirements, 129-130
    stages, 129-131
        service discovery, 137
        service inventory analysis, 131-132, 141
        service logic design, 137
        service-oriented analysis, 133-134, 141
        service-oriented design, 135

SOASchool.com SOA Certified Professional (SOACP), 11

SOA with Java, 4, 40

SOA with .NET & Windows Azure, 4, 40

standardization
    dynamic binding with, 302-304
    of HTTP headers, 177-179
    of HTTP response codes, 179-186
    of media types, 144
    of methods, 144, 175-177
    of resource identifiers, 194-201
    of REST constraints, 201-204

Standardized Service Contract design principle, 35, 44, 137
    profile, 411, 412
    REST constraints and, 104-105
    uniform contract and, 242-243

standards. *See* Web standards

state
    active versus passive, 527-528
    business data, 529-530
    context data, 529

session data, 529
stateless versus stateful, 528
types of, 527
state deferral, 524, 527
state delegation, 524, 527
stateful complex methods, design
considerations, 221-223
stateful compositions, Stateless
constraint and, 247-248
stateful services, 528
Stateful Services design pattern, 265, 511
stateless complex methods, design
considerations, 214-220
Stateless constraint, 54, 60, 98, 103, 111,
145, 272-276
composition design, 265
cross-service transactions, 266-281
*non-REST-friendly atomic
service transactions, 276-281*
*REST-friendly atomic service
transactions, 267-272*
*REST-friendly compensating
service transactions*
Event-Driven Messaging design
pattern and, 283-284
Fielding dissertation related
excerpts, 397
message polling and, 287-288
profile, 395-396
service compositions and, 263-265
Service Statelessness design principle
and, 246
standardizing, 201-202
stateful compositions and, 247-248
weakening, 115
statelessness
measuring, 530-531
weakening, 115
stateless services, 528

state management
explained, 522-523
measuring statelessness, 530-531
origins of, 523-526
State Messaging design pattern, 112,
265, 341, 509
State Repository design pattern, 265, 510
static business process definition, 233
Store and Confirm transactions, 267-272
Store method, 215-217
sub-controllers, 234
symbols
chorded circle, 25
for components, 39
legend, 9
plus (+), 88
REST triangle, 68
for state data, 523
synchronous service compositions,
asynchronous versus, 253-254

T

task services
composing entity services, 250-251
defined, 41
REST service contract design,
191-192
technology information abstraction, 108
templates, uniform contract profile
template, 362-367
case study example, 369-379
media type profile structure,
365-367
method profile structure, 364-365
uniform-level structure, 363
Termination Notification design pattern,
359, 512
Three-Layer Inventory compound
pattern, 167, 250, 513

transactions, 272-276
    cross-service transactions, 266-281
        non-REST-friendly atomic
           service transactions, 276-281
        REST-friendly atomic service
           transactions, 267-272
        REST-friendly compensating
           service transactions
Trans method, 221-222
triangle symbol notation, 68
Trusted Subsystem design pattern, 514

U

UI Mediator design pattern, 515
Uniform Contract compound pattern,
    339, 516
Uniform Contract constraint, 55-56,
    59-60, 62, 98-102, 145, 184
    breaking, 115
    composition coupling and, 248
    Fielding dissertation related
       excerpts, 402-403
    profile, 400-401
    REST service inventory modeling
       and, 141-147
    Service Abstraction design principle
       and, 108
    Standardized Service Contract
       design principle and, 104-105
    standardizing, 203
uniform contract modeling
    REST constraints and, 144-145
    REST service inventory modeling
       and, 141-147
uniform contract profile template,
    362-367
    case study example, 369-379
    media type profile structure,
       365-367

    method profile structure, 364-365
    uniform-level structure, 363
uniform contracts
    design considerations, 175-190
       for HTTP headers, 177-179
       for media type schemas, 188-190
       for HTTP response codes,
           179-186
       for media types, 186-188
       for methods, 175-177
    elements of, 68-69
    media types, 73-74, 350-354
    methods, 71-72, 349-350
    resource identifier syntax, 69-71
    REST services with, 79-80
    Service Loose Coupling design
       principle and, 243-244
    Standardized Service Contract
       design principle and, 242-243
    version identifiers, 358
    versioning, 346
uniform-level structure in uniform
    contract profile template, 363
URIs (Uniform Resource Identifiers),
    69-71, 388
    components, 196-197
    templates, resource queries and,
       86-87
URLs (Uniform Resource Locators),
    69-71
    service names for resource
       identifiers, 195-196
URNs (Uniform Resource Names),
    69-71
Utility Abstraction design pattern, 167,
    249, 517
utility logic, analyzing processing
    requirements, 169-172
utility service candidates, defining,
    170-172

utility services
    defined, 41
    design considerations for REST
        service contracts, 193

V

Validation Abstraction design pattern,
189, 342, 351, 518
validation constraint granularity, 45, 353
vendor diversity, 99-100
Version Identification design pattern,
355, 519
version identifiers, 355-359
versioning. *See also* **compatibility**
    explained, 346
    need for, 345
    REST service contracts,
        compatibility, 346-349
    strategies, 138
    version identifiers, 355-359
visibility (REST design goal), 61-62

W–Z

W3C (World Wide Web Consortium),
389-390
Web Service Contract Design and
Versioning for SOA, 4, 345
Web sites
    IETF, standards governed by, 389
    JavaScript, ECMA International, 390
    JSON (JavaScript Object
        Notation), 390
    W3C Web standards, 390
    www.cloudschool.com, 11, 551
    www.serviceorientation.com, 10,
        49, 552
    www.servicetechbooks.com, 10, 11,
        49, 551
    www.servicetechmag.com, 10, 552

    www.servicetechspecs.com, 10,
        388, 552
    www.servicetechsymposium.com,
        552
    www.soaglossary.com, 3, 10, 49, 552
    www.soa-manifesto.com, 39, 49, 534
    www.soa-manifesto.org, 38, 534
    www.soapatterns.org, 46, 49, 552
    www.soaprinciples.com, 410
    www.soaschool.com, 11, 551
    www.whatisrest.com, 10, 548
    www.whatissoa.com, 552
Web standards
    for application layer, 388
    IETF (Internet Engineering
        Taskforce), 388-389
    JavaScript, ECMA International, 390
    JSON (JavaScript Object
        Notation), 390
    W3C (World Wide Web
        Consortium), 389-390
World Wide Web Consortium (W3C),
389-390
WSDL, REST service contracts with,
82-83
WS-Security, 179

THE PRENTICE HALL SERVICE TECHNOLOGY SERIES FROM THOMAS ERL

SOA Governance: Governing Shared Services On-Premise and in the Cloud
ISBN: 9780138156756

This comprehensive book collects proven industry practices for establishing IT governance controls specific to the adoption of SOA and service-orientation and provides clear direction as to what does and does not constitute SOA governance.

Service-Oriented Architecture: Concepts, Technology, and Design
ISBN 9780131858589

Widely regarded as the definitive "how-to" guide for SOA, this best-selling book presents a comprehensive end-to-end tutorial that provides step-by-step instructions for modeling and designing service-oriented solutions from the ground up.

SOA: Principles of Service Design
ISBN 9780132344821

Published with over 240 color illustrations, this hands-on guide contains practical, comprehensive, and in-depth coverage of service engineering techniques and the service-orientation design paradigm. Proven design principles are documented to help maximize the strategic benefit potential of SOA.

SOA: Design Patterns
ISBN 9780136135166

Software design patterns have emerged as a powerful means of avoiding and overcoming common design problems and challenges. This new book presents a formal catalog of design patterns specifically for SOA and service-orientation. All patterns are documented using full-color illustrations and further supplemented with case study examples.

Several additional series titles are currently in development and will be released soon. For more information about any of the books in this series, visit www.servicetechbooks.com.

PRENTICE
HALL

PRENTICE HALL

REGISTER
THIS PRODUCT

informit.com/register

Register the Addison-Wesley, Exam Cram, Prentice Hall, Que, and Sams products you own to unlock great benefits.

To begin the registration process, simply go to **informit.com/register** to sign in or create an account. You will then be prompted to enter the 10- or 13-digit ISBN that appears on the back cover of your product.

Registering your products can unlock the following benefits:

- Access to supplemental content, including bonus chapters, source code, or project files.
- A coupon to be used on your next purchase.

Registration benefits vary by product. Benefits will be listed on your Account page under Registered Products.

About InformIT — THE TRUSTED TECHNOLOGY LEARNING SOURCE

INFORMIT IS HOME TO THE LEADING TECHNOLOGY PUBLISHING IMPRINTS Addison-Wesley Professional, Cisco Press, Exam Cram, IBM Press, Prentice Hall Professional, Que, and Sams. Here you will gain access to quality and trusted content and resources from the authors, creators, innovators, and leaders of technology. Whether you're looking for a book on a new technology, a helpful article, timely newsletters, or access to the Safari Books Online digital library, InformIT has a solution for you.

informIT.com
THE TRUSTED TECHNOLOGY LEARNING SOURCE

Addison-Wesley | Cisco Press | Exam Cram
IBM Press | Que | Prentice Hall | Sams

SAFARI BOOKS ONLINE

FREE
Online Edition

Safari Books Online

Your purchase of **SOA with REST** includes access to a free online edition for 45 days through the Safari Books Online subscription service. Nearly every Prentice Hall book is available online through Safari Books Online, along with thousands of books and videos from publishers such as Addison-Wesley Professional, Cisco Press, Exam Cram, IBM Press, O'Reilly Media, Que, Sams, and VMware Press.

Safari Books Online is a digital library providing searchable, on-demand access to thousands of technology, digital media, and professional development books and videos from leading publishers. With one monthly or yearly subscription price, you get unlimited access to learning tools and information on topics including mobile app and software development, tips and tricks on using your favorite gadgets, networking, project management, graphic design, and much more.

Activate your FREE Online Edition at
informit.com/safarifree

STEP 1: Enter the coupon code: KVXXDDB.

STEP 2: New Safari users, complete the brief registration form.
Safari subscribers, just log in.

If you have difficulty registering on Safari or accessing the online edition,
please e-mail customer-service@safaribooksonline.com

SOA Certified Professional (SOACP)

Content from this book and other series titles has been incorporated into the SOA Certified Professional (SOACP) program, an industry-recognized, vendor-neutral SOA certification curriculum developed by author Thomas Erl in cooperation with industry experts and academic communities and provided by SOASchool.com and training partners.

The SOA Certified Professional curriculum is comprised of a collection of 23 courses and labs that can be taken with or without formal testing and certification. Training can be delivered anywhere in the world by Certified Trainers. A comprehensive self-study program is available for remote, self-paced study, and exams can be taken world-wide via Prometric testing centers.

Dozens of public workshops are scheduled every quarter around the world by regional training partners.

All courses are reviewed and revised on a regular basis to stay in alignment with industry developments.

For more information, visit: **www.soaschool.com**

www.soaworkshops.com • www.soaselfstudy.com

Cloud Certified Professional (CCP)

The Cloud Certified Professional (CCP) program, provided by CloudSchool.com, establishes a series of vendor-neutral industry certifications dedicated to areas of specialization in the field of cloud computing. Also founded by author Thomas Erl, this program exists independently from the SOASchool.com courses, while preserving consistency in terminology, conventions, and notation. This allows IT professionals to study cloud computing topics separately or in combination with SOA topics, as required.

The Cloud Certified Professional curriculum is comprised of 18 courses and labs, each of which has a corresponding Prometric exam. Private and public training workshops can be provided throughout the world by Certified Trainers. Self-study kits are further available for remote, self-paced study and in support of instructor-led workshops.

All courses are reviewed and revised on a regular basis to stay in alignment with industry developments.

For more information, visit: **www.cloudschool.com**

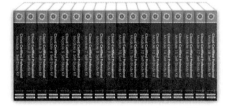

www.cloudworkshops.com • www.cloudselfstudy.com

SOASchool.com and CloudSchool.com exams offered world-wide through Prometric testing centers (www.prometric.com/arcitura)

Distributed Capability [457] How can a service preserve its functional context while also fulfilling special capability processing requirements?

 Domain Inventory [458] How can services be delivered to maximize recomposition when enterprise-wide standardization is not possible?

 Dual Protocols [459] How can a service inventory overcome the limitations of its canonical protocol while still remaining standardized?

 Endpoint Redirection [460] How can consumers of a specific service endpoint adapt when the service endpoint changes or is removed?

 Enterprise Inventory [461] How can services be delivered to maximize recomposition?

Enterprise Service Bus [462]

 Entity Abstraction [463] How can agnostic business logic be separated, reused, and governed independently?

 Entity Linking [464] How can services expose the inherent relationships between business entities in order to support loosely-coupled composition?

 Event-Driven Messaging [465] How can service consumers be automatically notified of runtime service events?

 Exception Shielding [466] How can a service prevent the disclosure of information about its internal implementation when an exception occurs?

Federated Endpoint Layer [467]

 File Gateway [468] How can service logic interact with legacy systems that can only share information by exchanging files?

 Functional Decomposition [469] How can a large business problem be solved without having to build a standalone body of solution logic?

 Idempotent Capability [470] How can a service capability safely accept multiple copies of the same message to handle communication failure?

 Intermediate Routing [471] How can dynamic runtime factors affect the path of a message?

 Inventory Endpoint [472] How can a service inventory be shielded from external access while still offering service capabilities to external consumers?

 Legacy Wrapper [473] How can wrapper services with non-standard contracts be prevented from spreading indirect consumer-to-implementation coupling?

 Lightweight Endpoint [474] How can lightweight units of business logic be positioned as effective reusable enterprise resources?

 Logic Centralization [475] How can the misuse of redundant service logic be avoided?

 Message Screening [476] How can a service be protected from malformed or malicious input?

 Messaging Metadata [477] How can services be designed to process activity-specific data at runtime?

 Metadata Centralization [478] How can service metadata be centrally published and governed?

 Multi-Channel Endpoint [479] How can legacy logic fragmented and duplicated for different delivery channels be centrally consolidated?

 Non-Agnostic Context [480] How can single-purpose service logic be positioned as an effective enterprise resource?

Official Endpoint [481]

Orchestration [482]

 Partial State Deferral [483] How can services be designed to optimize resource consumption while still remaining stateful?

 Partial Validation [484] How can unnecessary data validation be avoided?

 Policy Centralization [485] How can policies be normalized and consistently enforced across multiple services?

 Process Abstraction [486] How can non-agnostic process logic be separated and governed independently?

 Process Centralization [487] How can abstracted business process logic be centrally governed?

 Protocol Bridging [488] How can a service exchange data with consumers that use different communication protocols?

 Proxy Capability [489] How can a service subject to decomposition continue to support consumers affected by the decomposition?